Further praise for *Lincoln's Avengers*

"Well researched and written, a worthy memorial to a remarkable man." —Dr. Thomas P. Lowry, *Civil War Times*

"Abraham Lincoln's assassination has inspired a large literature often characterized by sloppy scholarship and bizarre interpretations. Elizabeth Leonard's well-researched, carefully argued study does an excellent job of framing the assassination and its aftermath within the political context of the first phase of Reconstruction—rather than as a tragic final act ending the Civil War. It also places Judge Advocate General Joseph Holt, a figure of crucial importance, at the center of the story." —Gary W. Gallagher, author of *The Confederate War*

"An important contribution to our understanding of the troubled, and troubling, era of Reconstruction." —Judith L. Holmes, *Law and Politics Book Review*

"The real contribution Leonard makes is to bring Joseph Holt to the front stage of the great trial of the Lincoln conspirators, and at the same time to make comprehensible the sense of personal vindication which fueled his relentless pursuit of the conspirators, then Wirz, and then Davis. . . . Leonard has done us an important service, since Holt, as Judge Advocate General, was the architect of the controversial military tribunals, which tried not only the Lincoln conspirators, but also will try the Guantanamo Bay internees." —Allen C. Guelzo, *Civil War News*

"Professor Leonard has expertly tackled an examination of the Lincoln assassination. Her special emphasis on Judge Advocate General Joseph Holt and his manipulations lends a clearer view as to how the aftermath of the assassination led to a more complex and difficult Reconstruction era for the United States." —Laurie Verge, director, Surratt House Museum

"In this important book, Elizabeth Leonard has rescued Joseph Holt from undeserved obscurity. Judge Advocate General and head of the U.S. Bureau of Military Justice during the Civil War and Reconstruction, Holt played a major part in prosecution of anti-Union conspirators, Lincoln assassination conspirators, and other alleged war criminals. Although at times overzealous, Holt merited the kind of careful presentations provided here. *Lincoln's Avengers* ties these prosecutions to the story of Reconstruction during Andrew Johnson's presidency in original and convincing fashion."   —James M. McPherson

"With her customary graceful pen and shrewd analytic abilities, Elizabeth Leonard unravels much of the previously misunderstood web of intrigue and nasty politics surrounding the trial of the Lincoln assassination conspirators and the botched prosecution of Jefferson Davis. In particular, Leonard elucidates the previously unexamined attitudes and role of Judge Advocate General Joseph Holt, the lead federal prosecutor. *Lincoln's Avengers* fleshes out the history of the failure of radical Reconstruction in new and significant ways."
        —Michael Fellman, author of *The Making of Robert E. Lee*

"A clear and understandable account of how Andrew Johnson . . . tried to cope with the task of readmitting the South and its former Confederate elite to the Union. . . . Elizabeth Leonard has produced a fascinating account of the period of transition from civil war to full-fledged Republican control of Reconstruction. . . . A very interesting book, highly recommended for those who prefer their history accurate and unbiased."
        —Dane Hartgrove, Fredericksburg, Virginia, *Free Lance-Star*

"Leonard's account of this crucial period in American history is thoughtful, compelling and insightful."   —Roger Bishop, *Bookpage*

"Leonard writes with clarity and balance about the oft-conflicting quests for justice, revenge and peace in the troubled early years of Reconstruction. . . . The book is exquisite history, as Leonard makes excellent use of overlooked primary materials to weave a taut narrative with fluid prose."   —*Publishers Weekly*

"A political page-turner. It was a remarkable time, and Leonard brings it to life with succinct, unfettered writing and the clarity of a historian's perspective."   —Gerry Boyle, *Colby* magazine

LINCOLN'S AVENGERS

OTHER WORKS BY ELIZABETH D. LEONARD

—

Yankee Women:
Gender Battles in the Civil War

All the Daring of the Soldier:
Women of the Civil War Armies

LINCOLN'S AVENGERS

—

JUSTICE, REVENGE,

AND REUNION

AFTER THE CIVIL WAR

—

Elizabeth D. Leonard

W · W · NORTON & COMPANY

NEW YORK LONDON

For information about permission to reproduce selections from this book, write to
Permissions, W. W. Norton & Company, Inc., 500 Fifth Avenue, New York, NY 10110

Manufacturing by Courier Westford
Book design by Margaret M. Wagner
Production manager: Anna Oler

Library of Congress Cataloging-in-Publication Data
Leonard, Elizabeth D.
Lincoln's avengers : justice, revenge, and reunion after the Civil War / by Elizabeth D.
Leonard.—1st ed.
p. cm.
Includes bibliographical references (p.   ) and index.
ISBN 0-393-04868-3 (hardcover)
1. Lincoln, Abraham, 1809–1865—Assassination. 2. Trials (Assassination)—United
States—History—19th century. 3. Assassins—United States—History—19th century.
4. Johnson, Andrew, 1808–1875—Impeachment. 5. Impeachments—United States—
History—19th century. I. Title.
E457.5 .L46 2004
973.8'1—dc22
                                                                         2003022245

ISBN 0-393-32677-2 pbk.

W. W. Norton & Company, Inc., 500 Fifth Avenue, New York, N.Y. 10110
www.wwnorton.com

W. W. Norton & Company Ltd., Castle House, 75/76 Wells Street, London W1T 3QT

1 2 3 4 5 6 7 8 9 0

To my sons,

Anthony and Joseph

Contents

—

From the first moment this conspiracy [secession] dis-closed its cloven feet in the Capital until now, I never doubted of my own duty, and had the entire race of man confronted me on the question, my convictions in regard to that duty would not have been the less com-plete. . . . From every church and praying household, aye, and from every devout heart in the land, a con-tinual prayer should go up that the fruits of this pro-longed and sanguinary conflict may not be suffered to perish. . . . If the knife is to be stayed while there remains a single root of that cancer slavery which has been eating into the national vitals, then in vain shall we have expended thousands of millions of treasure, and in vain will the country have offered on the red altars of war the bravest of its sons.

—JUDGE ADVOCATE GENERAL JOSEPH HOLT,
following the raising of the United States flag over
Fort Sumter, April 14, 1865

What a noble monument to Mr. Lincoln if we insist upon the rights of the oppressed, thus causing fragrant incense to arise perpetually from the altar on which he was sacrificed.

—WILLIAM WELSH TO JOSEPH HOLT,
April 21, 1865

Lee's surrender and Lincoln's assassination did not bring an end to the Civil War era. The fruits of the war appeared on the mangled tree of reconstruction as the country tried to solve the problems arising from the fratricidal conflict.

—FRANK KLEMENT, *The Limits of Dissent* (1970)

PREFACE

—

MANY BOOKS HAVE BEEN WRITTEN ABOUT THE ASSASSINATION OF ABRA-
ham Lincoln in the nearly 140 years since the event took place. Some
focus on the development of the conspiracy leading up to the murder
of the President and the virtually simultaneous attack on Secretary of
State William H. Seward. Others detail the events themselves and
their short-term aftermath: the capture and killing of John Wilkes
Booth roughly two weeks later, and the trial during May and June of
eight of Booth's co-conspirators. Most studies draw to a close with
the execution of four of the convicted conspirators on July 7, 1865,
although they generally also devote some limited attention to the subsequent pursuit, capture, and 1867 trial of John H. Surratt Jr., son of
the only woman among the four conspirators who were hanged two
years before.

Lincoln's Avengers takes a different tack. Early in my research on
the assassination I was struck by the fact that the majority of my
predecessors in the field depicted the dramatic events of the spring of
1865 as the final tragic act of the Civil War. To a great extent, of
course, this is appropriate. But it quickly became clear to me that the
assassination of Lincoln also constituted a crucial first act in the
period known as Reconstruction, for it significantly influenced the
debates over what the federal government's program for the van-

quished Confederacy should look like, and how the South's eventual return to the political fold should be effected.

Most obviously, Booth's murder of Abraham Lincoln put an entirely different sort of president in the Executive Mansion. Although he certainly had his detractors, Abraham Lincoln was a diplomat and a pragmatist, genuinely flexible in his response to changing circumstances. Furthermore, having seen the war through to a successful conclusion for Union arms on the battlefield, Lincoln yearned to ensure that the blood and treasure expended in the effort to save the Union and crush slavery should not have been in vain. Andrew Johnson, in contrast, was a stubborn, intractable scrapper whose ingrained hatred of the planter class failed to trump either his love for his native South or his deep-seeded racism. As such, Johnson's wartime loyalty to the Union and his early postwar comments about punishing the former Confederacy soon gave way to an attitude that combined forgiveness and amnesty toward former Confederates (including their leaders) with resistance to any sort of plan to ensure the social and political uplift of the freedpeople.

Booth's murder of Lincoln dramatically altered the future of Reconstruction, and of the nation, because it put Andrew Johnson in the Executive Mansion instead of Lincoln. At the same time, the assassination sharply exacerbated the already vengeful inclinations toward the former Confederacy of other key figures in Washington, including the Radical Republicans and also, notably, Joseph Holt (judge advocate general and head of the Bureau of Military Justice) and his boss, friend, and political ally, Secretary of War Edwin M. Stanton. Holt and Stanton, and others as well, believed that the assassination of Lincoln was nothing less than the ultimate crime of the slavocracy that had instigated secession and war in the first place. Thus, they believed that not just the assassins themselves but the former Confederate leadership, too, must be punished harshly and disempowered permanently. Toward the latter goal, they endorsed the granting of civil rights to the freedpeople and political rights to the freedmen, thousands of whom, after all, had borne arms for the Union during the war.

To put it simply, the federal government's ongoing and conflicted response to the Lincoln assassination became inextricably intertwined with the increasingly bitter debate over Reconstruction. And because of this, although *Lincoln's Avengers* begins with the more familiar story of the assassination and its immediate aftermath, the book also continues the story through the profoundly consequential presidency of Andrew Johnson, which ended with the inauguration of Ulysses S. Grant on March 4, 1869. Over the course of these four years, powerful disagreements concerning the punishment of the South as a whole influenced—and were, in turn, influenced by—powerful disagreements concerning the punishment of those remaining individuals, including Jefferson Davis himself, who were associated in one way or another with Booth's plot.

Lincoln's Avengers carries the story of the federal government's response to the Lincoln assassination through Johnson's presidency and situates it explicitly in the context of early Reconstruction. Additionally, the book substantially enhances our understanding of Judge Advocate General Joseph Holt, a fascinating and important federal official during the Civil War era whom historians and biographers have grievously neglected. All books that deal with the Lincoln assassination have to mention Holt, if only because he quickly became the chief investigator of the crimes of April 14, and then served as chief prosecutor at the trial of the original eight conspirators. *Lincoln's Avengers*, I believe, affords Holt something much closer to the attention and careful consideration he truly deserves. A Kentuckian by birth and a former slaveholder himself, Joseph Holt is not an easy character to understand. Nor is it a simple matter to come to grips with why exactly he was so determined to pursue convictions against not only the eight defendants who came before him in 1865, but others as well, particularly Jefferson Davis and John Surratt Jr. *Lincoln's Avengers* seeks to provide a fuller picture of Holt, whose principles and whose unbending resolve earned him great renown and enormous respect during this period, but also led him to commit some terrible errors in judgment. I confess in advance my sympathy and compassion for Joseph Holt. Still, I have tried to treat him evenhandedly and in accord with a fair reading of the historical record.

Finally, *Lincoln's Avengers* incorporates the capture, trial, conviction, and execution of Captain Henry Wirz, the notorious commandant of Andersonville Prison in Georgia, into the story of the federal government's response to the Lincoln assassination. Soon after the execution of the four assassination conspirators in July 1865, Joseph Holt turned the Bureau of Military Justice's energies toward the Wirz case. From Holt's perspective, Wirz was the next in a long line of Confederate criminals he intended to make pay with their lives for their ghastly misdeeds. Unknown to Holt at the time, however, the prosecution and conviction of Wirz in the fall of 1865 represented the last opportunity for virtually unobstructed punishment of one of the "nation's enemies." Even as Wirz climbed the steps to the gallows, Andrew Johnson was moving to supplant the avengers' agenda with an agenda of his own.

Acknowledgments

—

At the end of a major project like this one, it is always a pleasure, and something of an embarrassment, to look back and recall all the help one has received along the way. I am grateful to many people for their contributions to ensuring both the project's successful completion and my own continued mental health.

I would like to recognize the excellent staff of the Library of Congress Manuscript Reading Room. For years, various staff members have good-naturedly hauled out volume after volume of Joseph Holt's papers for my examination, along with portions of many other collections as well. Their efficiency and courtesy are exemplary. Special thanks to John Sellars, Library of Congress manuscript historian, who made me feel most welcome and who more than once took the trouble to make sure I was finding the sources I needed. Also, thanks to the staff of the Prints and Photographs Division for their expert help in locating and reproducing most of the images contained in this book.

The staff of the Surratt Society, in Clinton, Maryland, also merit great appreciation for their assistance. Laurie Verge, Joan Chaconas, and others made my time pouring over the archival materials housed at the society both pleasant and fruitful, and I now look forward to future visits to their newly constructed James O. Hall Research Center. The Surratt Society's efforts to encourage popular interest in the events and individuals surrounding the assassination of Lincoln, and to support serious scholarly research into the subject, deserve recognition and praise. So, too, does the unparalleled generosity of James O. Hall himself, who some years back invited me—as he has so many others—into his home, where he spent several hours answering my questions before sending me on my way armed with microfilm, photocopies, valuable tidbits of information, and a pinch of good advice. Mr. Hall later read and rigorously critiqued an essay I wrote about Mary Surratt, and for all of this, I owe him a great debt.

Anyone who studies the Lincoln assassination invariably must come to grips with the sixteen rolls of microfilmed documents and trial testimony known familiarly as "M-599." Although this microfilm collection constitutes only a piece of the research puzzle, it is a very substantial piece, and I would like to indicate here my appreciation that the National Archives has made this important material so readily accessible. I also want to thank John Rhodehamel, Norris Foundation curator of American historical manuscripts, and his colleague Lita Garcia for responding so kindly to my request for a microfilm copy of the entire collection of Joseph Holt's papers housed at the Huntington Library in San Marino, California. This collection had not previously been microfilmed; their willingness to do it for me saved me a lot of time and expense (although I also missed out on some good walks in the Huntington gardens).

Closer to home, I would like to express my sincere thanks to the staff at Colby College's Miller Library for all their efforts over the years to locate obscure sources for my use and for agreeing, at my request, to purchase for the library's own collection a copy of "M-599" from the National Archives. I would also like to acknowledge the Colby Social Sciences Division grant that I received in 1999 (Grant #01 2204), which helped to get my research for this project under way. Subsequently, Colby alumni Harriet S. and George C. Wiswell Jr. most graciously and unexpectedly endowed a permanent research fund to support my scholarly work, without which continuing my research and writing this book would have been a great deal more difficult. I offer my deepest thanks to the Wiswells for their financial support, and for their ready good cheer and enthusiasm whenever we meet.

The research process is often a lonely one, and as a researcher I tend to be more of a loner than many scholars I know. I find it exceedingly difficult to delegate tasks to others (even photocopying), and I like to run my own eyes over every document several times and, stubbornly, draw my own conclusions. Still, over the years I can admit to having enjoyed the assistance of some fine student workers, among whom in connection with this book I must name Erin Clark (Colby '02). I am sure I have never had a student I trusted as thoroughly as I trusted Erin to help me with a range of tasks, from photocopying to evidence interpretation. Ever consistent, Erin assisted my work in a prompt, thorough, and utterly intelligent manner, and I thank her sincerely for that.

As is true for me in the research process, I am also essentially solitary when I write, at least in the early stages. Solitary, but not stupid. I am deeply grateful, and so very fortunate, to have Amy Cherry, senior editor at W. W. Norton, in my corner. For the third time now Amy has provided her impressive editing expertise to trimming, shaping, and polishing one of my bulky, wordy manuscripts. If *Lincoln's Avengers* is readable and coherent and if it makes a meaningful contribution to historical understanding, it is much to Amy's credit, and that of Norton's splendid copyediting staff. I also want to acknowledge Professor Stephen Cushman of the Univeristy of Virginia for his careful reading of a portion of the manuscript. His wise and helpful suggestions served me very well throughout and have undoubtedly made the book better. And I thank Professor Raffael Scheck of Colby College, whose insightful comments have greatly strengthened the book as well. Among other things, Raffael reminded me how important it is to provide a strong and convincing answer to the fundamental question "So what?"

Finally I would like to thank my colleagues in the History Department at Colby, who provide such splendid examples of teaching and scholarly excellence and who are such a joy to work with besides. Thanks, too, to other friends and colleagues who help to keep me sane, and to my parents, Richard and Polly Leonard, for always acting like what I do is so amazing! And to RMS, *mein lieber Schatz*: how lovely to find such a great treasure at the end of such a long, bumpy road. Finally, I would like to thank my two precious sons, Anthony and Joseph, for being exactly who they are. Their deep love of reading makes writing books seem even more worthwhile.

LINCOLN'S AVENGERS

The people in the central part of the city, during the night after the assassination, were stricken with horror at the deed and terror at the consequences. The unusual noises, the shoutings of the news . . . the rushing "in hot haste" of single horsemen and bodies of cavalry, the blaring of bugles, the excited and determined faces of men, the blanched and terror-stricken faces of women, who were full of apprehension of further evils, made an impression which will never be forgotten upon those who were awakened that fearful night.

—*Washington Times*, February 9, 1898,
on April 14, 1865

We desire that, as regards the people of the Confederate States, by-gones shall really be by-gones. . . . But as regards the leaders . . . self-respect and respect for order, law and morality, forbid that they should ever find shelter or protection under the national flag, or that ever their bones should find a resting place in our soil.

—*New York Times*, April 16, 1865

The nation well remembers that had Joseph Holt failed us at that crisis when Sumter's provisioning was the grave question . . . the last prop in the national edifice [would] have gone! . . . I pray that in your present responsible [post as] Chief of Military Justice, you may have the same high quality of firmness & sagacity to weigh & fix the issues. A wrong step now might lose to us & to the world all that has been gain[ed].

—M. W. JACOBUS TO JOSEPH HOLT,
May 9, 1865[']

1

"That Fearful Night"

The Assassination and

the Making of an Avenger

On April 14, 1865, fifty-eight-year old Joseph Holt was tired. Nevertheless, he was pleased with the thought that he had finally completed the bulk of his hard but essential wartime work as judge advocate general and head of the United States government's Bureau of Military Justice. Just a few days before, like millions across the Union, Holt had exulted in the surrender of Robert E. Lee to Ulysses S. Grant at Appomattox Court House, Virginia, and the general collapse of Confederate arms it signified. Since then, Holt had traveled south from Washington into the almost fully defanged viper's nest to participate in ceremonies marking the resumption of federal authority at Fort Sumter in Charleston Harbor. The formal raising of the Stars and Stripes at the fort on April 14—four years to the day since Major Robert Anderson had yielded in the face of a ferocious thirty-hour onslaught by South Carolina batteries—was followed by a dinner at the Charleston House at which Holt lived up to his long-standing reputation as a brilliant orator. To an enthusiastic audience Holt offered a passionate and unforgiving speech entitled "Treason and Its Treatment," which the *New York Commercial Advertiser* a few days later described as a "masterpiece of oratory, in its conciseness, felicity of diction, breadth of views, and loyal statemanship."[2]

In his speech at the Charleston House, Judge Advocate General

Holt advocated mercy for the Southern people generally, but none for the Confederate leadership, to whose account he credited in full the last four years of cruel, relentless bloodshed. The Republic, Holt declared, had proved invincible in the face of the "conspirators'" betrayal; still, those who had deluded the Southern people into taking up arms against their Northern kin deserved the harshest possible consequences. Whereas a month earlier President Abraham Lincoln had promised "malice toward none," and even on that very day had articulated to his cabinet a generous vision of national reconstruction with the errant South, Joseph Holt vowed nothing but stern punishment for the guilty parties who had instigated and then prosecuted such a bitter war. Others also spoke at the Charleston House that evening, the *Advertiser* noted, and "but for the eclipsing effect of Judge Holt's eloquence," their presentations "would doubtless have been deemed remarkable utterances." On that night, however, Joseph Holt in all his charismatic fury was the star.[3]

Even as Holt was thrilling his audience in Charleston with "ebullitions of pure patriotism and unfettered sentiment,"[4] back in Washington a series of terrible events, in whose resolution Holt would play a crucial role, was unfolding. For on that same night, a small band of villains entered the final phase of their plan to take the lives of the President and those others in positions of power whom they deemed crucial to the stability and survival of the federal government. At approximately 10:00 P.M., the well-known actor John Wilkes Booth walked through the front door of Ford's Theater. There, seated in a comfortable chair in a private upstairs box, President Lincoln was enjoying a performance of the comedy *Our American Cousin* in company with his wife, Mary Todd Lincoln, and two young friends, Major Henry R. Rathbone and Miss Clara Harris, who were engaged to be married. Because his face was so familiar to the theater employees, Booth met no resistance as he moved through the lobby, up the stairs, and down the passageway leading to the President's box. Soon the handsome and beguiling Booth, a Maryland native and now a profoundly embittered secessionist, found himself separated from the President by a single door, into which a hole had already been bored to allow him a clear view of his target.

Seconds later, the President lay mortally wounded, the victim of the single bullet Booth fired at point-blank range into the back of his head. As Lincoln's wife and Clara Harris screamed in horror, Major Rathbone struggled briefly with the assassin, who now sought to make his escape by forcing his way through the box, onto the stage, and out a back door to an alley where his horse was being held by an unsuspecting theater employee. Rathbone's efforts to restrain Booth failed when Booth cut the major's arm deeply with a large knife he had brought to the scene. When Rathbone released Booth, the assassin leaped unexpectedly over the side of the box, dropping a dozen feet down to the stage where he stumbled briefly, his foot having caught in some bunting during his vault. Probably not yet aware that he had actually fractured his leg upon landing so awkwardly, Booth sped through a backstage passageway and out into the night, the sound of his angry words, *"Sic semper tyrannis"* ("Thus always to tyrants"), ringing in the ears of those who had witnessed his ghastly deed.[5]

Meanwhile, elsewhere in the capital one of Booth's loyal accomplices was in the process of carrying out his part of the conspirators' plan. Just as Booth was preparing to strike the President at Ford's Theater (located on 10th Street near D), Lewis Thornton Powell arrived on horseback at the Lafayette Square home of Secretary of State William Henry Seward, just a short distance from the Executive Mansion. There Powell dismounted and rang the bell, and when the door swung open he announced to one of the Seward family's young black servants, William Bell, that he had a prescription from a "Dr. Verdi" to deliver to the secretary, who had been confined to bed for the past few days with a broken arm, a broken jaw, and fever as a result of a severe carriage accident. Initially persuaded by Powell's ruse, Bell permitted the unusually tall and imposing stranger to enter the house. Informing Bell that he was under strict instructions from the doctor to deliver the prescription to Seward personally, Powell headed up the stairs. The sound of his heavy footsteps aroused the secretary's son, Frederick William Seward (himself an assistant secretary of state), who came out of his bedroom to see what was going on. Powell repeated his story, to which the alarmed assistant secretary

Secretary of State
William Henry Seward.
Courtesy of the
Library of Congress

replied that his father was not to be disturbed under any circumstances. Perhaps temporarily flustered, Powell started down the stairs, but he soon turned around and bounded back up, drawing a pistol from his coat and attempting to shoot Frederick on the spot. When the gun misfired, the intruder, undaunted, began to use it as a bludgeon, beating Frederick ferociously about the head and ultimately fracturing the young man's skull and breaking the gun at the same time.

As the bloodied Frederick fell, his frightened sister Fanny, who had been attending to her father, opened the secretary's bedroom door in order to discover the cause of the noise in the upstairs hallway. In so doing, she unwittingly allowed Powell to enter the room. There Powell encountered Sergeant George F. Robinson, a convalescent soldier who had been detailed for duty as the secretary's nurse and who now desperately tried to fend off the massive attacker. With his broken pistol in one hand and a large knife in the other, however, Powell was able to push past Robinson to the secretary's bed. He then brutally slashed Seward, who had been awakened by all the noise, in the face and neck. "I saw him cut Mr. Seward twice that I am sure of," Robinson later testified; "the first time he struck him on the right cheek, and then he seemed to be cutting around his neck." Fortunately, before Powell could complete the job he had come to do, Seward was able to roll himself off the bed, onto the floor, and out of reach. At the same time, Sergeant Robinson was joined by another of Secretary Seward's sons, Major Augustus H. Seward, who had been awakened by his sister's screams and now raced into the room in his shirt and drawers to join the attack on the assailant. Both of the secretary's defenders received several knife wounds, but they managed to drive Powell off. On his way out the door, however, Powell delivered one last vicious blow, stabbing Emerick Hansell, a messenger assigned to the Seward residence, in the back. With that, Powell fled, only a few steps ahead of William Bell, who rushed out into the street in a panic, crying for help.[6]

As a result of these clearly coordinated events, by about ten thirty on the night of April 14, 1865, Americans' hopes for the peace and reconciliation Robert E. Lee's surrender had seemed to augur were in tatters. Word of the disaster spread quickly across the capital, even as the District's finest doctors were being urgently summoned both to the Seward home and to a private house where Lincoln now lay. The dying President had been carried to the home of a family named Petersen, which stood across the street from Ford's Theater, in order to spare his family the shame of his having to pass his final hours in a theater, a place of uncertain moral value. Immediately upon hearing the news, stunned citizens poured into the streets of Washington to express their sorrow and, in some cases, to seek vengeance. At the same time, members of Lincoln's cabinet, Vice President Andrew Johnson, and General Grant—who at the time of the attacks was on board a train to Pennsylvania with his wife—were informed as quickly as possible and placed under the protection of armed guards dispatched for that purpose by the War Department. As the details of the night's events grew clearer, the fact that Johnson in particular had thus far escaped unharmed provided some relief, especially given the apparent likelihood that Seward would not survive. For, as scholars have noted, had Lincoln, Seward, and Johnson all been killed, the nation would have been thrown into a state of "electoral chaos":

although by law the president pro tempore of the Senate—the little-known Lafayette S. Foster of Connecticut—would have assumed the role of acting president, he would have done so in the absence of the necessary legal procedures for electing a proper successor, procedures that only the secretary of state could set in motion.[7]

Having received word of the events by telegraph in Charleston, an enraged and deeply saddened Joseph Holt returned to Washington right away. It undoubtedly came as no surprise to him that his friend and longtime colleague, Secretary of War Edwin McMasters Stanton, had already gotten the investigations under way. From the moment he learned of the attacks, Secretary Stanton had quite rightly assumed that he himself was, at least for the time being, the government official most responsible for the nation's security and the survival of the peace, both of which required that the killers and all of their associates be apprehended as quickly as possible and any further violence be forestalled. As such, Stanton had spent most of the night of April 14–15 at the Petersen house interviewing witnesses, including many who had been at the theater when Booth shot the President and had recognized the actor when he landed on the stage, before he disappeared into the night heading for his native Maryland. Other witnesses brought Stanton reports of strange goings-on around the theater and near the Seward house earlier in the evening.

During the night Stanton and his assistants gathered and sifted through whatever information came to hand. At the same time, they issued regular telegraphic messages to the press and to the military high command, updating recipients on the President's condition, naming Booth as his attacker, and hypothesizing about the identities and possible whereabouts of Booth's co-conspirators. Stanton also mobilized various forces to track down the criminals, even as he attempted simultaneously to calm the dying President's wife and to manage his own very real grief over the loss of his friend and mentor. Surely Stanton bemoaned Lincoln's repeated refusal over the years to tolerate substantial military protection. More than once during the war Stanton had boldly defied Lincoln's wishes, sending detachments of armed soldiers or cavalry troopers to accompany the President on his frequent trips away from the Executive Mansion. But Lincoln, who spent a great deal of time at the War Department's telegraph office monitoring the progress of Union arms, was famous for giving his escorts the slip, justifying his actions on the principle that "the presence of armed guards smacked too much of imperialism." Tragically, on this night, although an officer of the Metropolitan Police had been assigned to protect the President, Booth had succeeded in gaining access anyway.

Working out of the parlor at the Petersen house, Stanton struggled to ascertain how such a catastrophe could have occurred, all the while making regular trips into the back room where the President lay gasping for breath on a bed far too small for his vast frame. Through the night Secretary Stanton pressed on with the diligence and attention to detail for which he was famous: years later, his sister Pamphila recalled, "he was imperative where a duty was to be performed, for with him, where duty and obedience were involved, he knew no dallying, no turning aside."[8]

Shortly before seven thirty on the morning of April 15—long after Booth and one of his accomplices had made it safely across Washington's Navy Yard bridge into Maryland, and several hours after they had found temporary shelter and valuable medical assistance at the home of a fervent Southern nationalist named Dr. Samuel A. Mudd—Abraham Lincoln breathed his last. Three and a half hours later, Andrew Johnson—whose life, it would be revealed, had been spared by another conspirator's loss of nerve—was sworn in as Lincoln's successor by the Chief Justice of the United States, Salmon P. Chase. Perhaps predictably, this transfer of executive power, though smooth, did little, at least in the short run, to alleviate popular concern over the nation's future. For one thing, the question whether the murder of Lincoln and the brutal attack on the secretary of state were harbingers of further violence to be committed against the victorious Union leadership remained open. For another, it was hardly a source of reassurance that the new president himself was widely considered something of a buffoon: on more than one important occasion during his years in government service, Johnson had appeared in public obviously inebriated. Perhaps even more important, in the few weeks that Johnson had been vice president, there was little to suggest that Lincoln had intended to bring his new subordinate into his inner circle of advisers and confidants. Rather, Lincoln seems to have held the Unionist Democrat from Tennessee at a distance: sources indicate that the two men met with each other only once between the March 4 inauguration and the assassination, and then only very briefly.[9]

It must have seemed entirely fitting to most observers that throughout the day on April 15 a "cheerless cold rain" fell on the gloomy capital. Secretary of the Navy Gideon Welles informed his diary that among those who seemed to experience the greatest despair over the previous night's violence were the ones for whom the war's end had seemed to offer the greatest hope: former slaves whose bonds the Union victory had broken at last. "On the Avenue in front of the White House," Welles wrote,

> were several hundred colored people, mostly women and children, weeping and wailing their loss. This crowd did not appear to diminish through the whole of that cold, wet day; they seemed not to know what was to be their fate since their great benefactor was dead, and their hopeless grief affected me more than almost anything else, though strong and brave men wept when I met them.[10]

Not just for blacks but for whites across the country, too, the future was uncertain. For Stanton, however, some things were becoming crystal clear. Above and beyond the eyewitness accounts identifying the man who pulled the trigger at Ford's Theater, Stanton was soon convinced that the events of April 14 were by no means the work of this one man alone, or even the work of Booth in concert with a few well-coordinated local henchmen. Rather, the initial investigations Stanton conducted following the attacks only confirmed his belief that the Slave Power, which over the course of four years of bitter, fratricidal warfare had already proved itself capable of previously unimaginable evils, was at the root of this evil as well. In Stanton's mind, then, the attacks of April 14 could be understood only as the result of a vast conspiracy, masterminded at Richmond, Virginia, by the Confederate leadership, most likely including Jefferson Davis himself.

"President Lincoln's Funeral Procession in Washington,"
from Harper's Weekly, *May 6, 1865*

As it turns out, however, just at the time Stanton reached this conclusion, he found it necessary to turn over the responsibility for proving his theory to someone else. For within a few days of the
assassination Stanton himself was compelled to refocus his attention
on the task of bringing the war to a final close, something that
became significantly more complicated on April 18, when General
William T. Sherman, without War Department approval, authorized
an overly generous peace treaty with General Joseph E. Johnston,
commanding the last substantial Confederate forces in the field.
Therefore, on the twentieth, the secretary of war turned over the
assassination investigations to Joseph Holt and Holt's Bureau of Military Justice, an arm of the War Department. Needless to say, when
he handed over control of the investigations (and any subsequent
prosecution) to Holt, Stanton also transmitted to his trusted colleague
and friend his own preliminary reading of the accumulated evidence.
Significantly, it was a reading that Holt's own worldview, primed by
years of pursuing military justice against the enemies of the United

States, was more than ready to accommodate.¹¹ Indeed, looking back
over Joseph Holt's life, as well as his professional training and experience, it becomes clear that few if any in the federal government were
as well prepared as he was in April 1865 to play the role of Lincoln's
principal avenger.

Joseph Holt was born in Breckinridge County, Kentucky, on January 6, 1807. As a young child he attended a neighborhood school and
then, when he was fourteen, his ambitious parents—farmers who
owned a small number of slaves but were nevertheless not wealthy—
sent the bright and articulate young Joseph off to earn a proper
private college education, paid for by his maternal grandfather.
Although it is not entirely clear whether Holt actually graduated from
the respected and expensive Centre College in Danville, there is no
question that from the time he left home in 1821 he steadily made his
way along the path to social and financial betterment that his parents
wished for. By 1825 Holt was studying law in Lexington with one of
Kentucky's most famous attorneys, Robert Wickliffe, and by 1828 he
opened his first law office, in Elizabethtown. That year Joseph Holt
also became an active and committed supporter of Andrew Jackson's
Democratic Party, in whose service, as in his law practice, he soon
"won a name for oratory in competition with many notable rivals."
In 1832, having enjoyed considerable professional success in Elizabethtown, Holt moved his practice to Louisville, where he also took
on the job of assistant editor of the *Louisville Advertiser*. Three years
later, Holt, who was now twenty-eight years old, married, and the
formidable prosecuting attorney for the Louisville circuit, moved his
practice again. He set up shop first in Port Gibson, Mississippi, and
then in Vicksburg, where "the abundant litigation that accompanied
the development of this new cotton region" soon made him a rich
man.¹²

While pursuing his law career in Mississippi, Holt also continued
to expand his commitment to the Democratic Party. At the Democratic National Convention in 1836, Holt defended a controversial vice
presidential candidate, Richard M. Johnson, against the attacks of his
opponents in a speech that further enhanced Holt's fame as an effective and persuasive orator. As one observer described it: "His coal-

black hair, flashing eye, olive complexion, graceful figure, and thrilling voice electrified the convention. Never was there a more dramatic scene." Strikingly, Holt's devotion to Democratic Party politics did not translate into a personal desire for political office. On at least one occasion he turned down a nomination by the state legislature to serve as one of Mississippi's United States senators.[13]

Over the next several years, Holt's Vicksburg law practice continued to thrive, his reputation grounded in observers' recognition of his masterly courtroom style and demeanor. "There was nothing sparkling in Holt's courtroom presence," writes one biographer; rather, "it was the driving force of his sincerity that gave to his delivery such power over his audience." Holt's cases were not won by humor, cleverness, or glamour; instead, "Holt spellbound the jury by the crushing weight of evidence he could bring to bear on the case." Overall, Holt seems to have lived a work-centered life in Vicksburg, even undermining his own health with the demanding pace he kept. Indeed, during their time in Mississippi, both Holt and his wife, Mary, contracted what was diagnosed as tuberculosis. Their health severely eroded, by 1842 Holt deemed it prudent (and, fortunately, economically feasible) to retire from the law and return with Mary to Louisville to recuperate.[14]

In Louisville Joseph and Mary Holt lived a relatively quiet life, struggling to regain their health and strength. Only Joseph was successful on this score: in 1846, Mary died, plunging Holt into a period of deep, private despair. Two years later, he began to resume a more active life. He reengaged in Democratic Party politics to some degree and also began to give political speeches on the affairs of the day, in which his familiar eloquence was much in evidence. In 1850, Holt remarried. His second wife, Margaret, was the daughter of Kentucky's Democratic governor, Charles A. Wickliffe. The Holts traveled to Europe and the Middle East, where Holt later claimed his appreciation for American political institutions had been reconfirmed. Returning to Louisville, Holt devoted considerable time and energy to the Democratic Party's electoral successes in 1852 and 1856. Then, in April 1857 he and Margaret removed to Washington, D.C., where, half a year later, Holt accepted his first appointment from Democratic President James Buchanan, as the administration's commissioner of patents. According to the *New York Times*, the position "was one that in a high degree demanded perfect integrity of character, added to a practical sense and a good knowledge of the law." And among those public figures known for their manifestation of precisely these qualities, noted the *Times*, "Mr. Holt stood preeminent."[15]

Over the next three years as commissioner of patents and then, beginning in the spring of 1859, as postmaster general, Holt maintained his firm resolve, his effective, no-nonsense leadership, and his unrelenting reliability even in the face of personal tragedy: Margaret died following a protracted illness in the summer of 1860. Holt's work ethic steadily increased his stature in Buchanan's eyes, and when Buchanan's avidly pro-Southern secretary of war, John B. Floyd of Virginia, suddenly resigned on December 29, 1860, the President gladly heeded the advice of his recently appointed attorney general, Edwin Stanton, and appointed Holt to the post. According to one contemporary source, Stanton not only advised Buchanan to nominate Holt, but also urged Holt, in a midnight meeting at Holt's home, to accept the President's offer, "impress[ing] upon him the grave nature of the exigency, and the need of a man in that place whose sentiments they [the Unionists] knew."[16]

Buchanan's cabinet had been in crisis for several weeks by the time Holt replaced Floyd. Ever since the election of Abraham Lincoln in November, debate had raged among the cabinet officers, as elsewhere, over the future of the nation and, more immediately, of the federal forts located in those states where secessionist sentiment was becoming increasingly strident. On November 24, Holt's fellow Kentuckian Major Robert Anderson had requested federal reinforcements for the forts under his command in Charleston Harbor (Castle Pinckney, Fort Moultrie, and Fort Sumter). With three months still remaining until Lincoln's scheduled March 1861 swearing-in, President Buchanan and his closest advisers struggled over how to respond. Some rejected the idea of reinforcements purely as a consequence of their own secessionist views. Others believed that to reinforce Anderson would be to inflame the Southern nationalists further, to play into

Judge Advocate General
Joseph Holt.
*Courtesy of the
Library of Congress*

their hands. Still others took the stance that a bold display of federal power would effectively curtail secessionism, reminding the fire-eaters of the potential costs of rebellion. As for President Buchanan himself, his position was essentially, if perhaps hopelessly, conciliatory. On December 3 Buchanan declared publicly the illegality of secession, but also the impotence of the federal government to countermand it. In practical terms, the upshot was that Buchanan refused to send the reinforcements, Anderson continued to request them, and the cabinet began to collapse.[17]

Even before South Carolina's fateful decision, on December 20, to lead the slave states out of the Union, cabinet members on all sides of the argument began to tender their resignations. First to go was Howell Cobb of Georgia, Buchanan's secretary of the treasury, once an advocate of compromise but since Lincoln's election an outright secessionist. Buchanan filled Cobb's post with the equally pro-Southern Philip F. Thomas of Maryland. When Secretary of State Lewis Cass of Michigan, past promoter of the doctrine of popular sovereignty, quit in frustration over the President's refusal to respond to Major Anderson's pleas, Buchanan moved Attorney General Jeremiah S. Black, a staunch Pennsylvania Unionist, into his spot, and replaced him with Stanton, known by then as a strong Union man.[18]

Holt's late-December appointment to succeed Floyd as head of the Department of War did not go unnoticed by the public at large. The *New York Times* happily reported the change on January 1, 1861, praising Holt's designation as secretary of war as "a step in the right direction," despite the fact that Holt was a lifelong Democrat and a border state native. Indeed, the population of Kentucky in 1860 contained a significantly higher percentage of slaves (20 percent) than any of the other border states (Delaware, Maryland, Missouri, and even western Virginia), as well as the third highest number of slaveholders in the nation, following only Georgia and Virginia. Moreover, in recent years Holt had displayed considerable distaste for Northern extremists, especially abolitionists, and as a lawyer in both Mississippi and Kentucky he had been known to argue cases in favor of the slave institution, cases in which he firmly "upheld the rights of the States to protect slavery within their own bounds." Indeed at some point, like his family, Holt himself had actually owned some slaves, although never many, and all were manumitted long before the law required him to release them.[19]

Still, despite his deep roots in slaveholding Southern society, Holt was widely known above all as "a Union man—honest, straightforward and firm." On this question he stood proudly in the tradition of Henry Clay, his renowned fellow Kentuckian, for whom the preservation of the Union became the paramount concern of his life, and who famously declared in 1852, in the last great speech of his long political career, that he would prefer to die than see the Union sundered. Because Holt was known to share Clay's devotion to the Union, his appointment as secretary of war was a source of great reassurance to Unionists across the nation. In contrast, a letter dated the very next day from the passionate Southern nationalist senator Louis T. Wigfall of Texas to Milledge Bonham, a U.S. congressman from South Carolina who was then also commanding his state's militia forces, revealed in two curt sentences the consequences that Southern fire-eaters anticipated from Holt's taking over for the Virginian,

Floyd. "It means war," wrote Wigfall. "Cut off supplies from Anderson and take Sumter as soon as possible." Years later, the widow of a former Southern friend condemned Holt bitterly for having betrayed his Southern, slaveholding heritage: "Holt," wrote two-time Alabama Senator Clement C. Clay's wife, Virginia, "rose high in Federal honors . . . having sold his Southern birthright for a mess of Northern pottage."[20]

Having accepted the post of secretary of war, Holt busied himself immediately and tirelessly with the work of managing his department while trying to undermine secessionism and simultaneously enhancing Washington's defenses against the terrible conflict he was fast coming to believe inevitable.[21] Holt's task was complicated by the persistent opposition of the pro-Southern, pro-secession forces in the administration, in Congress, and even in the general population, opposition also experienced by the other members of the Unionist bloc in Buchanan's cabinet, Attorney General Stanton and Secretary of State Black. Among those who most urgently hoped to steer Holt away from what they considered his wayward path were several of his relatives, including his younger brother, who was then living in Mississippi. On January 10, 1861, Robert Holt sent the new secretary of war a letter in which he combined family chitchat with a scolding. "I deeply regret," wrote Robert, "that a sense of propriety or duty induces you still to remain among the advisers of the President. He is fast drifting into coersion, and coersion is war, war upon the south, upon your country, your friends, your kindred, and which will probably find its way with fire & sword to the very hearthstone of our childhood."[22] Robert was mistaken, of course, in his belief that Buchanan would ultimately adopt a policy of compelling the seceding states to return to the Union. But he was right about Holt's sense of propriety and duty, both of which represented powerful driving forces in Holt's character and undergirded his professional and personal conduct throughout his life.

Another essential driving force in Holt's personality was his persistent concern about the nature and responsibility of leadership and power. Quite simply, Holt believed that it was the express burden of those in power, such as himself, to dedicate themselves, their blood, and their treasure to sustaining common people's basic devotion to the good. In the context of the crisis of the winter of 1860–61, "the good" to Holt meant, most saliently, loyalty to the Union as a sacred and unbreakable trust. By way of corollary, Holt believed with equal fervor that when "the people" turned away from the good and toward evil (in this case, away from Union and toward secession), they rarely if ever did so of their own accord but only because they were seduced by corrupt and traitorous power-mongers who conspired successfully, albeit through subterfuge and deceit, to lead them astray. Such traitors and conspirators, though few in number relatively speaking, were nevertheless extremely powerful and must be flushed out and stopped by means of any and all available weapons. Only then, Holt believed, could the good be preserved.

As will be seen, these fundamental organizing principles of Holt's worldview, which endured long past the assassination of Lincoln, would prove powerfully influential in shaping his response to those dreadful events of April 1865. Even without the ability to foresee the horrors that lay ahead, however, it is clear that in the winter of 1860–61 Holt was profoundly alarmed, but probably not terribly surprised, by letters such as the vicious one he received from an unknown correspondent, written less than a week after he became secretary of war. Among other things, the writer warned Holt to live up to the supposed demands of his Southern roots, or face dire personal consequences. "My eye is upon you," wrote the author. "I am afraid you are about to play false to the South. You are a Kentuckian by birth, & you married 2 Kentucky wives. You made your fortune in Miss[issippi]. . . . If you by word or act favor the shedding of the blood of the people of your section I will be the Avenger that will strike you when you least expect it. Beware—Beware." Clearly the letter's author intended to frighten Holt with this explicit threat on his life. But one suspects that the words that followed provoked Holt even more: "woe betide the leaders & the abettors," wrote his anonymous correspondent, "if one drop of southern blood is shed." And he warned, "there is a secret band of avengers that will strike down every leader of the foes of the south, & then willingly die for their country."[23] Letters such as this only enhanced Holt's determination, in those first months of 1861 and ever after, to drive from the shadows where they lurked all conspirators against the Union, as well as their accomplices, the South's self-appointed "secret bands of avengers."

And so Holt set to work, according to at least one source summoning the general in chief of the United States army, Winfield Scott, to a private meeting within minutes of accepting his appointment. A primary focus for both Scott and Holt was the situation in Charleston Harbor, and as early as January 5, 1861, having previously ordered Major Anderson to assume a strictly defensive posture against potential attackers, Holt authorized the U.S.S. *Star of the West* to sail from New York to Charleston, carrying both supplies and soldiers, two hundred troops and four officers.[24] The vessel reached South Carolina on the night of January 8, and the next morning, as the ship approached Fort Sumter, shots rang out, first from Morris Island and then from Fort Moultrie, which had fallen into Confederate hands in late December. Because of the delayed arrival of orders issued on January 5 permitting him to respond forcibly, Major Anderson held his fire and before long, unable to complete its mission, the *Star of the West* headed back out to sea. A week later, when critics claimed that Anderson should have covered the ship's passage more vigorously, Holt rose to his defense. "You rightly designate the firing into the *Star of the West* as 'an act of war,' and one which was actually committed without the slightest provocation," wrote Holt reassuringly to Anderson.

> Had their act been perpetrated by a foreign nation it would have been your imperative duty to have resented it with the whole force of your batteries. As, however, it was the work of the government of South Carolina . . . and was prompted by the passions of a highly inflamed population of citizens of the United States, your forbearance to return the fire is fully approved by the President.[25]

Here Holt blamed the government of South Carolina, which he understood to be dominated by a few traitorous fire-eaters, as much for inflaming the passions of the state's common and presumably otherwise honorable citizenry as for the actual attack on the *Star of the West*.

In mid-January 1861, the moment of truth in Charleston Harbor had been postponed, but Holt's struggle for the Union against the bands of traitors and conspirators who threatened to destroy it had only just begun in earnest. Among the first to give way under the impact of Holt's uncompromising, pro-Union influence (reinforced by Stanton and Black) on the shape, policies, and actions of the Buchanan administration was Secretary of the Interior Jacob Thompson of Mississippi. Thompson had been a friend and supporter of Holt for many years, but a rift between the two men had developed in recent months over the cause of secession and now, even before the *Star of the West* had reached its home harbor, Thompson resigned (he was not replaced). Philip Thomas, who had just replaced Howell Cobb as secretary of the treasury in December, was the next to go; he was replaced by Unionist John A. Dix of New York.[26]

Meanwhile, Holt continued to engage actively in both discussion and diplomatic efforts relating to the unresolved crisis in Charleston Harbor, but reinforcing Major Anderson was only one of the new war secretary's goals. At the same time he devoted considerable time and energy to reorganizing and streamlining his department and purging it of insurrectionists, their allies, and their influence. Once Holt took the wheel, recalled two of Lincoln's chief advisers, John Nicolay and John Hay,

> Plots and plans of arsenals and forts, and reports of their armament and supplies, were refused to conspiring Members [of Congress] and Senators. The issue of advance quotas of arms to disloyal governors was discontinued. The practice of selling Government arms was abandoned. [Former War Secretary] Floyd's order to send . . . cannon south was promptly countermanded. The military precautions of General Scott were adopted, and as rapidly as possible carried out.

In short, as the final weeks of the uncertain Buchanan administration drew to a close, Joseph Holt moved quickly to transform the Department of War, at least, into an unequivocal agent of the Union's survival. Wrote friend and admirer Dr. H. Wigand of Springfield, Ohio, on January 24: "whatever may be the result of this mad Disunion scheme, the future historian will record your name as the only clearheaded noble and honest member of the former cabinet of Mr. Buchanan." In retrospect, Dr. Wigand's remarks seem unfair to Holt's allies in the cabinet, Stanton and Black. But they nevertheless reflect the confidence countless Northerners and determined anti-secessionists had in Holt's unflappable Unionism.[27]

As Holt cast a stern eye over the defenses of the federal capital in the early months of 1861, he found them lacking. On February 18, just a few days before President-elect Lincoln was due to arrive in the city, Holt issued a report to Buchanan expressing his concerns about Washington's ability to defend itself from attack by the seceded states—now numbering seven and organized, at least provisionally, into the Confederate States of America, with Jefferson Davis as president. In the report Holt explained his reasons for summoning to the District a "well-appointed corps" of regular soldiers, "admirably adapted for the preservation of the public peace." He began with a review of the steady and relentless challenge to federal authority that the last three months had witnessed in those states now engaged in "revolution" against the government. The revolutionaries, Holt pointed out, were "guided and urged on by men occupying the highest positions in the public service" who, "with the responsibilities of an oath to support the Constitution still resting upon their consciences, did not hesitate secretly to plan and openly to labor for the dismemberment of the Republic whose honors they enjoyed and upon whose Treasury they were living."[28]

Having succeeded brilliantly so far—capturing forts and vessels, seizing arsenals, stealing funds from the mint at New Orleans, and more—these revolutionists, Holt insisted, aspired to ever bolder depredations, including almost certainly the capture of Washington, D.C., preferably before March 4, in order to thwart Lincoln's inauguration. Holt, it is clear, had come to believe that a speedier response to the crisis in Charleston Harbor might have stopped the revolution in its tracks. He further believed that a strong display of military

might would offer the revolutionaries the best evidence of the administration's "determination, as well as ability, to maintain the laws" at
the same time that it would serve as the most effective means of "baf-
fling and dissolving any conspiracy that might have been organized,"
avoiding war, and bringing Lincoln safely into office. As such Holt
sought to concentrate additional armed soldiers in the federal capital.
Subsequently, he and General Scott also arranged for a grand parade
of the troops down Pennsylvania Avenue to commemorate George
Washington's birthday. At the end of his report to Buchanan, Holt
noted that the strong presence of federal troops in the city had, in
fact, already begun to achieve its purposes: restoring public confidence and disrupting the "machinations" of those "deluded, lawless
men" who were dedicated to the nation's destruction.[29]

Abraham Lincoln arrived in the capital on February 23. As his
inaugural, with all of its potentially grave implications, drew nearer,
Holt maintained a firm hold on the War Department while also keeping his eye on the military situations locally, in Charleston, and elsewhere. No doubt he read with both sadness and contempt his brother
Robert's mid-February suggestion that in the time remaining there
was but "one great service" which he might yet do the South and
"indeed the whole country," namely turning over the last military
posts still located in Southern states but held in federal control. Only
by doing so, Robert believed, could Holt aid the federal government
to avoid war with "the section which now as ever stands but on the
defensive, and claims but to enjoy its rights, the section which gave
you birth and which contains all your kindred and friends."[30]

Dismissing Robert's suggestion without hesitation, Joseph Holt
instead focused on his War Department work and protecting the
future president's life. Simultaneously, he prepared himself for the end
of Buchanan's administration, which would mean, at least for the
time being, his own departure from official government service as
the incoming administration took shape. As it turns out, Holt actually stayed on as secretary of war for several days after the peaceful
inauguration of Abraham Lincoln. ("To Joseph Holt's fidelity,"
declared the *New York Times* later, "and to his sagacity and courage
when clothed with the powers of the War Department, the present

Administration owes the fact that it was peacefully inaugurated, or, perhaps, inaugurated at all."[31]) Indeed, one of the first official documents to cross Lincoln's desk in the Executive Mansion was a letter from Secretary of War Joseph Holt, communicating the important news that Fort Sumter "must, in the lapse of a few weeks at most, be strongly reinforced or summarily abandoned."[32] Simon Cameron soon replaced Holt as secretary of war, but rumors—and hopes— continued to circulate widely that Lincoln would assign Holt to another cabinet post, or perhaps make him a Supreme Court justice. Holt's own papers contain a note from Lincoln, dated March 12, 1861, summoning him to a private interview in which such an appointment may have been discussed.[33]

It is also quite possible, however, that the March 12 conversation between Lincoln and Holt revolved around not the possibility of a bureaucratic appointment in the federal government, but rather the connection between the future survival of the Union and ongoing political developments in Kentucky, the home state Lincoln and Holt shared with other key players in the coming war, including Jefferson Davis. Lincoln's anxiety over Kentucky's shaky loyalty to the Union has been widely recorded: among his most famous documented remarks on the subject was his contention that "to lose Kentucky is nearly the same as to lose the whole game."[34] As in the case of Maryland and Missouri, scholars have overwhelmingly agreed that Kentucky's decision was a crucial one for the outcome of the war. As historian James M. McPherson has pointed out, "the confluence of the Ohio, Mississippi, Tennessee, and Cumberland rivers on the borders of Kentucky made the state a vital military nexus for the movement of troops and supplies," while the state itself offered a "rich source of horses, mules, leather, grain, and meat."[35] If Kentucky seceded, the consequences for the Union cause could be disastrous.

Determined to hold his beloved Kentucky in the Union (single-handedly if necessary), in the months following his departure from the War Department, Joseph Holt, now an independent citizen volunteering on the nation's behalf, launched a personal campaign to ensure his home state's loyalty. Central to the argument Holt brought to the divided people of Kentucky, through the press and in speeches he made while visiting the state in the spring and summer of 1861, was his now familiar notion that the rebellion itself was the work of a small but virulent conspiracy dedicated to the pursuit of an evil goal, a conspiracy that only the wisdom and the selflessness of the common people could overcome. In his mind, although the Kentucky legislature had initially endorsed a position of neutrality, there remained within its chambers a "band of agitators" whose primary and immediate aim was to push Kentucky into the arms of the Confederacy, for the sake of their own selfish political ambitions. As such, neutrality was not an option. "I can neither practice nor profess nor feel neutrality. . . . I would as soon think of being neutral in a contest between an officer of justice and an incendiary arrested in an attempt to fire the dwelling over my head," wrote Holt in a lengthy open letter to prominent Kentuckian and close Lincoln friend Joshua F. Speed, which was published first in the *Louisville Journal* and then in the *New York Times* and elsewhere (some 30,000 copies of the letter were disseminated in Kentucky alone). Though a noble aspiration in its own right, neutrality, Holt insisted, was by no means the same thing in the current crisis as outright loyalty to the Union. And in fact, if Kentucky's vaunted "neutrality" meant refusing to allow U.S. troops to march on her soil, then in practice it actually amounted to "aggressive hostility" against the federal government, for such a policy prevented the United States from defending itself against its avowed enemies. Not neutrality, Holt urged his fellow Kentuckians, but activism on behalf of the Union's survival was the key, and he summoned his compatriots to rise up, as he had done, to "twine each thread of the glorious tissue of our country's flag about our heartstrings," and to defend the Stars and Stripes in order to ensure that this "luminous symbol of resistless and beneficent power" might not be "sacrificed on the altars of a Satanic ambition," and thus disappear forever.[36]

In his speeches and in his writings about the situation in Kentucky, Holt sounded the same familiar themes for which he had come to be known, which so dominated his interpretation of the national crisis, and which later underpinned his response to Lincoln's murder.

Notably, Holt pressed the case of the Southern people, his country-men and women, whom he described essentially as the innocent vic-tims of a few evil fanatics. "Should you occupy the South," Holt told an audience of Kentucky volunteers in the Union army, "you will do so as friends and protectors, and your aim will be not to subjugate that betrayed and distracted country, but to deliver it from the remorseless military despotism by which it is trodden down." In con-trast, however, all restraint should be cast aside in confronting the "atrocious conspirators" who had set the revolution in motion: "strike boldly, strike in the power of truth and duty, strike with a bound and a shout, well assured that your blows will fall upon ingrates, and traitors, and parricides, whose lust for power would make this bright land one vast Golgotha." Show mercy to the deluded Southern people, Holt urged, but punish their leaders with unbridled severity. Nothing that took place in the years that followed, least of all the assassination of Lincoln, led Holt to alter his perspective.[37]

In the end, the crisis in Kentucky came abruptly to a head: in early September 1861, Confederate General Leonidas Polk's troops invaded the state; two days later, Ulysses Grant's forces accepted the Kentucky legislature's invitation to drive out the intruders. For the duration of the war, Kentucky remained officially outside the bounds of the Confederacy, and thus officially in the Union camp, though Kentuckians enlisted and fought in both armies. In Washington, Lin-coln experienced an enormous sense of relief upon learning the news of Kentucky's decision, as did Holt's Unionist allies back home. On September 19, longtime friend Theodore S. Bell sent words of pro-found appreciation from Louisville: "Kentucky has responded fully to your demands. Neutrality died here last Tuesday night, so suddenly that a coroner would be justified in issuing a writ of inquiry to ascer-tain whether it was a case of suicide."[38]

By the late fall of 1861 it is clear that a grateful Lincoln was con-templating finding an official place for Holt in his administration. In December Holt received a letter from their common friend Joshua Speed, informing him that Lincoln was searching for a way to repay Holt "in some form commensurate with the service you have rendered the country." Sensing, as many did, that Simon Cameron's days as secretary of war were numbered, Speed urged Holt to accept nothing short of his old War Department position.[39]

However, on January 14, 1862, Edwin Stanton—Holt's old friend, fellow Unionist Democrat, and staunch ally from the last months of the Buchanan administration—became Simon Cameron's replacement. Holt proved strikingly unembittered by this turn of events. On January 25, Stanton acknowledged Holt's generosity. Wrote Stanton, the "cordial approval you have given to my appointment is known and fully appreciated. Your regard and support strengthen my heart more than I can tell. My feelings toward yourself you already know. We stood together in the beginning of this mighty contest and by God's blessing we will stand together until the end." Stanton was right to be grateful: evidence suggests that Holt may well have substantially improved Congress's support for Lincoln's famously cantankerous new war secretary by means of his own broadly held reputation for integrity and reason.[40]

In any case, the two would soon have the opportunity to work closely together once more. On September 3, 1862, Lincoln designated Holt as his choice to fill a new spot in the federal bureaucracy, that of judge advocate general in Stanton's War Department. Holt held this position for more than a decade, until his retirement from government service in December 1875, first with the rank of colonel and after June 1864 when the Bureau of Military Justice was organized under his leadership, with the rank of brigadier general. A month after Holt's appointment, he publicly declared his resolute loyalty to the Union yet again in words that now have an eerie resonance: "I am for the Union as unconditionally as I am for protecting my own body, at every cost and hazard, from the knife of the assassin."[41]

As judge advocate general, Holt oversaw the War Department's policy regarding legal affairs within the military, as well as its policy with regard to civilian political prisoners—the latter soon to be extended by Lincoln's September 24, 1862, proclamation suspending the writ of habeas corpus and, for the first time, requiring military trials for "all Rebels and Insurgents, their aiders and abettors within the United States, and all persons discouraging volunteer enlistments, resisting militia drafts, or guilty of any disloyal practice, affording comfort to Rebels against the authority of the United States."[42] In Lincoln's eyes, at least, Holt was the ideal man for this demanding job: an unswerving and apparently tireless Unionist, a brilliant legal mind, and a man known for being thoroughly honest. More than a year before his appointment, Holt had told Kentucky Union troops stationed at Camp Jo Holt in Indiana, "I don't hesistate to say that any and every measure required to save the Republic from the perils that beset it, not only may, but ought to be taken by the Administration, promptly and fearlessly."[43] Hardly an inflexible defender of civil rights in wartime, Lincoln undoubtedly found Holt's attitude deeply reassuring.

In his capacity as judge advocate general, Joseph Holt was also charged with guaranteeing that "the administration of military law in courts-martial, courts of inquiry, and military commissions was uniform and just," and with determining precisely which sorts of offenses Lincoln's suspension of habeas corpus encompassed, and thus which offenses subjected the individuals who committed them to trial by court-martial (for military personnel) or military commission (for civilians). Over the months and years ahead, as he had always done in the past, Holt applied himself vigorously to his tasks, both transforming legal theory into policy and overseeing particular cases directly. In both realms, Holt based his approach on two fundamental principles, both of which were to be of crucial importance for those later charged with murdering Lincoln and attacking Secretary Seward. First, Holt insisted that so-called military offenses ("offenses aimed at impairing the validity of the military service or its success in the field") could be committed by civilians as well as by soldiers. Second, he maintained that, in wartime, crimes that otherwise fell under civil jurisdiction could also—at the discretion of the judge advocate general's office—come under the purview of the military court system.[44]

During the Civil War, a large proportion of Holt's time was occupied by trials internal to the military. Among the most important of these was the case of General Fitz-John Porter of New Hampshire, who was relieved of command in the Army of the Potomac on

November 10, 1862, on charges of dereliction of duty and failure to obey orders during the second Battle of Bull Run that past August. Between December 1862 and January 10, 1863, Porter—a staunch supporter of George B. McClellan—was tried by a court-martial on charges of disobedience of orders and disloyalty to his commanding officer, McClellan foe General John Pope.[45] (Holt upheld the guilty verdict and Porter's dismissal from the service.) Prior to the assassination of Lincoln, however, few individual decisions Holt made as judge advocate general were more important in the long run than the ones in May 1863 and October 1864 to sanction the trials by military commission of, respectively, Clement L. Vallandigham, a notorious antiwar activist, and Lambdin P. Milligan, an anti-Lincoln crusader.

Joseph Holt's deep concern over the rising and increasingly vocal antiwar sentiment linked explicitly with certain factions of the Democratic Party—his party—dated back at least to the fall of 1862. Not surprisingly, given his basic worldview, Holt was convinced that like Southern nationalism or rabid abolitionism, the political stance that soon came to be known as Copperheadism (so named because critics insisted that the antiwar "Peace Democrats" would prove as poisonous to the Union cause during the war as the venomous copperhead snake[46]) was the brainchild of a small number of extremists whose influence over the masses bordered on the demonic, and whose agenda further imperiled the life of the nation. As such, Holt was determined to muzzle rabble-rousers such as Vallandigham, a member of the Ohio legislature who on May 1, 1863, directly and intentionally violated the orders of General Ambrose Burnside, commanding the military district of Ohio, by making a public speech in which he explicitly denounced the war and Lincoln's policies with regard to military affairs as well as civil rights. As a consequence, Vallandigham was arrested, tried before a military commission, and sentenced to confinement for the duration of the war, his sentence later being converted to banishment into the Confederacy. Early in 1864, Vallandigham appealed his conviction, but in February the U.S. Supreme Court ruled against him, clearly influenced by the strong case the judge advocate general himself made in support of the military before the bench.[47]

Having slipped away in the meantime to Windsor, Ontario, an unrepentant Vallandigham boldly returned to the United States, giving more anti-administration, antiwar speeches and helping to write the Democratic Party's platform for the fall 1864 elections. He was not arrested again, and his influence faded with that of his party in the wake of its failure at the November polls.

Similarly, in October 1864, Lambdin P. Milligan of Indiana was arrested and charged with treason in consequence, among other things, of his association with a secret antigovernment Copperhead organization known as the Order of the American Knights. As judge advocate general and personally committed to uprooting antigovernment conspiracies wherever he found them, Holt oversaw Milligan's trial before a military commission in Indiana. The trial resulted in a guilty verdict and a death sentence for Milligan, although the sentence was never carried out.[48] Still, hardly insignificant was the fact that in the Milligan case Holt was ably assisted by Colonel Henry L. Burnett, judge advocate of the Union army's Northern Department, headquartered in Cincinnati, who presided over the trial. In pursuing Milligan, Burnett and Holt developed a relationship based on mutual respect, trust, and a common cause that would enhance their later collaboration in the prosecution of Lincoln's murderers. Also important was the fact that when Holt strove to punish those who had conspired to kill the President in 1865, those who opposed his actions in both the Milligan and Vallandigham trials resurfaced and severely hindered his efforts.

Throughout his wartime career as judge advocate general, Holt clearly took a special interest in certain cases that came through his office, but he did not have the time or the resources to devote equal attention to all of the cases under his purview. About a month before the assassination of Lincoln, in his March 1865 report to Secretary of War Stanton, Holt indicated that just since November 1863 the office had reviewed the case records of almost 34,000 courts-martial and military commissions and had issued approximately 9,000 reports "as to the regularity of proceedings on applications for restoration to the service, the pardon of offenders, the remission or commutation of sentences," and other miscellaneous questions. Eight months later, in

November 1865, Holt would claim that in the period since his last report the office had "received, reviewed, and filed" over 16,000 records of general courts-martial and military commissions and had completed more than 6,000 special reports. In addition to such grinding day-to-day duties, in the summer of 1864, at Stanton's request, Joseph Holt undertook an extensive examination of secret societies (such as Milligan's Order of the American Knights) whose influence and membership in the North and the West seemed to him to have reached epidemic proportions, especially in Ohio, Indiana, Illinois, Kentucky, and Missouri. Holt studied the aims of such organizations and concluded that they shared as their primary goals "the embarrassment of the Government in its military operations," the inciting of "armed opposition and rebellion," and the undermining of any efforts being made in the states where they were most active to enlist black soldiers in the Union army. On October 8, 1864, Holt delivered a lengthy report of his findings to Secretary Stanton.[49]

Holt's report focused on the Knights of the Golden Circle, for which he seemed to have the most concrete information, and which he characterized as "an inspiration of the rebellion," armed and drilling for revolution, dedicated to the perpetuation of slavery and the overthrow of the federal government. According to Holt, the organization's tactics included aiding Union soldiers to desert and harboring and protecting deserters; discouraging army enlistments and encouraging resistance to the draft; circulating disloyal and treasonable publications; communicating with and giving intelligence to the Confederacy; aiding the Confederacy by recruiting for its military within Union army lines; furnishing the rebels with arms, ammunition, and other supplies; cooperating with and sponsoring raids and invasions into federal territory; destroying federal property; persecuting people loyal to the U.S. government and destroying their property; and engaging in assassination and the murder of loyal civilians and soldiers. For Holt, the Knights of the Golden Circle was a frighteningly large and effective fraternity. Like spreading Copperheadism generally and, before that, Southern nationalism, it amounted to yet one more manifestation of the power of a few crazed conspirators at the top to corrupt the minds of otherwise mild-mannered folk, to arouse in them a fiercely "parricidal spirit," and to drive them into violent action against the benevolent institutions and leadership of the Republic and its loyal citizens. As he had believed in various contexts all along, the nation's very life depended on identifying and crushing the fomenters of such madness, male *and* female, for he noted that in his native Kentucky, at least, "two of the most notorious and successful" of the troublemakers were women. Only then could peace be restored and the nation's long-term survival be assured.[50]

As much as Joseph Holt believed the words and implications of his own report in October 1864, he believed them even more six months later, when John Wilkes Booth ended the life of Abraham Lincoln and Lewis Thornton Powell almost succeeded in murdering Secretary of State William Henry Seward.

I got back last evening at 5 o'clock. Met my wife on the street down town and enjoyed with her the enthusiasm that glowed on all sides in the faces of Union-loving friends. Baltimore street was red with the Stars and Stripes, soldiers were marching under arms from point to point to prevent the pent-up anger of loyal men from bursting forth in deeds of violence against the wretched minions of Jeff Davis and slavery. Every secessionist was compelled to throw out the flag from his place of business. The street was literally jammed and crammed with excited people.

—W. G. SNETHEN TO JOSEPH HOLT
from Baltimore, April 4, 1865[1]

Jeff. Davis and the other original conspirators have committed the most monstrous crime, and, in its consequences, the most terrible ever witnessed. If justice ever made a claim on earth, it claims these men for punishment.

—*New York Times*, April 21, 1865

2

"A Vindictive Clique of Villains"

The Pursuit and Capture

of the Suspects

On April 20, 1865, the day after Abraham Lincoln's memorial service in Washington and the day before his remains began their long, sad journey back to Springfield, Illinois, Joseph Holt and his Bureau of Military Justice took over the investigations into Lincoln's assassination and the attack on Secretary of State William Henry Seward. An immediate goal was to streamline the process that Edwin Stanton had initiated on the very night the attacks took place, but which had almost immediately become quite diffuse. Virtually from the moment the crimes became known, a number of different agencies had offered Secretary Stanton their expertise and manpower to ensure the investigations' success, including the Washington, D.C., Metropolitan Police, the Provost Marshal General's Bureau, and the United States Secret Service. Perhaps not surprisingly, Joseph Holt's subsequent efforts to bring all of these agencies under his supervision met with some resistance: on April 26, the *Pittsburgh Commercial* commented that the disjointed agendas of the different agencies were still creating a situation in which "disguised detectives arrest disguised detectives, and several amusing *embroglios* have occurred," although the paper did not elaborate. Nevertheless, within the next few days Holt was able to bring at least the bulk of the work of collecting and evaluating the evidence under the control of the Bureau of

"President Lincoln's Funeral:
Citizens Viewing the Body at
the City Hall, New York,"
from Harper's Weekly,
May 6, 1865

Military Justice. At the same time, he made it clear that from this point on he himself would be responsible for the official prosecution of the crimes.[2]

As has already been noted, in the investigations he subsequently conducted Holt was assisted closely and ably by Colonel Henry Burnett. At Holt's request, Burnett had been detailed for this purpose from his duty as a judge advocate in Ohio, where much of his time had been dedicated to prosecuting Copperheads such as Lambdin Milligan and other enemies of the federal government. Also brought in to assist were H. S. Olcott of the Metropolitan Police and Provost Marshal Colonel H. H. Wells. All were committed in practice to Stanton's and Holt's fundamental presumption—which many others also readily shared—that the well-coordinated and ghastly attacks of April 14 could not possibly have been masterminded by one angry actor seeking revenge for the downfall of the Confederacy. Rather, the attacks must have been instigated by the senior Confederate leadership itself, perhaps even working in concert with various antigovernment, anti-emancipation, pro-Confederate secret organizations such as the Knights of the Golden Circle, with which Burnett in particular was familiar. Indeed, shortly after Holt summoned him to Washington, Burnett reported to Secretary Stanton—who kept an eye on the investigations even while he attended to the war's conclusion—that as he studied the evidence before him, he found "the footprints of the old Order of the Knights of the Golden Circle crossing my path in all directions." Concluded Burnett: "There is reason to believe that many, if not all, the persons connected with the late assassination of the President were members" of this or other similar fraternities.[3]

Such presumptions shaped the investigators' efforts, leading them to cast their net wide and to authorize hundreds of arrests, sometimes on evidence that was quite flimsy. Moreover, according to some reports, the Bureau's investigators (and Holt himself) were also known on occasion to subject both witnesses and suspects alike to harsh and intimidating interrogations.[4] Thanks to Abraham Lincoln's own wartime suspension of the writ of habeas corpus, of course, Northerners had, albeit reluctantly, become accustomed to federal government violations of individual civil rights. And indeed to many observers in the anxious and vengeful atmosphere that pervaded the federal capital following Lincoln's assassination, such sweeping arrests actually seemed quite reasonable. In any case, they made perfect sense to Judge Advocate General Holt, who was determined to bring the Bureau's investigations to a swift and successful conclusion and to punish all guilty parties with appropriate severity. As Holt had informed the Kentucky recruits at Camp Jo Holt back in 1861, he believed that "any and every measure required to save the Republic" from the depredations of its enemies must be employed "promptly and fearlessly."[5] As Holt saw it, Robert E. Lee's and Joseph E. Johnston's surrenders notwithstanding, the attacks on Lincoln and Seward had proved that the survival of the nation was still in grave peril. If, like Lincoln himself, he must stretch both law and convention in some measure to save the Republic, Holt was quite prepared to do so.

Even before Holt took the helm, efforts to bring to justice to those responsible for the events of April 14 had produced some extremely significant results, laying the foundation upon which Holt and his assistants then worked assiduously to build the government's case. Among those already in federal custody by the end of the month were eight individuals who particularly commanded Holt's attention. According to his quite reasonable reading of the evidence, these seven men and one woman had been Booth's most important local accomplices and were responsible (with Booth) for doing the actual dirty work of the April 14 crimes: Samuel Arnold, George Atzerodt, David Herold, Samuel Mudd, Michael O'Laughlen, Lewis Powell (a.k.a., Lewis Paine), Edman Spangler, and Mary E. Surratt. A ninth important local accomplice, Mary Surratt's son John, who was known to be a good friend and frequent companion of John Wilkes Booth, had up to this point eluded the authorities' grasp.

As for Booth himself, at the time Holt and the Bureau of Military Justice took over the investigations, it was unclear whether Lincoln's killer would ever be brought to trial. He too had thus far managed to keep his pursuers at bay. Exiting Ford's Theater, the injured Booth had brutally shoved aside the theater employee who had, until then, unsuspectingly been holding his getaway horse at the ready. Booth then galloped off through the streets of the city toward the Washington Navy Yard bridge, which spanned the eastern branch of the Potomac from the southeastern corner of the capital. Quickly reaching the bridge, Booth halted before the young sentry posted there and, upon being questioned, calmly—even brazenly—gave his true name and stated his desire to cross into his home state of Maryland. As yet unaware of the terrible events that had just transpired, the sentry allowed Booth to pass with only a warning that the bridge was closed to inbound traffic for the night, should Booth seek to reenter the city. Booth, of course, had no intention of returning that night. Once he was in Maryland, Booth met up with his accomplice David Herold, and together they continued to lengthen the distance that lay between themselves and the capital. Over the next twelve days while the two men were on the lam, Herold proved to be a loyal companion and aide to the famously charismatic Booth, remaining by his side until their escape was finally cut off by federal troops on April 26.

Described later as Booth's "dog-like follower," David Herold was born on June 16, 1842, making him only twenty-two at the time of the assassination. The sixth of ten children (including seven daughters) born to native Marylanders Adam and Mary Porter Herold, David Herold was raised in relative prosperity in a large brick house just beyond the gates of the Washington Navy Yard, where his father had earned a good salary as chief store clerk. David seems to have had a better than average education for the time, studying pharmacy first at Georgetown College and then completing his studies at Rittenhouse Academy, which was attended by some of Washington's elite sons. After graduation, Herold worked as a pharmacist and then as a clerk to a doctor until the fall of 1864, when he appears to have become unemployed. Considered by many to be quite immature for his age and even fundamentally unreliable (undoubtedly the reason that Adam Herold explicitly rejected his only surviving son as the executor of his estate), Herold was nevertheless a sociable fellow with many friends. He was also an avid hunter who had spent a great deal of time as a youngster in the Maryland woods.[6]

As a consequence of this hobby, Herold came to know the geography of southern Maryland extremely well. And presumably it was the combination of his rich knowledge of the region, his broad acquaintance with its people, and his strong Southern sympathies that drew Herold to the attention of John Wilkes Booth, who had met him for the first time a couple of years earlier while Herold was working at William S. Thompson's drugstore (a block away from the Executive Mansion), where Booth may have been soliciting quinine and other medicine for purposes of running the blockade. During the almost two weeks Herold and Booth were on the run following the assassination, Herold's familiarity with the area and its people proved essential: it afforded the two men a series of hideouts as well as sufficient nourishment to continue and even, at the end, a boat to carry them across the Potomac into Virginia. All the while, Herold's savvy and his contacts allowed the two to elude their captors, even when the soldiers who sought them drew so close that the fugitives could hear the sounds of their horses and their equipment.[7]

The fugitives' luck ran out at last when a detachment of the Six-

David Herold.
Courtesy of the
Library of Congress

teenth New York Cavalry, following a series of leads, discovered them early in the morning of April 26 about three miles south of Port Royal in Caroline County, Virginia, where they were hiding in a barn located on the property of farmer Richard Garrett. Frustrated in their attempts to lure Booth and Herold out of Garrett's barn and into custody, some of the troopers set the barn on fire, at which point Herold's courage seems to have failed him (although it is also possible that Booth persuaded him to surrender). Unarmed, Herold exited the barn with his hands in the air. At roughly the same time, an eccentric soldier named Boston Corbett, acting without orders, took aim through a gap in the barn wall and shot John Wilkes Booth, who was easily visible by the light of the flames, in the neck. In that moment Corbett ensured that many questions pertaining to the assassination conspiracy would remain forever unanswered. For Booth's wound was mortal, although after the soldiers dragged him from the barn to the steps of Garrett's house, he suffered for a number of hours before he died.[8]

Shortly thereafter, the captive Herold—along with the dead Booth's body sewed up in a blanket—was placed on board the steamer *John S. Ide* and escorted under heavy guard back to Washington. There he was imprisoned overnight in double irons, with a ball and chain attached to his legs and a stifling hood over his head, on board the *Montauk*, an ironclad, before being transferred to a small individual cell in Washington's Old Arsenal Penitentiary. (A remnant of the penitentiary still stands on the grounds of Fort Lesley McNair, situated on Greenleaf's Point in Washington, about a mile southwest of the Capitol.)[9]

At the Old Arsenal Herold joined, among others already in custody, Lewis Powell, Secretary Seward's attacker, who had been captured virtually by accident only three days after the crimes. The army officers and detectives who took Powell into custody late on the night of April 17 had actually been on a mission (their second since the assassination, in fact) to question Mary Surratt, who owned a boardinghouse on H Street between 5th and 6th, not far from Ford's Theater. They had come to question her again about her son John's whereabouts and recent activities. Just as Major H. W. Smith and the other officers were in the process of arresting Mrs. Surratt and, for good measure, all the inhabitants of her household, the tall, burly young Powell arrived unexpectedly, dressed rather awkwardly in the clothes of a common laborer, covered with mud and carrying a pickax. Recalled Major Smith some weeks later: "While we were there, [Powell] came to the house. I questioned him in regard to his occupation, and what business he had at the house at that time of night. [It was close to midnight.] He stated that he was a laborer, and had come there to dig a gutter at the request of Mrs. Surratt."

Since several eyewitnesses had described the intruder at the Seward home as an unusually tall, muscular young man, the already suspicious officers remained unconvinced by Powell's explanation. So they took him into custody as well, escorting him first to the office of General Christopher C. Augur, then in command of the Union army's forces in Washington, D.C., where he was interrogated, stripped, and searched. In the process, blood was found on his clothing and it was determined, upon close examination, that one of his boots seemed to be marked on the inside with the name "J. W. Booth." When William Bell was summoned from the Seward house, he immediately confirmed Powell's identity as his employer's assailant. As a result, by

4:00 A.M. on April 18, Powell was in double irons aboard the iron-clad the *Saugus*—sister ship to the *Montauk*—where he was subsequently identified for a second time by the secretary's son Augustus Seward. On April 29, now wearing a hood like David Herold, Powell was moved to a private cell at the Old Arsenal.[10]

Soon to be styled, by a number of observers, the "mystery man" of the assassination conspiracy—thanks to his size, his youth, his good looks, his detached demeanor in the courtroom, and his extreme reticence—Lewis Powell was born in April 1844 in Randolph County, Alabama. His parents were Georgia natives George Cader Powell, a blacksmith, farmer, Baptist minister, and county tax collector and assessor, and his wife, Patience. Although for a time during Lewis's childhood the Powells owned a few slaves, they were hardly rich. Still, both were very well respected in their community. Like Herold, Lewis was the sixth of ten children; he was also the Powells' youngest son and, also like Herold, had received at least the standard amount of schooling for a boy of his background.[11]

Most of Lewis Powell's childhood was spent in rural Georgia, to which his parents returned with their children when Lewis was four. When he was fifteen, the Powells moved to Florida, apparently for financial reasons. Throughout his youth, Powell's family demonstrated a strong commitment to religion, and Lewis himself seems to have been no exception. His father later recalled that at the age of twelve, Lewis had expressed a desire to become a minister himself; at fourteen or fifteen, he was holding prayer meetings, presumably for his friends and family. In contrast with the picture that emerged in the weeks after Powell stabbed Secretary Seward, George Powell remembered his son as a "pious, kind, and tenderhearted" boy, the child he most expected to follow in his footsteps in the church. At the same time, he also recalled that his handsome son was a popular fellow, a "great favorite with the ladies." In short, Lewis Powell gave all the signs of being a promising young man with a bright future, both professionally and personally.[12]

Florida seceded from the Union on January 10, 1861. That May, seventeen-year-old Lewis Powell enlisted (giving his age as nineteen) in the so-called Hamilton (County) Blues, which would soon become

"Lewis Payne [Powell] the Assassin,"
from Harper's Weekly,
May 27, 1865

Company I of the Second Florida Infantry. Powell's three older brothers followed his example, though they enlisted in different regiments. Two, Oliver and Benjamin, died in battle; the third, George, was seriously wounded and lost a limb during the siege of Petersburg. As for Lewis, his family never saw him again. Dedicating himself to the cause of his native region, Powell was soon transformed from the gentle boy his father remembered into a hardened fighter—so hardened, in fact, that he was described as keeping among his belongings the skull of a Union soldier, which he occasionally used as an ashtray. Writes one biographer, Powell became "a most efficient soldier who often boasted that he never wounded the enemy, he either killed or missed." Powell's career with the Second Florida was cut short just before the Battle of Gettysburg in July 1863, when he sustained a wound to his right wrist. Following a period of hospitalization and convalescence, Powell spent time as a cavalryman with John Singleton Mosby's fierce partisan rangers. He then left the military altogether at the end of 1864 and, giving the appearance of a former Confederate soldier who had seen the evil of his former ways, swore an official oath of allegiance to the United States, though clearly with-

Lewis Powell.
*Courtesy of the
Library of Congress*

out conviction. Four months later Powell was in prison awaiting trial for his involvement in the Lincoln assassination conspiracy.[13]

If the eyewitness accounts identifying Powell as Seward's attacker seemed incontestable as early as April 18, no similarly substantial evidence had as yet accumulated for the woman in whose home Powell had been arrested: Mary Surratt. Nevertheless, in part because her son John had for some time been known to the federal government as a Confederate courier and, since April 14, had been identified as a close friend of the President's murderer; and in part because of Lewis Powell's untimely and ill-explained visit to her boardinghouse on the night of the seventeenth, Mary Surratt was hauled into custody, first in the Old Capitol Prison and then, like Herold and Powell, in the Old Arsenal Penitentiary. Born in 1823 to Elizabeth Anne and Archibald Jenkins on a tobacco farm in southern Maryland about a dozen miles from the capital, Mary was only two years old when her father died, leaving her mother to manage the family's estate, including a small number of slaves, and to raise Mary and her two brothers alone. As a property-owning widow only thirty years of age, Elizabeth Jenkins should have been able to remarry, but for whatever reason, she did not do so. Over the next decade she handled her family and financial affairs sufficiently well on her own to enroll Mary, at the age of twelve, in a private girls' boarding school in Alexandria, Virginia. Despite the fact that Elizabeth herself was an Episcopalian and her late husband had also been Protestant, the Academy for Young Ladies in Alexandria was Catholic, and over the course of her four years there Mary Jenkins converted to that faith. She remained an extremely devout and active Catholic for the duration of her life.[14]

Shortly after her return to Prince George's County in 1839, Mary Jenkins met John Harrison Surratt, a man ten years her senior whose ancestors had been among the early settlers of the region in the late 1600s. Although he agreed to convert to Catholicism so they could marry, John Surratt was hardly a model of moral behavior, having already fathered at least one child out of wedlock. Unfortunately for Mary, who married him when she was seventeen, John Surratt's character only became increasingly dissolute as time passed. Yet she bore him three children in quick succession: Isaac in 1841, Elisabeth Susanna ("Anna") in 1843, and John Jr. in 1844.[15]

Mary and John Surratt's marriage was troubled and their life together was hard. Like their families before them, Mary and John farmed tobacco with the help of a few slaves. Still, although John Surratt Sr. was a mediocre businessman at best, by 1854, with Mary's help, he had augmented their farmlands with a general store, a tavern, and a gristmill. He had also become the first postmaster of the newly established "Surrattsville" post office, transforming the Surratt family and its operations into the economic core of the small community that had arisen around it. At the same time, however, John Surratt Sr. proved to be the greatest threat to his own and his family's stability and survival. By 1857, through debt and misadventure, he had reduced the family's holdings in Maryland to less than six hundred acres. By the summer of 1862 he was dead presumably of alcohol abuse, leaving Mary, their nineteen-year-old daughter Anna, and their eighteen-year-old son John in dire financial straits. Son Isaac had left home the year before for a job as a pony express rider in Mexico.[16]

Like her mother before her, Mary Surratt did not remarry. Rather, she struggled on in Surrattsville for two more years, trying to hold the family, the farm, and the business together and managing the few remaining slaves. By the summer of 1864, however, forty-one-year-old Mary Surratt was weary to the bone and frustrated by the clamoring of creditors. One after another, her late husband's shady business deals, unpaid loans, and debts challenged her very best management skills. She decided to settle up affairs as best she could in Surrattsville, selling or renting various remaining properties and leaving the house and tavern in the charge of a former Washington, D.C., police officer named John Lloyd. With what personal and financial resources remained, Mary Surratt banked the family's future on an investment John Sr. had made over a decade before: a small, debt-free house in Washington. She, Anna, and John Jr. moved there in the fall of 1864 and immediately began to advertise rooms for rent.

It was because of the suspected goings-on at that house over the previous months—goings-on that seemed to be related to John Surratt Jr.'s activities as a Confederate courier and his association with John Wilkes Booth—that federal officers and D.C. police descended on the Surratt boardinghouse within hours of the assassination. They came at about two thirty on the morning of the fifteenth, after John Surratt's name arose repeatedly as a probable accomplice to Booth during Edwin Stanton's preliminary investigations at the Petersen house. Indeed, some of Stanton's early telegraphic messages even identified John Surratt as the presumed assailant of Secretary Seward, and some newspapers later published the same allegations. Not finding John Surratt home on April 15, the officers and detectives left empty-handed and unsatisfied.

By the time they returned on the night of the seventeenth, however, based on the evidence that had been gathered thus far, they had good reason to believe that perhaps John Surratt's mother may also have been involved in the murder plot. In any case, they felt certain that she must have known of her son's links to the Confederate secret service, and that she could not possibly have remained entirely oblivious of whatever plans her son and his friends—including Booth—were hatching under her roof. As Lewis Powell's biographer, Betty Owns-

Mary E. Surratt.
Courtesy of the Library of Congress

bey, puts it simply: "Not much can go on in an eight-room house and remain unnoticed for long." If nothing else, investigators hoped that by arresting Mary Surratt they might secure a lead to her son, whom they were having difficulty locating. And if they felt any hesitation about arresting her for that purpose, Lewis Powell's unexpected appearance at the boardinghouse dispelled it. As we have seen, Mary Surratt, too, went to jail on April 17, along with several members of her household (they were subsequently released).[17]

On the twentieth, yet another key suspect was brought into federal custody. That morning, a detachment of soldiers from the First Delaware Cavalry arrested German immigrant George Andrew Atzerodt in Germantown, Maryland, where he had been staying for the past four days at the home of his cousin, Ernest Hartman Richter. George Atzerodt was born in a small Prussian village in 1835. The fourth child of a blacksmith and his wife, Atzerodt moved with his family to the United States in 1844. Initially the Atzerodts took up farming in Germantown with the Richters, who had emigrated at the same time. Perhaps in an effort to become more independent or improve their standard of living, the Atzerodt family subsequently moved to Montross, Virginia, where George's father, Johann, ran a blacksmith shop in the early 1850s. After Johann died in 1856, the family returned to Maryland. Taking advantage of skills he had acquired as an apprentice while in Virginia, George Atzerodt initially worked for a couple of coach makers in Washington, but in 1857 he headed for the small community of Port Tobacco on the lower Potomac River, about thirty-five miles from the capital. There he established a carriage-making and painting business with his elder brother, John Ernest Christian Atzerodt.[18]

When the Civil War began, each of the Atzerodt brothers undertook a new line of work made possible by the war itself. John Atzerodt accepted a job as a military detective with the provost marshal's office in Baltimore, ironically a post that involved him in tracking down crime suspects such as his brother ultimately became. George, in turn, dissolved the business he and John had established together, but continued to do some coach painting. At the same time he began to earn additional money by ferrying spies and operatives (possibly both Union and Confederate) back and forth across the Potomac. Among those he rowed over the river on more than one occasion was John Surratt Jr., almost certainly the person who ultimately introduced Atzerodt to Booth. Indeed, as federal officials discovered after the assassination, during the first months of 1865 Atzerodt visited the Surratt boardinghouse on several occasions, including once staying overnight.[19]

Atzerodt's precise role in the plot against Lincoln was not yet completely clear on the morning he was arrested, though it was later learned that Booth had assigned him to murder Vice President Andrew Johnson. Still, the circumstantial evidence connecting Atzerodt, whom some of the boardinghouse residents had nicknamed "Port Tobacco," to the plot in some way or another was already quite strong. Among other things, on the morning of April 14, Atzerodt had taken a room at the Kirkwood House, on 12th Street and Pennsylvania Avenue, where the vice president had his living quarters. At the time he registered, Atzerodt paid in advance; he carried no luggage, and apparently occupied the room for only a few hours before disappearing. When Atzerodt's room was examined by the police on the fifteenth, after his name had surfaced in their early inquiries in connection with Surratt and Booth, a number of suspicious items were discovered, including a loaded revolver and three boxes of cartridges, a twelve-inch bowie knife, a black coat whose pocket con-

George Atzerodt.
Courtesy of the
Library of Congress

tained a bankbook belonging to John Wilkes Booth, and a map of the Southern states.[20]

Struggling to piece the assassination puzzle together, officials at first wondered whether it might in fact have been Atzerodt who attacked Secretary Seward. But they soon realized the true nature of Atzerodt's specific task in connection with the conspiracy and also recognized that somewhere along the line, perhaps even at the moment Booth and Powell were going into action, Atzerodt had balked. Though it was impossible to determine in the short term whether it was cowardice, or reason, or some mixture of the two that had stayed Atzerodt's hand, it was clear that he still potentially offered a wellspring of information. Moreover, in legal terms he could be found guilty of participation in the conspiracy even if he had, in the end, failed to complete his assignment.[21]

Around 9:00 P.M. on April 15, Edwin Stanton (then still overseeing the investigations firsthand) directed Assistant Secretary of War Charles A. Dana to issue a formal description of Atzerodt to the press. On the sixteenth local newspapers began to carry notices that the War Department was offering a $25,000 reward for his capture, and early on the morning of the twentieth, Atzerodt—who had care-lessly left a vivid trail for the investigators to follow—was quietly arrested. A few hours later, he, along with Richter, began the journey back to Washington under heavily armed guard. According to arrest-ing officer Sergeant Zachariah W. Gemmill, although he was ques-tioned several times along the way to the capital, Atzerodt never once inquired about the reasons for his arrest. On the contrary, over the next several days he fulfilled eager investigators' expectations by pro-viding an abundance of important information about the conspiracy and his own connection with it. Back in Washington, Atzerodt and his cousin (who was later released) were placed in double irons aboard the *Saugus*. On April 23, Atzerodt was removed to the *Mon-tauk* and hooded, and on the twenty-ninth, he was transferred to the Old Arsenal.[22]

Among the evidence the government had amassed by late April, that pertaining to the apparent involvement in Booth's scheme of David Herold, Lewis Powell, Mary Surratt, and George Atzerodt was undoubtedly some of the most damning. Also very strong, of course, was the evidence against John Surratt Jr., whose whereabouts Joseph Holt still urgently hoped to discover. As time passed, however, efforts to smoke Surratt out of hiding continued to prove unsuccessful, and suspicion mounted that he had in fact escaped to Canada, probably to Montreal, although a team of detectives sent there to find him had been unsuccessful. Even the government's offer of a $25,000 reward for John Surratt's capture failed to produce results. Frustrated by this apparent setback, Holt's investigators nevertheless continued to find plenty of material on which to develop their case against John Wilkes Booth's local accomplices, important pieces of which were provided by two of Booth's boyhood friends, Samuel Arnold and Michael O'Laughlen, both of whom had been taken into custody very early on.

Born in the Georgetown section of Washington, D.C., in Septem-ber 1834, Samuel Bland Arnold was the son of George Arnold, a well-known and respected baker, and his wife, Mary Jane. Samuel Arnold spent most of his youth with his parents and three siblings in Baltimore. In the early 1850s he attended St. Timothy's Hall, a mili-

Samuel Arnold.
Courtesy of the
Library of Congress

tary academy in Catonsville, Maryland, where he was a classmate of
Booth and where the two seem to have made something of a habit of
getting into trouble together. According to one source, Booth, Arnold,
and a number of other students once got into trouble with the administration after they stole some guns and began taunting the faculty.[23]
Perhaps such mischief foreshadowed their activities together in the
spring of 1865. In any case, after the Civil War broke out—unlike
Booth, who preferred to support the Confederacy as a noncombat-
ant—Arnold joined the Confederate army, serving with Company A
of the First Maryland Infantry Volunteers at the first Battle of Bull
Run in July 1861. He was discharged about four months later as a
consequence of his poor health, but returned after some rest to follow
the army in an unofficial capacity for several more months. He then
took a series of jobs as a clerk, first in Tennessee and then in Georgia.

In January 1864, having learned that his mother was gravely ill,
Arnold returned to Baltimore. Over the next several months he spent
time in the city and at the family's country home about six miles away
in what was then known as Hookstown. There, Arnold found life
increasingly "tedious and insipid." As summer faded, Arnold wel-

comed the diversion from his boredom that his old friend Booth unexpectedly offered. Sometime in late August, Booth made contact out of the blue and invited Arnold to join him for wine and cigars at Barnum's Hotel in Baltimore. When they met, Booth outlined a plan to capture President Lincoln and ship him south, where he was to be held as a hostage in exchange for the release by the federal government of Confederate prisoners of war, and perhaps even for the South's independence. Arnold signed on, probably for the excitement of the adventure as much as anything else. He later recalled the kidnap plan as "humane," "patriotic," and a "legitimate act of war."[24]

Someone else who signed on to the abduction plot that evening was Michael O'Laughlen.[25] Born in June 1840, O'Laughlen was the son of a well-respected Catholic family in Baltimore and he, like Arnold, knew Booth from their school days. One family member described O'Laughlen as having been a "very timid boy" who grew into an "amiable" young man, moderate in his sensibilities, and who became a fine craftsman, particularly skilled in engraving as well as ornamental plasterwork. Once the war began, however, O'Laughlen's Southern sympathies drew him away from such quiet activities and into the Confederate army. Like Arnold, O'Laughlen lasted in the service only briefly, however, probably for reasons of health, and by the fall of 1862 he was back in civilian clothes. Over the next two and a half years O'Laughlen worked in his brother's produce and feed business in Washington, D.C., and then as an agent for the business, traveling between Baltimore and Washington. Like Arnold, O'Laughlen undoubtedly welcomed the similarly unexpected invitation from Booth in late August 1864. It was on that occasion, at Barnum's Hotel, that Arnold and O'Laughlen met for the first time.[26]

Over the next several months the three men remained in loose but steady contact. In late December or early January they met again in Baltimore, where Booth placed into his old friends' possession a selection of "Spencer rifles, revolvers, knives, belts, handcuffs, canteens, boxes of cartridges and cartridge caps" taken from a trunkload he had acquired in New York, telling them to transport the weapons to Washington. A couple of additional meetings of the three followed shortly thereafter, but Booth gave Arnold and O'Laughlen little in the

Michael O'Laughlen.
Courtesy of the
Library of Congress

way of detail about how his abduction plan was progressing. Arnold later claimed that during this period he and O'Laughlen were "left entirely in the dark" while Booth "was always pressed with business with a man unknown to us then," a man by the name of John Surratt Jr. Meanwhile, in early February 1865, O'Laughlen and Arnold took rooms a few blocks away from both Ford's Theater and the Surratt boardinghouse. There, Arnold later recalled, he and O'Laughlen met quite often with Booth, as often as four times a week, but always for just a few minutes. To pass the time, O'Laughlen and Arnold occasionally took drives around the city, to Georgetown and elsewhere, and engaged in drinking and other "amusements." They also traveled frequently to Baltimore together; to curious inquirers they claimed they were in the oil business.[27]

On March 15, 1865, Booth, Arnold, O'Laughlen, Atzerodt, Herold, Powell, and the mysterious John Surratt all finally came together for the first time, at Gautier's Saloon on Pennsylvania Avenue for a midnight supper and conference. Clearly, while remain-

ing vague about his activities with Arnold and O'Laughlen, Booth
had spent the past months building a team of individuals willing to
participate in his abduction scheme. Recalled Arnold later, "This was
the only assembling or meeting of the parties held either in the City
of Washington or any other place in connection with the abduction of
Abraham Lincoln, President of the United States." At this meeting,
for which Booth rented a private parlor at Gautier's, the seven men
drank abundantly, ate oysters, smoked cigars, and discussed the plan
in great detail. Initially they focused on a plan Booth had devised to
capture Lincoln while he was at the theater, preferably Ford's,
behind which Booth had already rented a stable, and whose rear
exits—useful for escape—Booth had recently shown to Arnold and
O'Laughlen. In the face of this specific plan, however, Arnold
revealed strong misgivings. "To me," he later wrote, "it seemed like
the height of madness and would lead to the sacrifice of us all, without attaining the object for which we combined together." Arnold's
resistance provoked a harsh response from the determined Booth,
who chastised his old friend severely for displaying cowardice. Holding his ground, Arnold insisted that if the abduction did not go forward within the week, he would withdraw his support completely,
though he also swore not to betray the others.[28]

Perhaps it was Arnold's ultimatum that drove the plotters forward.
In any case, only two days later, on March 17, the seven conspirators
made an attempt to kidnap Lincoln, having learned that the President
was scheduled to attend a matinee performance of the play *Still
Waters Run Deep* at the Campbell Hospital, situated on 7th Street.
This was the same wide-open road that Lincoln frequently took to the
Soldiers' Home, where he often went for respite during the war.
Rather than capturing him at the theater itself, the conspirators
planned to intercept Lincoln's carriage, which they expected would be
only lightly guarded if at all, on the return trip. They would then
hijack the carriage and its occupant across the eastern branch of the
Potomac via Benning's Bridge into Maryland, transfer their prisoner
onto horseback, and flee through the pro-Confederate countryside to
boats waiting on the banks of the Potomac to carry them to Virginia.
The plan was well laid out, but at the last minute Lincoln changed his

agenda, choosing instead to remain in the city and address the soldiers of the 140th Indiana Volunteer Regiment. Thus, when the
would-be abductors went to seize the President, he was nowhere to
be found. Foiled, they scattered, and three days later, on March 20,
Arnold and O'Laughlen left the capital for Baltimore. A week after
that, Arnold wrote Booth a letter explaining why he was pulling out
of the kidnap scheme altogether.[29]

Officers Voltaire Randall and Eaton G. Horner arrested Samuel
Arnold on April 17 at John W. Wharton's sutlery near Fortress Monroe, Virginia, where he had recently begun working as a clerk. Randall and Horner found incriminating evidence among Arnold's things,
including "some letters, Papers, clothing, a [loaded] revolver, and
some cartridges." Moreover, almost immediately under questioning,
Arnold—"the first person closely associated with Booth to talk
openly of the conspiracy"—began to confess, though he insisted that
he had in fact withdrawn from the kidnap scheme at the end of
March and was thus uninvolved with the murderous attacks of April
14. Additionally, Arnold freely admitted to being the author of a
March 27, 1865, letter, signed "Sam" and found among Booth's
effects at the National Hotel in Washington on the night after the
assassination. This letter announced "Sam's" loss of confidence in
Booth's "manner of proceeding" and urged Booth to avoid acting
"rashly or in haste." Of great significance in the long run, not least of
all from the perspective of Joseph Holt and the Bureau of Military
Justice, was the fact that the "Sam" letter suggested that Booth "go
and see how it will be taken at R——d" (almost certainly a reference
to the Confederate capital at Richmond) before making another
move. As one contemporary later put it, the "Sam" letter, whose contents hit the press as early as April 15, "furnished the first and most
important clue to the Government and was one of the direct means of
unearthing the Conspiracy." Two years after the events in question,
Arnold himself posited the theory that Booth, angry at Arnold's withdrawal from the original conspiracy, had purposely left the letter in
his trunk—though Arnold had asked him to destroy it—in order to
"betray me into the hands of the Government when he perpetrated
his damning act."[30]

The "Sam" letter was an important piece of evidence for the assassination investigators and especially for Joseph Holt's shaping of the government's case, supporting as it did not only the theory of a small-scale conspiracy of local villains, but also that of a grand conspiracy involving the Confederate leadership at Richmond. As it turns out, the individual probably most responsible for swiftly linking the "Sam" letter to Samuel Arnold was the provost marshal general of Baltimore, James L. McPhail, who also happened to be the wartime employer of George Atzerodt's brother, John. McPhail knew Samuel Arnold, Michael O'Laughlen, and their families and was aware that the two men were longtime friends of Booth. He put investigators on O'Laughlen's trail as well as Arnold's. O'Laughlen upon learning that officials of the federal government were looking to question him, simply turned himself in to the Baltimore police on April 17.[31]

As for Arnold, following his arrest he was taken to Baltimore, where he was questioned initially by McPhail and produced a detailed written statement. Arnold was turned over to the commanding officer at Baltimore's Fort McHenry, birthplace of "The Star Spangled Banner" some fifty years before. There Arnold recalled being "placed in a loathsome and filthy cell" and then stripped and searched and put in a "dungeon beneath the Earthwork of the Fort, heavily ironed hand and foot, where not a ray of light could penetrate." Around midnight Arnold was awakened, ordered to dress, and removed to Washington for imprisonment aboard the *Saugus*, where he was secured with irons "so tightly fitting," he later wrote, "that the blood could not circulate and my hands were fearfully swollen, the outward skin changing its appearance to a mixture of black, red and purple color." A few days later, Arnold found himself not only in irons but also hooded like the other male prisoners. He theorized morbidly that their captors hoped to accustom each prisoner to the "death cap" all would be required to wear at their executions. Following his surrender to police, O'Laughlen, too, was taken to Washington and placed on board the *Saugus*, hooded and in irons. On April 29, like the rest of Booth's presumed key local associates who were already in custody, both men were transferred to the Old Arsenal Penitentiary.[32]

Also taken into federal custody on April 17 was an employee of

Ford's Theater whom investigators thought had facilitated Booth's escape from the scene of the crime. Born on August 10, 1825, in York County, Pennsylvania, Edman ("Ned") Spangler had lived in Baltimore for many years and had worked for John T. Ford for the last four.[33] Ford later recalled that Spangler, a quiet widower, had generally spent his summers (when the theater was on hiatus) crab fishing back in Baltimore, where his wife was buried. First as an intermittent and then as a steady employee at the theater, Spangler spent the bulk of his time during the war in Washington, however, working as a stagehand, scenery shifter, and general laborer during the evening performances, and doing unskilled carpentry at other times of day under the direction of the theater's official stage carpenter, James Gifford. Spangler's financial resources were very limited; for this reason and perhaps also because he so often worked late into the evenings at the theater, Spangler tended to sleep at Ford's, though he stored a valise and took his meals at a nearby boardinghouse owned by a Mrs. Scott.[34]

Those who knew Ned Spangler best described him as a decent sort, a "good-natured, kind, willing man" who socialized little, patiently endured being the regular butt of others' jokes, and kept his political sentiments to himself. According to John Ford, Spangler was essentially a private fellow, without affectation, his primary flaw being that he was "a little dissipated" and "fond of spreeing around." In other words, he occasionally drank too much, which caused his work to suffer, though he typically remained pleasant while under the influence. Most notably, in his day-to-day life Spangler seems to have served quite frequently as a "drudge" for the actor John Wilkes Booth, whom he had known for many years, having also worked as a carpenter for Booth's father in Baltimore. James Gifford explained later that Spangler's willingness to do odd jobs for Booth was not really that unusual, for Booth's gregarious, charming, and charismatic personality made all want to do his bidding. In any case, Spangler had earned a reputation around the theater for doing just that—Booth's bidding—and on the night of April 14, 1865, it got him into serious trouble.[35]

As Holt's investigators soon discovered, John Wilkes Booth's movements during the day he shot President Lincoln included a series of earlier visits to Ford's Theater. Shortly before noon, Booth

Edman Spangler.
Courtesy of the Library of Congress

appeared at Ford's for the first time that day. While he was on the road Booth typically had correspondents address their letters to Ford's, where he often performed, and he had come that morning to pick up his mail. While there, Booth engaged in conversation with Henry Clay ("Harry") Ford, John's brother and the treasurer of the theater, and learned that both President Lincoln and General Ulysses S. Grant were scheduled to attend the theater that night. Notice of their attendance also appeared in an early afternoon edition of the *Washington Evening Star*.

Clearly at some point following the failed kidnap attempt in mid-March, Booth's original abduction plan had mutated into a murder plan, although when exactly that change took place is not, and probably never will be, known for certain. Assassination scholar William Hanchett notes, however, that Booth's "zeal for the South and his abhorrence of what the North was doing were inflamed by Lincoln's visit to Richmond on April 4, 1865." Over a week later, when he (and perhaps some of his co-conspirators) joined a crowd to hear Lincoln speak from a second-story window at the Executive Mansion concerning his emerging Reconstruction policies, Booth became absolutely enraged. According to Hanchett, on that occasion Booth exclaimed: "That means nigger citizenship. Now, by God, I'll put him through." If Hanchett is right, it would certainly help to explain why, once Booth learned of Lincoln's and Grant's intentions to celebrate the Union victory with a viewing that night of the play *Our American Cousin* (Grant later changed his mind for personal reasons), he became possessed by the belief that his opportunity to strike a meaningful blow for the Confederacy had arrived at last. Virtually all of Booth's activity during the rest of that day, which included some heavy drinking, pointed toward the assassination.[36]

Around four thirty that afternoon, Booth brought a hired mare to Ford's and put her in the stable behind the theater that he had previously shown to Arnold and O'Laughlen. Then he went next door to a restaurant and had a few drinks with some of the theater staff, including Edman Spangler. Sometime between five and six o'clock, Booth left, but he returned around nine, removing the mare from her stable and calling for the trusted Spangler to come and hold her. She was a difficult horse to keep tied: Spangler later recalled Booth describing the mare as a "bad little bitch" who tended to break her bridle in order to get free. Busy with his work inside now that the play was already under way, Spangler came briefly to Booth's aid, but soon called Joseph ("Peanuts") Burroughs, another employee of the theater who was also familiar with Booth, to take his place. Recalled Burroughs later, "When Spangler told me to hold the horse, I said I could not; I had to go in to attend to my door. He told me to hold it, and if there was anything wrong to lay the blame on him; so I held the horse." Within the hour, Booth had reentered the theater, proceeded unhindered to the President's box, shot Lincoln, jumped down to the stage brandishing the knife with which he had slashed Major Rathbone, and escaped through the passageway that led from the left-hand side of the stage outdoors to the rear of the theater. There the unsuspecting Burroughs waited with the rented mare. Mounting the horse, Booth kicked or struck Burroughs violently in order to drive him back, and escaped down the alley.[37]

Spangler's movements immediately following Booth's escape are unclear, but he does not seem to have been among those brought into the parlor at the Petersen house, or anywhere else, for immediate questioning. Rather, he moved about freely, though quite anxiously

Ford's Theater with guards posted.
Courtesy of the Library of Congress

thanks to his well-known connection with Booth, whose name had so quickly been associated with the crime. At some point on the night of April 14–15 Spangler bedded down in the carpenter's shop, located in a building adjacent to the theater, rather than in his usual room. The next day, Louis J. Carland, another employee, ran into Spangler at the theater, which, despite being under close surveillance by the Washington Metropolitan Police and others, still remained accessible for theater workers to come and go essentially as they pleased.[38]

To Carland, Spangler confessed his concern about rumors that angry citizens planned to set fire to the theater and burn it to the ground. Commenting that he was afraid to sleep there anymore, Spangler gratefully accepted Carland's invitation to spend the night of the fifteenth with him instead, in a room that, like the carpenter's shop, also adjoined the theater but was not part of it. Spangler may well have felt safer as he drifted off to sleep in Carland's room on the fifteenth, but outside the building suspicions about his involvement in the assassination were multiplying. Indeed, late that very night Spangler was taken in for questioning by the police, at which point he admitted having known Booth for over a decade, having had drinks with him late in the afternoon of the fourteenth, and having been called on that night to hold the bridle of the hired mare Booth eventually used in his escape.[39]

Released on Sunday morning April 16, Spangler enjoyed only twenty-four more hours of freedom before he was formally arrested by officer William Eaton on the morning of the seventeenth—this time at the boardinghouse where he kept his things—and booked as an accomplice to Booth. A search of the valise Spangler stored at Mrs. Scott's boardinghouse had yielded some apparently meaningless odds and ends, but also a rope about eighty feet in length, long enough, apparently, to heighten suspicions about his possible involvement in Booth's deadly plans. As they had done with Mary Surratt, officials first placed Spangler in the Old Capitol Prison. Next they moved him briefly—in chains like the others—to the *Montauk*. From there, Spangler was transferred with the other suspects to the Old Arsenal Penitentiary to await his fate.[40]

By the time Secretary Stanton turned over control of the investigations and the prosecution of the crimes to Joseph Holt and the Bureau of Military Justice, Samuel Arnold, Michael O'Laughlen, Edman Spangler, Lewis Powell, George Atzerodt, and Mary Surratt were all in federal custody. Four days later, and just two days before Booth himself would be located and killed and his frightened guide and companion, David Herold, hauled in, the eighth of the nine key living suspects associated with Booth's local operations was also imprisoned in Washington. In this case, the suspect was Samuel Alexander Mudd, a country doctor who had set Booth's broken leg early on the morning of April 15.[41]

Born in December 1833, Samuel Mudd was raised on his Catholic family's farm near Bryantown and educated at St. John's College in Frederick, Maryland, and at Georgetown College in Washington. Mudd later attended Baltimore Medical College, from which he graduated in 1856 with a medical degree. Soon thereafter the young doctor returned to the Bryantown area, where he opened his own medical practice while also establishing his family (he and his wife, Sarah, had their first four children before 1865), running a tobacco farm, and managing a number of slaves and at least one white employee.[42]

According to Mudd's own statement, given to Holt's assistant Colonel Wells on April 21, it was at about four o'clock in the morning on the fifteenth that two men arrived at his home, one of them knocking hard on the door and waking him up. Opening the door after some hesitation, Mudd claimed that these "strangers" informed him that while they had been en route to Washington, one of the horses had fallen, causing its rider to break his leg. Mudd helped the injured man into the house, up the stairs, and on to a bed. "I had no proper pasteboard for making splints," Mudd told the officers questioning him, so he fashioned something out of an "old bandbox" instead and, cutting off the boot that held it, he mended the leg—a "straight fracture of the tibia about two inches above the ankle." Mudd worked as quickly and as carefully as he could under the circumstances. Meanwhile, the injured man's companion who, Mudd recalled, "appeared to be very youthful . . . a very fast young man" and quite loquacious, tended to the horses and then came into the house to join Mudd for breakfast.

In the course of their conversation, Mudd told Wells, it became clear that the younger man seemed to know a great deal about the surrounding area; for example, he mentioned the names of a number of neighborhood residents. Since riding seemed out of the question for his friend, the young man informed his host that he hoped to procure a carriage for traveling, at which point Mudd graciously escorted his guest to the home of his father, Henry L. Mudd. No carriage was available there, however, so the two men decided to search for one in Bryantown. They had traveled part of the way there together when the younger man turned back, apparently having decided to take his friend on horseback after all for the next portion of their trip. Dr. Mudd continued on to Bryantown alone to run some errands, and it was there that he learned about the terrible events that had taken place in Washington the previous night. Only after he returned home did the two visitors finally depart, mounting their horses around five

Samuel Mudd.
Courtesy of the
Library of Congress

in the afternoon after paying the doctor twenty-five dollars for his assistance. The injured man was still in great pain, but at least he now had the benefit of the splint and a rough set of crutches Mudd had made for him while he had rested fitfully during the day. "I do not know where they went," Mudd insisted to his interrogators on April 21, nor did he know who the men were, though in hindsight he admitted that it seemed extremely likely that the wounded man, who had kept his face hidden as much as possible and had spoken little throughout the day, was John Wilkes Booth, and his companion was David Herold.

Of great significance in this statement was the fact that Samuel Mudd admitted that he had met Booth once before—in November or December 1864, he claimed—and had even put him up for a night and been a witness to his purchase the following day (from one of Mudd's neighbors) of a "darkish bay horse" with a large head and a "defect in one eye." At the same time, although Mudd was able to describe to Wells the men who had appeared at his door on the morning of the fifteenth—giving their approximate heights and weights, commenting on their complexions, and so forth—he still declared firmly that he had not recognized either man that day. Moreover, according to Mudd's statement, even word of the assassination of Lincoln and the attack on Secretary Seward had failed to arouse any suspicions about the strangers to whom he had offered hospitality and medical assistance. Only when he began to piece together his knowledge of the events of April 14 and his realization, following the men's departure, that the boot he had cut from the injured man's swollen leg had the name "J. Wilkes" written inside, had his suspicions become elevated. Still it was only later, when he further recalled that at some point during their stay at the house the injured man had requested a razor and had shaved off his moustache, that Mudd finally decided to share his suspicions for the first time with his cousins George and William Mudd. This he did, he told Colonel Wells, on the sixteenth. The next day, George Mudd spoke with federal officers stationed in Bryantown, informing them that two strange visitors, one of whom had a broken leg, had spent most of April 15 at Samuel Mudd's home before riding away to whereabouts unknown.[43]

On April 18, military detectives led by Lieutenant Alexander Lovett came to the Mudd farm to question the doctor and his wife. They returned on the twenty-first, conducting the initial part of their interrogation that day at the farm, while also attempting to search the house. Then they took Mudd with them to Bryantown, where they subjected him to further questioning. The next morning, the officers interrogated Mudd a third time, again in Bryantown. Over the course of all this questioning, additional details about Samuel Mudd's strange visitors emerged, and the detectives became increasingly convinced that the good doctor knew even more than he was slowly letting on. Writing to General Christopher Augur back in Washington on April 22, Wells expressed his uncertainty about Mudd's veracity: "Dr. Mudd is either ignorant," Wells wrote, "or willfully conceals the direction that the fugitives took." Finally, on April 24, Wells ordered Mudd's arrest and his transfer to Washington. Like Mary Surratt and

Edman Spangler, Samuel Mudd was imprisoned first at the Old Capitol. Then, on April 29 he was transferred like the other seven to a
small, individual cell at the Old Arsenal.[44]

Three days later, on May 2, 1865, a *Philadelphia Inquirer* correspondent wrote with relief: "Justice and fame are equally and simultaneously satisfied. The President is not yet in his sarcophagus, but all
the conspirators against his life, with a minor exception or two, are
in their prison cells, waiting for the halter."[45] Although Holt and his
assistants continued to interrogate a wide range of possible suspects,
they were deeply relieved to have these eight already in hand. At the
same time, they remained convinced that Booth and his accomplices
must have acted at the explicit behest of Jefferson Davis and the Confederate leadership. Meanwhile, President Andrew Johnson requested
through Secretary Stanton, that Holt produce immediately a list of
those persons not yet in custody against whom sufficient evidence had
accumulated to indicate their clear involvement in the April 14
attacks.[46] Although Holt surely shared his assistant Henry Burnett's
suspicions about the possible involvement in the crimes of Western
conspirators as well as Southern ones, at this point he chose to focus
on the latter, most likely because he believed their guilt was more
readily apparent and could more easily be proven. After all, their
names were well-known, and their leadership in violent antigovernment activities over the last four years was indisputable. That the
crimes of April 14 were of a piece with the Confederacy's proven
determination to destroy the Union seemed self-evident to Holt, as it
did to many who mourned the loss of Lincoln and prayed in earnest
for the secretary of state's recovery.

And so on May 2, Holt took a bold and irrevocable step, officially
declaring to Stanton and President Johnson his certainty that none
other than Jefferson Davis himself stood at the head of the conspiracy responsible for the assassination of Lincoln. Holt's step was bold,
but hardly reckless or surprising. Stanton himself had reached the
same conclusion. Indeed, as early as the day Holt took over the investigations, the *New York Times* had explicitly linked the assassination
conspiracy with the leadership of the Slave Power itself, noting that

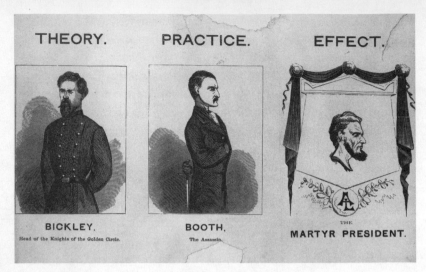

THEORY.   PRACTICE.   EFFECT.

BICKLEY.
Head of the Knights of the Golden Circle.

BOOTH.
The Assassin.

THE
MARTYR PRESIDENT.

"Theory. Practice. Effect.": Theorizing Booth's connection to the
Knights of the Golden Circle.
Courtesy of the Library of Congress

the attacks on Lincoln and Seward amounted to nothing less than the
"legitimate crowning of a whole system of crimes and atrocities" perpetrated by the South, beginning with slavery itself.[47]

With this thinking in mind, Holt also named several members of
the Confederate government's so-called Canadian Cabinet as high-
level suspects still at large, and as co-conspirators with Booth, whose
wartime work as a blockade runner and participation in other activities linked to the Confederate secret service were now coming to
light. The Canadian Cabinet was a group of highly placed agents who
had been operating primarily from Montreal on behalf of the Confederate cause since the spring of 1864. From among its ranks Holt
called for the arrests of Beverly Tucker, once a U.S. consul in Liverpool, England; George Sanders, famous for his open advocacy of the
assassination of tyrants; William Cleary; Jacob Thompson, his former
colleague in the Buchanan administration, who had resigned after the
failed attempt to reinforce Fort Sumter in January 1861; and Clement
C. Clay, his former friend, the Alabama senator. At a cabinet meeting
in Washington, D.C., on the afternoon of May 2 it was determined

that rewards ranging from $100,000 (for Davis) to $10,000 (for Cleary) would be offered for the arrests of these men. Posters were printed and circulated widely, and the nation's newspapers carried similar announcements.[48]

In the meantime, Holt and his assistants prepared for the trial of the eight alleged conspirators now being held under close guard at the Old Arsenal.

It is now settled that the regular trial of the . . . persons in custody for conspiring in the assassination plot, before a military commission, will begin in Washington on Monday of next week. . . . The trial will probably not be a secret one, and our readers will be enabled to hear of its development day by day through the *Journal*. It will be a trial of deep importance and interest. The Conspirators will all be hung. We hope soon to be able to report that Jeff Davis will be the first to be hung.

—*Lewiston* [Maine] *Daily Evening Journal*, May 5, 1865

If it seems too incredible to be true that the conspicuous rebel chiefs were accessory to the assassination of President Lincoln, it should be remembered that the crime is no more atrocious than many of which they are notoriously guilty. . . . Those who begin and prosecute a bloody war for the destruction of a mild and equal Government, and for the sole purpose of perpetuating the most odious outrage upon human enterprise—who deliberately spurn and deny the most sacred rights of man, embark on an enterprise of which arson, theft, assassination, and every form of inhumanity are the natural means and allies.

—*Harper's Weekly*, May 20, 1865

Justice is always sure, sooner or later, to overtake the murderer. For a brief time he may . . . be lost to the keen scent of the avenger. But the day must come, when he will meet his deserts. God's eye watches him, and when the hour arrives, the murderer is exposed and justice is at last satisfied.

—Peterson & Brothers' record of
the conspiracy trial, 1865[1]

3

"A Disposition to Preserve

Law and Order"

Joseph Holt and the First Trial

of the Assassins

At 10:00 a.m. on May 9, 1865, Judge Advocate General Joseph Holt, his two assistant judges advocate, and the nine United States army officers assigned to serve as military commissioners, or judges, came together for the first time for the trial of John Wilkes Booth's alleged local co-conspirators. They gathered in a courtroom arranged specifically for the trial on the third floor of the Old Arsenal Penitentiary, where the eight prime suspects were being held. Holt's hand-picked assistants for the prosecution were men he trusted politically as well as personally: Colonel Henry Burnett, who had spent most of the past three weeks at the heart of the Bureau of Military Justice's investigations into the assassination conspiracy, and John A. Bingham, a longtime U.S. representative from Ohio who had practiced law for more than twenty-five years and who had assisted Holt before, in the controversial Porter court-martial, while doing a stint as a judge advocate for the federal government in the West between 1862 and 1864.

As for the commissioners, they were selected by Assistant Adjutant General W. A. Nichols, undoubtedly also with considerable input from Holt. Most important among them was the commission's president, Major General David Hunter, a "stern, white-headed soldier, sixty-three years old" who was well-known for his devotion to Lincoln. Indeed, in February 1861 David Hunter had been among the troops who escorted the President-elect safely into Washington under then Secretary of War Holt's watchful eye; just over four years later, General Hunter had sat at the head of the late president's body as it "traveled from place to place on the triumphal progress to its burial." With Hunter—whom Holt had also appointed to preside over the Porter court-martial in 1862—sat Major General Lew Wallace (a prominent lawyer in Indiana before he joined the Union army in 1861), Brevet Major General August V. Kautz, Brigadier Generals Alvin P. Howe, Robert S. Foster, and Thomas M. Harris, Lieutenant Colonel David R. Clendenin, Brevet Brigadier General James A. Ekin, and Brevet Colonel Charles H. Tompkins.[2]

Throughout the trial, the nine military commissioners assigned to the case appeared in full uniform, as did Assistant Judge Advocate Burnett (technically, Holt was a civilian, as was Bingham). Not surprisingly, in fact, the blue uniforms of the United States army were abundantly visible for the duration of the trial both inside and around the Old Arsenal and all along the streets of Washington, as unprecedented trial-related security measures went into effect. Every day mounted troops escorted the commissioners, Holt, Burnett, Bingham, and numerous witnesses to and from the courtroom in army ambulances, remaining on duty while court was in session. Dozens of other soldiers reported daily to John F. Hartranft, the kindhearted and gentle special provost marshal general detailed for service at the Old Arsenal during the trial, and scores more secured the streets between the Old Arsenal and the Executive Mansion. Special guards were on duty at Holt's residence, and at the residences of Secretary of War Stanton, the gravely wounded Secretary of State Seward, and other members of the cabinet. In short, over the next few weeks hundreds of armed soldiers strove to guarantee that the trial would go forward without interruption or violence. To some in Washington, this display of military might became as much a source of annoyance as comfort. In his diary, Commissioner Kautz recorded a complaint from a neighbor who was miffed that Kautz's court-appointed escort routinely blocked the entryway to his house while waiting to pick the commissioner up in the morning.[3]

Indeed, on the first day the court was in session, Commissioner Kautz himself seemed rather annoyed with the way his current assignment was shaping up. A military man accustomed to action, Kautz grumbled in his diary that little in the way of actual business had been transacted on that day, although he noted that the eight defendants had been brought into the courtroom for their initial viewing. In his memoirs Kautz recalled that on that occasion the seven male prisoners were dressed entirely in black, with masks covering their faces and chains binding their legs together. In Kautz's mind, the mental imprint left by the prisoners' grim appearance was unnecessarily ominous: it "partook so much of what my imagination pictured the Inquisition to have been," he wrote, "that I was quite impressed with its impropriety in this age."[4]

Others must have agreed, and made their opinions known, for subsequently the prisoners appeared before the court with their hands and legs shackled but without their hoods, which were eventually discarded altogether (in deference to her sex, Mary Surratt was never required to wear a hood). Osborn Oldroyd, an early scholar of the assassination conspiracy and a passionate collector of Lincoln (especially assassination-related) memorabilia, wrote,

> The arms of the male prisoners were fastened at the wrists . . . by a bar of iron about fourteen inches long, which prevented the moving of one arm without a corresponding movement of the other. The left ankle was fastened by a shackle attached to an iron cone by a chain two feet long. This cone was a foot high and eight inches in diameter at the base. It would weigh about seventy-five pounds. When the prisoners were marched into the court room, two guards put an iron rod through the staple in the apex of the cone and carried it.[5]

Over the course of the next few days, the pace of events continued to seem almost unbearably slow, causing the restless Kautz to complain further about what looked to become "a long siege of duty" in the courtroom. Kautz's sense of inaction derived in part from the hours spent every day in the reading of the previous day's court

"Exterior View of the Cells in which the Conspirators Are Confined,"
from Harper's Weekly, *July 8, 1865*

record, a tedious practice that remained unchanged throughout the trial and that occasionally absorbed the morning hours entirely.[6] Also frustrating were the many bureacratic tasks that required completion before testimony could even begin to be heard. Much of May 10, for example, was taken up by the swearing-in of Judge Advocate General Holt, the commissioners, the assistant judges advocate, and a team of court stenographers led by Benn Pitman (who later published the federal government's official record of the trial), followed by the official reading of the lengthy charges against the accused. These charges, written and signed by Joseph Holt himself, included "maliciously, unlawfully, and traitorously . . . combining, confederating, and conspiring together" with Booth, John Surratt Jr., Jefferson Davis, and the same members of Davis's Canadian Cabinet who had originally been identified on the reward posters (plus a few others) to kill Lincoln, Andrew Johnson, William Seward, and Ulysses S. Grant. With regard to intent, Holt's charges cited the conspirators' desire to deprive the U.S. military of its leadership, to prevent the safe transfer of political power in the administration, to "aid and comfort the insurgents engaged in armed rebellion" against the United States, and to "aid in the subversion and overthrow of the Constitution" and its laws. In response to these charges, all eight of the accused, for whom defense attorneys were still in the process of being named, entered pleas of not guilty.[7]

Also on May 10, Holt, his assistant judges advocate, and the nine commissioners constituting the Court devoted considerable time to their discussion of the rules and regulations to be used in conducting the trial—including whether or not the courtroom should remain closed to the public and the press, as it had been during these first two days. In his capacity as overall manager of the trial, and since he was determined to tolerate as little interference as possible from outside sources, Holt recommended firmly that the proceedings be kept secret, except for such testimony and other elements of the proceedings as he himself proposed to select and provide daily to an agent of the Associated Press for dissemination. Holt reasoned that uncensored press access to (and publication of) the entire proceedings might endanger some of the proposed witnesses who were taking potentially grave risks by giving testimony and might also tip off additional suspects not yet in custody and permit their escape.

Members of the Court, as eager as Holt to effect the "speedy result which the loyal spirit of the country seemed to demand at the time," were prepared to comply with the judge advocate general's recommendation. In contrast, upon learning of the Court's decision, which the *New York Times* described as a great surprise, a significant proportion of the press corps understandably rejected the principle of secrecy as unconstitutional, and also as utterly unacceptable in a democracy no longer engaged in active war. Briefly, Holt held his ground against such opposition, but a flurry of hostile newspaper articles demanding free access for their correspondents, and his desire to preempt negative public opinion regarding the fundamental legitimacy of a military trial in the first place, led him to reconsider. On May 13, the courtroom doors were opened to the press and to ticketholding spectators, though Holt reserved the right to interview some witnesses in closed session and to hold some particularly sensitive portions of the testimony in confidence, at his own discretion.[8]

Holt's granting of access to the press and the public pleased many observers, but it failed to overcome all concerns about the convening of a military commission in this particular case at this particular time. There were many who believed, not without reason, that the assassination conspiracy suspects should be given a civil trial. Among the aspects of the case that indicated the propriety of a civil trial was the fact that the eight prime suspects in custody were civilians rather than soldiers at the time the crimes with which they were charged had taken place. Moreover, Robert E. Lee's April 9 surrender of the Army of Northern Virginia had removed the District of Columbia from immediate military threat and thus, in theory, the crime scenes themselves could be considered nonmilitary sites. Additionally, Washington's civil courts were open and operating in the spring of 1865, available to handle the case if it should be assigned to them.

However, crucial features of the assassination conspiracy case led Holt and others to insist on the incontrovertible legal authority of a military commission. As one *New York Times* correspondent put it, "It is the nature of the crime, and not the dress of the criminal, that determines the tribunal by which he may be tried." From this perspective, what was important was the fact that the war was not fully over on the day the crimes were committed: significantly, Joseph E. Johnston had not yet surrendered his army to General Sherman. Furthermore, although Secretary of State Seward was clearly a civilian, Lincoln, as commander in chief, could be construed as a military figure and thus his assassination could be called a military crime.

The argument could also easily be made that, regardless of whether the victims or the defendants were civilians or military figures, the crimes that had been committed fell squarely into the broad category of "disloyal practices" deemed—by Lincoln himself—to be within the purview of the judge advocate general's office. And after all, it was the War Department and Holt's Bureau of Military Justice that had dominated the investigations virtually since their inception. To Holt, at least, and also to Secretary of War Stanton, the necessary conclusion on the question of jurisdiction had been obvious from the start. So it was with appreciation and relief that they had read the May 1 opinion of Attorney General James Speed, in which he stated that "if the persons who are charged with the assassination of the president committed the deed as public enemies, as I believe they did," and if "the persons charged have offended against the laws of war, it would be palpably wrong for the military to hand them over to the civil courts, as it would be wrong in a civil court to convict a man of murder who had in time of war killed another in battle."[9]

Still, others remained unconvinced. Indeed, as the trial slowly got under way the issue of jurisdiction in the case became the first point of attack for the several lawyers who, on May 12, finally joined their clients in the Old Arsenal courtroom. Standing up for the accused on that day were two particularly illustrious figures, Maryland Senator Reverdy Johnson, a close friend of Lincoln who had served as a pallbearer at the late president's funeral, and Union General Thomas Ewing Jr., formerly the chief justice of the Supreme Court of Kansas, the son of a U.S. senator, and the brother-in-law of General William Sherman. Although these men's motivations for participating in the defenses of Mary Surratt (Johnson) and of Spangler, Mudd, and Arnold (Ewing) were mixed and by no means entirely transparent, they explicitly included opposition to the employment of a military commission to try civilians in peacetime. (In Ewing's case, his own Catholicism and that of defendants Arnold and Mudd was also almost certainly a factor; Ewing may well have hoped to make use of his own unquestioned patriotism to shield his clients from any potential negative bias due to their religion in the courtroom, a concern Mary Surratt surely shared.) Also present on behalf of the accused were three somewhat less well-known but hardly inexperienced attorneys: Frederick Stone, a lawyer in George Atzerodt's home base of Port Tobacco, Maryland, who defended Herold; Walter S. Cox, a graduate of Harvard Law School and a longtime lawyer in Washington, who served both Arnold and O'Laughlen; and William E. Doster, a former provost marshal of the District of Columbia, who was present on Atzerodt's and Powell's behalf. Finally, teamed with Reverdy Johnson for the defense of Mary Surratt were the considerably less accomplished Frederick Aiken, a twenty-eight-year-old graduate of Harvard Law School, and John W. Clampitt, age twenty-five, who had been admitted to the bar only a year before.[10]

The nine military commissioners and at right Bingham, Burnett, and Holt.
Courtesy of the Library of Congress

Once all defense counsel were present on May 12, they requested
that the not guilty pleas lodged on behalf of their eight clients on May
10 be withdrawn and replaced with challenges to the military commission's jurisdiction. Needless to say, it is highly unlikely that the
accused or their lawyers actually imagined that Holt and the commissioners would seriously reconsider the limits of their own jurisdiction.
Thus it is safe to assume that these challenges were offered primarily
for the record, and perhaps with an eye toward appealing the matter
before the Supreme Court at some point down the line. Still, as
required, the pleas to jurisdiction were debated and then, predictably,
overruled. Next, perhaps hoping to stall the trial further or reconfig-
ure it altogether, defense counsel put forward requests to permit each
of the accused to be tried separately from the others, presumably with
the goal of limiting the impact on each individual case of the weight
of the prosecution's evidence against any other. These requests, too,
were debated by the Court and then denied. Out of options for the
time being, the lawyers for the accused now resubmitted their clients'
pleas of not guilty, and the stage appeared to be set at last for Holt
and his assistants to begin presenting the government's case.[11]

Meanwhile, just as the commission's wheels were beginning to turn
a bit more rapidly in Washington, dramatic events were unfolding
hundreds of miles to the south. These events involved the man

believed by so many to be the true prime mover of the assassination conspiracy, and thus most deserving of the federal government's revenge: former Confederate President Jefferson Davis, who had been on the run for over a month since fleeing Richmond in advance of the federal troops Lincoln had sent to occupy the captured Confederate capital. Early on the morning of May 10, near Irwinville, Georgia, federal cavalry troops at last spotted the camp of Davis and his entourage, which included his wife, Varina, and their children, as well as several aides, armed soldiers, and black servants. The excited federal troopers quickly surrounded the camp, the wagons, and the horses, and began their search for Davis who, on the advice of his wife, was attempting to make good his escape on foot. Spied and confronted by Corporal George Munger of the Fourth Michigan Cavalry, Davis surrendered after a brief display of defiance. Soon after, the proud former leader of the Confederate States of America was headed north under close guard, first by train, and then by boat.

On the way, Davis and his wife were joined by Clement Clay, whom Stanton and Holt had already publicly identified as a co-conspirator with Davis and Booth in the assassination of Lincoln, and who was now under arrest, along with his wife. The ship bearing the Davises and the Clays arrived at Hampton Roads, Virginia, on May 19. Three days later, Clay and Davis were imprisoned, not—as might have been expected—at the Old Arsenal Penitentiary in Washington, but rather in individual cells within the casemates of Virginia's Fortress Monroe, and their wives were released. "The arrangements for the security of the prisoners seem to me as complete as could be desired," Assistant Secretary of War Charles Dana telegraphed Stanton on May 22. According to Dana, the casemate windows were "heavily barred," individual sentries were posted in front of the case-mate doors, the doors themselves were "secured by bars and fastened on the outside," and additional sentries were posted on the prison grounds, atop the parapets, and across the moat. Lights were to be left on at all times in the cells, and guards were ordered to check on the prisoners every fifteen minutes. Neither Davis nor Clay, who were to be kept incommunicado, had been placed in irons yet, Dana admitted, but the Union army commander of the fort, General Nelson

Jefferson Davis.
Courtesy of the
Library of Congress

Miles, had been instructed to "have fetters ready if he thinks them necessary." Meanwhile, Clement Clay's anxious wife, Virginia, wrote to Holt in Washington urging him to show leniency toward her husband, on the basis of the friendship that had existed between the Clays and the Holts before the outbreak of the war. Hardly in a mood to show mercy to any he associated even indirectly with the crimes of April 14, Holt was not moved, and Clay remained in jail with Davis to await his own fate.[12]

Although the Northern public celebrated the long anticipated imprisonment of Jefferson Davis (and, to a lesser extent, that of Clement Clay), popular attention remained riveted on the events now under way at the Old Arsenal. "Even the news of the capture of Jeff. Davis falls quietly upon the public ear, so much is the universal eye and ear turned toward the great assassination trial," claimed the May 16 *New York Times*. Even so, bureaucratic wrangling continued to interfere with the trial's smooth progress. Although the commission-

General David Hunter,
president of the commission.
*Courtesy of the
Library of Congress*

ers finally began hearing testimony on May 12, yet another hurdle appeared the next day, when Commissioner Thomas Harris abruptly expressed his resistance to accepting Reverdy Johnson as one of Mary Surratt's defense attorneys. Harris was not alone in his objection to Johnson's participation in the trial: General Hunter quickly chimed in that if Harris had not raised the objection, "I should have made it myself." Although as manager of the trial he was careful not to express his opinion openly, Joseph Holt almost certainly objected as well, having come into open conflict with Johnson at least once before, over the Fitz-John Porter case, at which Johnson had served as the general's defense counsel. (In the wake of Porter's conviction, Johnson had written a stinging critique of Holt's case review.)[13]

When Commissioner Harris raised the objection to Senator Johnson, however, he understandably made no reference to the Porter case. Instead, he explained what troubled him personally about Johnson's participation in this trial: while serving as a U.S. senator in October 1864, Johnson had written a letter questioning the constitutionality and the "legal and binding effect and bearing" of a loyalty oath recently prescribed in politically divided Maryland for those who sought to vote on the border state's newly proposed Unionist constitution. According to the rules of the military commission now under way, General Harris argued, all legal counsel for the prisoners must be able to prove that they had taken a loyalty oath themselves, and if Johnson in fact failed to recognize the "moral obligation of an oath designed as a test of loyalty," then what right did he have to serve as Mary Surratt's counsel?[14]

It is difficult to read Harris's questioning of Johnson's qualifications as anything but a direct challenge to the Maryland senator's loyalty to the Union, which for Holt, his assistants, and at least some of the commissioners was the sine qua non for being permitted to participate in the case, even on the side of the defendants. And although Commissioner Harris himself did not enumerate them, there were other reasons to doubt Reverdy Johnson's Unionism, too: he had supported General George McClellan rather than Lincoln in the 1864 presidential election, and he was known to have taken a good deal of money over the course of the war years to defend Confederates charged with various offenses against the Union.

On top of all this, and perhaps most important, Johnson had a reputation for being a splendid lawyer. Indeed, at the heart of Harris's objection may well have been a concern that Holt certainly would have shared, whether or not he was able personally to admit it: namely, a concern that even one of the accused should have access to such a brilliant but Southward-leaning defense counsel, especially one whose lifetime of accomplishments prevented his being easily cowed by both the real and the symbolic presence in the courtroom of the victorious Union army. As if to prove this last point, it is worth noting that Commissioner Harris's challenge provoked a vehement and lengthy self-justifying rebuke from Johnson (widely reprinted in the national press), in which Johnson stressed his years of service to the nation in an array of capacities. In the wake of Johnson's speech, although Harris did not seem to regret having made the objection in the first place (as some suggested he should), after considerable deliberation the commissioner withdrew it. But for all practical purposes, his unspoken goal was achieved. Deeply insulted by the provocation (and perhaps also not anticipating much personal or professional glory from his participation in the case anyway), Reverdy Johnson failed to reappear for most of the rest of the trial. At the very end he offered a long, strongly worded denial of the military commission's jurisdiction. But in the meantime he left the bulk of Mary Surratt's defense in the hands of the much less experienced, though not incompetent, Aiken and Clampitt.[15]

As Johnson withdrew, the testimony phase of the trial finally got under way in earnest. If Joseph Holt's singular influence over the proceedings of the military commission had not been entirely apparent before, it became so within short order. As judge advocate general, Holt was in charge of the military commission as a whole, and of the formulation and presentation of the prosecution's case in particular. He therefore had great latitude for shaping events in the courtroom to suit his own vision of justice, which was hardly distinguishable at this point from revenge. It was Holt, indeed, who oversaw the schedule each day, who reread the previous day's testimony, and who called and usually interrogated the witnesses.

In addition to his unique degree of influence over the proceedings in the courtroom, there is no question that Holt also played a central role in molding—both directly and indirectly—the commissioners' responses to the testimony they heard. After all, although he was not a military man himself, as judge advocate general, Joseph Holt was officially the nation's chief arbiter and executor of military law, and as army officers first and foremost, these commissioners (most of whom were trained for battlefield rather than courtroom service) undoubtedly felt at least some degree of deference to Holt and his assistant judges advocate with respect to the law.[16]

Similarly, they shared a strong sense of duty to take the side of the government for whose cause, as soldiers, they had fought and bled and watched others die, against those who were presumed to be the government's enemies, or at least its enemies' agents on the ground. Routinely described as a modest man, Holt nevertheless surely knew the potential magnitude of his influence in this trial, and it is clear that he aimed to use it, not haphazardly or for personal gain, but effectively, and relentlessly, to guarantee a just outcome as he understood it. And by the spring of 1865 it is clear that Holt's notion of a just outcome derived not from his roots in Southern slaveholding society, but from the sum of his personal and political convictions as they had evolved in the course of his professional experience since becoming secretary of war for President Buchanan during the secession winter. Nothing he had experienced over the past four years, either as chief agent in Washington in 1861–62 for the preservation of his beloved Kentucky's loyalty to the Union or, beginning in the fall of 1862, as the federal government's leading crusader against "disloyal practices" in whatever form they took, had caused him to feel more generous toward the slaveholding South or its supporters.

Rather, as has already been noted, all of Joseph Holt's personal and professional history since 1861 brought him to the inevitable conclusion that John Wilkes Booth, the murderer of the chief executive Holt had loved and served at great personal sacrifice, and Lewis Powell, the would-be murderer of Secretary of State Seward, had not acted alone. Instead, they had combined and conspired with a small local band of awkward goons and lackeys in order to execute—thankfully with only partial success—the Confederacy's consummate crime, a crime inspired and perhaps even directed by its leadership in Richmond. It bears noting again that many within the federal government—not least of all, Stanton—shared Holt's views from the very beginning, as did a significant proportion of the Northern public. The "bloody barbarous conspiracy" that committed the dreadful deeds of April 14, the *Pittsburgh Commercial* had declared three days after the events took place, "was part of the plans of that Confederacy. . . . It was their mode of warfare, in perfect accord with the deliberate starving [of] thousands of prisoners, in keeping with the slaughter at Fort Pillow and elsewhere, and entirely consistent with the barbarism of slavery for which they rebelled."[17]

This is certainly how Joseph Holt understood the events of April 14, and thus it is clear why Holt and so many others within and beyond the Old Arsenal courtroom were determined that all of the relevant parties—including those present in chains, those under heavy guard at Fortress Monroe, and those still eluding the government's grasp—should be found guilty and punished to the full extent of the law. Although, as the official manager of the trial, Holt was bound to ensure that the proceedings were aboveboard and evenhanded (and

indeed, Holt received many compliments in the press for his fundamental fairness[18]), all of his wartime experience and his position as
chief prosecutor of the federal government's enemies also convinced
him that he must make certain that the commissioners interpret the
evidence as he did and draw the same conclusions he drew. Only then
would the guilty receive their proper punishment, and only then
would Holt feel that he—along with his badly wounded, deeply
beloved Union—could rest, having avenged not only the crimes of
April 14, but indirectly also the rebellion of the Slave Power in the
first place.

In practice, what all this meant was that in his capacity as chief
prosecutor of the government's case against the accused conspirators
(somewhat distinct from his role as trial manager), Holt's key goals
were: a) to ascertain and prove the precise role each of the eight prisoners at the bar had played in the events of April 14; b) to uncover
any relevant connections between the individual defendants and
members of the Confederate leadership at Richmond, Montreal, or
elsewhere; and c) to establish that the crimes of April 14 could be
understood only as of a piece with a host of similarly heinous crimes
committed over the course of the war by representatives and supporters of the Southern Confederacy. With this end in mind, on May
12 Holt began the prosecution's questioning of approximately 200
witnesses. Over the next few weeks the days were long: court was
usually in session from ten in the morning until after six in the
evening, with a break for lunch (to save time, members of the Court
and Holt's staff were served lunch in a nearby room, at the expense
of the War Department). Sundays were the only days off, except for
two days scheduled for a final grand review of the victorious armies
(May 23 and May 24), as well as Thursday, June 1, set aside by the
federal government for "humiliation and prayer." Virtually the only
change from the standard routine came on May 16, when the Court
met at Ford's Theater first thing in the morning, "in order to acquaint
ourselves with the scene of the assassination." Otherwise they met in
the Old Arsenal courtroom which tended to become extremely stuffy
thanks to the warm spring weather and crowds of eager observers. It

is noteworthy that, according to the *New York Times*, the majority of the public present were women, whose sheer numbers and elaborate dress did little to ease the congestion.[19]

In his effort to develop the prosecution's case Holt called witnesses right from the start who spoke in a focused way to the questions surrounding the assassination conspiracy as it had taken shape at the local level: on May 13, for example, John Lee, a member of the military police in Washington, described in detail the investigation of Atzerodt's room at the Kirkwood House following the attacks, and the discovery there of various items that seemed to confirm Atzerodt's involvement with Booth and the others in their deadly plot. Lee was followed by a host of other witnesses who filled in the details of Booth's activities on and before April 14, as well as the activities of the prisoners at the bar. Other witnesses Holt summoned early on provided testimony that linked the Confederate leadership and its agents in both America and Canada to the attacks carried out by Booth and his local associates, as well as to other schemes that had been designed during the war to destabilize the federal government and the Union war effort—in all, he painted a rich picture of the Confederacy's fundamental depravity. With the help of his assistants, Henry Burnett and John Bingham, Holt strove to weave these threads together.[20]

Prosecution witnesses whose testimony was most relevant to the matter of the "grand conspiracy" into which Holt firmly believed that Booth, Powell, Herold, and the others fit answered questions pertaining to the Confederate leadership's involvement in planning various examples of "irregular warfare" against the United States, such as an October 1864 attack on St. Albans, Vermont, in which Confederate raiders from Canada robbed three banks, for a haul of over $200,000, and killed one civilian. Others helped to create an indelible image of a vicious rebel leadership determined to destroy the Union army with whatever means were available, when they discussed the ghastly conditions captive Union soldiers had been forced to endure as prisoners of war in the South.

Still other witnesses answered questions posed by Holt and his assistants concerning the members of Davis's Canadian Cabinet, such as Jacob Thompson, Clement Clay, and George Sanders, whose connection to Booth Holt clearly aimed to uncover. On May 12, the very first day testimony was taken, for example, one prosecution witness claimed that as far back as the summer of 1864 he had heard members of the Canadian Cabinet in Montreal conversing about a plan to "rid the world of the tyrant Lincoln, Stanton, Grant, and some others." That same day, another witness testified that when he had met Booth shortly after the Battle of Gettysburg, the actor insisted that if the Confederacy's chances of gaining its independence came to seem too gloomy, killing Lincoln might become the "final resource" for achieving the goal. From that point on, the witness explained, Booth had worked with a group of "rebel officers" reassigned to posts in Canada to plot a strategy to "lay Northern cities in ashes, and finally to get after the members of the Cabinet, and kill the President," which, he emphasized, was really their main purpose. Other witnesses added further details to the picture of the South's relentless desire to crush the federal leadership by any means, including one who claimed that while he was a resident of Richmond he had routinely overheard conversations among Confederate army officers concerning reward money for "any person or persons [willing] to go North and assassinate the President." Yet another witness discussed his participation in a meeting in mid-February 1865 in Montreal at which Canadian Cabinet member George Sanders "named a number of persons," including Booth, "who were ready and willing . . . to engage in the undertaking to remove the President, Vice-President, the Cabinet, and some of the leading Generals; and that there was any amount of money to accomplish the purpose, meaning the assassination."[21]

Undoubtedly the most significant, and ultimately also the most controversial, witness Joseph Holt called to develop the government's case against Jefferson Davis and his high-level associates as conspirators with John Wilkes Booth was the man initially known to the Court as "Sanford Conover," but whose name later proved to be Charles Dunham.[22] Beginning on May 20, the day after Jefferson Davis and Clement Clay arrived at Hampton Roads, Conover began his testimony for the prosecution. That day he described in extensive detail his service, under the alias "James Watson Wallace," to the

Confederate government while in Canada, where he also claimed to have been acting as a secret correspondent for the *New York Tribune* (in which capacity he said he had written a number of stories in 1864 concerning Confederate plots against Lincoln). During his time in Canada, he came to know a number of the Confederacy's agents who were later charged in the assassination conspiracy, including Sanders, Thompson, Clay, Beverly Tucker, and William Cleary. Also known to him, Conover told the Court, was John Surratt Jr., whom he had met several times in Montreal in early April 1865 when Surratt was there conveying "dispatches from Richmond." On one occasion in particular, Conover recalled, Davis's Canadian agents had met with both himself and Surratt, had explicitly discussed "the plot to assassinate Mr. Lincoln and his Cabinet" as well as General Grant, and had invited Conover to participate.[23]

Although other prosecution witnesses provided related evidence of the "grand conspiracy" Holt hoped to delineate for the commissioners (and the Northern public), there is no question that Conover's particular and extensive testimony at the trial was essential for Holt's goal of linking the assassination plot not only to the Canadian cabinet members but also to Davis himself, to Surratt and Booth, and to other plots against the United States such as the St. Albans raid. Indeed, Conover made a point of mentioning a number of other anti-Union schemes of which he had become aware at one time or another while in Canada, such as a planned attack on Camp Douglas, outside Chicago, to secure the release of Confederate prisoners, and an attack on the Croton Dam in New York, designed to deprive New York City of water. On May 22, Conover further enhanced his previous testimony with details about a plot apparently favored by Thompson and Cleary to deliver "goods infected with yellow fever" to New York, Philadelphia, and Washington. All in all, Conover's testimony— especially in combination with other evidence—should have gone a long way toward proving the judge advocate general's theory that the events of April 14 had their origins with the Confederate leadership and were part of the vast Confederate conspiracy to destroy the nation.[24]

As it turns out, however, Sanford Conover was a liar and, while the trial of the conspirators was still in progress, the Canadian and American press began publishing letters and affidavits to that effect, challenging Conover's reliability and, to a lesser extent, the reliability of some of Holt's other "grand conspiracy" witnesses and the evidence they had brought forward. Holt and Stanton also received a number of letters with similar accusations against Conover and others. Such intense attacks on the veracity of the federal government's key witnesses against Davis and his associates were disturbing, although one could argue that they were also, at some level, eminently predictable given the bitter hostility still gripping so many hearts in the vanquished Confederacy. But when Union loyalists and army officers also joined in the challenge to Conover's testimony in particular, it put Holt and his assistants in a difficult spot. In a June 24 letter to Stanton, for example, Union General John Dix explained his reservations about Conover. The man's character, Dix explained, was known far and wide to be, simply, "bad." Without corroboration from more credible witnesses, wrote Dix, Conover's testimony should be dismissed altogether.[25]

If Dix was right about Conover, and it seems that he was, Holt simply should have set his testimony aside. Indeed, contemporaries as well as later scholars of the trial have insisted that Holt's refusal to do so was both irrational and unconscionable. What must be recalled, however, is the fact that Holt's wartime experiences, his unshakable and widely shared conviction concerning the guilt of the accused, and his determination to bring about the results he sought in this trial combined to make it virtually impossible for him to denounce or abandon even such a flawed witness. And so, even when one revelation after another (including an affidavit from the real James Watson Wallace denying many of Conover's claims) effectively compromised Conover's integrity and the credibility of his testimony, Holt stood by him.[26]

Similarly, Holt stubbornly refused to discount any evidence that was brought before the Court if it served his primary purpose of bringing the accused to justice, as he interpreted it. Holt failed to acknowledge, for example, the uncertain origins of the "Lon letter," which a prosecution witness named Charles Dawson introduced in early June. The Lon letter was purported to have been written by one Leonidas ("Lon") McAleer to "Friend Wilkes" on April 6, 1865; its contents linked Booth to a network of Confederate spies, and employed language ostensibly pertaining to Booth's oil speculations in order, apparently, to send him a coded message about the assassination plot ("when you sink your well go deep enough; don't fail, everything depends on you and your helpers"). Even after he had been alerted to the letter's possible fabrication, Holt allowed this piece of evidence to stand. Ironically, in so doing, Holt inadvertently guaranteed that while he may well have been correct about the Confederate leadership having been behind Booth and his accomplices and the assassination plot—and to the present day, some scholarship persuasively supports Holt's theory—his attempts to prove it would be unsuccessful.[27]

For in the end, the precipitous decline in Conover's credibility at the 1865 trial, along with serious questions that were raised concerning some of the other witnesses Holt had subpoenaed, meant that the prosecution's case against Davis and the Confederate leadership remained unproven. For the duration, then, Davis and Clay were left at Fortress Monroe to await a separate justice, although it was certainly within Holt's (and Stanton's) authority to haul them in to the Old Arsenal to face charges along with the others already in custody. But one suspects that despite his steadfast determination to prove their culpability in the assassination scheme—determination that, needless to say, led him to make some very bad decisions—Holt himself was aware that his case against Davis, Clay, and the others at the top was falling apart in his own hands. In the meantime, of course, he also had the case against Booth's local co-conspirators to prove. And so, even while he scrambled to bolster Sanford Conover's credibility (or at least to evade challenges to it), Holt and his assistants pressed on with the task of delineating the shape of the conspiracy. On this score the prosecution team was much more successful, largely thanks to the contributions of a good-looking, persuasive, apparently upstanding young man named Louis Weichmann, who testified on May 13, 15, 18, and 19.[28] To put it simply, in the government's case against the locals (including the still absent John Surratt Jr.), Weichmann succeeded where, in the case against Davis and the rest of the Confederate leadership, Conover had failed.

Age twenty-two at the time of the trial, Louis J. Weichmann was born in 1842, the same year as David Herold, in Baltimore. His parents were German immigrants, and his father was a tailor. In 1845 the Weichmanns, who were Catholic, moved to Washington, D.C., and then north to Philadelphia in 1853. After graduating from high school, Louis enrolled at St. Charles College, about twenty-five miles from Baltimore, as a divinity student.[29]

Described in one brief sketch of his life as an "exceptional student" who spoke seven languages and had also mastered a contemporary version of shorthand, Weichmann nevertheless did not complete the course of education offered at St. Charles to prepare him for the Catholic priesthood (his brother, Frederick, did become a priest). Indeed, Weichmann later described his experience at St. Charles with considerable distaste: "The studies," he recalled grimly, "were severe, and the discipline was rigid. The young men had no intercourse whatever with the outside world; their only privilege being permission to write letters to their parents and friends." Unhappy with this harsh regime, and with the fact that he did not seem to be advancing toward the priesthood as quickly as he thought he should, Weichmann left the college in July 1862. He took up teaching, first at Pikesville, Maryland, and then, beginning in January 1863, at St. Matthew's boys' school in Washington.[30]

Weichmann did make at least one friend of enduring significance while he was at St. Charles: John Surratt Jr., who arrived there in the fall of 1859, about six months after Weichmann, also—presumably—to study for the priesthood. "Well do I recall," Weichmann later wrote wistfully, "his first appearance and my impressions. . . . He was tall, erect, slender, and boyish, with a very prominent forehead and receding eyes. His nose was sharp, thin, and aquiline; his face bore an unusually keen and shrewd expression." John Surratt seems to have done very well at the seminary. According to the admiring Weichmann, he was a very "orderly" student who "could not have been excelled by anyone. His reputation for conduct and deportment was most excellent." Unlike Weichmann, who remained more reticent about his true political sentiments, Surratt also quickly revealed himself to be a staunch supporter of the Southern cause. Years later, Surratt recalled himself to have been, "like all Southern boys at that time," or so he thought, "a red-hot rebel."[31]

Once he moved to Washington, Weichmann lived at St. Matthew's, where he also received calls from friends, including Surratt, who had left St. Charles at roughly the same time as Weichmann. Surratt's visits were always pleasant, Weichmann recalled, and the two young men spent much of their time chatting about their years together. Although in the months since leaving the college and since his father's death Surratt had apparently become somewhat more of "a man of the world" with a "brusquer air" than the self-consciously refined Weichmann was accustomed to, Louis still nevertheless found him charming and good-natured. "There was never the slightest jar between us," he recalled, "and during the entire period of our acquaintance we never quarreled once." To some extent, Weichmann attributed this easy friendship to Surratt's "clean habits": Surratt was "entirely free of small vices" such as smoking, drinking, and chewing tobacco. When he visited, Surratt also frequently brought with him fruits and vegetables from his family's home in Surrattsville. And around Easter 1863, he extended an invitation to Weichmann to accompany him home. There Weichmann met Surratt's mother, Mary, whom he described as being "rather above medium height with a ruddy and fair complexion," dark brown hair and steel gray eyes that were "quick and penetrating." Mrs. Surratt welcomed Weichmann warmly into the Surratt home, where he also met John's sister, Anna, who was twenty and, in Weichmann's eyes, a "tall, well-proportioned, and fair-complexioned young woman" who resembled her brother.[32]

In January 1864, Weichmann—who seemed to have no appetite for military service with either the Union or the Confederate army—left teaching and took a clerkship in the office of the Union army's Commissary General of Prisoners, associated with Edwin Stanton's War Department. The work was challenging, and it offered a much higher salary than he had been getting as a teacher, as well as the company of numerous "gentlemanly and kind-hearted clerks" in the office.

Louis J. Weichmann.
Courtesy of Alfred A. Knopf,
a division of Random House, Inc.

Weichmann moved to a boardinghouse on 19th Street and Pennsylvania Avenue, not far from the Executive Mansion, where he continued to receive regular visits from John Surratt, with whom he remained very close despite the apparent disparity in their politics, and who was "always welcome; whatever I possessed was his own, as much as mine." Apparently Weichmann was equally welcome in Surrattsville, even though he was an employee of the federal government: in September 1864, he visited there again, at which time he learned that Mary, John, and Anna Surratt, financially strapped and burdened with the late John Surratt Sr.'s numerous and complicated debts, were themselves preparing to move to Washington.[33]

As a result, Weichmann moved from his previous lodgings to the Surratts' H Street home in early November 1864. He was followed by several other boarders and "thus," he later recalled, "the house was well filled almost from the beginning, and was a paying institution." Weichmann himself paid Mrs. Surratt thirty-five dollars per month, almost half his monthly salary, to stay there. At least during the last two months of 1864, he considered it well worth the price to reside in a home he considered "just as orderly, decent, and respectable" as any in Washington, and even better, really, because he shared it with his good friend John and John's family.[34]

Around Christmas, however, things at the boardinghouse began to change as a result of John Surratt Jr.'s increased activism on behalf of the Confederate cause. Although he had long been aware of Surratt's strong pro-Southern sentiments, once Weichmann moved into the H Street house he could no longer avoid acknowledging his friend's work as a courier and a blockade runner. "No one knew the people of his own and the adjacent counties better than he," Weichmann later wrote, in words that also might have described David Herold: "An excellent horseman, a good pistol shot . . . he was familiar with every main, cross-, and byroad in Lower Maryland, and was thoroughly posted in all the secret recesses and hiding places of that section."[35]

In fact, John Surratt had become engaged in this sort of activity long before the family's move to Washington: Weichmann himself described the Surratts' home in Maryland as a veritable "resort for blockade runners, spies, and parties who wanted to cross the Potomac . . . a regular secession headquarters," although he claimed—not quite credibly—not to have realized this, or precisely what sort of work John was engaged in, while he was first visiting there. Looking back, however, Weichmann now asserted his belief that, in addition to the financial incentives, one of Mary Surratt's key reasons for moving to Washington was actually to separate John from the "baleful influences" that were increasingly associated with his childhood home. In any case, Weichmann could not help noticing that his erstwhile school chum's pro-Southern activities had increased dramatically as the year drew to a close. They also became more dangerous. Perhaps most important, in these months Surratt began to make portentous connections with a number of individuals who would ultimately bring tragedy to his family, his friends, and to the nation. Among those individuals was John Wilkes Booth.[36]

According to Weichmann, he and John Surratt were together on the evening of January 15, 1865 (he later revised the date to December 23, 1864), when they met Booth (Weichmann for the first time) while strolling on 7th Street, the broad avenue that led out to the Soldiers' Home frequented by Lincoln and upon which the aborted kidnap attempt would take place on March 17. That evening Weichmann and Surratt were heading up 7th Street from Pennsylvania Avenue, presumably heading home, when they encountered Booth in the company of Dr. Samuel Mudd, whom Weichmann understood to be an old friend of John's from Maryland. Weichmann recalled Booth as a nattily dressed young man, "of medium figure, apparently

John H. Surratt Jr.
Courtesy of the Library of Congress

about twenty-eight years of age," with a black moustache, fair complexion, and a head of thick, curly black hair, a man whose voice was "musical and rich in its tones," and who carried himself as Weichmann clearly yearned to himself, like "a man of the world and a gentleman."[37]

Introductions accomplished—Weichmann claimed in his testimony not to have recognized the famous actor and to have initially understood Booth's name to be "Boone"—the four men went for drinks and cigars, first to Booth's room at the National Hotel, and later to the much seedier Pennsylvania House on C Street, where Mudd was staying. Over the course of the evening, group conversations were interspersed with more private ones from which Weichmann was excluded. (Weichmann even recalled being left alone in Booth's room at one point while the other three men conversed outside.) Although he claimed—again, not quite credibly—not to have found any of this behavior particularly strange at the time, in later months it all came to seem much more meaningful and ominous. At the time, Weichmann insisted that he took his companions' actions in stride, even when Booth took out an envelope and wrote mysterious markings on it while Mudd and Surratt watched intently. Nor did Weichmann attempt to question John Surratt's explanation later that night, to the effect that "Booth desired to purchase Mudd's farm" and that Surratt "was to be an agent in its purchase." Perhaps Weichmann, who enjoyed socializing (especially with John Surratt), was absorbed in the pleasure of making new and distinguished acquaintances. Perhaps he also sought to maintain at least a veneer of ignorance in the face of the increasingly suspicious activities to which, wittingly or not, he was becoming party.[38]

It is noteworthy that Weichmann's feelings with regard to the events taking place in and around the H Street boardinghouse changed dramatically as he came to recognize the deep bond that was forming between his beloved friend Surratt and John Wilkes Booth. As the winter of 1864–65 progressed, Booth began to visit the boardinghouse on a regular basis, and he always received a warm welcome from its residents, including both Mary Surratt and her daughter, Anna, for whom Weichmann's affections appear to have grown substantially. Moreover, to Weichmann's dismay it seemed as if John, as a result of his relationship to Booth, was yielding moral ground daily, heading further down the path of becoming the "evil genius" Booth's "principal associate, ally, and fellow conspirator." Weichmann later recalled, with a mixture of sadness and resentment, that Surratt eventually came to be bound to his actor friend "as completely as Doctor Faust belonged to Mephistopheles." And it was out of this evil compact that other troubling alliances developed between John Surratt and a handful of unsavory individuals—George Atzerodt, for example, and Lewis Powell—who then also found their way to the boardinghouse. One could certainly make the case that Weichmann's bitterness toward Surratt arose at least in part from his sense of abandonment by his friend in favor of a more elegant, worldly, and accomplished companion. "I never could understand the sympathy and affection which existed between Booth and Surratt," he wrote much later in his life. As Weichmann saw it, Surratt and Booth were, presumably unlike Surratt and himself, "so dissimilar in their natures, education, and the social position they held in life. . . . Never were two individuals thrown together so utterly at variance with one another." On the other hand, it is also possible that Weichmann secretly envied John Surratt's exciting and mysterious connection to Booth while resenting, at some level, his own exclusion from whatever schemes they seemed to be cooking up together. At the same time, once the assassination conspiracy was revealed and the boardinghouse and its occupants, including Weichmann, came under suspicion, Booth was the logical target for Weichmann's wrath.[39]

In any case, according to Weichmann, George Atzerodt visited the H Street house for the first time in January 1865. Introduced to Atzerodt by Surratt, Weichmann described the former with obvious disdain, as "swarthy" of complexion, thick of accent, with a "figure low and squat," "ugly eyes," and a "badly shaped head."[40] Atzerodt, wrote Weichmann, was neither learned nor refined, but he was a man "full of fun, country humor, and quaint stories." As for Lewis Powell, Weichmann recalled that his first visit to the boardinghouse had been in February, when he introduced himself as "Mr. Wood," a clerk in a Baltimore china store, and stayed overnight. Weichmann described Powell as "silent and uncommunicative," but with "the eye of an eagle" and "very self-possessed." Later that month, John Surratt introduced yet another visitor to the house, Mrs. Sarah Antoinette Slater, who turned out to be a Confederate courier. Another suspicious visitor to the boardinghouse during this period was Augustus Howell, also a courier and a blockade runner acquainted with Mrs. Slater.[41]

Throughout the early weeks of the new year, even though John Surratt's pro-Confederate activities became more and more pronounced and intruded more noticeably on life at the boardinghouse, any misgivings Weichmann felt still failed to cause him to move elsewhere. Rather, he remained as a lodger, enjoying the company of the Surratts and their other guests, and working at his job at the War Department, where he had joined, in August 1864, a reserve regiment composed of ten fully equipped companies of volunteers, called the War Department Rifles. During this period, Surratt was "continually on the go and away from his home much of the time," acting the part of a man "thoroughly preoccupied with important business affairs." Notably, Surratt seemed unconcerned about money, indicating to Weichmann that he had plenty of it to spend, although he had no steady, regular employment.[42]

On March 14, Lewis Powell returned to the boardinghouse, this time identifying himself not as "Mr. Wood" but as "Lewis Paine," and claiming to be a Baptist minister. During this second visit, which lasted three days, Powell and Surratt spent a good deal of time in private conversation up in the attic in the room Surratt and Weichmann shared when Surratt was at home. At one point, Weichmann recalled entering the room unexpectedly and finding the two deep in conversation, handling an array of suspicious articles: eight new spurs, two revolvers, and two bowie knives. Finally demonstrating some concern, Weichmann reported to Mary Surratt what he had observed ("Mrs. Surratt, I do not like this," he recalled saying), but he received a lukewarm response. According to Weichmann, Mary Surratt told him that he should not bother himself about such things, and that John "was in the habit of riding into the country, and that he had to have these things as protection." Once again Weichmann opted not to pry. On the night of March 15, Surratt, Powell, and two female boardinghouse residents, Honora Fitzpatrick and Apollonia Dean, attended a play at Ford's Theater. Weichmann, perhaps disgruntled by not being invited, remained at home. (This was the same night Booth, Herold, Powell, Atzerodt, O'Laughlen, Arnold, and Surratt met at Gautier's Saloon very late in the evening to discuss the kidnapping scheme.)[43]

Occurrences that Weichmann now acknowledged to be suspicious multiplied during Lewis Powell's second visit to the boardinghouse. On March 17, Weichmann returned from work to find both Surratt and Powell unexpectedly absent. Curious about their whereabouts, Weichmann summoned a servant for information. From this man Weichmann learned that Surratt had departed from the house at around 2:00 P.M. with a group of six or seven other men. Hearing this, Weichmann turned again to Mary Surratt, who appeared, he said, to be emotionally overwrought, unable to eat, and who wept as she told him to "make the best of dinner that you can. John is gone away, John is gone away." At supper that evening Weichmann got a taste of Anna Surratt's anxiety as well, when she suddenly "grew very excited and, bringing the handle of her knife with great force upon the table, exclaimed, 'Mr. Weichmann, do you know that if anything were to happen to my brother John through his acquaintance with Booth I would kill him.'" As Weichmann later admitted, there could no longer be any doubt in his mind that something dreadful was afoot. His misgivings were confirmed shortly, when Surratt, Powell, and Booth reappeared at the H Street house displaying obvious signs of distress. The three men went upstairs for a private conversation, then dispersed. Apparently unknown to Weichmann, their attempt to abduct Lincoln had just failed.[44]

In the days that followed Weichmann finally decided to articulate some of his concerns about the goings-on at the Surratt house to a colleague in the War Department, Captain D. H. Gleason. According to Weichmann, Gleason suggested only that he track any further developments and report them to Secretary of War Stanton later. Gleason remembered their conversation differently, indicating that he had urged Weichmann to go straight to Stanton with his suspicions, advice that Weichmann, whom he described as "physically and intel- lectually . . . a giant, but in bravery . . . a dwarf," then willfully ignored. In the end, whether Gleason actually recommended that he do so, it is clearly the case that Weichmann chose not to convey his suspicions to anyone higher up in the War Department, perhaps because he feared the implications of his proximity to the schemers. Later, of course, he insisted quite predictably that he deeply regretted his decision. Even so, he argued defensively that "no man in my posi- tion would have acted differently . . . no one would have suspected from the facts stated that these men had on that day tried to effect the capture of the President or, that failing, his murder." Moreover, Weichmann continued, he had always had "too high an opinion of John Surratt" to believe that he could be involved in a crime of such magnitude. It is perhaps true that the circumstantial evidence accu- mulating before Weichmann's eyes (which included a false moustache Weichmann had found among Powell's things during the latter's sec- ond visit) may well have been insufficient to indicate definitively that a scheme to assassinate the President and other high officials—or even just to kidnap the President—was evolving. At the same time, it seems absurd to let Weichmann off the hook so easily, knowing that he was in possession—at least by March 17, if not before—of infor- mation to which the federal government should have been made privy immediately. After all, Weichmann himself acknowledged that he was

a "sworn officer of the Government . . . bound by every consideration of honor. . . ." Needless to say, he was also in the midst of an
emerging conspiracy, about which the extent of his intimate knowledge remains, even today, unclear.[45]

In any case, after describing the events of the seventeenth to Captain Gleason, Weichmann decided to keep his own counsel. The following evening Surratt invited Weichmann to accompany him to see
Booth perform at Ford's Theater. Herold and Atzerodt also attended,
separately, and after the play (Booth's last official performance) all
four men joined Booth for drinks, at which time the excitement of the
previous day apparently went undiscussed, at least in Weichmann's
presence.

Over the next two weeks things seemed to quiet down again,
although Weichmann recalled receiving, on March 23, a cryptic
telegram from Booth in New York City demanding that he "tell John
to telegraph number and street at once." Weichmann also noted a
March 26 visit by Booth to the H Street house, theoretically made at
Mary Surratt's request. Then, on April 2, Weichmann accompanied
Mary Surratt, who had become something of a surrogate mother to
him, to St. Patrick's Church, after which they strolled over to the
Herndon House, a short distance away. There, as he later learned,
Mary Surratt had a brief private visit with Powell, who was staying
in a room arranged for him by her son. (Weichmann later surmised
that Booth's cryptic March 23 telegram had been a request for information on the correct address of the Herndon House, so that Booth
could tell Powell, who was then with him in New York City.) Also on
the second, Mary Surratt sent Weichmann to the National Hotel, supposedly to summon Booth to the boardinghouse in order to discuss
the possibility of borrowing a horse, which she claimed was actually
her son's but which was in Booth's possession. Finding Booth absent,
Weichmann sought out Atzerodt, to whom he understood Booth had
given the responsibility of caring for his horses. Weichmann brought
Atzerodt to the boardinghouse, but to no avail: for whatever reason,
Atzerodt refused to lend the horse. The following day, April 3, John
Surratt briefly returned to Washington with the courier Mrs. Slater in
tow, and carrying a great deal of money. Surratt announced that he

was on his way to Montreal, and indeed he and Mrs. Slater left early the next morning. That, Weichmann later claimed, "was our final farewell."[46]

Weichmann had a few more encounters with John Wilkes Booth in the week that followed. At the Surratts' on April 10, he made a joke about the fall of Richmond to Booth, to which the actor supposedly responded energetically that the end of the Confederacy had not yet arrived. On the eleventh, at Mary Surratt's request, Weichmann went again to the National Hotel to ask Booth's permission to use his horse and buggy in order to drive her to Surrattsville on business. Instead, having sold his horse and carriage, Booth lent Weichmann ten dollars to rent a rig for the trip. In Surrattsville that day, Mary Surratt transacted some business with one John Nothey in connection with a debt he owed on property purchased from her late husband some years back. During that trip Weichmann and Mary Surratt also ran into John Lloyd, her Surrattsville tenant, and Lloyd's sister-in-law, Emma Offutt. According to Weichmann's account, Mary Surratt and John Lloyd had a brief private conversation. Three days later, on the day of the assassination, Weichmann drove Mary Surratt back down to Surrattsville around 2:30 P.M. for another business meeting with Nothey. On this occasion Mary Surratt carried with her a small, nondescript, paper-wrapped package, between six and eight inches in diameter, which Booth had brought to the boardinghouse just as she and Weichmann were about to leave.

When they reached Surrattsville, Nothey was nowhere to be found. Instead, they stopped again at John Lloyd's, where Mary Surratt handed Booth's package over to Emma Offutt, with whom she spoke briefly. Mary Surratt then summoned Weichmann from the carriage to write a letter to Nothey regarding the debt, and the letter was handed to a neighbor to deliver. Around six o'clock, just as they were preparing to leave, Lloyd himself returned, and Mary Surratt spoke with him for a few moments in the backyard ("No portion of this conversation did I hear," Weichmann insisted). Not long thereafter, once Lloyd had fixed a spring on the buggy that had come loose during the day's driving, Weichmann and Mary Surratt headed back to Washington. They arrived home around 9:00 P.M. Just over an hour later, John Wilkes Booth murdered Lincoln, and Lewis Thornton Powell viciously attacked Secretary Seward.[47]

As is already known, within a few hours after the crimes were committed, the Washington, D.C., Metropolitan Police descended on Mary Surratt's boardinghouse. Looking back, Weichmann remembered the period of time between his return home with Mary Surratt and the arrival of the police as replete with mysterious incidents. Among other things, he had a conversation with his landlady in which she suddenly informed him that Booth was now "done acting" and that he was "going to New York very soon, never to return." On this occasion Mary Surratt also purportedly told Weichmann that Booth was "crazy" on some unspecified subject, for which she planned to "give him a good scolding" the next time she saw him. According to Weichmann's recollection, Mary Surratt appeared that night to be unhappy, "agitated and restless," having just received a brief letter from her son, dated April 12 and posted from Montreal. Also on that evening she entertained an unknown visitor (whom Weichmann believed to be Booth) for a short time in the front parlor before she retired. And at some point Mary Surratt asked Weichmann to "pray for her intentions," a not uncommon Catholic practice at the time, although she did not define what those intentions were, and he did not say whether he acceded to her request. Regardless of this odd mixture of occurrences, however, Weichmann seems to have been able to maintain his composure, if only because, as he later claimed, when he himself went to bed just before ten, he was "as ignorant of the coming murder as was Mr. Lincoln himself." Perhaps a bit too fervently, Weichmann added that his sleep that night "was the sleep of innocence and of clear conscience. I had done no wrong and meditated none."[48]

When the detectives first arrived that night, still looking only for Booth and John Surratt, they aroused all of the residents of the boardinghouse, including the peacefully sleeping Weichmann. Not finding either of the men they sought and learning from Mary Surratt that her son had left town for Canada, the police and their detectives departed. But they left the previously sanguine Louis Weichmann profoundly shaken, though more on behalf of his good friend John, he insisted, than himself. As he later explained: "I returned to my room—no more sleep that night. My God! My God! What agony I endured until the morning light came through the windows. Providence alone is witness. I said to myself repeatedly, 'It cannot be that Surratt has been guilty of this crime. . . . No, no, it cannot be!'"[49]

Over the next few hours, in his highly agitated state, Weichmann pondered what to do. Regardless of the innocence he later proclaimed, his mind surely churned with anxiety about the possible consequences for his future of his longtime association with the Surratt family, his residence in their home, and his acquaintance with Booth and others who seemed likely to have been involved in the night's horrible crimes. Weichmann clearly knew that serious questions would be asked about the numerous things that he had seen and heard over the course of the months since moving in with the Surratts, not to mention the various people whom he had met there. As he considered his own extreme vulnerability in connection with the night's events, Weichmann came to a position of firm resolve: namely, as he put it, "that under all circumstances I would stand by the cause of justice and the Government," arguably the only tactic available to him if he hoped to save his own neck. And so, shortly after breakfast on April 15—just as weeping cabinet members were bidding their sad farewells to the late president, and John Wilkes Booth and David Herold were seeking assistance at the Maryland home of Dr. Mudd—Weichmann, accompanied by fellow boarder John Holohan, voluntarily headed for police headquarters. Weichmann intended, he said, to "answer truthfully every question put to me, with an unblushing countenance and a sinless soul." After all, he noted with his usual, if only partly believable, self-righteous tone, "an upright man never has anything to fear, and I knew that my life had been correct and honest."[50]

At police headquarters, Weichmann and Holohan met with Superintendent Almarin Colley Richards and detectives James McDevitt and John Clarvoe, who had been at the Surratt boardinghouse the night before. Without much difficulty, Weichmann was able to persuade Superintendent Richards of his willingness to assist the police in any way possible.[51] Indeed, not long after he arrived at the station,

Weichmann was essentially deputized (even as he was also being held for questioning) to participate in the pursuit of Booth and the other assassins. Over the next several days, Weichmann worked with the police as they tried to track the conspirators' whereabouts, traveling both south to Surrattsville, where they interviewed John Lloyd, and north to Baltimore, where they hoped to locate Atzerodt. Weichmann and Holohan also accompanied the group of detectives who on the seventeenth headed for Montreal hoping to pick up John Surratt's trail. "I was convinced that I was doing the right thing in going to Canada in pursuit of Surratt," Weichmann later wrote, as if he sought to persuade at least himself of his upright motivations. "I went with the kindest intentions towards him." Although it is not clear that Weichmann's assistance made a great difference in the early stages of the investigations and the pursuit of the key suspects, his willingness and determination to assist—if only in order to counteract the authorities' suspicions about his own possible role in the emerging conspiracy—portended the central role he would play in the trial itself.[52]

On April 29 Weichmann and the police detectives returned empty-handed from Canada. That night, the eight prime suspects already in custody were transferred to the Old Arsenal Penitentiary. On April 30, Secretary of War Stanton himself questioned Weichmann for roughly two hours about his background, his life, and his knowledge of the events surrounding the assassination and of the individuals who may have been involved in it. According to some reports, if Weichmann had not yet fully realized the gravity of his own situation—though his actions suggest that he had—he certainly had to have done so after speaking with the secretary of war. Weichmann was then placed in the custody of Colonel Lafayette C. Baker, the federal government's controversial chief detective, who had been summoned from New York to participate in the investigations. Weichmann was held in the Carroll Prison, an annex of the Old Capitol Prison, where his former landlady had been held when she was first taken into custody.

At the prison Weichmann appears to have felt gratified to find himself surrounded by virtually every witness "possessing any important evidence for the Government" in the conspiracy case. Interrogated again, he insisted that he still felt no fear: "I saw but one line before me," he wrote later, "the straight line of truth and honor, and to that I adhered." As for any anger Weichmann might have felt about being held prisoner during this period, he justified it—at least after the fact—as a consequence of the War Department's desire to protect the government's witnesses against its enemies. "I really believe," Weichmann explained in retrospect, "that my own life, and that of others who were ready to stand up for the Government, were saved by the wise though stern measures of the War Secretary."[53] Given the vengeful sentiments alive in Washington in May and June, Weichmann may well have been right that his imprisonment vouchsafed his survival. Whether that was because he was a government witness whom pro-secession forces would have targeted, or because his close connections to several of the key players in the assassination would have provoked pro-government forces to seek his life, is less clear.

In any case, imprisoned for about thirty days, Louis Weichmann repaid the federal government well for its efforts on his behalf with his testimony, which remained consistent even under harsh cross-examination by defense counsel. His highly persuasive and detailed testimony tied at least four of the prisoners at the bar—Mary Surratt, Lewis Powell, George Atzerodt, and Samuel Mudd—not only to one another but also to Booth and John Surratt. Already on May 22 (only ten days into the testimony phase, and in the wake of Weichmann's four appearances before the Court), the *New York Times* reported that the prosecution's case was virtually complete, and that Powell, Herold, Atzerodt, Mudd, and Mary Surratt had clearly been proven guilty. Indeed, "Mrs. Surratt," the paper commented, "appears to have been cognizant of the intended crime almost from its inception, and became an active participant in overt acts . . . a general manager." Of the involvement of Spangler, O'Laughlen, and Arnold in the events of April 14, the correspondent was less certain. Of the involvement of Jefferson Davis, the Confederate leadership, and the Canadian Cabinet, the *Times* said nothing.[54] Meanwhile, Davis and Clement Clay were locked up in their casemate cells in Fortress Monroe, and John Surratt Jr. remained beyond the government's grasp.

The country has much reason to congratulate itself on the wisdom, vigor and faithfulness with which the investigation has been prosecuted, and the enormity of the conspiracy, in its vast ramifications, exposed. The case has been prepared with great skill and labor which, we understand, has been performed principally by that unswerving patriot, Judge Holt.

—*Pittsburgh Commercial*, May 20, 1865

It was too horrible to imagine that the ghost of the martyred Lincoln should walk unavenged. So stupendous a calamity must of necessity be the outcome of as stupendous a conspiracy, and must in the very justice of things be followed by as stupendous a retribution.

—DAVID DEWITT,
The Judicial Murder of Mary E. Surratt, 1895[1]

4

"A Stupendous Retribution"

Conviction and Punishment of

Eight Co-Conspirators

Long after the conspiracy trial reached its conclusion in early July 1865, Commissioner Lew Wallace (later best known as the author of *Ben Hur*) recalled Louis Weichmann with both appreciation and a sort of paternal respect. "I have never seen anything like his steadfastness," exclaimed General Wallace.

> There he stood, a young man only twenty-three years of age, strikingly handsome, intelligent, self-possessed, under the most searching cross-examination I have ever heard. He had been innocently involved in the schemes of the conspirators, and although the Surratts were his personal friends, he was forced to appear and testify when subpoenaed. He realized deeply the sanctity of the oath he had taken to tell the truth, the whole truth, and nothing but the truth, and his testimony could not be confused or shaken in the slightest detail.[2]

Commissioner Wallace's unqualified praise for Weichmann— Joseph Holt's key witness in the case against the local conspirators— is striking. It is especially so in light of the fact that, despite any actual merits of the case Holt aimed to construct with their aid against Jefferson Davis and the Confederate leadership, witnesses such as

Sanford Conover were sized up by so many observers, so quickly and quite rightly, as both unsavory and unbelievable. Moreover, it appears that a majority of observers (and, most important, the commissioner-judges themselves) viewed Louis Weichmann in a favorable light. At best they saw him as Lew Wallace did: a noble, trusting and trustworthy young man who wisely managed to avoid getting caught up in the ghastly plans that his close friend John Surratt, his beloved landlady Mary Surratt, the charismatic John Wilkes Booth, and a motley crew of disagreeable, dangerous characters had laid right before his innocent eyes. How brave this young man was, such observers agreed, that he could overcome strong ties of affection and loyalty to serve the federal government and bring the whole wretched gang to justice.

Needless to say, it helped Holt and the prosecution that Weichmann was an articulate and attractive fellow from a "good" family with links not only to troublesome Maryland but also to loyal Pennsylvania. Furthermore, he was well educated and well spoken, devoutly Christian (even if he was a Catholic), a federal bureaucrat, and a member of a Union army reserve regiment. It also made a difference that Holt called Weichmann so early in the trial, so that—as the previous chapter revealed—his extensive and persuasive testimony offered an elaborate framework into which so much subsequent testimony could fit.

Of course, Weichmann had his critics, including those who perceived him as a credulous dupe in the hands of the wily Booth and his equally crafty local associates, especially John Surratt Jr. And then there were those who declared him, like Conover, an outright liar. The most ardent of these was twenty-two-year-old John P. Brophy, a close friend of the Surratt family and the principal of St. Aloysius, a Catholic boys' school in Washington. In a detailed affidavit addressed to Mary Surratt's lawyer, Frederick Aiken, almost a month after Weichmann completed his testimony, Brophy feverishly assailed Weichmann's credibility. He claimed that Weichmann, whom he had known for some time, had in fact recanted his testimony after being released from custody on May 29, had made assertions about being pressured relentlessly by the prosecution to testify against Mary Surratt, and had declared himself an "ardent secessionist who wanted to go to Richmond to get a clerkship." In his affidavit Brophy also actively defended Mary Surratt in the most vigorous terms, proclaiming that *she* was in fact the innocent in the story and that she had been maligned, not only by Weichmann's testimony against her, but also by the press. "I cannot allow her character to be so wantonly destroyed," Brophy declared. "She is sorrowfully feeble, but strong in conscious purity." How was it possible, Brophy wondered, that in the hands of Weichmann and the press Mary Surratt's mere ownership of a boardinghouse in which others had laid their nefarious plans could be used to condemn her? After all, hers was not a private home but a public lodging house, "open to all comers," wrote Brophy. "If the mere fact of the presence of bad men in her boarding house argue[s] complicity in their crime, what keeper of a public house, what host who entertains his friends, what member of society who mingles with the world, as it passes, would be safe?"[3]

There were others who, quite reasonably, found Weichmann's story as a whole, as well as his proclamations of innocence, rather hard to believe. In the summary report of his pretrial examination of Weichmann, for example, investigator Colonel John A. Foster wrote that he found it "extremely improbable" that Weichmann could be as ignorant of the implications of the developments he described as he would have others believe. Foster doubted Weichmann's honesty; others saw him as nothing more than a coward determined to extricate himself from the messy tangle of the conspiracy, a task of some magnitude given his long and extremely close relationship with John Surratt, his months of residence at the boardinghouse, and his acquaintance and numerous interactions with Booth and at least some of the prisoners at the bar, including his almost filial bond with Mary Surratt. Even while the trial was still in progress, the anxious Weichmann acknowledged the challenges brewing against him, and wrote defensively to Assistant Judge Advocate Colonel Henry Burnett: "I have acted from principle throughout this entire affair and have no doubt made many *personal* enemies."[4] (He had indeed, as he would soon discover.) But it is nevertheless true that, in contrast with Sanford Conover, in the late spring and early summer of 1865 the significance of Weichmann's credibility and his testimony were considerable, even definitive, in the development of the prosecution's case against Mary Surratt and her fugitive son as co-conspirators with Atzerodt, Herold, Powell, and Booth.

Fortunately for the prosecution, too, Weichmann's testimony did not have to stand alone. Rather, it was augmented and corroborated by the testimony of scores of other witnesses who helped to fill in the picture of just how the events of April 14 had come to pass, although it is also questionable how much testimony was even necessary against some of the "alleged conspirators" the federal government already held in its grasp. Herold, after all, had been caught on the lam with Booth; Atzerodt had already confessed more than once about his involvement in the plot, even if the content of his confessions was not always consistent. Since his bizarre capture at the Surratt boarding-house on April 17, Lewis Powell, too, had not once denied his attack on Seward. In order to leave nothing to chance, William Bell, the servant at the Seward home who had tried to stop Powell at the door, and George Robinson, the convalescent soldier-nurse on duty in Secretary Seward's room, both returned to identify Powell at the trial, as did Augustus Seward, one of the secretary's sons.[5] As early as May 4, before the trial was even under way, the *Philadelphia Inquirer* was among those newspapers already prepared to condemn these three men, as well as Mary Surratt, whom it dubbed Booth's "anchor" and whom it described as "coarse, and hard, and calm . . . worthy of companionship with Booth." Noted the *Inquirer*, "When Booth cast around him for an assistant, he naturally selected those men whom he could control. The first that recommended himself was one Harold, a youth of inane and plastic character, carried away by the example of an actor." Of Atzerodt the *Inquirer* reported, he had "led a desperate life at Port Tobacco," and when Booth "broke the design to him, with a suggestion that there was wealth in it, he embraced the offer at once, and bought a dirk and pistol." Powell, the paper concluded simply, was nothing more than a "professional murderer." A few days later, the *Inquirer* called Powell "the assassin of Seward . . . a regular contract villain . . . sent here to do his work of blood for a stipulated price."[6]

The team for the prosecution (from left): John Bingham,
Joseph Holt, Henry Burnett.
Courtesy of the Library of Congress

Still, Judge Advocate General Holt and his assistants called one prosecution witness after another, adding important details to the framework Weichmann's extensive testimony had constructed. For example, Robert R. Jones, a clerk at the Kirkwood House, identified George Atzerodt as the suspicious person who had paid in advance for a room on the morning of April 14, but did not sleep there. It was in this room—located directly above Vice President Andrew Johnson's—that John Lee of the Washington, D.C., military police had testified that he and a team of detectives discovered a bowie knife, a loaded pistol, and other articles linking the renter of the room to Booth. The prosecution also called liveryman Brooke Stabler, who described seeing Atzerodt, Booth, and John Surratt Jr. often at his place of business, where Surratt kept two horses, one of which was identified positively as the horse Powell rode—and abandoned—on the night of the assassination.[7] Similarly, John Fletcher of J. Naylor's livery stable recalled his business dealings both with Atzerodt (which also involved Powell's getaway horse) and with Herold, who late on the evening of April 14 hired a horse that he ended up never returning—despite Fletcher's having pursued him as far as the Navy Yard bridge, over which Herold and Booth escaped into Maryland that night.[8]

The active complicity in Booth's assassination scheme of Herold, Atzerodt, and Powell was relatively easy for Holt and his prosecution team to demonstrate. On the other hand, it was somewhat more difficult to substantiate convincingly the involvement of Mary Surratt, although the popular press was quick to condemn her. "She, it will be remembered," commented the *Philadelphia Inquirer* on May 10, "was the leading spirit next to Booth." Certainly Mary Surratt's ownership of the boardinghouse that Booth and so many of the others had frequented, combined with her son's known reputation as a Confederate courier and ardent Southern nationalist, and the post-assassination appearance of Lewis Powell at her home, apparently in disguise and on the run, seemed damning. But additional evidence was necessary in order to position her firmly in the midst of the conspiracy. On this score, the most important prosecution witness against her—besides Weichmann—turned out to be John Lloyd, the manager of the Surratt property in Maryland and the individual with whom, according to Weichmann, Mary Surratt had had mysterious, private conversations during their trips to Surrattsville on April 11 and April 14. On both occasions, Lloyd claimed, Mary Surratt's brief conversations with him revolved around some "shooting-irons" (in this case, carbines) hidden in the Surrattsville house. On the eleventh, declared Lloyd, Mary Surratt warned him that the guns would be "wanted soon"; three days later, "she told me to have those shooting-irons ready that night,—there would be some parties to call for them." On the fourteenth, Lloyd added, the paper-wrapped package Mary Surratt had brought down from Washington at Booth's request proved to contain a set of field glasses. And she told him to get two bottles of whiskey ready as well, since "they were to be called for that night."[9]

If Weichmann's testimony put Mary Surratt's H Street boarding-house at the heart of the conspirators' planning process, and her in the thick of it at least by association, Lloyd's testimony—given largely in response to questioning by Holt himself—proclaimed her to be an active, material accomplice before the fact. It also strengthened Holt's cases against some other defendants: in answering the question of where the "shooting-irons" stored at Surrattsville came from in the first place, Lloyd claimed that Atzerodt, Herold, and John Surratt Jr. had brought the guns to Surrattsville, along with ammunition, a rope, and a monkey wrench, some weeks before the assassination, presumably in the wake of the failed March 17 abduction scheme. "Surratt asked me to take care of them," Lloyd testified, "to conceal them." As it turns out, the first stop Booth and Herold made on their way south after the assassination was not the home of Dr. Samuel Mudd, but the Surrattsville house and tavern. According to Lloyd, they arrived there around midnight, Booth demanding the guns "in such terms that I understood what he wanted." Lloyd delivered the guns, of which they only took one, apparently due to Booth's injury. Then the fugitives downed some whiskey and rode off, but not before one of the men announced that they had killed the President. Declared Lloyd somewhat disingenuously, he was "so astonished" by this news "that I do not think I made any reply; but if I had had a carbine in my hand, I would have shot him on the spot." An option Lloyd might also have pursued was to inform the police immediately of what he had heard. He failed to do this as well, however, almost certainly because he quite reasonably feared being linked to the assassination plot.[10]

John Lloyd gave his highly incriminating testimony on May 13 and May 15; Louis Weichmann was done by May 19. It is hardly an exaggeration to say that by the time these two left the witness stand—only six days into the testimony phase of the trial—the evidence presented against Mary Surratt, David Herold, Lewis Powell, and George Atzerodt—and even against Mary Surratt's fugitive son, John—was virtually insurmountable for the defense. On the other hand, the task of providing sufficient evidence to prove the guilt of Arnold, O'Laughlen, Spangler, and Mudd remained somewhat more problematic for Holt and the assistant judges advocate.

Holt called a host of witnesses to shed light on the participation in Booth's conspiracy of these four defendants. Mary Van Tyne, the former landlady of Arnold and O'Laughlen, testified about their strange comings and goings and their frequent encounters with Booth while renting rooms at her boardinghouse in the spring of 1865. Bernard J. Early, an acquaintance of both Arnold and O'Laughlen, placed the latter in Washington on April 13–15 and also testified that O'Laughlen had made a visit to the National Hotel—where Booth was staying—on the morning of the fourteenth. Another friend of O'Laughlen, Samuel Streett, spoke of the intimate nature of O'Laughlen's association with Booth, and David Stanton, son of the secretary of war, identified O'Laughlen as the mysterious man he had seen briefly lurking in the shadows of the crowd that gathered in the secretary's front hall on the night of April 13, when General Grant was also present at the house. With regard to Edman Spangler, Sergeant Joseph M. Dye raised suspicions about the possibility that Spangler was indeed the "ruffian" with whom he saw Booth conferring outside Ford's Theater on the night of the assassination. William Withers Jr., a member of the orchestra at the theater, indirectly suggested that Spangler, as scenery changer, may have cleared a path for Booth's escape after the assassination, and may even have held the exit door for him. John Miles, also a Ford's employee, confirmed that it was Spangler whom Booth summoned to hold his horse that night, and claimed that after Booth escaped Spangler explicitly told him (Miles) to keep silent about what had happened. In addition to the testimony provided by such witnesses, the prosecution appealed to other evidence. In Arnold's case, there were his confessions following his arrest (which also implicated O'Laughlen, Herold, Atzerodt, and John Surratt), as well as the notorious "Sam" letter found in Booth's trunk at the National Hotel the day after the assassination. In the case of Spangler, the evidence clearly indicated that he had been Booth's preferred drudge at Ford's Theater for a number of years, had gone drinking with Booth on the evening of the assassination, and had been called to hold Booth's getaway horse, even if he had ultimately deputized fellow employee Joseph Burroughs to do it for him.[11]

Building a solid, unassailable case for Samuel Mudd's premeditated involvement in the assassination conspiracy was also more difficult for Holt and his assistants, although Booth's appearance with Herold at Mudd's home on the morning after the assassination was extremely incriminating, as was Mudd's failure to contact authorities more quickly, especially once he himself knew of Lincoln's murder. Weichmann's testimony, too, was relevant for the prosecution's case against Mudd, for it tied Mudd directly to John Surratt Jr., Booth, and, loosely, others among the defendants. Most important, Weichmann's testimony suggested that Mudd knew Booth, and perhaps quite well, long before Booth's and Herold's visit to his home seeking medical assistance.

Then there was the testimony of Lieutenant Alexander Lovett, who explained at considerable length the circumstances surrounding the initial interrogations and the subsequent arrest of Mudd, and of Colonel H. H. Wells, who described his own interviews with Mudd, which left him confident that Mudd was lying. Daniel J. Thomas, the doctor's neighbor, testified that he had heard Mudd make a prediction sometime in March to the effect that Lincoln and his whole cabinet ("and every Union man in the State of Maryland besides that") would be killed within the next few weeks. Eleanor Bloyce and her daughter Beckie Briscoe testified to having seen Samuel Mudd riding toward Bryantown on April 15 in company with a stranger, and noted that, in contrast with the information Mudd had given his interrogators prior to his arrest, the news of Lincoln's assassination had indeed by that time already spread to the area. Soldiers were even then stationed there gathering information, had Mudd wanted to offer any. In addition, a number of Mudd's former slaves testified that John Surratt Jr. had been a frequent visitor to the Mudd home, bolstering the impression that the "good doctor" was not only a Southern sympathizer but also perhaps an active member of the Confederate underground operating in Maryland. Still, when Judge

Advocate General Holt announced on May 23 that the "case on the part of the prosecution was closed," significant doubts persisted regarding the depths of Mudd's prior knowledge of the assassination scheme.[12]

When Holt declared the prosecution case closed, he nevertheless reserved the privilege "to call witnesses at any time" thereafter, "during the progress of the trial, as to the general conspiracy charged" and with regard to "the nature, extent, and character of the Rebellion." His ultimate goal, of course, was unchanged: to show that the Rebellion itself, characterized as it was by an array of horrid crimes against humanity, was the very wellspring of the assassination plot, and its leaders—Jefferson Davis and his high-level cronies—were as responsible for the murder of Lincoln as they were for the war itself, and all the death and destruction that had resulted from it.

Indeed, throughout the next four weeks Holt repeatedly exercised his right to introduce new witnesses, some of whom brought forward additional evidence pertaining to Confederate plots against not only Lincoln, but also an assortment of Union targets. Some later witnesses' testimony dealt in a focused way with specific horrors, such as the treatment experienced by Union soldiers in Confederate prisons like Libby and Andersonville, with the goal of placing the Lincoln assassination scheme within the larger context of what Holt (and those who shared his perspective) considered the limitless potential of Confederate brutality against the Union.[13] Nevertheless, it seems to be the case that by May 23 Holt was becoming aware that the best he and the federal government could hope for at the moment—in terms of immediate revenge for the assassination of President Lincoln—was the conviction and punishment of the eight prisoners present in the courtroom. Justice for John Surratt Jr., Jefferson Davis, the members of Davis's Canadian Cabinet, and other leading Confederate criminals would simply have to wait.

In the meantime, as Holt's presentation of the prosecution's case wound down, the work of the defense attorneys began in earnest. It was by no means an easy task. As attorney William Doster later wrote, "this was a contest in which a few lawyers were on one side, and the whole United States on the other."[14] Still, the defendants' lawyers had made regular efforts throughout the trial to challenge the government's case in cross-examination and to raise various objections. Then, in late May, defense counsel began to present their own case: character witnesses who emphasized individual defendants' moral natures and pro-Union sentiments or who disputed the veracity of those who had testified for the prosecution, as well as other witnesses whose testimony was designed to distance one or more of the defendants from Booth's assassination scheme, or to implicate others—especially those who were not on trial—more heavily in it.

Not surprisingly, the defense could offer little on behalf of David Herold, whose decision to assist Booth in his escape was tantamount to suicide, even if he did not actually participate directly in the April 14 attacks. While in custody on board the ironclad *Montauk*, Herold had given a thoroughly unconvincing statement to the effect that he had met up with Booth quite by accident on the night of the fourteenth, that he had tried to resist Booth's efforts to persuade him to come along, and that he had only discovered Booth's crime the next night. "I knew nothing at all of it," Herold had insisted. "I never knew any party in existence that had the slightest idea of injuring the President or any of the Cabinet." Herold's own protests aside, as early as April 17—nine days before his capture—an article in the *Washington Evening Star* had identified a man named "Harld" as one of Booth's most important accomplices. Four days later, Secretary of War Stanton received an anonymous letter, identifying some of Herold's links to the Confederacy. On May 1, the *New York Times* described Herold as Booth's "nearest accomplice" in the Lincoln assassination, and three weeks later the same newspaper declared that there could be "no doubt whatever of his guilt, and he will suffer the penalty of his crime."[15]

In this light, the best—probably the only—hope the defense had was to present Herold as a fool. It was an image his surrender to authorities at Garrett's farm on April 26 may well have bolstered, albeit ironically, in contrast with the more heroic (or antiheroic) image of Booth, shot to death by Boston Corbett in a burning barn while defying orders that he give himself up.[16] "From what I know of him," remarked Dr. Charles Davis, a longtime neighbor, during his May 31 testimony, "I should say he is very easily persuaded and led; I should think that nature had not endowed him with as much intellect as the generality of people possess." Added a former employer for good measure: "I consider him a very light, trivial, unreliable boy. In mind, I consider him about eleven years of age." (Herold was twenty-two.) In his final argument, defense attorney Frederick Stone denied that there was any reasonable evidence linking Herold to the planning of the murder itself, insisted that his client's only crime was to assist Booth in his escape, and then explained Herold's reasons for doing so in terms that echoed the words of the witnesses he had called. "Who is Herold?" asked Stone. "A weak, cowardly, foolish, miserable boy . . . trifling, easily persuaded . . . and ready to do the bidding of those around him. Such a boy," he concluded, "was only wax in the hands of a man like Booth." As such, Stone implored the Court to show him mercy.[17]

Witnesses called for George Atzerodt's defense could do no more for him than Herold's had done. "He excited no sympathy from anyone," recalled Commissioner Kautz some years later. On top of the testimony against him, Atzerodt's own confessions to authorities linked him firmly to the assassination plot, though at one point he asserted that it was not he but Herold to whom Booth had assigned the task of killing Vice President Andrew Johnson. Atzerodt also claimed that he had backed out of any involvement whatsoever before the actual events took place on the night of April 14. The circumstantial evidence, of course, strongly suggested otherwise, and his confessions—and even their inconsistency—further undermined Atzerodt's attempts to extricate himself from responsibility. It is worth noting, too, that in the nativist context of mid-nineteenth-century America, Atzerodt's status as a German immigrant of the laboring class worked against him as well, both at the trial and in the press. On April 24 the *Richmond Times* called him a "villainous-looking man, and a German by birth," adding that "there is but little doubt of his criminality." Two days later the *New York Times* described him stereotypically for the period, as "a German by birth. . . . His complexion is dark and swarthy. . . . His forehead is low, and the general contour of his features stamp[s] him as a man of low character, who would stoop to any action, no matter how vile, for money."[18]

Some of Atzerodt's defense witnesses seem to have been summoned simply to cloud the meaning of his actions, either on the night of April 14 or on the days leading up to it. Much more effective, however, were those whose contributions demonstrated that a core characteristic of Atzerodt's nature was unmanly cowardice, which would have prevented him from participating in any meaningful way. It was a theme the press coverage reflected as well: throughout the trial Atzerodt was typically described as "restless and nervous," one "whose whole bearing indicates the craven coward." Indeed, defense attorney William Doster himself consciously and purposefully chose this line of argument, much as Frederick Stone chose to argue for Herold's basic idiocy. "May it please the Court," Doster explained on May 30, when questioned by prosecutor John Bingham about his rather surprising tactics, "I intend to show that this man is a constitutional coward."[19]

In postwar Victorian America, where the blood of male honor and heroism had been shed for four long years, to construct the defense of an accused criminal on the basis of his cowardice must have seemed to some—perhaps even to prosecutor Bingham—a shameful exercise in humiliation. It was, however, the best defense to be had for him. Alexander Brawner, who had known Atzerodt in Port Tobacco for seven or eight years, testified, "I never considered him a very courageus man, by a long streak. . . . I have seen him in little difficulties and bar-room scrapes, where there were pistols drawn, &c.; and he generally got out of the way." Other acquaintances of Atzerodt agreed: "He was always called a man of not much courage," commented Washington Briscoe. Doster concluded in his closing argument: "Coward conscience came to his rescue. . . . He tried to become a hero, but he was only a coachmaker."[20]

To Herold's foolishness and Atzerodt's faintheartedness, William Doster tried to add an image of Lewis Powell's tragic lunacy, the roots of which lay, he argued, in the hardships Powell had experienced as a common soldier during the war. Right from the start Doster had experienced a great deal of frustration trying to learn something about the very reticent Powell. "During the first two weeks of the trial," Doster later wrote, "I could get nothing out of Payne [Powell's assumed name, usually spelled as Paine] either as to his previous history, or as to anything he might have to say in his own defense, or as to whether he wished to be defended at all. During this time I knew very little more of him than the public generally, and not near as much as the prosecution." As a result, recalled the unfortunate defense counsel, he concluded "that the only thing possible to be done on his behalf was to let the court know all that I knew about his mental and moral nature and his previous education. This," he went on to explain, "could only be done under the plea of insanity." In some ways, the door to this defense strategy had been opened by one of Holt's own witnesses, Augustus Seward, when he testified that during their struggle following the attack on the Secretary of State, Powell had even "repeated in an intense but not strong voice, the words, 'I'm mad! I'm mad!'"[21]

And so on June 2 Doster called Dr. Charles H. Nichols, superintendent of the Government Hospital for the Insane in Washington, D.C., who defined "moral insanity" as a situation in which "the moral or affective faculties seem to be exclusively affected by a disease of the brain," in the case of Powell probably caused by the "fatigues of a soldier's life," for which as a young country boy he may not have been fully prepared. "Is great taciturnity considered a symptom?" asked Doster, no doubt hoping to turn his client's striking reticence in his favor. He continued,

> If one should try to murder a sick man in his bed, without ever having seen him before. . . . If the same person should, besides, try to murder four other persons in the house without having seen them before. . . . If the same person should make no attempt to disguise himself, but should converse for five minutes with a negro servant, walk away leisurely, leave his hat and pistol behind, [and] throw away his knife before the door . . . would not such conduct . . . corroborate the suspicion of insanity?

"I think it would," responded Nichols. Guided by Doster, Nichols also linked insanity to severe constipation, and several witnesses then offered testimony to the effect that Powell had suffered from precisely that condition throughout his imprisonment, and presumably before.[22]

However, Holt called a number of witnesses in rebuttal who, as doctors themselves, were able to undermine the defense counselor's case by declaring Powell sane. This left Doster scrambling, without much hope, for a new angle. As he recalled some years later, once he realized that the insanity plea had failed, "this was practically the end of my case, as far as any show of legal defense was concerned. The rest was firing pistol shots against siege guns." In the end, Doster chose to defend Powell as a very good boy gone very bad: the defendant, Doster explained in his final argument, had begun his life as an innocent country youth and, but for the evil influences surrounding him, might have become a good honest farmer. Instead, growing up within the context of slavery and racial prejudice and then being caught in the whirlpool of the late war's horrors, this otherwise fine young man's basic simplicity and goodness were corrupted. He lost his early moral footing and became a ruthless murderer, though an extremely brave one. Pushing his argument even further, and implicitly contrasting Powell with Atzerodt (a coward whose timidity led him to shirk the job Booth had assigned to him), Doster developed the notion that Powell the soldier might well have become a hero—given what heroism means in wartime—if only he had fought for the right cause. The Civil War, Doster claimed, "took him from honest pursuits and professions, and left him to make his living without any other accomplishments than dexterity in murder." On the other hand, what had Powell done "that every rebel soldier has not tried to do? Only this: he has ventured more; he has shown a higher courage, a bitterer hate, a more ready sacrifice," and thus, "if you praise men who are ready to die for their country, you will praise him; and if you applaud those who show any courage superior to the rest of mankind you will applaud him." In short, having abandoned any hope of persuading the commissioners that Powell was crazy, Doster instead posited the paradoxical argument that Powell was a shining example—for better or worse—of what bad institutions and bitter war make of the good, common man. Too bad, one can almost hear him urging the commissioners to agree, Powell was one of theirs, not one of ours. "It was a rather remarkable defence," noted Commissioner Kautz in his diary that night.[23]

Herold, an idiot; Atzerodt, a coward; Powell, a fallen hero. Needless to say, the case of the only woman among the prisoners at the bar demanded yet a different sort of defense strategy. On the one hand, the prosecution's evidence against Mary Surratt was clearly flawed, at least in terms of its ability to prove her full participation in—or even her full knowledge of—Booth's scheme to assassinate Lincoln. On the other hand, at the time the trial took place, the sentiment both within and beyond the courtroom in favor of convicting her was overwhelming, more than sufficient to transform the circumstantial evidence against her into what appeared to be a series of vivid indicators of her total, conscious complicity with Booth and the others. In other words, regardless of how the prosecution's case against her appears in retrospect, at the time it seemed very persuasive indeed. Her defense attorneys had to exert a significant effort in order to try and save her.

Not surprisingly, some of those called on behalf of Mary Surratt's defense strove to undermine the credibility of John Lloyd and Louis Weichmann, the two prosecution witnesses who had given the most damning evidence against her. For example, Lloyd's own sister-in-law, Emma Offutt, told the Court in no uncertain terms that Lloyd was thoroughly drunk at the time Mary Surratt came by the house on April 14, bringing into question his ability to remember accurately anything at all that had been said to him that evening. From a different angle, the testimony of George Cottingham, a detective involved in arresting John Lloyd, suggested that Lloyd himself had been aware of the assassination plot and perhaps even actively involved in it, thus casting doubt on all his testimony. With regard to Louis Weichmann's trustworthiness, the defense called none other than the Confederate blockade runner Augustus Howell, whom Weichmann himself had identified as a visitor to the Surratt boardinghouse. Howell's lengthy testimony addressed the issue of Weichmann's own political sentiments (suggesting that they were in fact strongly pro-Confederate), as well as his strong interest in Howell's activities. The witness's obvious and not so easily dismissed implication, of course, was that Weichmann may have been much closer to the conspiracy than he was admitting, and was just trying to save himself.[24]

Mary Surratt had claimed that, despite the fact that Lewis Powell had previously boarded at her home more than once, she had been unable to recognize him on the night of April 17. As might be expected, Holt and his assistants had presented Mary Surratt's denial—repeated consistently under questioning by various investigators before the trial—as evidence of her essential duplicity, as well as her complicity with Powell and Booth in the assassination scheme. To challenge this interpretation, the defense hoped to prove that Mary Surratt's eyesight was indeed poor enough to explain how she could have failed to identify her former guest. Among the witnesses who testified to this effect were Emma Offutt, boarders Honora Fitzpatrick and Eliza Holohan, a former servant, Rachel Semus, and Mary Surratt's own brother, J. Z. Jenkins.[25]

By far the strongest theme in the case for Mary Surratt's defense, however—and in fact quite a predictable one in mid-nineteenth-century America—was the notion that her nature, sex, and piety made it impossible for her to have been engaged in the sort of treacherous behavior of which she stood accused. In choosing this defense strategy, attorneys fought against a history of women during the Civil War—particularly pro-Confederate women—defying precisely such presumptions by engaging in countless forms of treasonable behavior on behalf of their side. The lawyers also fought against the popular opinion, already formed, that Mary Surratt was in fact a perfect example of proper womanhood gone awry. "She is about fifty to fifty-five years old," claimed the *Philadelphia Inquirer*—in error (she was in her early forties)—on May 10. "She is large in form; very stout; has a keen grey eye; a resolute look; rather ugly; has light hair, and any man would set her down at once for a perfect virago."[26]

Limited in their options, defense attorneys Frederick Aiken and John Clampitt called a number of priests to the stand, all of whom strove to identify Mary Surratt as an innocent representative of true uncorrupted womanhood who could not possibly have been involved in such horrible deeds. To this end, the defense's witnesses praised Mary Surratt's character in the most glowing terms: she was "estimable" (Reverend Francis F. Boyle); "a lady and a Christian" (Reverend B. F. Wiget); "a proper Christian matron" (Reverend Charles H. Stonestreet); and simply "a good Christian woman" (Reverend Peter Lanihan). "Her reputation," commented the Reverend N. D. Young, "is that of a Christian lady in every sense of the word. . . . I have heard her spoken of with the greatest praise by all her acquaintance within my knowledge. I never heard any thing but what was highly favorable to her character."[27]

Laypersons testified similarly. Former servant Rachel Semus recalled that Mrs. Surratt was so good and generous that she routinely fed the many hungry Union soldiers who stopped by her Washington boardinghouse. Others emphasized that Mary Surratt's own basic goodness prompted her to shun rather than to embrace those whose character was questionable. Two of her young female boarders, Eliza Holohan and Honora Fitzpatrick, recalled that Mary Surratt had disliked George Atzerodt from the start and had banned him from the house, and they suggested that she had not thought very highly of Lewis Powell either.[28]

Undoubtedly Mary Surratt's most powerful defense witness was her twenty-two-year-old daughter, Anna. Although not extensive, Anna Surratt's testimony basically echoed that offered by others concerning her mother's fundamental kindness and generosity—even toward unsavory characters like Atzerodt—and her bad vision. In addition, the tremendous grief Anna demonstrated while delivering her testimony moved many observers deeply. Noted the *New York Times* on May 31:

> During the intervals between the questions and answers, whilst she was upon the witness stand she closely scanned the audience, turning in all directions as if to discover some familiar face. Shortly before the close of her examination and after glancing rapidly over the room she enquired aloud "where is she?" All eyes were turned toward her, and she seemed indifferent to the gaze of curious eyes fastened upon her. She was again questioned, and her answer being given, she was told that she could retire. She lingered and searched with her eyes in every part of

the room, apparently much disappointed. Her face became flushed, her eyes filled to overflowing, and as she was almost forced out of the room, asked earnestly, "Where is ma?" She had looked in vain for her mother's form. A crowd of persons standing intervened between the wretched daughter and the criminal mother. Mrs. Surratt was for the first time since the commencement of the trial bowed down with grief, and she wept like a child as her daughter's form passed out of the court-room.[29]

Anna and the other witnesses called for her mother's defense aimed to create the impression that Mary Surratt was a discerning woman who steered clear of evil as best she could, and that her motherly nature and basic Christian charity drove her to treat most people with courtesy and in good faith—and perhaps even "too kindly," as Anna described Mary's treatment of Louis Weichmann. Collectively these defense witnesses strove to prove that Mary Surratt—woman, mother, Christian—simply did not realize how truly evil were those (especially her own son!) who ultimately plotted assassination right there under her very roof.[30]

If in the early twenty-first century such unvarnished appeals to the defendant's womanhood, motherhood, and essential Christian goodness seem improbable or ineffective, it should be remembered that in mid-nineteenth-century America they had the potential to be quite persuasive indeed. This is not to say, however, that in the end Mary Surratt came significantly closer to being exonerated than did Herold, Atzerodt, or Powell. On the contrary, as press reports suggest, the likelihood of her conviction was extremely high right from the start, trapped as she was in a matrix of troubling circumstantial evidence, damning testimony, and her errant son's absence, not to mention the backdrop of Northern outrage—which Holt surely shared—over pro-Confederate women's years of anti-Union treachery, in which many Union observers believed they had engaged with virtual impunity. "Treason never found a better agent than Mrs. Surratt," remarked the Washington correspondent of the *Philadelphia Inquirer* as early as May 4. "She is a large, masculine, self-possessed female, mistress of her house, and as lithe a rebel as [the Southern spies] Belle Boyd or

Mrs. Greensborough [Rose Greenhow]. She has not the flippantry and menace of the first, nor the social power of the second; but the Rebellion has found no fitter agent."[31] On May 11 the *Philadelphia Inquirer* called Mary Surratt a "female fiend incarnate, who figures as the '*mater familias*' of these criminals." On May 16, a Maine newspaper described her as "the arch criminal among those before the Commission," and on June 3, before the testimony was even complete, *Harper's Weekly* wrote, "In regard to Mrs. Surratt, there can scarcely be any doubt of the deepest guilt on her part. She not only harbored the principal criminals, but took a prominent part in the whole conspiracy."[32]

For numerous reasons, Mary Surratt's chances of being acquitted were negligible from the moment she was hauled into custody. Regardless, defense attorneys were duty bound to put up some sort of argument in her favor. In his final argument, Frederick Aiken therefore urged the commissioner-judges to recognize Surratt as

a woman born and bred in respectability and competence—a Christian mother . . . whose unfailing attention to the most sacred duties of life has won for her the name of "a proper Christian matron;" . . . [and whose] maternal solicitude would have been the first denouncer, even abrupt betrayer, of a plotted crime in which one companion of her son could have been implicated, had cognizance of such reached her. Her days would have been agonized and her nights sleepless, till she might have exposed and counteracted that spirit of defiant hate which watched its moment of vantage to wreak an immortal wrong— till she might have sought the intercession and absolution of the Church, her refuge, in behalf of those she loved. . . .[33]

Defense attorneys thus sought to prevent Mary Surratt's conviction by arguing that the combination of her sex, nature, and religious faith made her participation in such a heinous crime impossible.

In the cases of Samuel Arnold and Michael O'Laughlen, the defense argued simply that these men were not involved in the murderous attacks of April 14. Arnold was clearly linked to Booth and to the earlier plan to abduct Lincoln: he had admitted as much in his confession, after all, and the contents of the "Sam" letter offered further confirmation. On the other hand, his return to Maryland following the failure of the kidnapping and his move, at the very end of March, to Fortress Monroe in Virginia (both of which defense witnesses corroborated persuasively) made it "physically impossible," as Arnold's attorney Walter Cox pointed out, "for him to participate in the murder or assaults in Washington. Nor is there the slightest evidence, or even pretense," Cox added for good measure, "that he had any part to perform in the execution of the deadly plot." Of Arnold's participation in the plans to kidnap Lincoln there could be little doubt, Cox basically conceded. But once that scheme fell through, he explained, Arnold had distanced himself physically and otherwise from Booth and the rest of the conspirators, and thus could not be held to account for their subsequent actions, which were, after all, the fruits of a different plot.[34]

Making a similar case for O'Laughlen was more difficult. Witnesses had placed O'Laughlen in Washington—and even possibly in communication with Booth—on April 14, raised the suspicion that Booth had assigned O'Laughlen to kill General Grant, and offered evidence that he was perhaps preparing to do so on April 13, when someone who resembled O'Laughlen was seen lurking around Edwin Stanton's home, where Grant was celebrating that night.[35] Nevertheless, defense attorney Cox offered a similar interpretation of the evidence presented against O'Laughlen, insisting that neither O'Laughlen nor Arnold "had anything to do with the execution of the alleged conspiracy" under consideration. Rather, by virtue of their having to all intents and purposes cut their ties with Booth after the failed abduction attempt in mid-March, Arnold and O'Laughlen "*could* not have had any knowledge of the intended murders." In essence, Cox's argument on behalf of these two defendants revolved around the issue of their making wise choices and showing good judgment (in relative terms, of course). Crucial to their defense was the theme that each man chose, after all, to separate himself from

Booth weeks before the conspiracy mutated into its final deadly form. "That the accused were wrong in ever joining the rebellion against their Government, no one will deny," exclaimed Cox; "that they were wrong in ever listening for a moment, if they ever did, to any proposition from that wicked schemer, Booth, inimical to their Government, no one will deny." But the most important thing to remember, he concluded, was that both men had made the decision to break with Booth long before April 14. On this basis above all, Cox demanded for Arnold and O'Laughlen not just mercy, but "an absolute and unqualified acquittal."[36]

What of Edman Spangler? Needless to say, no one tried to deny that this generally solitary workingman was well-known to be a faithful lackey of John Wilkes Booth, at least when the actor needed things done around the theater. According to proprietor John T. Ford's own rather unflattering testimony, "Booth was a peculiarly fascinating man, and controlled the lower class of people, such as Spangler belonged to, more than ordinary men would." Nor could it be denied that Spangler had been present in the theater on the night of April 14, and of course a good number of witnesses had testified that it was he whom Booth had summoned to hold the skittish horse upon which the murderer later escaped (Spangler, of course, had admitted as much in the statement he gave to investigators on the day after the assassination).[37] In Spangler's case, then, there were only two basic points upon which there was any debate: first, whether he knew in advance about the crime that Booth was planning to commit; and second, whether he aided Booth consciously and in any way premeditatively, such as by arranging in advance to hold the getaway horse, clearing a path from the stage to the exit, boring the hole in the door of the President's box through which Booth observed his victim, tampering with its lock to make the box more accessible, or preparing the piece of wood Booth used to wedge the door closed in order to buy time for his escape onto the stage and out into the alley.[38]

The defense strategy in Spangler's case was to plead his ignorance of Booth's plotting. The attorneys argued that Spangler knew nothing whatsoever of any plot—abduction or murder—that Booth and other conspirators might have been hatching, and they insisted that it was merely a matter of coincidence if any of Spangler's actions on or about April 14, and especially at the time of the crime, smacked of complicity. Defense witnesses testified that the preparations made in advance in the President's box at the theater must have been effected either by Booth himself or by an unknown third party; that the passageways at the back of the stage needed to always be kept unobstructed; that Spangler had been at his post on the stage throughout the play; and that although he had been called to hold Booth's horse, he had turned that job over to someone else. In summing up Spangler's defense, Thomas Ewing Jr. made a strong effort to persuade his listeners that, with all the evidence in, there still remained more than a reasonable doubt of Spangler's having been in any way a deliberate accomplice of Booth. As he put it, in all the testimony given "there is nothing shown to have been said or done by anybody prior to the moment of assassination . . . tending at all to show that Spangler had any intimation of Booth's guilty purpose, or was in any way, even innocently, instrumental in effecting it."[39]

On the surface, Samuel Mudd's chances for acquittal must have seemed significantly lower than Spangler's, although perhaps not to the defendant himself. Reported the New York Times on May 14, just as the trial was getting under way, "Dr. Mudd looked calm, collected, and attentive."[40] Mudd's purported serenity notwithstanding, little or no doubt was attached to the bulk of the basic evidence. He had met Booth (and probably also several others associated with the conspiracy, including John Surratt Jr.) before the assassination. After the assassination, Booth and Herold had come to his house seeking medical attention for Booth's broken leg. Mudd had then housed and fed Booth and Herold that day and had failed to inform authorities promptly of their visit. Finally, when interrogated by investigators a few days later, his answers had been inconsistent and, seemingly, evasive. Holt and his assistants had pieced together these and other bits of evidence into a persuasive picture of Mudd's complicity in Booth's scheme.

In the face of the prosecution's strong evidence against him,

Mudd's defense counsel struggled to show that each bit of potentially incriminating data—data that seemed like an indication of premeditated involvement in the scheme to murder Lincoln and others—was in fact no such thing, and could, moreover, be explained in another way. The defense called far more witnesses than for any of the other defendants, including several members of Mudd's large, extended family. These witnesses testified that although Mudd had met Booth before April 1865, his reasons for doing so had had nothing to do with the conspiracy—at least, from Mudd's perspective. He had helped Booth purchase a horse, but he did not know what the horse would be used for. Although Mudd had been in Washington in December 1864, he had gone not to meet with Booth and Surratt but to purchase a stove. When he traveled to Washington again on March 23, 1865, it was only to "attend a sale of Government-condemned horses," not to connect with Booth and his fellow conspirators. And although Mudd had indeed been in Bryantown on April 15 and 16, at that time few people were talking about the attacks of the fourteenth. Moreover, among those who were talking, none could name the individual who had killed the President, and furthermore, the name associated with the attack on Seward was "Boyle," not "Booth." In addition, defense witnesses claimed, once the details of the attacks became clearer on the morning of April 17, Mudd had come forward immediately and voluntarily. George D. Mudd testified that his cousin had at that point promised to "give every information in his power relative" to the crimes, beginning with describing the "suspicious parties" who had been at his house on the fifteenth. Then there were Mudd's own statements to investigators, in which he confessed to setting Booth's leg and providing Herold and Booth with other assistance, but staunchly insisted that he had no idea who they were and claimed, implicitly, that he was simply providing the sort of help any good country doctor and gentleman would have done.[41]

Defense witnesses built on the image Mudd projected of himself. Perhaps persuaded to a certain extent, Commissioner Kautz later commented that Mudd was certainly "the most intelligent looking" of the accused. Defense witnesses testified as well that, despite Holt and the prosecution's presentation of him as a passionate Southern nationalist, Mudd was in fact a Union man and a "good citizen." One witness who had known Mudd since childhood recalled, "He has always been amiable and estimable . . . a good neighbor, honest, correct." Former slaves even went so far as to testify (sometimes against the word of other former slaves) that Mudd was a kind master, although they agreed that he had once shot one of their number, presumably for troublesome behavior. Other defense witnesses specifically challenged the credibility of those called by Holt to testify against Mudd—particularly Daniel Thomas, who had testified that Mudd asserted in March that Lincoln and the whole cabinet were to be killed soon. Still others strove either to undermine prosecution testimony linking Mudd to various members of the Confederate underground in Maryland, including John H. Surratt, or to suggest that any of Mudd's associations with known pro-Confederate operatives had come to an end years before Lincoln's assassination.[42]

In his long summary argument on behalf of Samuel Mudd, defense lawyer Thomas Ewing Jr. took the offensive right away. "As to Dr. Mudd," he declared, "there is no particle of evidence tending to show that he was ever leagued with traitors in their treason," nor had he participated in any way in the murder of Lincoln, and as such was not guilty of the charges against him. As for the evidence against Mudd, Ewing stressed that Booth and Mudd were clearly not intimates, nor were Mudd and John Surratt, whom Mudd may, in fact, never even have met. Moreover, Mudd's trips to Washington were unconnected to Booth's conspiracy, and Mudd had never actually predicted the assassination. As for Booth's appearance with Herold at the Mudd house on April 15, that was driven by Booth's need for a doctor (had he not broken his leg, the assassin never would have gone there). Any actions taken by Mudd on that day were, therefore, acts rooted in his basic kindness and his sense of professional responsibility, and had been performed on behalf of men whom he assumed to be complete and innocent strangers. When the facts of the assassination became clear to him, Ewing insisted (not quite accurately), Mudd "moved more promptly in communicating his information" than the authorities did "in acting on it." In short, Mudd, doctor and gentleman (albeit, slaveholder), was "a man of most exemplary character—peaceable, kind, upright, and obedient to the laws," a man "never known or reported to have done an act or said a word in aid of the rebellion, or in countenance or support of the enemies of the Government." Clearly, therefore, he should not be convicted.[43] One can almost hear Ewing's implicit encouragement to the commissioner-judges to recognize the contrast between Mudd, on the one hand, and cowards like Atzerodt, fools like Herold, thugs like Powell, Jezebels like Mary Surratt, and even lackeys like Spangler.

According to the rules of the commission, once the defense attorneys' closing arguments had been heard, the prosecution had the last word. Perhaps because of his own role as trial manager as well as chief prosecutor, Holt delegated responsibility for the prosecution's closing statement to Assistant Judge Advocate John Bingham, who summarized (at enormous length) the federal government's case against the accused. First, Bingham reasserted, in forceful terms, the propriety and the legality of the government's decision to try the accused before a military commission. Then he restated clearly and in great detail the government's presumption that the local conspiracy upon which Holt and his assistants had in the end focused most of their energy was in fact the brainchild and the logical conclusion of an overarching conspiracy designed by Jefferson Davis and the Confederate leadership. Finally, Bingham reviewed the evidence Holt and the prosecution's witnesses had presented against each of the defendants, and he concluded with an important reminder about the law pertaining to conspiracies, namely, that "all the parties . . . must be held as principals, and the act of one, in the prosecution of the common design, [is] the act of all." According to Commissioner Kautz, the argument Bingham made was "well prepared and very conclusive," though Kautz criticized as its "principal defect" the "volume of words in which it is enveloped." Bingham, as the recent historian William Hanchett notes, "was a formidable, even a fearsome prosecutor, and his closing statement," at least to a marked extent, "determined the outcome of the trial."[44]

On June 29 and 30, the military commissioners gathered behind closed doors to deliberate. Years later William Doster recalled that among the attorneys for the defense, the very context of the trial had offered little hope for the success of their painful chore, and when the commissioners gathered to decide the verdicts, the defense attorneys were hardly optimistic. "The circumstances under which, and the place where, the trial began," Doster wrote, "were not of a character to cheer counsel in their task. More than all, it was the period proper for punishment of the rebellion, and somebody must be hanged for example's sake." Doster was almost certainly correct, although to say so is hardly to vindicate the accused of the crimes with which they were charged, or to diminish the quality of much of the powerful evidence Holt and his assistants had compiled. It does, however, offer a reminder of the significance for the outcome of the trial of the atmosphere of vengeance that prevailed in Washington, and across much of the North in the spring and early summer of 1865.[45]

The commissioners reached their conclusions quickly on June 30. However, the announcement of their decisions—both to the public and to the prisoners themselves—was delayed for five days, due to the fact that President Andrew Johnson had fallen ill and appears to have been too indisposed during that period to review the case and approve the commissioners' findings. "The President is ill," wrote Secretary of the Navy Gideon Welles in his diary as early as June 27. "[He] is feeling the effects of intense application to his duties, and over-pressure from the crowd." Meanwhile, the commissioners began to take their leave of the capital; Kautz was on his way as early as July 2.[46]

On July 5, less than three months after the assassination and "after mature deliberation," Johnson finally endorsed the commissioners' recommendations as they were presented to him by Judge Holt, who brought all the relevant paperwork from the trial to the White House for Johnson's review. The commissioners' decisions were then announced in the press that day. All the accused had been found guilty to a greater or lesser degree of the charges lodged against them. Spangler received a sentence of six years in prison at hard labor; O'Laughlen, Arnold, and Mudd were condemned to life imprisonment, also at hard labor; and Atzerodt, Herold, Powell, and Mary Surratt were sentenced to hang. President Johnson scheduled the executions for July 7, between 10:00 A.M. and 2:00 P.M. The time allotted to the four condemned prisoners for "preparation" seemed uncommonly short to many. "Surprise is expressed, almost unanimously," reported the New York Times, "that the execution should be fixed for a day so immediate after the promulgation of the sentence," although in fact such speed was typical for courts-martial (if not for civil trials) at the time.[47]

On July 6, the reaction on the streets of the federal capital to the news of the trial's conclusion and the verdicts of the commissioners was somber and intense, as it was within the walls of the Old Arsenal for the four who now faced the gallows. According to a reporter for the Philadelphia Inquirer who gained access to the condemned, Mary Surratt was "extremely depressed and wept bitterly." Powell "manifested little or no emotion," having already "evidently nerved himself to meet his death with firm resolution." Herold at first appeared typically indifferent, but according to the Inquirer's account finally came to realize at least in some measure "the solemnity of his situation" (in contrast, the New York Times claimed that Herold "was full of levity almost to the very hour of his death"). As for Atzerodt, the reporter claimed, his response was to become "violently agitated and almost paralyzed with fear." The New York Times correspondent corroborated this new evidence of Atzerodt's purported cowardice by noting that when he learned of the news about his sentence, Atzerodt "trembled and grew deathly pale."[48]

Shortly after learning of their sentences from General Hartranft and General Winfield Scott Hancock, in command of the Union's armed forces in the federal capital, the four prisoners awaiting execution were offered the opportunity for religious counsel. Mary Surratt immediately requested two Catholic priests, Fathers Jacob A. Walter and B. F. Wiget (Wiget had testified on her behalf). Powell requested one Dr. Stracker, a Baptist minister. Herold does not seem to have sought spiritual counsel, but Atzerodt willingly agreed to meet with a Lutheran clergyman recommended by General Hartranft.[49]

Meanwhile, on July 6, soldiers worked to build a scaffold in the south yard of the prison—"a simple wooden structure of very primitive appearance . . . elevated about twelve feet from the ground, and . . . about twenty feet square," according to one reporter—on which the four condemned prisoners were to be executed simultaneously. (In a cruel twist, and for reasons that are difficult to discern, the other four prisoners were left uninformed about who among their number was condemned to die, although they could hear the hammers pounding away in the prison yard.) That afternoon, Atzerodt had an emotional meeting with at least one of his brothers, a visit whose sad tone reportedly moved several witnesses, including hardened prison guards, to tears. The previous day, five of David Herold's seven sisters had come to visit him bearing cakes and delicacies, and Anna Surratt was at this point in almost constant attendance on her mother. "When the time came for separation," reported one observer, "the screams of anguish that burst from the poor girl could be distinctly heard all over the execution ground." As had been the case throughout the trial, not one member of Lewis Powell's Florida family tried or was able to come and see him.[50]

In the brief period that remained before the scheduled execution, a range of efforts got under way to save Mary Surratt, the first woman in American history who was condemned by the federal government to die. Indeed, as the time proposed for the execution drew near, General Hancock stationed mounted soldiers at regular intervals between the White House and the prison grounds in anticipation of the need to relay a last-minute presidential pardon.

Among those involved in attempting to persuade President Johnson to spare Mary Surratt's life was John Brophy, who had so vigorously challenged the veracity of Louis Weichmann's testimony, and who had delivered an affidavit to that effect to Mary Surratt's lawyers on June 21. Early on the morning of July 7, the day scheduled for the execution, Brophy penned yet another lengthy statement to President Johnson, urging him to put a halt to Mary Surratt's execution on the basis of Weichmann's—and Lloyd's—obvious duplicity. Both men, Brophy claimed, had been "testifying with ropes around their necks," so implicated were they themselves in the conspiracy in which Mary Surratt stood accused of participating.[51]

There is much in Brophy's statement that arguably might have worked to Mary Surratt's advantage, especially given the fact that the federal government had never yet executed a woman and the fragility of some of the evidence against her. Nevertheless, Johnson refused to consider Brophy's statement, quite likely on the advice of Joseph Holt, to whom Johnson referred all pleas for mercy, and whose vision of justice precluded Mary Surratt's exoneration. Indeed, neither Holt nor Johnson was willing to consider with any seriousness any of the pleas on Mary Surratt's behalf with which they were besieged during the two days between the announcement of the convicted prisoners' sentences and the execution, including a signed statement from General Hartranft at the Old Arsenal Penitentiary claiming that Lewis Powell himself had declared Mary Surratt "innocent of the murder of the President or any knowledge thereof."[52]

Andrew Johnson also refused several attempts by a desperate Anna Surratt to speak with him on her mother's behalf, sending her to see Joseph Holt instead, who remained absolutely unshaken in his resolve. Years later, John Clampitt bitterly recalled Holt's attitude: "His heart was chilled, his soul impassive as marble. . . . He said: 'I can do nothing.'" However, Holt passed the buck to Johnson when he told Anna Surratt that, "The President is immovable . . . and you might as well attempt to overthrow this building as to alter his decision."[53]

According to one report, when she was denied access to the President, "Miss Surratt threw herself upon the stair steps, where she remained a considerable length of time, sobbing aloud in the greatest anguish, protesting her mother's innocence, and imploring every one who came near her to intercede in her mother's behalf." In vain, Anna Surratt also sent others to the White House—including Father Walter, Frederick Aiken, and the widow of Democratic Senator Stephen A. Douglas—to implore Johnson to pardon her mother. Two of David Herold's sisters also went to the White House, to plead for mercy for their brother, but they, too, were forbidden to see the President.

Meanwhile Samuel Mudd's wife, Sarah, attempted to plead with Holt on her husband's behalf. Months later, she wrote the judge advocate general of that meeting: "Your dignified and reserved manner somewhat awed me. I thought I could see through the reserve a kind heart, and you felt for me in my deep distress." Kind heart and empathy aside, Holt did not change his mind. Instead, he and President Johnson allowed the wheels to continue to turn.[54]

On the morning of July 7, a blisteringly hot day in Washington, soldiers on special duty tested the gallows traps with three-hundred-pound weights and readied the ropes for their task. The *Philadelphia Inquirer* offered a graphic description: "The rumbling sound of the trap as it falls in the course of the experiments which are being made to test it, and to prevent any unfortunate accident occurring at the critical moment, is heard . . . and all eyes are involuntarily turned in that direction for curiosity is excited to the highest pitch to view the operations of the fatal machinery." Around noon, General Hancock ordered Hartranft to get ready, "the signal," noted the *Inquirer*, "for the interviews of the clergymen, relatives and friends of the prisoners to cease, and for the doomed to prepare for execution."[55]

Then, around 1:15, the condemned, their guards, and their spiritual advisers moved slowly through the prison door, across the courtyard, and up the thirteen steps to the gallows platform, where a small chair and an umbrella to block the sun—"whose rays shot down like the blasts from a fiery furnace"—were made available, somewhat ironically, for Mary Surratt. After a few minutes each of the prisoners underwent final preparations: pinioning of the arms and tying of the legs (in Mary Surratt's case, cotton strips were tied around the skirt of her dress below the knees), placing of the heavy rope around the neck and a hood over the head. Defense attorney William Doster recalled, "To me the most harrowing part of [Mary Surratt's] execution was to see her bonnet removed by two soldiers and the rope put around her neck. It was the meeting of the extremes of what is esteemed sacred and what is deemed infamous."[56]

Seconds later, Captain Christian Rath, the official executioner, gave the signal by clapping his hands, and four members of Company F of

The execution.
Courtesy of the Library of Congress

the Fourteenth Veteran Reserves caused the drops to fall by knocking out the supporting posts. In that moment more than a thousand people, including ticket-bearing spectators, soldiers on guard duty, officers, government officials, members of the press, and friends and family of the prisoners, witnessed what the *Philadelphia Inquirer* called the "last scene of the terrible tragedy of the 14th of April." About thirty minutes later, once doctors had confirmed their deaths, the bodies of Atzerodt, Herold, Powell, and Mary Surratt were cut down and placed in the plain pine coffins ("similar to those used for packing guns in") that had been visible throughout from the platform on which the condemned had stood. Into each coffin officials placed a glass vial containing a slip of paper on which the victim's name was written for identification purposes. The coffins were then buried in shallow graves against the prison wall, just a few steps from the hastily constructed gallows.[57]

Meanwhile, Michael O'Laughlen, Samuel Arnold, Samuel Mudd, and Edman Spangler awaited their fate inside their cells within the

Old Arsenal Penitentiary. Jefferson Davis and Clement Clay awaited theirs in their well-guarded casemates at Fortress Monroe. And as Anna Surratt, brokenhearted and "perfectly crushed with grief," stumbled back to the barricaded boardinghouse on H Street under the eyes of hundreds of curious spectators, her brother John was still nowhere to be found.[58]

The result of the Washington Court-martial, as announced by the Washington telegrams this afternoon, seems to be in accordance, generally, with the anticipations of the public, only it was considered pretty sure that more than four of the parties would be hanged. A mawkish sort of sympathy seems to be expressed in some quarters for Mrs. Surratt, on account of her sex, coupled with the wish that the President would pardon her; but the same sort of people, I dare say, would sympathize with Satan himself, if there was any possibility of bringing him to justice.

—*Philadelphia Inquirer*, July 7, 1865

I congratulate you upon the great vindication of the laws in the conviction & punishment of the rebel tools, the Conspirators.

—T. S. Bell to Joseph Holt,
July 7, 1865'

There is yet one great criminal upon whom the majesty of the law is yet to frown. He is imprisoned in the casemates of Fortress Monroe. The despotic cause of the death of hundreds of thousands of innocent men, the cruel destroyer of thousands of unarmed prisoners by the torture of starvation, must not escape the punishment which he has defied. For him it is now the duty of the Government to demonstrate that justice, although slow, is sure.

—*Philadelphia Inquirer*, July 8, 1865

5

"In Violation of the Laws and Customs of War"

Going After Henry Wirz of Andersonville

For fully nine days after the execution of Atzerodt, Herold, Powell, and Mary Surratt, the four remaining convicted conspirators waited to learn of their own sentences. Arnold later recalled the excruciating uncertainty of this period: "I thought at times they intended executing us in sections," he wrote, "and thus days came and passed under the strain of horrible conjectures." Although it is not known why Holt and others withheld this information, the decision to do so certainly mirrors the judge advocate general's stern refusal at this point to display signs of mercy toward any whom he associated with the crimes of April 14, or even toward their family members and friends. While the four prisoners waited for word of what would happen to them now that the others had been hanged, each spent his two hours of daily allotted exercise time in the prison yard, where he could see the scaffold and the "four mounds of new heaped Earth" marking the graves of those who had just been hanged.[2]

Then, on July 16, the men were abruptly informed of their sentences, which initially consigned them to imprisonment in Albany, New York. The following night at midnight, however, Arnold, O'Laughlen, Mudd, and Spangler boarded a steamboat for Fortress Monroe, where Jefferson Davis and Clement Clay were being held.

There they were transferred to a warship, the *Florida*, each man heavily guarded and bound in double irons as well as leg shackles. On July 24, the four men arrived at Fort Jefferson, a federal prison located on one of a series of small islands off the southwestern coast of Florida, dubbed the Dry Tortugas. Fort Jefferson lay about sixty miles beyond Key West and, as Mudd's attorney Thomas Ewing Jr. noted, beyond the jurisdiction of any civil court in the United States. Still, Ewing wrote reassuringly to Samuel Mudd's wife a week after the men arrived, "the place is better for [Samuel's] health than almost any other. The island is dry, and the climate good." On August 24, Mudd himself confirmed Ewing's reassurances to Sarah: "This place continues to be unusually healthy," he noted; but he added with unknown prescience: "the only fear manifested is that disease may be propagated by the arrival of vessels and steamers from infected ports."[3]

In his memoir Samuel Arnold recalled Fort Jefferson, which occupied an area of about seven acres (more than half the island), as a "huge and massive structure" made of brick and mortar, hexagonal in shape, and surrounded by a broad, deep moat, designed not so much to keep the prisoners in (where would they go, after all, upon escaping?), as to "prevent the surging of the sea from washing against the main structure itself." At the time the conspirators arrived, about six hundred prisoners were confined at Fort Jefferson for various breaches of military law. According to Arnold, all of the inmates "were compelled to labor daily from morn to night upon limited and loathsome subsistence." In his mind, Fort Jefferson was "without exception . . . the most horrible place, the eye of man ever rested upon." Historian Gary Planck concurs, calling it "an American version of Devil's Island, complete with dark dungeons, torture chambers, and a shark-infested moat . . . virtually an escape-proof prison, isolated from the outer world, in the heart of the yellow fever belt." To be condemned to life at Fort Jefferson, many prisoners believed, was virtually the same as being condemned to death.[4]

Brigadier General Levi A. Dodd, the Union army officer responsible for overseeing the prisoners' safe transport to Fort Jefferson, submitted an official report concerning the trip to the War Department. Dodd claimed that all four prisoners had spoken with him during their trip about the conspiracy case and their respective roles in it. According to Dodd, Arnold's comments had remained consistent with his pretrial confession to federal authorities, namely that he was involved in the abduction scheme but not in the scheme to murder, and that when the abduction scheme had failed, "he considered himself out of it, and never knew anything about the assassination." Arnold believed that Booth had devised the final plan and logistics only a few hours before the event, and it seems quite likely from the evidence that he was correct. Dodd's report further claimed that, like Arnold, O'Laughlen freely admitted to participating in the kidnapping plot, but denied "that he had part or knowledge in the plot to assassinate the President, Gen. Grant, or any one else." As for Spangler, Dodd reported that he "expressed some impatience at his own stupidity" for not having remembered, at the time he spoke with investigators, that the door through which Booth had escaped from the theater had been fixed with a spring so as to close automatically, a point of information Spangler apparently thought would have worked to his advantage somehow. But, wrote Dodd, Spangler also said while on board the *Florida* that he "supposed the court had done right," and that if he had work to do and food to eat during his upcoming six years in prison, "he was satisfied."[5]

As far as these three men were concerned, Dodd's report offered nothing new. In Mudd's case, however, the report claimed quite sensationally that the doctor had actually made a rather elaborate confession in which he acknowledged that Louis Weichmann's testimony against him was essentially correct, and that he had in fact recognized Booth when the actor arrived with Herold on the morning of April 15, but that he had been afraid to say anything to the authorities, "fearing the life of himself and family would be endangered thereby." According to General Dodd, Mudd even went so far as to tell him that "the Military Commission, in his case, had done their duty, and as far as they were concerned, the sentence in his case was just," though Mudd also supposedly commented that some witnesses had intentionally and maliciously given false testimony.[6]

Years later Louis Weichmann recalled the sensation of utter vindication he had experienced when he read Dodd's report of Mudd's "confession." Not surprisingly, when Mudd himself learned of Dodd's account late in August, he denied it immediately and unequivocally, along with many other accusations that had been leveled against him at the conspiracy trial.[7] In truth, it must be noted that even without a confession Mudd, as assassination expert Roy Chamlee has expressed it, seemed "by far the most guilty of those given lesser sentences." Certainly the evidence of his direct involvement with Booth, both before and after the assassination, is at least as strong as that assembled against Mary Surratt. As such, had Mudd made the sort of confession Dodd attributed to him either before or during the trial, it would undoubtedly have resulted in his execution. If in fact he did make such a confession while en route to the Dry Tortugas, however—which seems unlikely, given all of his previous denials—it had no practical effect on his fate, even though it raised some eyebrows and set tongues wagging for a time when the press announced it.[8]

In any case, by the end of July, Arnold, O'Laughlen, Spangler, and Mudd were settling in as best they could at Fort Jefferson, but the transition was, understandably, painful. For a large portion of their time in prison the men would share a single cell, an arrangement initially designed to isolate them from the other prisoners, which then persisted to a great extent because the four of them simply preferred remaining together. Still, the cell they shared was hardly pleasant: according to Arnold it was nothing more than a small, dark, "damp and ill ventilated dungeon." Arnold further described the rations at the prison as ghastly: "The bread was disgusting to look upon," he recalled vividly, "being a mixture of flour, bugs, sticks, and dirt." The meat was so foul, he noted, that "dogs ran from coming in contact with it"; virtually no vegetables were provided, and as for the coffee, it was "brought into our quarters in a dirty greasy bucket, always with grease swimming upon its surface."[9]

In September, Edman Spangler used similar language in a letter to a "dear friend" detailing the dreadful conditions of life in captivity in the Dry Tortugas. For one thing, Spangler wrote, there was the relentless, searing heat. The food was horrible and scant: "whe have hard grub, sult horse and one pc. of bread. . . . Whe some times gets soup.

There is some small fish in the break water that we can catch from our cell window but we have no fish hooks small enough," and no way to get any. The poor quality of the food and the harsh living conditions were not the only things that claimed Spangler's attention; so, too, did the presence of what Samuel Mudd called the "detested and abominable negro regiment" which had been assigned to guard duty at Fort Jefferson (in late September the Eightieth and Eighty-second U.S. Colored Infantry Regiments replaced the white 161st New York as prison guards). All in all, Fort Jefferson struck Spangler as a "purty hard place to live." If indeed Spangler had suggested to Dodd some weeks before that he thought the military commission had done its job correctly, now—faced with six years of what had quickly come to seem like hell on earth—he saw things differently. "Before God and all that is sacred," Spangler insisted to his friend, "I am perfectly innocent of all charges and specifications brought against me by the prosecution. I have no knowledge of enything nor did I aid or assist the villain or the assasen of the President either before or after the assanation."[10]

Although Fort Jefferson was associated with brutal hard labor for its inmates, there has been some dispute over how hard their labor actually proved to be. One historian has claimed that Mudd and the others barely labored at all, instead passing their time "making little boxes and picture frames out of shells and colored wood" that were later sold. Other historians disagree, saying that the prisoners were indeed expected to do what Arnold described as "the filthiest jobs the Provost Marshal could hunt up," although at some point he himself was given a post as a clerk in the prison adjutant's office, Spangler was able to do some carpentry, and Mudd was assigned to serve as assistant to the prison's surgeon in charge. Still, Mudd's letters home over the years also indicate that he (and probably the others, too) did a considerable amount of custodial labor at the prison.[11]

As late summer gave way to autumn in 1865 Mudd's adjustment seems to have been the slowest and most reluctant of the four. Indeed on September 25, after much consideration, he actually tried to escape on board a military transport bringing troops to the fort. "Providence was against me," Mudd wrote about a week later to his brother-in-law. "I was too well known and was apprehended five or ten minutes after being aboard the steamer." Unsuccessful, temporarily deprived of his relatively privileged position in the prison hospital, and fearful that further attempts to escape would be interpreted as an admission of guilt and undermine any hopes for an early release, Mudd did not try again. Still, for the next several months, he and the other convicted conspirators suffered for his error in judgment: they were chained, held in their cell at least twelve hours a day, and deprived of the opportunity to exercise.[12]

Meanwhile, in Washington, the period since the execution had been a study in frustration for Judge Advocate General Holt, even though he also saw the arrival of many heartfelt tributes to his steadfastness during the conspiracy trial. Wrote one V. O. Taylor from Des Moines on July 7, "Permit a stranger, who knows the sentiments of the people of the 'far west,' to express to you his thanks for the results reached by the Court which you have so ably & honorably represented, in the case of the assassins of our late beloved President." With similar enthusiasm, Holt's good friend Margaret E. Crosby wrote from New York on July 10: "Please receive my congratulations for the issue—so happy for justice and order in our dear country—of your efforts in the late distressing trial." Such adulation notwithstanding, Holt's efforts to move forward after the trial with the larger project of avenging the death of Lincoln specifically, and the crimes of the Confederacy and its leadership generally, were bumping up against a series of stubborn obstacles.[13]

Among other things, Holt found himself contending with the unpleasant task of sorting through the claims—coming from every possible direction, it seemed—on the various reward moneys the federal government had offered for information as well as for the arrests of key suspects associated with the conspiracy case.[14] Far more troublesome than this was the burst of popular sympathy that the execution of Mary Surratt had generated almost immediately. This sympathy arose in part from public recognition of the gaps in the evidence against her and also drew on substantial pockets of popular discomfort with the concept of hanging a woman, guilty or not, in the first place. "No sooner had the decree of the Commission . . . been carried into effect," recalled Louis Weichmann years later, "than a great outcry was raised . . . by those sympathizing with the rebellion and by certain elements in the church of which she was a member, that the Government had executed" a woman, and perhaps even an innocent one (or at least one who was not nearly as guilty as those with whom she had been executed). Many in midcentury America, both North and South, Catholic and non-Catholic, found the act abhorrent, even if they believed deeply in Mary Surratt's guilt and in the need to punish her somehow. Indeed, the majority of the commissioner-judges themselves had doubted both the justice and the wisdom (or both) of hanging a woman. Although all nine commissioners had resoundingly convicted Mary Surratt of conspiracy in the plot to assassinate Lincoln and officially sentenced her to hang, five of them—David Hunter, August Kautz, Robert Foster, James Ekin, and Charles Tompkins—had also signed a petition recommending clemency in her case, "in consideration of [her] sex and age." Word of this petition, which was then attached to the paperwork forwarded with Joseph Holt to President Johnson for approval on July 5, was reported (or leaked) immediately to the popular press.[15]

Andrew Johnson's failure to grant the commissioners' request for executive clemency for Mary Surratt subsequently became a source of a bitter dispute between the President and Holt.[16] In the immediate aftermath of the execution, however, far more controversy erupted over Johnson's failure to entertain any of the other requests for mercy on Mary Surratt's behalf—the anguished cries of her daughter, Anna, and others that he issue a stay of execution, for example, and a habeas corpus petition presented just hours before her death.[17] Years later, Commissioner Kautz recalled anticipating with trepidation such an outpouring of support for Mary Surratt should she in fact be executed. "In these early days after the assassination," Kautz wrote in his memoir, "the country seemed to require victims to pay for the great crime. It was apparent to me, however, that there would be a reaction and that those who were instrumental in causing her execution would regret that they had permitted Mrs. Surratt to be hung." Within days—even hours—of her death, Kautz's prediction proved correct. "The friends of the late Mary E. Surratt," warned the *New York*

Times as early as July 13, "are resorting to ill-judged action in endeavoring to prove her innocence." Over the course of the summer, growing sympathy for Mary Surratt manifested itself in a series of public debates, particularly concerning the workings of Holt's military commission, and the presumably unfair treatment the convicted woman had received in her final days.[18]

With respect to the workings of the commission, one of the most serious challenges revolved around the credibility of Louis Weichmann—Joseph Holt's key witness, especially against Mary Surratt—who came under fresh attack. On July 17, the *Philadelphia Inquirer* published a statement from Weichmann clearly demonstrating that the attacks against him, which John Brophy had initiated during the trial and then reiterated in his July 7 statement to President Johnson, were gaining momentum. Not surprisingly, Weichmann responded by characterizing Brophy's challenges as "a tissue of lies from beginning to end"; in his statement to the *Inquirer*, Weichmann delivered what he hoped would be a stinging counterattack against Brophy's own reliability: "He is an alien," wrote Weichmann, as if the negative implications of Brophy's "alienness" were obvious. Moreover, Weichmann continued, Brophy "has never been naturalized, and has not taken the oath of allegiance to the Government which he attempts to assail in the person of its chief witness."[19]

In his statement Weichmann also shamelessly defended his own character, insisting that "no person throughout the whole trial had his good character so fully vouchsafed for as I have. It is beyond reproach, either as regards loyalty, veracity or morality." He maintained that his testimony against Mary Surratt had been accurate in every detail. "Conscious of my integrity and of my desire to do right to all," Weichmann wrote rather melodramatically and with his now familiar air of self-righteousness, "I stand to-day in the pure light of heaven without one sin on my soul to answer for as regards the trial of the conspirators." Although Weichmann agreed in his statement that it was just possible that Mary Surratt—like O'Laughlen and Arnold—had known only about the kidnapping scheme and not the plot to kill, still, he declared, she "deserved death." She was a woman and a mother, after all, he wrote, essentially turning the defense attorneys' argument on behalf of Mary Surratt on its head. "She should have exercised a woman's influence and a mother's love, and then she could have prevented all."[20] It hardly represents a great leap of imagination to suggest that lingering anxiety about his own ultimate exoneration in the public eye prompted Weichmann to condemn in the harshest possible terms the woman in whose home he had enjoyed the status of an adoptive son.

The *Philadelphia Inquirer* defended Weichmann unequivocally that day, but on July 18 the *New Haven Register* claimed with equal confidence that Mary Surratt's execution "was nothing less than murder."[21] In the weeks and months ahead the debate about Weichmann's credibility persisted, as did entirely reasonable questions about his own proximity to—and even his own possible culpability in—the conspiracy. Doubts about Weichmann were exacerbated by growing popular discomfort with Holt's stern attitude of resolve regarding the punishment of the assassins and all of their associates, which had apparently induced him to support duplicitous witnesses such as Sanford Conover. Among some observers, concerns arose that the judge advocate general had either bought Weichmann's testimony or coerced it out of him simply in order to convict Mary Surratt.

At the same time, popular distress over Mary Surratt's death also manifested itself in a discussion in the press about the quality of her last days—specifically, whether she had been allowed the sort of religious succor she sought and deserved at the end of her sad, pious life. Soon after the execution, the *New York Times* published a short piece relaying an accusation that Mary Surratt had been denied a crucial visit from her "spiritual advisers" in the hours before her death. A week later, the *Philadelphia Inquirer* reprinted an article from the *New York Tribune* which intimated that on July 6, the day after she learned of her sentence, Mary Surratt had requested a visit from the Reverend Jacob A. Walter of St. Patrick's Church in Washington, but that Reverend Walter had been turned away from the Old Arsenal, supposedly for lack of proper authorization from the Department of War.[22]

According to Reverend Walter (notably, a pro-Southern native of Maryland), as well as his (and Mary Surratt's) supporters, the real reason he was turned away was that he had openly expressed his bitterness about Mary Surratt's conviction and her death sentence, and federal authorities feared he would speak his mind, both inside the prison and at the execution itself. General James A. Hardie, the assistant to Secretary of War Stanton responsible for issuing passes to the prison, claimed, however, that Walter's expressing in "violent and excited language" his revulsion at the trial's results had nothing to do with his being denied access to Mary Surratt's cell, which was really no more a temporary administrative blunder. "Mr. Walter's convictions as to the innocence of the prisoner . . ," Hardie wrote, "were not made matters of objection." Moreover, once the mistake was detected Father Walter gained access almost immediately—although not, Hardie confessed, before the general took the opportunity to counsel the priest about keeping his thoughts on the trial to himself.[23]

As the summer drew to a close, to Holt's frustration and dismay, popular sympathy for Mary Surratt continued to grow. During this period Holt also found himself the recipient of an extended plea on Samuel Mudd's behalf from the doctor's wife, Sarah. Calling her husband "the innocent victim of the nation's wrath," Sarah Mudd challenged item after item of the evidence presented by the prosecution against him and went on to describe her own agony during the trial as she heard her husband falsely accused again and again. She pleaded with Holt, whom she deemed "all powerful in the case of my husband," to accept Mudd's innocence and release him. Should he do so, she promised, "I will teach my children to love and pray for you as long as they live."[24]

Sarah Mudd's plea fell on deaf ears. Holt felt no more merciful toward the good country doctor at the end of the summer of 1865 than he had all along. As Holt saw it, there were far more pressing and complicated matters to deal with at this juncture, especially how exactly to proceed with Jefferson Davis and Clement Clay, and whether to go after the rest of those named in the original charges against the assassination conspirators. Some of these Confederate leaders had already declared themselves innocent in the press and then, apparently like John Surratt, slipped across the northern U.S. border into Canada. Indeed, in response to Johnson's May 2 proclamation identifying them and others presumed by Holt to be involved in the assassination conspiracy, George Sanders and Beverly Tucker had written an open letter to Andrew Johnson from Montreal; it was published in the *New York Times* on May 7, even before the conspiracy trial got under way. "Your proclamation is a living, burning lie," wrote Sanders and Tucker with heat, "known to be such by yourself and all your surroundings."[25] How to handle such denials, how to deal most effectively with the men who issued them, what to do next about those high-ranking Confederate leaders already in custody, and how to go about the task of finding John Surratt and bringing him to justice were all questions that demanded clear answers before Holt would even consider a plea of mercy on behalf of one of Booth's convicted co-conspirators.

Had Holt been able to proceed unfettered along the path he believed in his heart lay before him, he almost certainly would have focused at this point on bringing Jefferson Davis, the former president of the Confederacy, to trial. Certainly Holt had received, and continued to get, plenty of encouragement from a number of correspondents to do just that. In a May 18 letter, friend J. M. McAlpine had urged Holt to set aside any concerns he might have about transforming Davis into a martyr by trying, convicting, and executing him, too. True patriots, wrote McAlpine, would never consider Davis a martyr, nor would they "care for the good feelings of individuals or Governments, who would tender the name of martyr, to one of the most damnable scoundrels, that this or any country has ever produced." As such, McAlpine expressed his fond hope that Holt would bring Davis to trial promptly. "The Government," he declared, "must get rid of all such men, before she will be entirely free from such bloody scenes as they have been enacting during the past four years." Other correspondents agreed: "There is general feeling in the West," wrote a concerned stranger to Holt the day of the four conspirators' execution, "that Robert E. Lee, (as well as Jeff Davis) should be *executed*." Holt's own Aunt Mary wrote to him from Kentucky on August 10: "I think if its found out that he had a hand in killing Lincon that [Davis] ought to be hung."[26]

As early as July 18, Secretary of the Navy Gideon Welles noted, the subject of pursuing a legal case against Davis had come up for discussion in a cabinet meeting, and the cabinet officers themselves were divided. Since Holt was not a cabinet member, he did not attend. However, his friend, ally, and boss at the War Department, Secretary of War Stanton, readily put forth views (on this question and on others) that were similar to Holt's. At the same time, Stanton routinely communicated relevant information from cabinet meetings back to Holt, with whom his bond would only grow closer over time. It is important to note that by July 18, Holt and Stanton shared not only a stubborn determination to punish Davis and the Southern leadership for the full complement of the Confederacy's many wartime crimes, but also a growing conviction that real meaning could be given to the Union victory only if the South could be reorganized permanently in such a way as to transfer a measure of social and political power from those who had defended the institution of slavery to those who had been its victims—namely, by enfranchising the freedmen.

According to Secretary Welles, a range of opinions about the Davis case was aired at that cabinet meeting. The moderate Secretary of State Seward—who had returned to duty just over a month after Powell assaulted him—said he saw no hurry, but that he believed the trial of Davis should ultimately take place before a military commission. On this occasion Stanton concurred with Seward, though one suspects that the secretary of war (like Holt) hoped to move more quickly against the "arch rebel" than Seward seemed to consider necessary. Welles himself maintained that a swift trial was best, but he supported a civil trial for treason over a military commission to determine the extent of Davis's involvement in the assassination scheme. Three days later the debate continued, by which point Welles had come to feel even more strongly that a civil trial, conducted within the jurisdiction of state of Virginia (since the Confederacy's headquarters had been in Richmond), was the only possible course. "I had no doubt he was guilty of treason and believed he would be convicted, wherever tried," Welles recalled. Although in late April Attorney General James Speed had endorsed Holt's recommendation for a military commission for the first eight assassination conspirators, this time he fell into line with Welles. In contrast, Secretary of the Interior James Harlan expressed his uncertainty that Davis could be convicted of treason—especially in Virginia! Harlan declared that it would be "much better to pardon Davis at once than to have him tried and not convicted," for such a result would be "most calamitous" for the nation, undermining any hope the federal government might have of being able to assert its dominance over the South in the nation's reconstruction. In the end, the cabinet failed to resolve the question, though the majority seemed to be leaning toward the Welles position. Meanwhile, perhaps reluctantly, Stanton brought to his colleagues' attention a letter from an officer at Fortress Monroe stating that "Davis' health had been failing for the last fortnight," "the execution of the assassins had visibly affected him," and Davis had expressed the opinion that, in the case of the convicted conspirators, "President Johnson was 'quick on the trigger.'"[27]

Joseph Holt would have liked nothing more than to be "quick on the trigger"—at least in a legal sense—with regard to the former president of the Confederacy and his high-level henchmen. But how to bring about swift justice in their cases? Somewhat ironically, one prod to quick action on the part of the War Department and Holt's Bureau of Military Justice came from the imprisoned Clement Clay, who by late summer was writing to Secretary Stanton complaining that the federal government was taking far too long to bring about a resolution in his case. "I can imagine no satisfactory reason why I am still denied a trial," Clement Clay wrote to Stanton on August 19. "Every day's delay . . . diminishes my chance of being fairly tried & is a denial of justice." Moreover, Clay informed Stanton, the conditions at Fortress Monroe were unbearable. "The nightly draining of half an ounce of my blood would inflict less torture," he wrote, than all the intrusions the prisoners were forced to endure, day and night, from their guards.[28]

No matter what the President's cabinet thought, as summer faded Holt still hoped to bring Davis before a military commission, over which he and his Bureau of Military Justice would have control, in order to prove that Davis had been involved directly in the assassination scheme. The "chiefs of the rebel confederacy," Holt continued to believe, as "the instigators and leaders of the rebellion, should be held responsible" for the crimes for which the eight conspirators had been convicted; the latter, after all, had functioned essentially as the local agents of the Confederate leadership and especially of Davis, who must now be called to account.[29]

However, the serious problems that had arisen during the conspiracy trial in connection with the testimony of Sanford Conover and others made it clear that new evidence would have to be gathered against the ex-president of the Confederacy if his complicity in the assassination scheme—and that of others like Clay—was to be proved conclusively. But how to gather this evidence? As Judge Advocate General Holt confronted the vexing problems of the present, one imagines his recalling nostalgically the cathartic execution of July 7. Doubtless Holt cursed the fact that the task of punishing Davis and the rest of the Confederate leadership seemed to have become more complicated with each passing day. Back on May 14, just as the conspiracy trial was getting under way, a correspondent had written to Edwin Stanton of the recently captured Davis: "surely he should be tried & executed as a traitor. . . . He can be convicted now easier than in [the] future."[30] By the end of the summer of 1865, the letter writer's words were proving most prophetic.

Moreover, to Holt's disgust the image of Jefferson Davis as a martyr did seem to be increasing, in some circles at least, as Davis's imprisonment at Fortress Monroe continued and reports of his failing health multiplied and became public. Davis was suffering from "erysipelas and a carbuncle," noted Secretary Welles in late August. Indeed, even Southerners who had been lukewarm to Davis during the war now began to see him as "a symbol for the lost Confederacy"; considering themselves innocent of any crime in having sought independence, they believed that Davis was innocent as well and saw his incarceration as a sign of an unforgiving and relentlessly oppressive federal government. At the same time, many Northerners who were growing anxious for a speedy and generous reconstruction of the Union began to see the pursuit of Davis's conviction—either as a traitor or a conspirator—in an increasingly negative light. In fact, the Executive Mansion began to be besieged with letters and petitions demanding Davis's release, leaving President Johnson (who in the early weeks of his presidency had "stated unequivocally that he wanted Davis punished") no longer sure of what to do. Jefferson Davis received mail of his own at Fortress Monroe, both supportive and not, including some from freedpeople "congratulating him on his captivity and their freedom." Davis was of course aware of the debate concerning his fate. According to one biographer, when he was informed of the charge that he had been involved in the conspiracy to assassinate Lincoln, Davis responded with derision. Andrew Johnson, he said, must know that such an accusation was unfounded. The two men had clashed often in Congress before the war, and Johnson, Davis insisted, must know "that I would a thousand times rather have Abraham Lincoln to deal with, as President of the United States, than to have *him*."[31]

In late August, in an effort to break the impasse in his quest for justice against Davis, Joseph Holt asked Francis Lieber, a prominent German-born scholar of the law and a professor at Columbia University, to examine the mass of Confederate government documents that federal troops had seized after the fall of Richmond. Under instructions to find all relevant material linking Davis and his associates to the assassination conspiracy, or any of the other nefarious plots against the United States that had been identified during the conspiracy trial, Lieber set about his task with grim determination. "I send you 5 sheets of note papers," he wrote to Holt on September 15, "containing writing by K. J. Stewart, a correspondent of Jeff. Davis, from Canada, showing the perfect connexion of Jefferson Davis with the [St. Albans] *raiders &c*—if, indeed, this connection were not already proved."[32] In the weeks ahead, Lieber continued to sort through the Confederate archives in search of similarly incriminating information.

Meanwhile, Holt attempted to speed justice further along by turning once again for assistance to the slippery Sanford Conover. Against all evidence to the contrary, the determined judge advocate general persuaded himself that this time Conover would deliver the goods on Davis, as he had consistently promised but failed to do in the past. At first glance, Holt's gullibility when it comes to Conover is somewhat startling, given his vast experience, his long and accomplished career, his impressive legal mind and his basic intelligence. One can begin to understand such credulousness, however, when one considers that Holt had been anxious for years about the possibility of Lincoln's being assassinated, and that he had struggled throughout the war to identify, isolate, and punish the enemies of the President and of the nation.

Now the nation appeared to have been saved, but Lincoln was dead. Was it possible that John Wilkes Booth and a few "hirelings of the basest and meanest description" (as one Maine newspaper described Booth's local accomplices) could conceivably have acted alone, thwarting all the efforts of Holt and the rest of Lincoln's loyal supporters in positions of power to keep him alive? What could possibly make up for the hideousness of such a crime, the culmination of four years of relentless Confederate treachery? "It is understandable," wrote Holt biographer Roger Bartman almost fifty years ago, "that the War Department and the [Bureau] of Military Justice should feel themselves cheated. Holt, in particular," Bartman added, "had staked his entire career of the Civil War on the assumption that the entire war was the work of some of the Southern leaders. . . . How could he believe that Booth manipulated this scheme alone," or even with a mere handful of local associates?[33] It simply was not possible, and Joseph Holt was determined to prove what he believed to be absolutely true: Davis was the mastermind of the plot. Now that eight of the local agents of the plot were dead or in prison, Holt was equally determined to bring Davis to justice and, through him, in some sense, the Confederacy itself.

Most unfortunately, Holt's determination became desperation, clouding his judgment and permitting him to adopt any tools available—including the highly problematic Conover—to accomplish his mission. In turn, Conover made superb use of Holt's desperation. Having thus far managed to evade capture by those who believed he should be thrown in prison himself, Conover wrote to Holt from a variety of locations over the course of the late summer and the fall of 1865, offering tantalizing bits of evidence that kept the judge advocate general hooked. Most important, Conover wrote of uncovering potential new witnesses, all of whom seemed eager to testify that Davis was involved in the assassination scheme. Conover pumped Holt constantly for financial resources to fund his investigative expedition and, supposedly, to loosen the tongues of his witnesses even more.[34]

Meanwhile, as Holt negotiated with Conover and pondered the future of his case against the Confederate leadership and its crimes against Lincoln and the Union, he found one small stretch of what must have seemed unmistakably firm ground upon which to tread—namely, the pursuit of justice against Henry Wirz, former commandant of the Confederacy's prison at Andersonville, where over the course of a single year some 13,000 Union soldiers had lost their lives.[35]

Born in Zürich, Switzerland, in 1823, Heinrich Hartmann Wirz, the son of "estimable parents," according to one contemporary source, came to the United States in 1849, leaving behind a checkered past that included at least one run-in with the law, a brief imprisonment, and a broken marriage. Eventually settling in the South, Wirz worked as a physician on a Louisiana plantation, although he had little or no formal medical training. In 1861, "Dr. Wirz" enlisted in Company A of the Fourth Louisiana Infantry Regiment. In the 1862 Battle of Seven Pines / Fair Oaks he took a bullet in his right arm, the wound so severe that the arm became permanently useless. Following Wirz's convalescence—during which he was promoted "for bravery" to the rank of captain—Brigadier General John H. Winder, who was in charge of Union prisoners of war, briefly placed Wirz in command of a military prison in Tuscaloosa, Alabama. In December 1862, Wirz, who spoke German, French, and English, was assigned to serve as a special envoy for Jefferson Davis in Europe (Wirz himself later claimed he was on furlough during this period). When he returned to America in February 1864, Wirz assumed command of the newly constructed Confederate prison at Andersonville, located in southwest Georgia. At the end of March Wirz moved to Andersonville with his second wife, an American whom he had married in 1854, and their children.[36]

The first prisoners had already begun to arrive at Andersonville shortly before Wirz took up his command of the site. Although Confederate prisoners of war also suffered from crowding, bad food and water, a lack of supplies and medicines, and other harsh conditions, reliable statistics indicate that their rates of survival were generally far higher than was the case for Union soldiers imprisoned in the South. According to Civil War historian James McPherson, "Confederate prisoners were 29 percent less likely to die in Yankee prisons than to die of disease in their own army, while Union prisoners were 68 percent more likely to die in Southern prisons than in their own army." And among Southern prisons Andersonville was indisputably one of the worst. Built to house about 15,000 prisoners, by August 1864 Andersonville held nearly 33,000. In addition to being subject to the extreme shortages of food, supplies, and medicines characteristic of all Southern prisons (and the South generally) by this time in the war, the prisoners at Andersonville were not permitted to build decent shelters for themselves. Furthermore, their primary water supply was a "sluggish stream" that also served as the prison's sewer system.[37]

It will be recalled that in the trial of Booth's local conspirators, Holt and his prosecution team had worked hard to place the assassination of Abraham Lincoln and the vicious attack on Secretary of State William Seward in the context of a series of heinous crimes plotted—and in many cases successfully committed—by agents and supporters of the Confederacy, and presumably initiated at Richmond. Among those crimes Holt had included in his portrayal of the Confederacy's treachery was the appalling treatment received by Union soldiers held in Confederate prisons, specifically Libby (in Richmond), Belle Isle (an island in the James River not far from Richmond), and Andersonville. On May 25, May 26, and June 10, 1865, Holt had summoned Union soldiers to testify for the prosecution regarding Confederate prison conditions. One former inmate who testified was William Ball, who spent almost a full year at Andersonville, most of it with nothing more to wear than "a pair of drawers and a shirt." According to Ball, the prisoners at Andersonville were, without exception, deprived of all their personal goods—clothing, blankets, money, shoes—and compelled to live without shelter under a blazing sun in what amounted to a swamp with a hill on either side. As for the food, said Ball, it was both inadequate and inedible. "Every morning, between nine and ten," he recalled, "they would bring a wagon with corn-meal ground up, cobs and all, full of stones and one thing and another, and give each man half a pint, and two ounces of [spoiled] bacon, and half a spoonful of salt, which was to last for twenty-four hours." Under these conditions, somewhere between 60 and 100 prisoners died of starvation or disease every day; on one particular day in the fall of 1864 that number rose to 133. Ball testified that other prisoners—sometimes 6 or 8 a day—were simply shot for crossing the "dead line," the internal perimeter of the prison beyond which guards watched and waited with their fingers on the trigger. "It was said they got thirty days' furlough for shooting a Yankee"—even a Yankee, Ball remembered bitterly, who merely poked his nose over the line by mistake. As for prisoners who fell ill, Ball stated that the standard "medicine" at the prison was nothing more than vile, useless pills made out of pine pitch and vinegar. Those who died every day of disease or malnutrition were piled on wagons with pitchforks, hauled away, and dumped into trenches.[38]

Charles Sweenay, who spent about six months at Andersonville and whose brother died there, concurred with William Ball's testimony. Sweenay testified that he had twice tried to escape from the prison, but was captured both times and punished severely. On one occasion Sweenay was left gagged and out in the cold for six hours straight; on the other, he was put in stocks for an entire day in the open sun, which made him terribly sick for several days afterward. Recalling his experience at Andersonville, Sweenay commented, "It is only God who has let me live this long." According to former prisoner Lieutenant J. L. Ripple, the Andersonville guards were known to use bloodhounds to chase down escapees such as Sweenay, and although Ripple himself had never witnessed such a pursuit, "I have heard some of the men who went after them say that there were persons who had been torn [apart] by the dogs." Significant for the case Holt was trying to build, linking such crimes as the treatment of Union prisoners at Andersonville with the assassination of Lincoln,

was Ripple's assertion under oath that he had twice heard rebel officers at the prison saying that if Lincoln was reelected in November
1864, he would be killed before his inauguration, as would Seward.[39]

Witnesses who testified at the assassination conspiracy trial concerning their experiences at Andersonville did not hesitate to blame
Commandant Henry Wirz for making the prison even more brutal.
According to William Ball, on one occasion, "the men inside got up
a committee," which then requested redress from Wirz, particularly
in relation to the water situation. Noted Ball, Wirz simply replied
that "he did not care a damn whether the water got through or not,
or whether we got any or not." On another occasion, when the federal government dispatched to Andersonville some material supplies
for the desperate inmates, Wirz "took it himself, and put it into his
own house and sold it,—blankets, pants, socks, and other things."
Sweenay told a grisly story about Wirz's incitement of the already
trigger-happy guards stationed at the prison. "Old Captain Wurtz
there," he said,

> had told the guard that they must shoot every Yankee whom
> they could catch with his hand or his head over the dead-line;
> and every one who did so would get a furlough of forty days to
> go home. So they used to kill our men the same as though they
> were brutes. I saw a cripple, a one-legged man, get shot there.
> We were digging tunnels, and doing one thing and another to try
> to make our escape. There was a one-legged man who told the
> captain about that. Some of the boys got down on him, and
> abused him; and he ran inside of the dead-line next the gate, so
> as to get protection from the guard; and Captain Wurtz stood on
> the post, and told the guard, if they did not shoot that man, he
> would shoot the guard. So the guard had to shoot the man.

As for complaints brought to Wirz by the prisoners, Ripple recalled
that the commandant responded only, "It is good enough for you:
you should all die!"[40]

As it turns out, by the time William Ball and others rose to give
their testimony, Captain Henry Wirz was already in prison in Wash-

ington, having been captured at Andersonville in early May, just around the time Davis and Clay were captured. On May 7, Wirz wrote to Brevet Major General James H. Wilson, commanding the Union forces at Macon, seeking mercy. "Like hundreds and thousands of others," Wirz claimed, "I was carried away by the maelstrom of excitement and joined the Southern Army," for which his only apparent reward was to receive a permanently debilitating wound. As for his job as commandant at Andersonville, Wirz insisted that he had found his duties "arduous and unpleasant," and that he had only been following orders. "I am satisfied," he wrote, "that no man can or will justly blame me for things that happened here and which were beyond my power to control. I do not think that I ought to be held responsible," though he realized that former prisoners might now feel a need to "wreak their vengeance upon me for what they have suffered." Still, Wirz urged Wilson to recognize him as a "tool in the hands of my superiors" and to offer him assistance, at least in the form of safe-conduct or some sort of "guard to protect myself and family against violence." Promised Wirz, "My intention is to return with my family to Europe as soon as I can make the arrangements." As such, he implied, he would be out of the federal government's hair for good.[41]

If in fact Henry Wirz actually believed his letter would evoke Wilson's sympathy—all good soldiers follow the orders of their military superiors, after all—he was mistaken. Nor did his promise to depart the country meet with approval, for in the eyes of Holt and countless others, to let him go meant to abandon any hope of punishing him for his involvement in the deaths of 13,000 of the Union army prisoners who had been under his "care." Moreover, one could argue (and Joseph Holt certainly would have done so) that too many other Confederate criminals were already using a similar strategy, escaping to Canada to dodge justice. It seems quite safe to assume that Wirz's Swiss origins further disadvantaged him, for two opposing reasons. On the one hand, the notion of a foreign national treating American soldiers so badly can only have increased the animosity toward Wirz that was felt in many circles. On the other hand, one suspects that Wirz's foreign roots may well have made him seem, at least to some and perhaps even to Kentuckian Joseph Holt, more readily expendable than a "true" American.

Despite Wirz's May 7 plea for mercy, on May 16 General Wilson notified the adjutant general at Washington that the former commandant of Andersonville had been placed under arrest and sent under guard to General George H. Thomas, commanding the Department of the Cumberland, at Nashville. At the same time Wilson sent to Washington "all the records, &c., of the prison that could be found, and also other papers relating to his cruel treatment of our men," adding a personal request "that this miscreant be brought before a general court-martial in Washington, D.C., where the evidence in his case can be more readily obtained." General Wilson duly forwarded Wirz's request for mercy to General Thomas, who then forwarded it to Washington. "The writer of this," General Thomas scribbled on the outside of Wirz's letter, "will be sent under guard, in charge of Captain Noyes . . . this day to Washington for final disposition."[42]

Wirz awaited the "final disposition" of his case in a cell in the Old Capitol Prison, where some of the assassination conspirators had been confined for a time. Meanwhile, Joseph Holt and the Bureau of Military Justice continued to gather information about life at Andersonville and to identify potential prosecution witnesses for Wirz's trial. Almost seven weeks after the execution of Herold and the others, on August 23, 1865, Wirz's trial began before an eight-man military commission under Joseph Holt's authority.

In language reminiscent of the charges against the eight Lincoln conspirators, General Court Martial Orders No. 607 charged Wirz with "maliciously, willfully, and traitorously . . . combining, confederating, and conspiring, together with John H. Winder . . . and others unknown, to injure the health and destroy the lives of soldiers in the military service of the United States, then held and being prisoners of war within the lines of the so-called Confederates States . . . to the end that the armies of the United States might be weakened and impaired, in violation of the laws and customs of war." The orders further charged Wirz with "murder, in violation of the laws and customs of war" and the specifications went on to describe the ghastly conditions that had prevailed at Andersonville and to offer details of more than a dozen cases in which Wirz personally attacked and killed individual Union soldiers who were incarcerated there. These court-martial orders named General Lew Wallace, who had served on the commission that convicted the Lincoln assassination conspirators, to preside over Wirz's trial. "I sincerely hope," wrote former Anderson-ville inmate H. T. Drinkhouser to Joseph Holt five days after the trial began, "that Wirtz and his coadjutors will receive their just deserts, so that the world may see that our civilization will not tamely brook the perpetration of such atrocious barbarities."[43]

Wirz pleaded not guilty to the charges and specifications against him. His legal team offered numerous objections to his being tried in the first place, among other things arguing—as the assassination con-spirators' lawyers had also done—that a military commission had no jurisdiction in his case. As in the previous case, however, and equally predictably, the commissioners overruled any such pleas and quickly began to hear testimony. The trial lasted almost two months and included testimony from almost 150 witnesses as well as a large amount of documentary evidence both from Andersonville itself and from the Confederate files at Richmond. In the end, the eight com-missioner-judges assigned to the case found Wirz guilty of both charges and most of the specifications.[44] Tellingly, they also amended the language of the original charges to include the names of Jefferson Davis and other members of his cabinet as co-conspirators with Wirz, bringing the official charges even more into line with those against Mary Surratt and the others in the assassination conspiracy trial.

In a synopsis of the Wirz trial and its findings that he sent to Pres-ident Andrew Johnson on October 31, Joseph Holt praised the com-mission's findings and added his own personal indictment of the defendant. As might be expected, in his summary remarks Holt depicted Wirz's crimes as just one hideous aspect of a vast complex of related crimes perpetrated over the past four years by the Confed-erate leadership. "Language fails," Holt wrote with eloquent and familiar fury,

> in an attempt to denounce . . . the diabolical combination for the destruction and death, by cruel and fiendishly ingenious

"Court-room in which Captain Wirz,
the Andersonville Jailer, is being tried,"
from Harper's Weekly, *September 16, 1865*

processes, of helpless prisoners of war who might fall into their hands, which this record shows was plotted and deliberately entered upon, and, as far as time permitted, accomplished by the rebel authorities and their brutal underlings at Andersonville Prison. Criminal history presents no parallel to this monstrous conspiracy.

Four days later Holt followed up with a letter to Secretary of War Stanton urging that a number of other Confederate officers whose

names had come up during the Wirz trial in connection with the cru-
elties inflicted on Union soldiers at Andersonville also be tried before
military commissions.[45]

The commissioner-judges in the Wirz case convicted the defendant
summarily. On November 3, President Andrew Johnson approved the
Wirz commission's proceedings, findings, and sentence, and ordered
that Wirz be executed on November 10, sometime between 6:00 A.M.
and noon. In the intervening days, Andrew Johnson received a number of letters and other requests for Wirz's reprieve, and for the commutation of his sentence to life in prison. Indeed, Wirz's lawyer, Louis
Schade, had begun to plead with Johnson as early as October 26,
when he wrote to remind the President that "one of the principal pre-
rogatives of your high position is that of mercy and pardon." Others
followed suit in the days after Wirz's doom became public. "Mercy
will become you before the people," wrote Estwick Evans, a self-
proclaimed "Northern man and a Union man," on November 8; "it
will be acceptable to God." Evans wrote again on November 9, asking Johnson to bear in mind "that war is not civil life. It is rough and
cruel, and thousands even of our own soldiery have not been too merciful." That same day, John Hitz, consul-general of Switzerland (a
nation "proverbial," Hitz insisted, "for magnanimity toward enemies"), urged Johnson to demonstrate mercy on the principle that,
although "in the annals of civil war there is . . . no greater conception
of atrocity than the prison pen at Andersonville," yet Wirz was
merely "the detestable tool of monsters in human form. Shall the
hand suffer for the arm that wielded it, for the soul and mind that
controlled its ultimatum of crime?" Hitz pleaded with Johnson, in the
spirit of Christianity, to commute Wirz's sentence to solitary confinement for life. "The harrowing thoughts which must then constantly
be his companions," Hitz urged, "will inflict a greater and far more
impressive penalty for any crimes he may be guilty of against fellow-
man than death in his present condition."[46]

Meanwhile Schade made repeated requests for an interview with
the President on behalf of his client, all of which were turned down.
Johnson—like Holt—was immovable, as both had been in the case of
the Booth co-conspirators in July. On November 10, Henry Wirz was

"Execution of Wirz—Adjusting the Rope" and
"Execution of Wirz—Lowering the Body,"
both from Harper's Weekly, *November 25, 1865*

hanged on the grounds of the Old Capitol Prison. Once his death was confirmed, Wirz's body was taken to the Old Arsenal Penitentiary grounds where, as General Christopher Augur reported the following day, it was buried alongside the bodies of the executed assassination conspirators, right next to that of Wirz's fellow-immigrant, George Atzerodt.[47]

I am glad Lincoln was killed. We were at least saved the humiliation of being under his rule. He would have completed the ruin the war had so fearfully begun. The Southern people would have had their chains riveted with iron. Andy Johnson is more inclined to be just.

—ELLEN RENSHAW OF TENNESSEE
in her diary, November 1865[1]

Rosina [Holt's sister-in-law] said she wished it had have been old Andrew Johnson . . . that had been killed instead of Lincon for Johnson was nothing but an old Drunken tyran I told her it was time for her to shut up for I had often heard her call Lincon a drunken tyran & now said I Lincon is killed you can begin to see a little virtue in him but none while alive so I soon closed her up.

—AUNT MARY STEPHENS TO JOSEPH HOLT,
August 1865[2]

The trouble with [Andrew Johnson's] course was that it amounted to throwing away a splendid opportunity to initiate a promising racial policy.

—HANS L. TREFOUSSE,
Andrew Johnson (1989)[3]

6

"Forbearance and Forgiveness"

Andrew Johnson's Vision

for Southern Restoration

On November 13, 1865, three days after the execution of Anderson-ville Prison Commandant Henry Wirz, Joseph Holt summarized the work performed by the Bureau of Military Justice over the last seven and a half months for Secretary of War Stanton. In his report, Holt provided some statistics: the Bureau had "received, reviewed, and filed" some 16,591 records of courts-martial and military commissions; it had also prepared 6,123 special reports "upon the numerous miscellaneous subjects and questions referred for the opinion of this office." In other words, Holt explained to Stanton, despite the war's end, the amount of business transacted by the Bureau had actually increased since March, and he predicted that the agency's workload would almost certainly not decrease for some time yet. In the report, Holt also praised his bureau staff—from officers to clerks—for their "ability and efficiency," and he urged that Congress extend the life of the bureau, which had been created by Lincoln during the war primarily for wartime service, for at least another year.[4]

Holt also drew the secretary's attention to what he considered by far the most significant business the Bureau of Military Justice had conducted since March: overseeing the two military commissions by which the federal government had brought Commandant Wirz and eight of John Wilkes Booth's co-conspirators to justice. Holt reviewed for Stanton and the War Department's records the makeup and duration of each of the two commissions, the number of witnesses examined, and each trial's outcome. He went on to point out what he called a "peculiar characteristic" the two commissions shared—namely, that in both cases the evidence presented by the federal government had proved unequivocally not only the guilt of those who stood trial in the courtroom, but also—in absentia—the complicity of the "chiefs of the rebellion" in the crimes of the accused. Each of these two military commissions, wrote Holt, had demonstrated that the convicted were in fact "the hirelings and accomplices of the cabal of traitors of whom [Jefferson] Davis was the acknowledged chief." Moreover, in each case Davis and his "cabal" were revealed to be "in fact, as well as in law, equally with the accused, responsible for the detestable deeds which were adduced in evidence."[5]

Having stressed to Stanton the particular significance of these two commissions within the broad scope of the Bureau of Military Justice's charge and responsibility, Holt concluded his report with a discussion of the merits of military commissions generally during the war for "bringing to justice . . . a large class of malefactors in the service or interest of the rebellion, who otherwise would have altogether escaped punishment." Military commissions, Holt explained, were "unincumbered by the technicalities and inevitable embarrassments attending to the administration of justice before civil tribunals." As such, a military commission could make use of the government itself "for the execution of its processes and the enforcement of its orders," and it could investigate crimes with a freer hand than was the case in civil trials; this latitude allowed it to uncover such things as "the element of conspiracy" so noteworthy in the trials of Wirz and the Lincoln assassins. Furthermore, no other form of trial could produce results so efficiently, declared Holt, tacitly brushing aside any possible complaints about the potential for civil rights violations, as Stanton, and probably also Lincoln himself, would have done. In sum, as an "arm of the military administration" for the successful prosecution of the nation's enemies, Holt insisted, the military commission had proved itself invaluable, in its own way contributing powerfully to the Union's victory.[6]

In the fall of 1865, Holt clearly had great confidence in the work his bureau had performed, particularly over the past several months, on behalf of the government and the nation. As Holt saw it, by means of military commissions and courts-martial, the Bureau had tried thousands of enemies of the United States, investigating and punishing their individual crimes and also exposing, where appropriate, their connections to Jefferson Davis and others in the Confederate leadership. Holt's report rang with pride.

But there were other tones in the report as well, undertones of anxiety that the Bureau's ongoing work might be obstructed, or worse, brought to a close prematurely. Should such a thing happen, Holt worried that he and his staff would be prevented from fulfilling in any true and final way the preliminary successes they could already claim. Only three days after the hanging of Henry Wirz, and just over four months after the execution of Herold, Powell, Atzerodt, and Mary Surratt, Holt displayed deep concern over his ability to achieve his goal of ensuring the appropriate punishment of the arch-criminal of the Confederacy himself, Jefferson Davis, along with as many of his high-level accomplices as possible.

Had he been able to do so at this point, Joseph Holt undoubtedly would have been content to devote all his time to sorting out the details of his case against Davis, and piling up evidence against the former Confederate president in preparation for a trial. By mid-November, it should be recalled, Davis and Clement Clay had already been in jail for approximately six months without any formal charges being brought against them. Shortly after their capture, Davis had in fact been indicted for treason by a federal grand jury in Norfolk, Virginia. But according to his biographer William Cooper, the indictment was "literally lost and never became part of the record."[7] Now a clear and even relatively prompt resolution of their cases seemed even less likely than it had in May.

Nevertheless, throughout the late summer and fall, with blind optimism and determination, Holt had remained in regular contact with the duplicitous Sanford Conover. "Believing that I can procure witnesses and documentary evidence sufficient to convict Jeff. Davis and C. C. Clay of complicity in the assassination of the President, and that

I can also find & secure John H. Surratt," Conover had written to Holt from New York less than three weeks after the execution of the local conspirators, "I beg leave to tender the Government, through you, my services for these purposes." Holt had complied with Conover's request, and by November 1, Conover was back in Washington with some results. That day, he sent a note from the National Hotel, the same hotel at which Booth had been a guest at the time of the assassination, informing Holt that he was finally ready to "produce the witnesses for examination." Over the next few days, Holt's time and attention were partly occupied with taking depositions from some of the "witnesses" Conover introduced, including William Campbell and Joseph Snevel. Another witness, John McGill, had been deposed back in August. Others were to follow.[8]

Could Holt have given all of his attention to the Davis case, he gladly would have done so. But too many other balls were also up in the air in November 1865, some of which were not only distracting and time-consuming, but also distressing. Certainly the extremely high-profile trial of Henry Wirz just finished had consumed a significant amount of Holt's energy and focus. Also true was the fact that Holt had spent the past several weeks confronting anticipated as well as unanticipated consequences of the trial at the Old Arsenal Penitentiary in May and June. And then there were the written requests and personal visits from Sarah Mudd seeking the release from Fort Jefferson of her imprisoned husband, Samuel, and inquiries from the families of the executed conspirators regarding the final dispensation of their loved ones' corpses.[9]

Beginning in mid-October, too, none other than star prosecution witness Louis Weichmann had begun to nag Holt (and Stanton) to help find him a paid position within the federal bureaucracy, either in Philadelphia, where he had relocated in order to be with his family and to escape the hostility he faced from Mary Surratt's supporters in Washington, or in Boston. Needless to say, Weichmann considered such a post fair reward for the service he had provided to Holt and the federal government during the conspiracy trial. Surely Holt's relief was almost as great as Weichmann's when in mid-December he was able to garner a position for his former witness as a clerk at the Philadelphia Customs House.[10]

And there was more. Holt's focus on the goal of bringing Davis, his cohorts, and ultimately the Confederacy itself to justice was compromised even further by a number of more personal developments, including the September 12 death of his beloved Aunt Mary, perhaps the only member of Holt's large Kentucky family who had steadily stood by his choice for the Union during the war. The family requested that Holt assume full responsibility for the execution of her will. Meanwhile, his staunchly pro-Confederate brother Robert had taken up the habit of lobbying Holt on a regular basis for aid in gaining a pardon from the federal government.[11]

Into this mix one must also add the grave and long-term impact on Holt's ability to pursue his agenda of a new and painful political controversy in which he found himself immersed in the late summer and early fall of 1865. In late August, fellow Kentuckian Montgomery Blair, who had been Abraham Lincoln's postmaster general until 1864 (when he was replaced by William Dennison) gave an alarming speech in Clarksville, Maryland. During the critical weeks before Lincoln's inauguration and the start of the war, Blair claimed, Seward, already a close adviser to the incoming President, then Attorney General Stanton, and then Secretary of War Holt had worked together purposefully not to save the Union but rather to undermine President James Buchanan's ability to respond effectively to the fledgling Confederacy's threats against the nation's life. Speaking at length, Montgomery Blair accused Joseph Holt in particular of essentially having abandoned Fort Sumter to South Carolina. Blair even went so far as to suggest that as Buchanan's secretary of war, Holt had in fact engaged in a secret agreement with an agent of the rebel government to let Sumter go in order to instigate the war. According to Blair, four years of bloody, costly war had really begun as a result of Holt's treacherous dealings with the Southern agents, and because of the ways in which Holt, Seward, and Stanton had obstructed Buchanan's attempts to pacify the secessionists.[12]

A few days after Blair's incendiary speech, Secretary of the Navy

Gideon Welles recorded his reaction in his diary. Welles was a good friend of the Blair family. At the same time, he was not particularly fond of Seward, and he liked Stanton even less (indeed, Welles seemed to dislike Stanton more and more with each passing day). Nevertheless, even Welles was surprised by the content, tone, and implications of Blair's remarks, and he expressed particular concern about the effects of such an unworthy and untimely attack on Holt, whom he considered a "stern, stubborn, relentless man," but nevertheless a "true patriot and a statesman of more than ordinary ability"—probably the best of Buchanan's cabinet members and outstanding among his peers for having sought to "sustain the national integrity" during early 1861. In Welles's mind Blair's attack was most unjust. Moreover, he rightly noted that the attack came at the worst possible time, just when the national focus should have been on finishing the business of the bitter war so recently ended and healing the wounds it had inflicted. Such a speech was more salt than balm. Welles struggled to interpret Blair's attacks with an attitude of "forbearance," but he did not find it easy, especially because he normally considered Blair an individual of "great political sagacity, tact, and ability."[13]

If Gideon Welles took Blair's speech badly, Holt's response was one of utter outrage. In mid-September the judge advocate general delivered a lengthy and detailed rebuttal to the New York Times in which he declared himself shocked "that a statesman supposed to be well instructed in public affairs, and in the history of his country, and who, from the high position he has occupied, must be expected to have an honorable solicitude for the protection of the fair fame of the public men laboriously engaged in administering the government, should, without provocation, have brought against them an accusation so dishonoring, and so utterly groundless." Holt went on to deny with passion all of Blair's accusations: the notion that he had entered into a secret agreement with representatives of the Confederacy; that he had actively resisted reinforcing Fort Sumter ("No man," wrote Holt, "rejoiced more than I did when the Star of the West was ordered with munitions and provisions to Sumter"); that he had somehow—individually or in concert with Seward and Stanton—tied Buchanan's hands, or those of the commander at Fort Sumter; that prior to the war's outbreak he had resisted congressional efforts to enable Union men in the South to organize into military units for defensive purposes; that he had been lukewarm himself in opposition to secession.[14]

Point by point, with eloquence and vigor, Holt challenged Blair's accusations. He also presented testimonials from various officials, including General Winfield Scott, with whom he had worked so closely as secretary of war during the months under consideration. "It gives me great pleasure," wrote General Scott in Holt's defense, "to say that during the last two or three months of Mr. Buchanan's Administration . . . I found you a steady and efficient opponent of secessionism, and prompt . . . in doing everything in your power to preserve and vindicate our happy Union." In his extended response to Blair—which he soon after published as a pamphlet and circulated widely among friends and supporters for further distribution—the proud but deeply wounded judge advocate general offered the public at large the opportunity to weigh the case for themselves.[15]

Montgomery Blair gave his damaging and ungenerous speech on August 26; Holt's angry self-defense appeared in the New York Times on September 16. But the aftershocks of the clash continued for many weeks to come, as Holt's supporters rallied faithfully behind him. "I have just been reading your extinguisher of M Blair," wrote Frank Ballard from New York the day before Holt's response appeared in the Times. "You have him on the hip, and I should think he would have to limp through the rest of his useless life." That same day W. G. Snethen, who had heard Blair's "miserable harangue" in person, wrote from Baltimore: "You ask what effect Blair's speech has had on public sentiment in our State? It has only served to make honest people more disgusted with him than ever."[16]

Although Joseph Holt was considered by many to be a profoundly modest and reserved man, by the time Montgomery Blair attacked him, the judge advocate general was prepared to defend his honor before the public. At the same time, for Holt, the vindication of his own name and, by association, the names of those with whom he had linked arms to save the nation back in the months before the fall of Fort Sumter, was essential work, too. Even more important, he believed it was work that bore deeply not only on the past, and not only on him personally, but on the nation's future, even its survival. For as he saw it, the Blairs of the world must not be ignored even for a moment, nor should they be allowed to claim even the smallest victory. To surrender to their "calumnies" was, in essence, to give up the game, and Holt was still a long way from being ready to do that.[17]

It may seem curious at first to link Joseph Holt's determination to preserve the patriotic luster associated with his own name (or Stanton's, or Seward's) on the one hand, with the future of the Union on the other, especially given that the war on the battlefield had already been won. Yet it is essential to note that Holt himself saw the connection clearly, as did many of those who pondered Blair's motives for attacking him in the first place. Seeking to understand Blair's purpose, Holt's friend D. H. Hoopes offered two possible explanations. He suggested that perhaps Blair was using mind-altering drugs when he gave the speech: "I am reminded of those Asiatics," wrote Hoopes in the language and from the uncharitable perspective of his times, "who, under the influence of opium, are said to run *amuck*. Blair, it seems to me, has been doing something of the same kind, and possibly, under the same influence." Alternatively, Hoopes suggested, Blair had hoped to "induce the country to believe that when secession was rampant, *he alone* of all our public men, stood firm," presumably with the goal of furthering his own political career. Even Gideon Welles suggested that Blair's attack on Holt had a lot to do with Blair's desire to highlight and perhaps even to exacerbate the political divisions between Stanton's allies and his own.[18]

Holt's loyal colleague Henry Burnett also made the connection between Blair's speech and Holt's role in guaranteeing the future of the Union. It will be recalled that Holt and Burnett had investigated secret antigovernment organizations in the West in 1864 together, and subsequently prosecuted the Clement Vallandigham case. Burnett had also served as one of the assistant judges advocate in the Lincoln assassination case. Holt's friends and Stanton's, Burnett wrote Holt on September 5, "feel outraged at the unwarranted malignant and cowardly attack of Montgomery Blair. . . . We feel all the more indignant and apprehensive from the fact that it has been generally understood and believed that . . . [Blair] was on specially confidential relations with the President and that the President was greatly under his influence. There is a trembling fear abroad in the land—with the loyal—lest Mr Johnson should be bound over to the consortium."[19]

What did Burnett mean? What possible connection did Andrew Johnson have with the controversy brewing between Holt and the Blair family? What did Johnson have to do with a dispute over whether Holt (or Stanton, or Seward) had stood sufficiently firm for the Union during the winter of 1860–61? And why might Holt and his supporters be concerned about such things, when instead they could have been celebrating the conclusions of the trials of Wirz and the assassination conspirators, and looking forward to extending their list of achievements with the successful prosecution of the "chief rebels"? The answers to such questions are simultaneously complex and simple. They are also closely interrelated, deriving as they do from the overarching conflict that had been developing in Washington since that fateful night when Lincoln was murdered, Seward was viciously attacked, and George Atzerodt, the man assigned to assassinate Johnson, lost his nerve and stayed his hand. Destined to become as vicious in many ways as the war that preceded it, this conflict pitted against one another distinct visions of how to "reconstruct" the former Confederacy, embedded in which were equally distinct visions of the future of the nation as a whole, and more specifically, of the rights therein of millions of former slaves.

Andrew Johnson, writes his biographer Hans Trefousse, "inherited problems of staggering proportions when he became President of the United States." Not the least of Johnson's problems revolved around the aftermath of the Civil War, especially the future of the emancipated slaves, which remained most uncertain.[20] As is now well-known, during his presidency Johnson became bitter enemies with the Radical Republicans in Congress and their allies outside it. For over time, Johnson entrenched himself in opposition to any and all whose vision of Reconstruction was predicated upon the vigorous punishment of the South's social and political leadership along with the entire region's submission to a national future that included, among other crucial details, the extension of civil rights to the freedpeople. Most troubling to the Democratic Johnson was the view that freedmen should have the right to vote (particularly the right to vote as Republicans). Johnson failed entirely to sympathize with the Radicals' idea that the provision of voting rights to black men, at least, would ensure that ultimately black Americans could begin to protect themselves against the worst ravages of race discrimination and could begin to seek true social equality by means of their legal participation in the democratic process.[21]

In the earliest days of his presidency, however, Johnson played his cards extremely close to his chest while simultaneously signaling his support to all sides of the debate. For example, in the cabinet meeting following his April 15 swearing-in at the Kirkwood House, Johnson vaguely stated that his own policy toward the vanquished South would be "in all its essentials . . . the same as that of the late president."[22]

To those who put their hope for the nation's future in the forgiving words of Abraham Lincoln's second inaugural speech, such promises offered encouragement. Lincoln, after all, had urged the soon-to-be-victorious North to approach the end of the war "with malice toward none; with charity for all." He had spoken of "bind[ing] up the nation's wounds," not retribution. Indeed, as early as December 1863, Lincoln had issued a Proclamation of Amnesty and Reconstruction in which he had offered to pardon and restore the property (except slave property) of those rebels who swore an oath of allegiance to the United States and who further swore to uphold its laws regarding slavery (Lincoln exempted some individuals and categories from his offer, including civil and diplomatic officials of the Confederate government and high officers of the Confederate army and navy). In this proclamation, Lincoln had also promised, by means of executive edict rather than legislative action, to restore to equal status within the Union any Confederate state wherein 10 percent of the state's (white) voters took the oath of allegiance and that established a new state government simply affirming the emancipation of the slaves but offering no provision for black suffrage. Those in both the North and the South who yearned for the Confederate states' swift and essentially painless restoration to equal status within the federal Union put great faith in this 1863 Proclamation and in Lincoln's

President Andrew Johnson.
*Courtesy of the
Library of Congress*

words at the second inaugural, and they hoped Johnson's promise to carry out the federal government's business "without interruption" meant that he saw things their way.[23]

Even as he comforted those who yearned for a smooth and generous reconciliation of the sections, however, Andrew Johnson also initially gave the Radical Republicans good reason to believe that he could be counted on as a faithful ally in the work of harshly chastising the political and social leaders of the Confederacy for their heinous crimes (including the murder of Lincoln). Similarly, he made comments that seemed to suggest that he supported their plan for restructuring the former Confederate South in such a manner as to disempower the planter class and simultaneously ensure the uplift of the former slaves. To Holt, Stanton, and others who specifically perceived the trials of Booth's co-conspirators and of Henry Wirz as essential components in this larger postwar mission of avenging the South's misdeeds and setting the whole region on the proper path to contrition, redemption, and restoration within the Union, Andrew Johnson offered clear indications that he was on board. On April 14, just hours before the assassination, Johnson had even made a special trip to the Executive Mansion to speak with Lincoln and to urge him "not to be too lenient with traitors." Then, on Sunday, April 16, the day after his own swearing-in, Johnson made it clear to his entire cabinet, including Stanton, that he did not intend to be merciful toward traitors, and that he planned to punish "the chief Rebels" with "exemplary severity."[24]

Just over two weeks later, on May 1, Johnson issued an executive order declaring that the assassination conspiracy suspects would be tried by a military commission. The following day he issued the proclamation that offered rewards for the capture of Jefferson Davis, five members of his "Canadian Cabinet," and John Surratt Jr. in connection with the assassination. On July 5, it was Johnson who signed the order approving the execution of four of the convicted conspirators and the imprisonment of four others. In the next forty-eight hours, he consistently rejected all pleas for clemency, even in the case of the first woman ever to be hanged by the federal government. On August 23 Johnson ordered the formation of a military commission to try Henry Wirz, and two months later he approved the conviction of the Andersonville commandant and ordered that he, too, be hanged until dead. Setting aside Johnson's more conciliatory remarks to supporters of a kinder and more forgiving attitude toward the postwar white South, actions such as these tempt one to assume—as many did—that in the early months of his administration the new president was of precisely the same mind-set as men like Holt and Stanton, at least with respect to the punishment due to traitors and anti-Union conspirators of pro-Southern sympathies. One might be tempted further to extrapolate a belief that Johnson would enthusiastically underwrite whatever plan for the postwar South the Radical Republicans intended to propose, even if the goal of that plan was to force the former Confederacy to elevate the social status of black people.[25]

After Lincoln's assassination, optimistic Radical Republicans such as Ohio Senator Benjamin F. Wade had already begun to express their enthusiastic support of Andrew Johnson.[26] Just one year earlier, Benjamin Wade and Senator Henry Winter Davis of Maryland had coauthored the Wade-Davis Act, proposing a much harsher stance toward the South than Lincoln's December 1863 proclamation had done (Lincoln pocket-vetoed the Wade-Davis Act in July 1864). Already at that time congressional Radicals such as Wade, Davis, and Massachusetts Senator Charles Sumner believed that Lincoln's proposed generosity toward the South was misguided. With vivid prescience, such men took the stance that offering the former Confederacy too much forgiveness too soon represented a dangerous prescription for the nation's future, for it would lead only to impudence and arrogance. Once vanquished militarily, the South would then rise again and shamelessly remount its challenge to the federal government's supremacy in other ways. In short, these men associated Lincoln's gentle plan for Reconstruction with the resurgence of a revitalized and unrepentant South. To avoid such dire consequences, like Holt they insisted instead that the federal government chastise severely those who, as they saw it, had caused the war in the first place, those on whose shoulders the burden of years of fratricidal bloodshed must rest.

As early as 1864, then, Radical Republicans determined to treat a defeated Southern Confederacy as a conquered enemy, to control the peace, and to define the nation's future course, not least of all with respect to the prospects facing the 4 million slaves for whom Union victory would mean permanent emancipation. Simply put, in the eyes of the Radical Republicans—among whose most committed supporters Holt and Stanton, despite their shared roots in the Democratic Party, came to number themselves—the leaders and the supporters of the former Confederacy must be forced to submit to whatever terms the victorious federal government saw fit to impose. Such men, studying Johnson's actions so far, hoped that he was on their side. They were wrong. Notes Johnson biographer Trefousse, "While Johnson's emphasis on stern retribution for individual rebels probably represented his firm conviction at this time, it also continued to be a convenient way of avoiding any definite commitment to a specific policy or Reconstruction."[27]

While he pondered the direction his administration's policy would take at the very beginning of his presidency, however, Johnson spoke of both forgiveness and vengeance. He thus offered something to everyone. In those early days, Johnson's true intentions remained veiled, and his future policies toward the South and Reconstruction were left unclear. In the weeks ahead, however, as Johnson's vision for the vanquished Confederacy and his policies for Reconstruction took shape, the comforting reassurance his earlier ambiguity had provided to all sides of the debate slowly gave way to bitter divisions and ideological battles, both within the federal government and beyond it. Indeed, even as he was taking steps to further the work of Holt's Bureau of Military Justice in the pursuit of justice against Henry Wirz and Booth's local co-conspirators, Johnson—a native of North Carolina who had spent virtually all of his prewar life in Tennessee and who had also been a slave owner—was already working at cross-purposes to the very goal Holt and the Radicals aimed to achieve.[28]

As early as May 29, only three days after Edmund Kirby Smith had surrendered the last of the Confederacy's forces to Brigadier General Edward R. S. Canby, Johnson took advantage of the fact that Congress was out of session to issue two executive proclamations, the first of which sounded a good deal like Lincoln's generous December 1863 Proclamation of Amnesty and Reconstruction. Like Lincoln, Johnson offered amnesty from prosecution and the restitution of property (with the exception of slaves) to a wide range of former Confederates, exempting Confederate civil and diplomatic officials, high-ranking officers, and other such types. Notably, in this proclamation Johnson also exempted "those who had mistreated prisoners of war or were under arrest for other military crimes" (the imprisoned conspirators at Fort Jefferson, Wirz, Davis, and Clay) and "all persons owning taxable property with an estimated value of more than $20,000," a category that comprised essentially the entire planter class, which the low-born Johnson famously despised. Those to whom Johnson offered amnesty were required simply to take an oath of allegiance and to pledge their support for emancipation (though not for black civil and political rights). And even those individuals who fell within the categories exempted from the amnesty offer could apply directly to the President for individual pardons, as Robert Holt, frustrated with his brother's refusal to help him, would seek to do in the weeks ahead.[29]

Johnson's second proclamation addressed the issue of restoring the former Confederate states to equal status in the Union. In it Johnson named a provisional civilian governor, William W. Holden, for North Carolina, and instructed him to call for the election of a group of delegates from among the white men of the state who had already received federal pardons. These delegates would then convene for the purposes of framing a new state constitution, and once that new constitution came into line with the federal constitution (including the Thirteenth Amendment freeing the slaves), the state's restoration would be essentially complete. In this proclamation, then, Johnson established a process similar to Lincoln's 1863 plan by which former Confederate states could regain their stature as full members of the Union. The process was simple and hardly harsh. It allowed the rebel states significant room to maneuver while sparing them the humiliation of even more dramatic threats of federal intervention and perhaps long-term military oversight. Not insignificantly, this proclamation also shored up the time-honored principle of white supremacy. The freedpeople, notes historian Eric Foner, "had no role to play in [Johnson's] vision of a reconstructed South."[30]

In the weeks ahead, similar edicts followed for six other former Confederate states: Mississippi, Georgia, Texas, Alabama, South Carolina, and Florida. Also during this period Johnson officially recognized the Unionist government Francis Harrison Pierpont had created late in the war in those counties in northern Virginia occupied by Union troops; the Unionist government of Tennessee, which Johnson himself had established in early 1865 when he was the state's military governor; and the Reconstruction governments Lincoln had earlier approved in Louisiana and Arkansas, according to the dictates of his 1863 proclamation. Significantly, none of the governments Johnson recognized during the summer and early fall of 1865 took steps toward protecting blacks' civil rights, let alone enfranchising the freedmen. Rather, they eagerly set about the work of constructing so-called black codes, supposedly in order to delineate the civil rights and responsibilities of the freedpeople, but ultimately most effective in turning back the clock and reviving as many of the constraints associated with slavery as possible, short of reestablishing the actual institution itself. To the great frustration of the Union army's occupation troops, the new state governments in the South also began, with the President's blessing, to reorganize and rearm their state militias, a sure sign to many that Johnson intended to hold the freedpeople down. From his distant vantage point at Fort Jefferson, convicted assassination conspirator Samuel Mudd rejoiced to learn of all these developments, which he understood as serving the vital purpose of keeping in check those he called the "idle, roving, and lawless negroes that roam unrestricted through the country" where his wife and children were struggling on without him.[31]

In the century and a half since the Civil War, some historians have suggested that the Reconstruction policies ultimately put forward by Andrew Johnson did in fact mirror Lincoln's intentions, in contrast with the Reconstruction plan proposed and, in the end, partly carried through by the Radical Republicans. For evidence such historians have pointed, among other things, to Johnson's May 29 proclamations. According to Stanton biographers Benjamin Thomas and Harold Hyman, however, although the parallels between the vision and sentiments expressed in Lincoln's December 1863 proclamation, and those expressed in Johnson's proclamations of May 29, 1865, are clear, and although both Lincoln and Johnson refused to accept the notion that the rebel states had ever actually left the Union (which both considered perpetual), there are important differences in the approaches the two presidents took to the problems of reconstruction and restoration.

For one thing, as Thomas and Hyman explain, Lincoln, "in advancing his [own] plan of reconstruction, had declared that he did not mean to rule out other plans." Indeed, at his last cabinet meeting, held on the very day he was shot, Lincoln had thoughtfully entertained a very different plan for Reconstruction. That plan, advanced by none other than Secretary of War Stanton, involved dividing the conquered South for a period of time into military districts under the control of military governors, in order to guarantee that certain fea-

Secretary of War Edwin M. Stanton.
Courtesy of the Library of Congress

tures of the former Confederacy might be thoroughly and decisively reshaped, particularly those aspects pertaining to the economy, the institution of slavery, and the civil and political subordination of blacks. Only when these changes were accomplished, Stanton argued, should the former Confederate states be restored to full status in the Union. Lincoln considered Stanton's plan carefully and called on his other chief advisers to give it serious consideration as well. Whether he would have adopted the Stanton plan in the end will, of course, never be known. What is certain, however, is that in ways very unlike his predecessor, Andrew Johnson was an immensely stubborn man. Although he claimed simply to be following the path laid out by Lincoln's 1863 proclamation, Johnson either failed or refused to acknowledge that Lincoln never meant the proclamation to be his last word on Reconstruction. Rather, he designed it as a "flexible . . . wartime weapon" that he hoped to wield in order to "hasten the coming of peace," but not, by any means, to set forth "the final form which that peace must assume."[32]

In short, Andrew Johnson was not testing the postwar waters, as Lincoln might have done, when he laid the official foundation of his Reconstruction policy. Rather, even as the Bureau of Military Justice's wheels of vengeance were turning against the men whom Holt, Stanton, and others believed to be the chief enemies of the nation, an only partly supportive Johnson was making his first moves toward enacting the swift, undemanding reconciliation with the South he had essentially decided to effect by executive means, with or without congressional approval. In so doing, Johnson ensured that the debate within the federal government over the shape of the new South, the future of the nation, the question of the freedmen's rights (no one was giving much thought to the rights of the freedwomen), and in many ways, the meaning of the war itself would be bitter and protracted. He further guaranteed that for the duration of his presidency the resolution of seemingly all other political questions—including the futures of Jefferson Davis, Clement Clay, and others in the Confederate leadership—would be subject to the vicissitudes of this larger struggle.

It bears mentioning that during the first days and weeks after the May 29 proclamations, Andrew Johnson seems to have enjoyed the strong support of the Northern public, the bulk of whom were enraged by the murder of Abraham Lincoln, but also tired of the war and eager for peace. Most Northerners also generally shared Johnson's racist perspective and his lack of concern for the post-emancipation security (not to mention political enfranchisement) of the former slaves.[33] As Ulysses Grant himself wrote years later, "I do not believe that the majority of the Northern people at that time were in favor of Negro suffrage. They supposed that it would naturally follow the freedom of the Negro, but that there would be a time of probation, in which the ex-slaves could prepare themselves for the privileges of citizenship before the full right would be conferred."[34]

Pro-Confederate Southerners, too, were encouraged by Johnson's apparent generosity, especially given their anger over the "Negro problem," which seemed to have been imposed on them by a coalition of crazed abolitionists and federal government operatives determined to punish the South savagely for the war as a whole. Most Radical Republicans and their allies, on the other hand, were horrified by Johnson's May 29 proclamations. If they had previously hoped that Johnson saw things their way, they now knew better. It seemed that the new president had made up his mind to act—and to act alone—in order to restore the Southern states to full equality in the Union as quickly and as benevolently as possible, with the goal of completing the task before Congress reconvened in early December.[35] Radicals were appalled not only by the speedy pace for Reconstruction that Johnson's proclamations projected, but also because they were sure that the South could not be trusted to live up to the unspoken assumptions underlying such a lenient policy.

The reports coming in from the South seemed to prove the Radicals right. In the first weeks after Lee's surrender and the assassination of Abraham Lincoln, pro-Confederate Southerners had seemed prepared for the absolute worst in terms of retribution by the North, including a federal program for Reconstruction that compelled them not only to free their slaves, but to grant them suffrage.[36] Guided by the implications of Johnson's emerging policies, however, former Confederates recovered from their initial humiliation and began to act with defiance rather than compliance toward all on their soil who represented the victorious North, especially those whose presence suggested that the end of the war should be followed by the economic, cultural, and social transformation of the region and a complete repudiation of the Old Order based on slavery. As the memory of Johnson's first harsh words gave way to what looked quite convincingly like an attitude of near absolution on his part, supporters of the late Confederacy regained their composure. Meanwhile, Holt, Stanton, the Radical Republicans, and their allies grew increasingly discouraged.

At the end of June, just as the military commissioners were preparing to debate their verdicts in the assassination conspiracy case, a delegation of Radicals including Senators Wade and Davis and Pennsylvania Congressman Thaddeus Stevens traveled to Washington to request that Andrew Johnson call Congress into special session so that the legislators' opinions on Reconstruction might at least be taken into consideration. Johnson refused the request, having determined in his own mind that Reconstruction was an executive issue rather than a legislative one. News of Johnson's response rejoiced his growing number of supporters in the former Confederacy, who continued to take measures to revive their influence over political and social affairs in the region. Just over a month later, even Secretary of the Navy Welles—whose hatred of the Radicals and whose support for Johnson's policies were unswerving—confided to his diary that "the tone and sentiment and action of the people of the South is injudicious and indiscreet in many respects . . . the Rebels appear to be arrogant and offensively dictatorial. . . . From various quarters we learn that the Rebels are organizing through the Southern States with a view to regaining political ascendancy."[37]

Moreover, in mid-August, Johnson took yet another important step toward defining the process by which he hoped to complete Reconstruction quickly and smoothly. He ordered General Oliver Otis Howard, whom Lincoln and Stanton had appointed at the end of the war to head the Bureau of Refugees, Freedmen, and Abandoned Lands, to return to all pardoned Confederates the property that had been confiscated from them, with the exception of slave property. General Howard was appalled, having spent the weeks since assuming the leadership of the Freedmen's Bureau placing thousands of former slave families on land that Southern planters had abandoned or that the Union army had confiscated during the war. Predictably, the freedpeople had set about cultivating and nurturing their fields with gratitude, enthusiasm, and boundless hope.[38]

Not surprisingly, however, in the wake of Johnson's May 29 proclamations, former Confederate landowners began to try to reclaim acreage being farmed by the freedpeople. On the pretext that he believed abandoned and confiscated lands to be exempt from Johnson's proclamations, initially General Howard had refused to recognize the planters' claims, and on July 28 he issued a circular to that effect. But on August 16, Johnson issued a direct order commanding Howard to restore the occupied lands to their former owners. Howard could not refuse. Less than a month later, on September 11, a delegation of white representatives from nine Southern states visited Andrew Johnson to express their "sincere respect" for his "desire and intention to sustain Southern rights in the Union." In response, Johnson—who at this point was issuing an average of 100 pardons per day to individuals officially excluded from his May 29 amnesty proclamation—confirmed his "love, respect, and confidence" toward Southerners and the South, and his desire to be "forbearing and forgiving." In line with this attitude of "forbearance and forgiveness," by October, only six months after Appomattox, Johnson had granted paroles to several members of Jefferson Davis's cabinet, as well as Davis's vice president, Alexander H. Stephens, who had served a brief term of imprisonment at Fort Warren in Boston harbor.[39] In the first days of November, thanks to Johnson's determination to effect Reconstruction on his own terms as quickly and painlessly as possible, four former generals, five former colonels, and even former Vice President Stephens were elected from the newly "reconstructed" states of the vanquished Confederacy to serve in the United States Congress.[40]

Among those in the North and in the South who were happy with the new president's posture toward the former Confederacy were many members of Johnson's own Democratic Party—including, notably, the Montgomery Blair family—who had feared that the collapse of the Confederacy, combined with emancipation and the possibility of a Republican-led push for enfranchising the freedmen, might result in the permanent demise of their political clout. To these Democrats, Johnson's proposals augured well for a restoration of the Union without black suffrage, which they rejected for reasons of racism as well as because they presumed (rightly) that the freedpeople's political loyalties would lie with the Republican Party associated with their liberation. As Eric Foner writes, "Northern Democrats quickly realized that Johnson's plan embraced ideas central to the party's ideology and essential for its political revival—control of local affairs by the individual states, white supremacy, and the quick resumption of the South's place within the Union."[41]

Democrats further rejoiced in the failure during October and November 1865 of three referenda in the Northern states (in Connecticut, Minnesota, and Wisconsin) designed to extend the vote to black men at the state level. Such developments made Johnson's course appear all the more reasonable to those already inclined to support him, for they suggested that not only pro-Confederate Southerners but also a large proportion of the Northern public stood behind his view of the future. In contrast, in the words of Gideon Welles, such developments "caused a great howl to be set up" among Johnson's Radical Republican opponents.[42]

Of course, there were lifelong Democrats who joined the list of Johnson's increasingly anxious opponents, too, including Joseph Holt. Holt's personal correspondence during the summer and fall of 1865 was replete with letters from Unionist friends across the South and the border states, informing him that the pro-Confederate enemies of the nation were once again on the rise. The "treacherous Secessionists of Charleston are conspiring to recover power," wrote Tal P. Shaffner from South Carolina in late June. "Their conversation seems to indicate that they are as hostile at heart to the supremacy of *Nationality* over *State Sovereignty* as before the war. They do not appreciate the fact that the late waste of blood was to maintain a Nationality that existed, legally, since the adoption of the Constitution." On July 19 C. B. New wrote from Holt's home state of Kentucky: "I fear the mode pursued by [Johnson-appointed provisional] Govs Wells and Sharkey of La and Miss instead of harmonizing will distract and divide our people. The old issues of slavery and state rights will be revived and sectional parties arise, from the appointments now being made in those states. . . . It seems to me the Southern states can not be made truly loyal by placing the offices in the hands of such." From Vicksburg, Mississippi, came word in August of the crisis that was shaping up in that state: "The people see late Generals colonels &c placed in office and they naturally conclude that rebellion is not so bad after all, and that loyalty is not a virtue, at least one not to be rewarded. . . . I think we have daily proofs that we have been in too much hurry to have restoration of what is called civil rule. . . . Every thing convinces me that this people needs to be told plainly & at the point of the bayonet, that for the present Military Law & rule prevail." Even Holt's Aunt Mary, a few weeks before she died, had voiced her concern: "In your letter to me you described exactly how the rebels would return home," she wrote. "I can't tell how you knew it but you are a correct prophet, for they came back blustering & insulting."[43]

What all this means is that in the late summer and early fall of

1865, Holt's angry dispute with Montgomery Blair only ostensibly pertained to the quality of Holt's prewar Unionism. At a deeper level, it really concerned his postwar association with Stanton and with the Radical Republican agenda for Reconstruction and for the freedpeople, in contrast with that of Andrew Johnson. Like Stanton and the Radical Republicans, Democrat Joseph Holt believed that in order to avenge the death of Abraham Lincoln and fulfill the promise of the Union's victory at Appomattox, the federal government must now approach the former Confederacy and its leaders unashamedly as conquerors who meant to chastise their erstwhile enemies severely, while also reshaping the postwar South in such a manner as to ensure the rights of the freedpeople and, if possible, their loyalty to the federal government.

It also means that at this point, his concern with such larger issues caused Holt to make what otherwise might seem to have been a strange and uncharacteristic decision: namely, to abandon, at least for the time being, his pursuit of military justice against John Surratt Jr., the last known member of Booth's local team of accomplices, who had thus far eluded capture. As it turns out, on September 27, five and a half months after Surratt vanished from Washington, Vice Consul Henry Wilding in Liverpool, England, had notified Secretary of State William Seward (who passed the word immediately to Holt and Stanton) that the wanted man was, indeed, in that city.[44] In fact, Surratt had been in England only very briefly, having spent most of the time he had been in hiding in Canada. Surratt's first stop had been Montreal, where on April 18 he had registered under his most common alias, "John Harrison," at the St. Lawrence Hotel, a favorite gathering spot of the Canadian agents of the Confederacy. When Surratt received word that the United States government—on Holt's recommendation—had put a $25,000 price on his head, friends persuaded him that Montreal was far too obvious a hiding place, a presumption soon confirmed by the appearance there of Louis Weichmann, John Holohan, and the Washington, D.C., detectives assigned to follow Surratt's trail. (Surratt later claimed to have caught a glimpse of Weichmann in Montreal, though Weichmann did not see him.)[45]

After moving the fugitive into a private home in the city, Surratt's friends piloted him a few days later across the St. Lawrence River to a village named St. Liboire about forty-five miles away. There, under the alias Charles Armstrong, Surratt took shelter in the home of a Catholic priest, Father Boucher, to whom his escorts explained that Mr. Armstrong was ill and also in some sort of undefined trouble on account of the American war. Whether Father Boucher came to know his guest's true identity and situation is unclear. Regardless, he permitted Surratt to remain at his house through most of the summer. Such limited information as Surratt received about the trial going on in Washington was still sufficient to make him anxious on his mother's behalf, and there is evidence that at one point during the trial he actually sent word to one of her lawyers, Frederick Aiken, to the effect that he was willing to return to Washington. John Surratt was hardly willing to play fast and loose with his own freedom in the long term, however, or to commit himself to implicating anyone else in the assassination conspiracy simply in order to save his mother. Thus, in exchange for his return to the federal capital he demanded that the government agree to "certain stipulations," one of which was that he, Surratt, would not be called as a witness in any trial of Jefferson Davis.[46] Such a demand can only have intensified Joseph Holt's suspicions that Booth, Surratt, and Davis had plotted the assassination together from the start.

In the end no such deal was made, and Surratt remained underground in Canada until the end of July or early August, by which time his mother was dead. At that point, Surratt's friends decided to move the fugitive again, fearing that his presence at Father Boucher's had been exposed by a careless, nosy servant. Surratt returned briefly to Montreal, where he took up hiding in yet another Catholic home (this time the homeowner's son was a priest). On September 15, wearing glasses and with his naturally light brown hair cut short and dyed a darker color, Surratt traveled on board the steamer *Montreal* to Quebec, where he transferred to another ship, the *Peruvian*, destined for London.[47]

On board the *Peruvian* John Surratt apparently spoke freely to the ship's surgeon, a Canadian doctor named Lewis J. A. McMillan. Surratt had been introduced to Dr. McMillan as "Mr. McCarty" by one of the friends who put him on board, but perhaps because of his relief at having escaped, or because of overconfidence or sheer bravado, once he was in international waters Surratt revealed his true identity to Dr. McMillan. In the course of their conversations, he apparently also discussed his self-imposed exile to Europe. Subsequently, Surratt left the ship in Londonderry, Ireland, but he then headed for Liverpool, where Dr. McMillan himself disembarked. In Liverpool the two men met up again, and further conversation finally convinced Dr. McMillan that he should approach the American consulate and divulge what he knew. So it was thanks to Dr. McMillan that by late September Vice Consul Wilding was aware that Surratt had come within range of his grasp; as quickly as possible he sent word to Secretary Seward to that effect, following up with two additional letters—on September 30 and October 10—detailing Surratt's movements in Liverpool.

Given his eagerness to convey this intelligence to the State Department, Wilding must have been quite surprised to receive Acting Secretary of State William Hunter's response, dated October 13, informing him that "it is thought advisable that no action be taken in regard to the arrest of the supposed John Surratt at present." Hunter's letter, written while Seward was out of town, described Seward's discussions on the matter with Holt and Stanton and essentially tied Wilding's hands. As a result, John Surratt slipped away again, to France and then to Rome, where he enlisted in January 1866 as a member of the Vatican guard known as the Papal Zouaves. Under the new alias John Watson, John Surratt was stationed at Sezze, about forty miles from Rome. Meanwhile, back in Washington, on November 24, 1865, a presidential executive order had abruptly revoked the $25,000 reward offered for his capture, as well as similar rewards for the capture of Jacob Thompson, Beverly Tucker, George Sanders, and William Cleary. These, of course, were the individuals named, back in early May, as co-conspirators with Jefferson Davis, Clement Clay, John Wilkes Booth, and Booth's local accomplices in the assassination of Lincoln and the murderous attack on the secretary of state.[48]

How can one explain what appears to be a sharp turning away from the goal of capturing Surratt and others implicated in the crimes of April 14 less than two weeks after Holt issued his November 13 report to Stanton? In testimony given to the House Committee on the Judiciary over a year later, in January 1867, Edwin Stanton explained—albeit not very persuasively—that Johnson's November 1865 order resulted from three considerations: the lack of any recent response to the offer of a reward; the federal government's desire not to pay rewards to foreign officers of the law, under the assumption that Surratt and the others must by now be out of the country; and the hope that rescinding the reward offers might, paradoxically, work to lure the suspects to return to the United States and put themselves at risk of capture.[49]

Three months after Stanton testified, in April 1867, Joseph Holt gave equally unpersuasive testimony to the Judiciary Committee, essentially arguing that when he learned in October 1865 of Surratt's escape to England, he assumed that it was beyond the bounds of his bureau's responsibilities to pursue him. Such testimony, by both Stanton and Holt, seems odd to say the least. What is most important here is that, in October 1865, armed with knowledge regarding Surratt's location, the Bureau of Military Justice—along with the State Department, the War Department, and the President—actively determined *not* to follow up and, furthermore, on November 24 these parties explicitly demonstrated their willingness to back off on the pursuit of Surratt, as well as the pursuit of others they had previously associated as co-conspirators in the assassination conspiracy. The question is, why?[50]

As his November 13 report to Stanton clearly indicates, in Joseph Holt's case at least it was not for lack of confidence in these men's guilt, or for lack of the desire to prove that guilt conclusively to the world at large. In light of Andrew Johnson's emerging policy with respect to Reconstruction, however, the conditions under which Holt was operating had changed dramatically, and the prospect of bringing John Surratt back to American soil to stand trial—however satisfying on one level—on another level seemed both foolish and dangerous. For one thing, the possibility of achieving any further justice against the nation's enemies appeared to be slipping away more quickly than Holt and others like himself could ever have anticipated, and as such it now seemed as if the time had come to concentrate exclusively on the big prey, Jefferson Davis, at the expense even of someone who seemed as readily punishable as John Surratt. At the same time, complications potentially associated with John Surratt's return surely also served as deterrents as Holt considered his options. Might not Surratt's return further enliven the nettling popular sympathy his mother's death had generated? And what if Surratt returned, went on trial, and testified that Davis had nothing to do with the assassination after all? It was a chance that neither Holt nor Stanton was willing to take, at least for now.

In his September 1865 response to Montgomery Blair's attack on his prewar record as a pro-Union man, Holt recalled how,

> during the trying and gloomy period preceeding the outbreak of the war, while holding office, with such light as God gave me, and with such limited powers and opportunities as I possessed, I labored unceasingly . . . to strengthen the hands of the government to meet the impending rebellion, and to unmask and baffle the machinations of those conspirators, who with perjury on their souls, were daily and nightly plotting the ruin of the government and country in whose service they were.[51]

As 1865 ground to a frustrating close, Joseph Holt remained eager to complete the work he had set out to do more than four years before, even as he grew increasingly uncertain about the possibility of doing so with Andrew Johnson in the Executive Mansion. Throughout the war, the task of bringing the nation's enemies to justice had always been linked, for Holt, to the larger issue of avenging the death and destruction those enemies had wrought by starting the war in the first place. As Johnson's troubling vision for the restoration of an unreconstructed South took form, Holt's desire and ability to pursue his version of justice against John Surratt Jr., Jefferson Davis, Clement Clay, and other chief rebels seemed likely to be swallowed up in the maelstrom that swirled around Johnson's vision, the agenda of the Radical Republicans, and the debate over which program represented the more meaningful outcome of the war, not least of all in terms of the freedpeople's future.

The experience of the world has shown that great crimes never have been and never can be repressed without punishment, and that laws which are not vindicated when violated are, in effect, no laws at all. Should the statute against treason, for lack of its enforcement, cease to be a terror to ambitious men wickedly lusting for power, whatever protection might remain for individual life, there would be none whatever for the life of the nation, which would be exposed to the stabs of every traitor who might choose to lift his dagger against it.

—JOSEPH HOLT TO EDWIN STANTON,
November 23, 1865[1]

It is complained that the President treats the Rebels and the Copperheads kindly. It is not strange that he does so, for kindness begets kindness. They treat him respectfully, while the Radical leaders are arrogant, presuming, and dictatorial. . . . It is an incipient conspiracy.

—GIDEON WELLES to his diary,
February 1866[2]

Andrew Johnson's obsession with keeping blacks in order led inevitably to abandonment of the idea of destroying planters' economic and political hegemony.

—ERIC FONER, *Reconstruction* (1988)[3]

It was politics, not law, that governed [Jefferson] Davis's case.

—GLYNDON VAN DEUSEN,
William Henry Seward (1967)[4]

7

"TRAITORS, CONFESSED PERJURERS

AND SUBORNERS"

THE UNRAVELING OF REVENGE

IN THE WAKE OF APPOMATTOX AND THE MURDER OF ABRAHAM LINCOLN, Joseph Holt numbered himself among those who had devoted the past four years of their lives to saving the Union, and now demanded the South's acceptance of the consequences of Union victory. To Holt, as to others, this meant that the people of the former Confederacy must repudiate their former leaders (from Jefferson Davis and Robert E. Lee on down), provide security for Unionists and Northerners residing in the South, and guarantee the basic rights of the freedpeople. Equally important, Holt believed that in their words, attitudes, and behaviors former Confederates should demonstrate remorse and a readiness to accept their defeat with grace. Until they did so, the reconstruction of the nation would remain incomplete. If necessary, those in power in Washington must compel compliance.[5]

Many of Joseph Holt's longtime correspondents shared his views on the subject of how the former Confederacy should confront its defeat and were deeply disturbed to discover that over the course of 1865, a very different attitude had developed—one not of remorse and graceful submission, but of arrogance and denial. On December 4, T. H. Duval wrote to Holt from Austin, Texas. Duval hoped to convey to his friend of many years his grave concerns about how political affairs were shaping up there, and elsewhere below the

Mason-Dixon line. Speaking of the actions being taken by the state constitutional conventions organized under Andrew Johnson's generous rules for restoration, Duval wrote:

> So far as I have any knowledge . . . none of them (except that of North Carolina) have come up to what I have supposed Congress would require. They repeal the ordinances of secession but leave the *right of secession* still an open question. While abolishing slavery, they *dodge* the ratification of the proposed [Thirteenth] amendment to the Constitution of the U. States [abolishing slavery], and at the same time fail to make any provision to secure the freedmen in their rights of life, liberty & property. Only one or two of them, so far as I am advised, have repudiated their state debts contracted for war purposes. All these failures & evasions evince anything but a sincere and *bonafide* disposition to do what their duty requires, & what the Nation expects.[6]

Duval indicated to Holt that, as far as he could tell, the states of the former Confederacy were moving quickly and essentially painlessly toward full status within the federal government, having shown little if any contrition for their crimes of the past four years, and virtually no intention of changing their wicked ways, particularly with regard to the former slaves.

Over the past several months hundreds of reports from individuals living or traveling below the Mason-Dixon line had found their way into the hands of federal officials or ran in the Northern press, and the news they brought was not good. Rather than being compliant with the occupation forces, white Southerners routinely challenged the Union troops stationed in the region, most notably those who were members of the United States Colored Troops. Witnesses also described former Confederates actively, openly, and sometimes even violently expressing their disloyalty to the Union, their disdain for the Unionists in their midst, and their determination to restore as much of the Old Order as they possibly could. Two crucial aspects of this vision of a resurgent Confederacy were Democratic Party dominance and black civil and political subordination. Reports such as these led many who had initially put their faith in Johnson and his agenda of simple forgiveness and rapid reunion to feel betrayed. In response, not a few of those who had formerly supported Johnson now began to throw their weight in with those who had doubted the merits of the Johnson plan right from the start.[7]

Holt may have been dismayed by the contents of T. H. Duval's letter from Texas, but he surely was not surprised. Long before April 14, 1865, Holt had vividly displayed his conviction, grounded in personal experience, that those who had guided the pro-Confederate South through four years of deadly assaults on the nation's life and welfare would never come to heel on their own. Furthermore, as far as Holt was concerned, if those who had plotted the destruction of the nation were forgiven too soon and too easily, they would simply rise again, reorganize their conspiracy, and find new ways to revive the Old Order, including white planter supremacy. Subsequently the struggle between the sections would be resumed, if not on the battlefield (though a return to armed conflict was by no means unimaginable), then in the halls of Congress and the public arena. At all costs, therefore, Davis and the rest of the leadership in the unrepentant South must be tried, disarmed, disbanded, and repressed. But as fall gave way to winter in 1865, Holt grew increasingly concerned that the work he and others had set out to do back in early 1861 was about to be wrecked by none other than the man who had benefited most directly from George Atzerodt's failure of nerve on April 14: President Andrew Johnson.

It is interesting to note that on December 4, 1865, the same day that T. H. Duval was penning his letter to Holt regarding political developments in the postwar South, the 39th Congress of the United States was meeting in Washington for its first session. Thanks to the electoral rules in place at the time, membership in this Congress for those states who had remained loyal to the Union had been determined by the elections that had taken place in November 1864 (not 1865). Representation for the states of the former Confederacy, however, was a different matter altogether, and before Congress could commence its business, the question remained whether these representatives elected in postwar state conventions should be allowed to take their seats. Andrew Johnson believed that they should. How better to expedite Presidential Reconstruction, after all, than to allow the states of the former Confederacy to send their newly elected officials to Washington?

In contrast with Johnson, however, most Republican congressmen arriving for the session—both the moderates, who at this point constituted the majority in the party, and the Radicals—had come to share, at least in some degree, Duval's and Holt's concerns about the evolution of Johnson's politics over the past few months. They feared that Johnson would permit a virtual revival of the Confederacy—even perhaps the return to national political power of the former Confederate leadership. As a result, after serious consultation, the Republican moderates and Radicals (who together enjoyed a better than three-to-one majority in both the House and the Senate) decided to join forces and take the first real opportunity to arrest Johnson's single-handed redemption of the South, at least to give them time to consider its long-term ramifications and perhaps, if necessary, to begin to work effectively against it. To this end they refused to accept the representatives sent to Washington by the former Confederate states.

In addition, a number of the more Radical members, led by Pennsylvania Congressman Thaddeus Stevens, engineered the immediate passage of a resolution in both the House and the Senate to create a joint committee of senators and representatives to review the whole process of Reconstruction up to this point. If necessary, the Joint Committee on Reconstruction would also develop a new and more just plan for national reunion. The Joint Committee had fifteen members—nine representatives and six senators—and was headed by Senator William Pitt Fessenden of Maine, himself a Republican moderate. Included on the committee were two members who had been intimately connected with the assassination conspiracy trial during the summer: Republican Senator John Bingham of Ohio, who had served as Joseph Holt's chief assistant judge advocate; and Democratic Senator Reverdy Johnson, the famed Maryland lawyer and legislator who had participated in Mary Surratt's defense.[8]

Andrew Johnson and his supporters had hoped to complete the

work of reuniting the broken nation politically by the time the 39th
Congress convened in early December 1865, but they were destined
for disappointment. Instead, as 1865 entered its final month, Presidential Reconstruction itself was under siege. In the eyes of many
proud and weary defenders of the Union, both within and outside the
federal government, Johnson's vision and plan represented a thoroughly unsatisfying conclusion to the war, a conclusion which suggested that the war's unspeakable expenditure of blood and treasure
had ultimately been for naught. Where was justice, many Northerners and Southern Unionists asked, if the former Confederacy's guilty
leaders and their henchmen could not be punished, and if the South
as a whole—a vanquished enemy, after all—could not be compelled
to adhere to strict conditions established by its conquerors, including
guarantees of the civil and political rights of the freedpeople? Could
the nation have any reasonable hope for its own future, or the freedpeople any hope for theirs? To demand anything less, many believed,
was to put the meaning of the war itself in grave doubt.[9]

Johnson, of course, continued to have his defenders. Learning of
the 39th Congress's refusal to seat the representatives elected from the
states of the former Confederacy and of the formation of the Joint
Committee on Reconstruction, Secretary of the Navy Gideon Welles
grumbled to his diary that such moves on the part of Congress represented "a blow at our governmental system" that was nothing less
than "revolutionary." Subsequently Welles's disgruntlement turned to
alarm and resentment as he came to believe that the federal government was being subjected to a violent attack from within, spearheaded by the Radical Republicans (for whom he had never had
much sympathy anyway), and prodded along by the man he liked
least among his cabinet colleagues, Secretary of War Stanton. Specifically, Welles complained that the legislative branch of the government—with the assistance of Stanton and his allies (including Joseph
Holt)—was subverting the executive branch on the question of how
best and most quickly to restore the Union. Furthermore, Welles
anticipated that the creation of the Joint Committee represented only
the first wave of the battle, and that already by December 1865 there
was evidence in the press of support in Congress for the impeachment

of the President, presumably for acting to effect Reconstruction without waiting for Congress to reconvene or seeking the legislators' consent.[10]

Welles believed the President's actions were well within the bounds of both propriety and law, and that Johnson's plan for restoration was not only generous but wise and fair. In his diary Welles described a recent discussion with Radical Republican Senator Charles Sumner of Massachusetts, whom Southerner Preston Brooks had beaten literally senseless with a cane in 1856 on account of Sumner's uncompromising abolitionist views (Sumner was unable to return to his Senate seat for three years following the beating). After the discussion, wrote Welles, he tried to persuade Sumner that "conciliation, not persecution" should be the federal government's policy toward the former Confederacy, for from Welles's perspective only such a policy could heal the wounds of the past and reunite the nation quickly. Sumner, however, had responded that a stern policy toward the states of the former Confederacy was not necessarily a policy of persecution. It was, rather, the best policy for ensuring the goal of taming the apparently unrepentant South and leading it into a more just future.[11]

Perhaps not surprisingly, in this same conversation the two men also discussed their opinions regarding the fate of the Confederacy's former president. In what may seem at first like a paradox, it was the Radical Republican Sumner who at this point explicitly advocated clemency in Jefferson Davis's case, whereas Welles, a Democrat from Connecticut, was as yet unprepared to let Davis off the hook. As had been the case for Andrew Johnson initially, for Welles the harsh punishment of a few leading figures like Davis seemed to have the potential politically to obviate the need for punishing the pro-Confederate Southern people as a whole. Sumner, in contrast, believed that punishing Davis as harshly as Henry Wirz and Booth's co-conspirators had already been might lead to a false sense that justice in the South and retribution for the Confederacy's crimes could be achieved simply by punishing a few, and that further action on the part of the federal government to remodel the region entirely was unnecessary. Like many Radicals who were deeply committed to transforming the

South wholesale, it was this false conclusion that Sumner hoped to avoid. If demonstrating clemency toward Davis could aid the Radicals in furthering their more expansive vision for a whole new (and demonstrably contrite) South, it was well worth the sacrifice.[12]

Joseph Holt disagreed. In the late fall of 1865 he still clung to the belief that the two agendas—punishing the Confederate South and its leaders, and transforming the region for the future—were intertwined. And he dearly hoped that both agendas could still be fulfilled, although it was coming to seem less and less likely that they would be. Holt's own daily work continued to focus overwhelmingly on the former task, specifically bringing the rebel chiefs and their leading co-conspirators to justice. At the very least, Holt yearned to prevent such evildoers from receiving pardons from Johnson, whose ability to discriminate between the deserving and the undeserving seemed, in the minds of many, to have completely broken down.

In view of this concern, on November 23 Joseph Holt sent Secretary of War Stanton a long, angry letter denouncing the efforts of William Marvin, whom Andrew Johnson had appointed provisional governor of Florida, to secure pardons for three former Confederates. These Floridians were D. L. Yulee, once a U.S. congressman, who had supported secession as well as the unlawful seizure of federal property in his state (and who was, incidentally, related to Holt through marriage); Stephen R. Mallory, former Confederate secretary of the navy; and A. K. Allison, former president of the Confederate Senate and, briefly, the state's wartime governor. Holt wrote that Marvin's applications on their behalf, sent to the President a month before, "ignore totally the criminality of these men, and evidence a singular unconsciousness that there is anything to be considered beyond their personal interests and comfort in determining the question of their longer imprisonment."[13]

Rather, in their cases Holt recommended "arraignment and trial upon an indictment for high treason," as they had all engaged actively and persistently in "the conspiracy for the destruction of the Government." In conclusion Holt passionately reiterated his conviction that "this Republic might exist for ages without developing in its bosom a

band of conspirators and parricides more steeped in guilt or more surrounded with aggravations of criminality than those recently conquered by its arms, and who, covered with the blood of our people,
are now standing in the presence of the Government, and, happily,
completely in its power." For Holt, failure by the federal government
to exercise its power and exact retribution against such "conspirators
and parricides" was, to all intents and purposes, the same as com-
mitting national suicide.[14]

Holt was concerned about the federal government's very survival,
and there was little in the Johnson program to reassure him. The May
29 proclamations had offered extremely generous terms for amnesty
and the restoration of federally approved governments in the former
Confederate states. As has been discussed, over the past few months
Johnson had pardoned hundreds—even thousands—of former Confederates, including several members of Jefferson Davis's cabinet and
his vice president. There were even rumors that Johnson was now
willing to consider a pardon for Davis himself, although it seemed
highly unlikely that Davis would stoop to request one, since doing so
might suggest that he acknowledged having committed a crime.[15]
Johnson had also displayed a ready willingness to recognize the new
state governments emerging across the late Confederacy, as well as
their representatives to the U.S. Congress. And he had gone so far as
to insist that the confiscated and abandoned Confederate lands Oliver
Howard and the Freedmen's Bureau had parceled out to eager freedpeople and their families be returned to their former white owners.

For some, of course, Johnson's emerging policies shone like a bea-
con of hope in a dark night. Around this time, for example, Samuel
Mudd's wife abandoned her previous efforts to persuade Joseph Holt
to release her husband from Fort Jefferson and, by means of the same
sort of long, emotional letter she had previously sent to the judge
advocate general, now began to devote her energy to persuading President Johnson instead.[16] To Holt and those who shared his viewpoint,
however, these developments signaled that Johnson was abdicating
his own and the federal government's responsibility toward the
nation and toward the former slaves.

Of great practical concern to Holt, too, was the fact that Johnson's

"President Andrew Johnson Pardoning Rebels at the White House,"
from Harper's Weekly, *October 14, 1865*

policies also dramatically transformed the context in which he was
struggling to achieve his own immediate goal of avenging the crimes
committed by the Confederate leadership and their chief agents and
operatives. True, Johnson had approved the prosecution of the assassination conspirators and had sanctioned the hanging of some and the
imprisonment of others. True, he had also endorsed the trial of Henry
Wirz and had signed Wirz's death warrant. True, Johnson had
not made any moves—yet—toward actually pardoning his longtime
nemesis in the prewar Congress, Jefferson Davis, or for that matter,
Clement Clay, both of whom remained in captivity at Fortress Monroe. (Possibly for health reasons, Davis at least had been removed
from his casemate cell in October and placed in a more congenial
room on the second floor of the fortress's Carroll Hall.) But by
December 1865, such early victories for Holt's agenda were coming
to seem more like isolated remnants of a previous incarnation of
Andrew Johnson. It increasingly appeared as if Johnson, although
willing to sacrifice a few significant former Confederates, meant in
the end to bring about a sweeping redemption of the entire region.[17]

It was clear that opportunities were slipping away to make good on the harsh and punitive rhetoric toward the former Confederacy and its leadership for which Johnson had been known during the first weeks of his presidency. On the other hand, the fact that the Republicans serving in the 39th Congress seemed willing to challenge Johnson and wrestle him to the ground politically if necessary, offered Holt and Stanton a slim ray of hope that their work might be still brought to completion. At the same time, on a practical level Holt recognized that he would do best to concentrate the energies of the Bureau of Military Justice on a few key cases, if he hoped to effect satisfying outcomes in any, and, in the immediate moment, the Jefferson Davis case interested Holt most.

In Holt's mind the federal government's case against Davis and, to a lesser extent, Clement Clay as co-conspirators with Booth in the assassination still seemed quite promising, at least if Sanford Conover's witnesses and the testimony they had given in their depositions could be trusted. Additional cause for optimism could be found in the apparent willingness of Johnson's staunchest opponents in Congress to throw their support specifically behind the effort to prove Davis's guilt. Indeed, some of the more extreme Radicals in Congress demonstrated their willingness to entertain the notion that Johnson himself was linked to the assassination conspiracy. After all, was he not the tragedy's greatest beneficiary? Although it is unlikely that Holt was prepared to extrapolate Johnson's complicity in Booth's plot from the evidence he had at his command, it is also clear that he was utterly committed to pursuing his case against Jefferson Davis, even if it meant grasping at straws.

To this end, as the year 1865 waned, Holt became party to what might be characterized as a somewhat awkward three-way alliance with Stanton, whose alienation from Johnson and the rest of the cabinet was growing more pronounced with each passing day, and with the Radical Republicans in Congress. In this tacit yet mutually supportive alliance the collaborating parties hoped to achieve two complementary goals. They hoped to undermine Johnson and his plan for speedy Southern redemption, thereby making way for a more demanding Congressional Reconstruction plan. They also hoped to bring to light the true nature of Jefferson Davis's crimes, expose as many of his co-conspirators as possible, and ensure their proper punishment. For Holt, participating in this awkward alliance meant, most important, that he could continue to pursue his goal. For Johnson's opponents in Congress, the alliance offered a means to destabilize Presidential Reconstruction and its chief proponent in favor of a different, more just vision. For Holt's boss, friend, and ally Stanton, as he rapidly moved toward complete isolation within the Johnson cabinet, and as he became more and more sympathetic towards the Radical Republicans' plan for Reconstruction, it offered an opportunity to do both.

Even with so many eyes turned toward him as the immediate target of their respective but interlocking agendas, however, the question remained, what exactly was to be done about Jefferson Davis? How was the federal government's case against him to be pursued? On December 6, two days after Congress convened, Holt wrote a long letter to Stanton in which he reminded him, "The formal and deliberate judgment of the military commission, by which the accomplices of Booth were tried and convicted," was that "Davis and other rebel leaders [were] implicated in the treasonable conspiracy of which the prisoners on trial were the mere instruments, and that the assassination was but the consummation of that conspiracy." For good measure, Holt also recapped the testimony against Clement Clay given at the trial during the summer, on the principle that if Clay was guilty, surely Davis was, too. He then offered new information that had been provided by one of Sanford Conover's "entirely faithful and reliable" witnesses. According to Holt, this new evidence further supported the charge that Clay, as Davis's agent, had been connected to various "guerrilla raids and schemes of rapine" and had been involved in a plot to introduce into the United States "clothing infected with virulent contagious disease." As Holt saw it, a trial of Clay, at least, was imminent, based on all of the testimony presented against him. Predictably, Holt recommended that Clay "be brought before a military commission" to face charges of "complicity in the plot of assassina-

"Gallow's Bird's" and "Jeff Davis on the Right Platform"
(next page).
Courtesy of the Library of Congress

tion" as well as "violation of the laws of war." Six weeks later, on January 18, 1866, Holt informed the secretary of war that he now had four additional depositions to support the case against Clay that he still hoped to bring to trial.[18]

As Holt pressed on at the Bureau of Military Justice, developing the government's case against Davis, the Senate also began to apply pressure on Johnson to do something about the former Confederate president. On December 21 the Senate issued a resolution requesting that Johnson inform Congress "upon what charges and for what reasons . . . Jefferson Davis is still held in confinement, and why he has not been put upon his trial." Two weeks later, Attorney General James Speed brought Johnson up to date on the Davis case. Despite the cessation of "active hostilities," Speed explained in his letter, the persistence of a "state of war" across the unreconstructed South per-

JEFF DAVIS ON THE RIGHT PLATFORM,
or the last "act of secession".

mitted Davis's continued incarceration at Fortress Monroe. However, although Davis was currently a military prisoner, the opportunity had passed for trying the former president of the Confederacy for violation of the laws of war before a military tribunal, which would have placed his trial under Holt's oversight. Rather, Speed—who had been leaning in this direction since the summer—now argued conclusively, and to Holt's great disappointment, that Davis should be tried in civil court for treason. Speed wrote that Jefferson Davis (and any other "insurgents" still in custody) "ought to be tried in some one of the States or districts in which they in person respectively committed the crimes with which they may be charged," once the courts in those states were open and the law could be "peacefully administered and enforced."[19]

That same day, January 4, 1866, Edwin Stanton wrote to Johnson, countering that Davis's continued confinement without trial was

largely the result of the fact that Virginia was the jurisdiction recommended for his civil trial for treason. Because the civil courts were not
yet open in that state, and because there was no clear indication when
they would be, trying Davis in civil court was, at least for the time
being, impossible. As for the charge of treason itself, Stanton went on
to remind Johnson that official accusations pending against the former president of the Confederacy included "the crime of inciting the
assassination of Abraham Lincoln" and "the murder of Union prisoners of war by starvation and other barbarous and cruel treatment
toward them," both of which could be interpreted as violations of the
laws of war. For all these reasons, Davis could and indeed should be
tried by a military court, under Joseph Holt's authority.[20]

As Speed's and Stanton's letters to Johnson indicate, by the beginning of 1866, the federal government's case against Jefferson Davis
had descended into indefinite limbo thanks to the warring between
the President and his political opponents, and both sides' intransigence. As historian William Cooper has pointed out, Jefferson Davis
had emerged as an essential "part of the political equation" in Washington, a symbol of the struggle over Reconstruction and even over
the meaning of the war itself. "Drumming the message that they had
saved the Union from traitorous rebels," writes Cooper, "Republicans depicted Davis as the archfiend of the rebellion." At the same
time, "Johnson needed Davis in prison to show he held the head of
the Confederacy accountable," although it was becoming clear that
Johnson did not intend actually to prosecute him. In short, politically
Johnson could not afford to let Davis go free, and the Republicans
and their allies were unwilling to do so.[21] Meanwhile, Joseph Holt
was caught between his commitment to bringing Davis to trial and his
frustration over the fact that there appeared to be no obvious or simple way to prosecute and punish him, either for treason or for
involvement in the Lincoln assassination conspiracy.

Over the next few months Holt's hands continued to be tied as the
problem of what to do about Jefferson Davis grew even more complex and perplexing in light of the escalating tensions between Johnson and the Republican-led Congress. Meanwhile, observing these
developments from his cell at Fort Jefferson, Samuel Mudd shrewdly

recognized the possible implications of the conflict for his own future. Aware that his wife, Sarah, had begun to lobby Johnson for her husband's release, Mudd warned her in a letter to exercise caution. He agreed with her that any hope for an early release lay with the President, but he instructed Sarah to avoid making any public remarks that might serve to focus the Radicals' negative attention on his particular situation. "Be careful," Mudd counseled, "lest you produce an antagonism which certainly will not tend to shorten my stay at this woeful place."[22]

Throughout the first months of the new year, Congress's Joint Committee on Reconstruction began to gather evidence from a range of sources concerning the political situation in the South, especially that of freedpeople and of Unionists living within the borders of the former Confederacy. Most of the evidence that came before the committee mirrored the contents of T. H. Duval's December letter to Holt, indicating that unrepentant former rebels were fearlessly flexing their political muscles, strengthening their local Democratic parties and the former planters' hold on local government machinery, and tyrannizing the former slaves and their allies.

In response to this information, the Joint Committee concluded that it had indeed become necessary to take drastic steps to nullify the Johnson plan for the South and replace it with one more likely to effect the former Confederacy's submission to Northern (not to mention Radical Republican) rule. This in turn meant compelling the region's adherence to a plan that offered greater justice for the freedpeople, including suffrage for black men. If the committee expected Johnson to yield easily on the question, they were of course mistaken. As would soon become clear, rather than seeking some sort of compromise with the Joint Committee—or even with the more moderate Republicans in Congress, simply in order to ensure that in the end the Radicals' agenda would not hold sway— Johnson prepared to dig in his heels. This meant becoming a better friend than ever to precisely those leading lights within the former Confederacy, and his own resurgent Democratic Party, whom the Radicals sought to hold in check.

Even loyal Johnson supporter Gideon Welles wondered whether

the President was moving too fast toward reconciliation with certain elements of Southern society. On January 31 Welles noted in his diary that "a large number of the denizens of Washington who have not heretofore been visitors and whose sympathies and former associations were with the Rebels" had attended an official reception hosted by Welles's wife. "So many who have been distant and reserved were present" at the reception, Welles wrote, that they aroused "her suspicions, and led her to ask if I [as Johnson's ally] was not conceding too much."²³ To those on both ends of the Reconstruction debate who had initially held out some hope for it, compromise was coming to seem impossible.

And indeed, as winter gave way to spring in 1866, Johnson and the Radical Republicans (increasingly supported by moderates within the Republican Party who were growing tired of Johnson's obstinacy) established a pattern of attack and counterattack. In February, by recommendation of the Joint Committee on Reconstruction, Congress passed a bill to extend the life of the Freedmen's Bureau and to confirm the freedpeople's possession, at least for three more years, of the abandoned and confiscated lands they had been allowed to occupy. President Johnson vetoed this bill, explicitly rejecting the notion that the federal government was in any way responsible for the freedpeople's welfare. On March 13, Congress passed a civil rights bill, which for the first time granted the former slaves citizenship, permitted them to rent or own property, guaranteed them the right to make and enforce contracts, and opened the nation's court system to them as plaintiffs as well as witnesses. (Significantly, the bill did not enfranchise the former slaves, or require desegregation of schools and public accommodations.) On March 27, Johnson vetoed this bill as well, once again arguing explicitly against federal protection of blacks' civil rights, and even going so far as to suggest that guaranteeing civil rights to the freedpeople somehow undermined the civil rights of white Americans.

Then, on April 2, Johnson proclaimed unilaterally (and apparently without even consulting his cabinet) that the rebellion was at an end, except in Texas, and that the other Southern states were once more full members of the federal Union, and as such there was no longer any reason for a military occupation of the South. (Texas was restored under the Johnson plan in August.) Congress denounced the proclamation, and on April 9 the legislators successfully overrode the President's veto of the civil rights bill, which they had been unable to do in the case of the Freedmen's Bureau bill in February. (A somewhat revised Freedmen's Bureau bill would pass over Johnson's veto in July.) "All of Stanton's pets" in Congress, wrote an embittered Welles in his diary the next day, "were active in opposing the veto," and although "not a word escaped the President to-day on the subject, it was evident he felt deeply" the sting of his defeat. It is worth noting that historians consider both the original Freedmen's Bureau bill and the civil rights bill to have been expressions of the moderate rather than the Radical Republican viewpoint. As such, Johnson's harsh repudiation of the bills says a great deal about the limitations of his vision for the postwar South, and his unwillingness to work even with the moderates in the Republican Party.[24]

The increasingly acrimonious battle between Congress and the President for control over the process and the outcome of Reconstruction had many consequences. Significantly, the conflict only further obstructed the ability of Holt and others to pursue their goal of punishing leading Confederates—at least Jefferson Davis!—for their crimes against the nation. Even justifying the continued incarceration of those already convicted became somewhat more difficult, and in such a climate, supporters of Samuel Mudd and his cell mates at Fort Jefferson grew bolder again in their efforts to press the case for a pardon. On February 18, Jere Dyer, Mudd's brother-in-law, wrote to Sarah Mudd about a long meeting that John Ford, owner of the theater where the assassination had occurred, had recently had with the President. Dyer reported that the interview seemed to bode well for all four prisoners, but especially for Mudd. According to John Ford, previously Edman Spangler's employer and still his loyal advocate, the President had given "every assurance he would release Sam at the earliest moment he could consistently do so," remarking that Mudd "was a mere creature of accident" whose imprisonment was unjust.

Still, Johnson warned Ford that releasing Mudd and the others would require time, since "in the present state of political excitement he did not think it prudent . . . to take any action, as it would be another pretext for the radicals to build capital on."[25]

Meanwhile, at the Bureau of Military Justice, Holt remained on alert for any indications of a possible breakthrough in favor of his agenda, at least with regard to the case against Jefferson Davis. Not unlike Johnson, Holt refused to back down. At the end of March, he wrote Stanton that more new evidence against Davis and Clay had come in to the Bureau, linking them both directly to the assassination plot. Holt urged the secretary of war to agree (despite Attorney General Speed's advice to Johnson) to have the men tried before a military commission after all, and he reiterated his position that only a military commission—which he himself would undoubtedly oversee—was truly "competent to ascertain and pass upon the guilt of these men."[26] It is clear from this letter that Holt was as aware as anyone that the opportunity for bringing Davis or Clay (or any former Confederates, for that matter) before a military court was rapidly fading. He, too, had heard the rumors—confirmed on April 2—that the President was preparing to proclaim the war completely at an end. Time was of the essence, and Holt strove to act quickly before his time ran out.

When Johnson proclaimed the end of the war on April 2, he officially threw the question of the propriety of military commissions altogether—and the future of Holt's Bureau of Military Justice—up in the air. "The proclamation of the President is unofficially before me," wrote Major General Charles R. Woods to Joseph Holt from his post in Mobile, Alabama, on April 4. "I have several cases ready and pending against citizens before commissions. Shall I proceed with or suspend them . . . ? Please advise me what course I shall pursue." Uncertain, Holt forwarded Woods's inquiry to Stanton. "It was," Stanton expressed to a friend, "additional evidence of the politicians' willingness to sacrifice the best interests of the Army," which needed the civil government's support to sustain it while on occupation duty. "Only if Johnson could resurrect the 300,000 Union dead," Stanton wrote angrily, would the nation accept it. On the following day Stanton fashioned a more diplomatic response to Major General Woods: the President's proclamation should not be understood to "invalidate" current proceedings, but rather to show "the President's purpose to dispense with such tribunals to the utmost possible extent consistent with the public peace and welfare" and rely instead on the "appropriate action of civil authorities." As much as possible, but only in accordance with the judgment of the local military commander, Stanton continued, should cases that were now pending be "transferred to the civil authorities or discharged."[27]

Stanton's advice to Woods almost certainly went beyond what Johnson himself would have offered. Clearly Stanton was digging in his own heels on the side of the Radical Republicans, having become less and less convinced that Johnson's policies toward the postwar South deserved his—or the military's—support. At the same time, Johnson had already reached the conclusion that Stanton and Joseph Holt were not to be trusted. As a result, Johnson declined to contribute further, in any meaningful way, to Holt's efforts to punish Jefferson Davis and the rest of the Confederate leadership. On February 1, 1866, Johnson confided to Gideon Welles that he "wished to put no more in Holt's control than was absolutely necessary," for he had come to believe "that Holt was cruel and remorseless, made so perhaps by his employment and investigations," and that "his tendencies and conclusions were very bloody." Noted Welles, "I have never heard him express himself so decidedly in regard to Holt, but have on one or two previous occasions perceived that his confidence in the Judge-Advocate-General was shaken."[28]

Although it is unlikely that Holt had received explicit word of Johnson's loss of confidence, he probably would not have been surprised by it. Regardless, by early April he considered it more urgent than ever that the Bureau of Military Justice go after Jefferson Davis with or without Johnson's official endorsement, even though the likelihood of achieving a satisfying judgment against him (or Clay, or even the fugitive Surratt) had come to seem remote. Holt was well aware that yet another important development in Washington threatened to obstruct the path to justice even further. On April 3—just one day after the President declared the Civil War over—the U.S. Supreme Court issued its preliminary opinion in the case *ex parte* Milligan. This case appealed the 1864 conviction of Copperhead Lambdin Milligan by a military commission, presided over by Holt's assistant Judge Advocate Henry Burnett, at a time when Milligan was a civilian, the civil courts had been in operation, and "a state of war did not exist" in Indiana. The Supreme Court's preliminary opinion (final opinions were handed down in December) repudiated the use of a military commission in Milligan's case, arguing that "a citizen, not connected with the military service, and resident in a State where the courts are all open, and in the proper exercise of their jurisdiction, cannot, even when the privilege of habeas corpus is suspended, be tried, convicted or sentenced otherwise than by the ordinary courts of law." As such, the Court ordered that Milligan (among others) be discharged from custody. Nine days later, on April 12, Milligan walked out of the Ohio State Penitentiary in Columbus a free man.[29]

Holt was hardly alone in his distress over the Supreme Court's preliminary opinion in *ex parte* Milligan. In the eyes of the congressional Radicals, the Court's opinion—like the virtually simultaneous announcement by the President that the war was over—threatened to undermine the revised Reconstruction program they were developing to supersede Johnson's program, and that they were hoping to institute as soon as possible. The implementation of such a program, which would among other things establish martial law in the former Confederacy until its compliance with congressionally dictated terms for Reconstruction was fully assured, required that all relevant parties—rulers and ruled—admit that a state of war still existed. This in turn would justify the use of arms to enforce the laws and the use of military courts to try offenders. Johnson's declaration of peace and the Supreme Court's decision in *ex parte* Milligan had entirely the opposite effect.

In practical terms the Supreme Court's opinion struck a severe blow to Joseph Holt's agenda. Holt clearly believed that military commissions were appropriate, and also supremely efficient, in the context of war, as well as in the current situation, where a meaning-

ful peace remained quite elusive. The Court's decision made the convening of military commissions for any purposes virtually impossible.
Moroever, the decision added new fuel to the fire being stoked by
those who criticized the trial of the Lincoln assassination conspirators, and the treatment they (especially Mary Surratt) had received as
a consequence of the commissioners' judgment. Such critics' underlying motives varied, but there were many for whom the trial itself
smacked too much of vengeance toward the former Confederacy. The
Supreme Court's decision also further encouraged the convicted conspirators at Fort Jefferson to envision their own releases in the not too
distant future—for instance, Samuel Mudd declared himself "much
delighted." He also rejoiced over news of the President's veto of the
civil rights bill and his April 2 proclamation of peace.[30]

Of primary importance to Holt at this point was the impact of the
Court's decision on the possibility that Davis, Clay, or John Surratt
would ever be tried before a military tribunal under the Bureau's and
his supervision. Indeed, only two weeks after the Supreme Court's
opinion became public, Clement Clay was released on parole from
Fortress Monroe on the sole condition that he swear his allegiance to
the United States and give his word "to conduct himself as a loyal citizen of the same."[31]

Other military prisoners whom Holt had been keeping his eyes on
were freed, without trial, in short order. The famed Confederate
raider Raphael Semmes, who had "made it his business to rob and
destroy the ships and property" of Northern merchants, had been
arrested in December 1865 and brought to Washington for trial. On
a number of occasions since Semmes's capture, Secretary of the Navy
Welles had pointed out that the President might have something to
gain, politically, from pursuing a stern course against Semmes, in the
same way that Johnson's refusal explicitly to show mercy to Jefferson
Davis could be used politically to obscure his generosity toward the
white South as a whole. "I told him," Welles explained to his diary
on February 21, "I thought it a good opportunity to show that he was
ready to bring criminals to trial when the duty devolved on him."
Instead, Johnson chose to delay the Semmes case. Then, on April 7,
he allowed the raider to walk free, just four days after the publication

of the Supreme Court's decision in *ex parte* Milligan, a day after Alexander Stephens, the former vice president of the Confederacy, made a stunning appearance at General and Mrs. Ulysses S. Grant's final public reception of the season, and ten days before the release of Clement Clay.[32]

Judge Advocate General Holt was infuriated by the growing number of head-on and seemingly irrefutable challenges to his attempts to bring the former Confederacy's leadership and their flunkies to account for their war crimes. Meanwhile, he received a directive via Stanton from the Judiciary Committee. Chairman James F. Wilson, requested "such evidence as may be in your Department" pertaining to Davis's (and Clay's) complicity in the assassination conspiracy, including "copies of such reports of the Judge-Advocate-General concerning the said complicity of said parties as may be in your possession." The roots of Wilson's request lay in a resolution passed by the Joint Committee on Reconstruction, which had been submitted by George Boutwell of Massachusetts, one of the most radical Republicans in Congress. Boutwell's resolution urged that the details in Davis's case be sorted out quickly in order to expedite his trial.[33]

It is likely that Holt initially saw in the Judiciary Committee's request some cause for optimism: while the President and the Supreme Court were busy undermining his prosecution of the nation's archenemies, the legislature showed signs of standing firm. Even Samuel Mudd recognized this development. Frustrated that the Supreme Court's decision in *ex parte* Milligan had failed to result in the immediate release of himself, O'Laughlen, Arnold, and Spangler, and certain that lawyers Thomas Ewing Jr. and Frederick Stone were "doing nothing" on the men's behalf, Mudd grumbled to his wife: "I expect nothing will be done toward our relief until after the adjournment of Congress."[34] Meanwhile, Holt duly gathered together his evidence against Davis and Clay, and prepared to testify before the Judiciary Committee.

Holt appeared before the committee on April 13 and 14, 1866.[35] Recalling the tragic events exactly a year before, Holt explained to the members of the Judiciary Committee that even before the trial of the conspirators began, he had heard enough verbal testimony to cause him to suspect Davis, Clay, and other Confederate leaders of complicity in the assassination plot, and as such had urged Andrew Johnson to issue his original May 1865 proclamation indicting them. The conspiracy trial itself, Holt went on, had produced additional testimony indicating these same men's involvement in the plot and, once that trial was over, Holt had felt bound to follow up. With Secretary Stanton's approval and the assistance of a number of "agents of intelligence," Holt had pursued the investigation, generating enough additional evidence by January 1866 to produce a full report for the secretary of war. The evidence he had compiled over time from depositions given by Sanford Conover and his witnesses, Holt noted, "would impress any court with its truthfulness"; moreover, it proved Davis's guilt conclusively, if not also the guilt of the others named in Johnson's proclamation. To the question of whether he believed Johnson's very recent declaration of peace should have any effect on the sort of trial to which Davis would be subjected, Holt rather boldly and defiantly replied that as far as he was concerned, his orders came not from the President but from Stanton, and that he himself still supported a military trial for the Confederacy's former leader. Holt then presented to the committee for their review the full complement of communications (letters and telegrams) between Sanford Conover and himself pertaining to Conover's investigations, dating back to July 1865.[36]

Over the next few weeks the Judiciary Committee continued its hearings as the battle for control of Reconstruction raged on. Most notably, on April 30, 1866, the Joint Committee on Reconstruction submitted to Congress a draft of the Fourteenth Amendment to the Constitution, much of which had been crafted by Holt's associate in the 1865 conspiracy trial, John Bingham. Among other things, the proposed amendment disfranchised a significant proportion of the former Confederate leadership, and at the same time guaranteed citizenship and equality before the law to the former slaves. "The Central Directory," wrote Gideon Welles derisively of the Joint Committee, "have submitted their plan of Reconstruction, which means division for four years longer at least." Having unburdened himself to his diary, Welles also expressed his vehement opposition to the proposed amendment in a subsequent cabinet meeting. "I said that I was not in favor of any Constitutional Amendment in the present condition of the country," Welles recalled, and "that I knew not what right Congress had to pass amnesty laws or prescribe terms to the States." According to Welles, Secretary Stanton responded angrily that, as far as he could tell, the secretary of the navy (and, by extension, Johnson) was "opposed to any terms with Congress," and furthermore "had not only fifteen-inch guns leveled against Congress, but was for running [his] prow into them."[37]

By fashioning some of their key principles for Reconstruction into an amendment to the Constitution, congressional Republicans (moderates and Radicals) strove to avoid having to contend with a presidential veto. At the same time, the legislators placed their faith in the fairness of the (largely Northern) public, whose votes in special state conventions would constitute the bulk of those necessary to add the Fourteenth Amendment to the Constitution (this had been the case with the Thirteenth Amendment abolishing slavery, which had been ratified in December). By adopting this strategy, the legislators left to Johnson only the right to express his opinion on the proposed amendment, a right that he exploited vigorously, but to no avail. By June 13, both houses of Congress had passed the Fourteenth Amendment, and on the twenty-second, an enraged and temporarily weakened Johnson was compelled by law to transmit it to the states for their consideration.[38]

Pleased with these developments, Holt nevertheless was bound to focus on the case against Davis and his own testimony before the House Judiciary Committee. At his urging, the committee interviewed Sanford Conover and a number of the individuals he had produced as witnesses over the last few months. The committee also interviewed Francis Lieber, now chief of the Archive Office of the War Department. Lieber reported on his efforts to find evidence linking Davis to the assassination plot in the Confederacy's official records. "So far," he admitted, "we have not discovered offers of assassination except of a general character," though he fully anticipated finding some eventually. The committee also sounded out Attorney General Speed about the sort of trial Davis should face; he responded, as he had to Johnson in January, that a civil trial for treason, whenever Virginia's courts permitted it, was called for. If not entirely encouraging to Holt, the Judiciary Committee's inquiries at this point must have nevertheless seemed fair and thus not particularly *dis*couraging.[39]

By early May, however, while the debate over the Fourteenth Amendment was just getting under way in the shadow of a deadly race riot in Memphis, the House Judiciary Committee's efforts produced some very disturbing results.[40] On May 8, Conover witness William Campbell admitted not only that he had been operating under an alias (his true name was Joseph Hoare), but also that the deposition he had given to Joseph Holt the past November was completely false. "I was informed by Mr. Conover," Hoare told the Committee, "that Judge Holt had offered a reward of $100,000 for the capture of Jefferson Davis, that he had no authority really to do it, that now Jefferson Davis was taken they had not enough against him to justify them in what they had done, [and] that Judge Holt wanted to get witnesses to prove that Davis was interested in the assassination of Prest. Lincoln so as to justify him in paying the $100,000 reward." Asked if he had received some compensation for making his deposition in November, Hoare admitted that he had been paid by Holt only for his expenses ($625), though he added that he had been led by Conover (*not* by Holt) to expect something more. Hoare then said that he was not the only witness against Davis produced by Conover who had—with Conover's knowledge—given Holt false testimony under a false name. Hoare further informed the committee that Sanford Conover's true name was Charles Dunham. Later that same day, Conover himself confirmed Hoare's revelation and went on to share other details of his own rather slippery past, though he insisted that his reasons for sustaining the alias (in fact, a pseudonym he had used as Canadian correspondent for the *New York Tribune*) were honorable. Shortly after his examination before the Judiciary Committee, Sanford Conover—who was not under arrest at the time—returned to New York, and disappeared.[41]

As the Judiciary Committee's investigations continued through May and into early June, to Holt's horror and dismay, other Conover

witnesses came forward to confirm Hoare's accusations and to confess their own duplicity. The committee also solicited testimony from
James H. Fowle, formerly of the Confederate secret service, who
seemed to have turned state's evidence. Although he spoke freely of
such matters as John Surratt Jr.'s involvement in Confederate espi-
onage, Fowle insisted that the Confederate leadership would never
have countenanced a plot such as Booth's, and would indeed have
had him arrested had they been aware of what he was up to.[42]

The committee also interviewed Colonel L. C. Turner, whom Holt
had sent to New York as a special judge advocate in late April to
locate Conover and his witnesses and bring them back to Washington. While in New York, Turner had learned much about the aliases
and shady pasts of Conover and his associates. Louis Weichmann
appeared as well. Mary Surratt's former boarder, who had been a key
witness at the assassination conspiracy trial, offered little new information, although he "corrected" a few significant dates in the story
he had presented the previous summer. As he had done before, Weichmann took the opportunity to assert his own innocence, and to reem-
phasize "conclusively the guilt of Mrs. Surratt."[43]

On June 18, an angry and deeply humiliated Joseph Holt returned
to face the committee. He struggled to explain why he had ever put
any confidence in Sanford Conover, or his witnesses. As calmly as
possible, Holt restated and reaffirmed his original reasons for believing that Davis, Clay, and the others named in Johnson's May 1865
proclamation were indeed guilty of complicity with Booth. Holt
explained that he had learned about Conover in the first place from
Conover's former employer at the *Tribune*, a Mr. Gay, whom he
described as "a citizen of well known character for loyalty and
integrity." Moreover, Holt insisted,

> There was nothing in the previous history of Sanford Conover
> . . . to excite any distrust either in his integrity, in his truthful-
> ness, or in the sincerity with which he had made his propositions
> to the Government that led to his being employed as an agent for
> the collection of the testimony which was supposed to exist in

reference to the assassination of the President. On the contrary, there was much in his intelligence, which was marked & striking, and his apparent frankness and his known connection with important sources of information, to inspire faith in his professions and promises.[44]

At the conspiracy trial, Holt testified, Conover had proven that he "possessed unusual opportunities for acquiring information" concerning the "plans and movements" of the "rebel refugees and conspirators in Canada." Unfortunately, the fact that during the same trial Conover had also proven his willingness to engage in outright perjury seems to have left little impression on the judge advocate general. Rather, Holt appears to have been blinded by a dangerous mix of his own unrelenting honesty, which often made it difficult to question the honesty of others, and his fierce determination to prove Davis's guilt. Thus, when the already problematic Conover had contacted him in late July 1865, "alleging the existence of testimony implicating Davis and others and of his ability to find the witnesses, & profferring his services to do so," Holt had accepted "his statements and proposals as made in good faith and entitled to credit and consideration." With funds placed at his disposal by Secretary Stanton, Holt had set Conover loose; subsequently he had received Conover's evidence with open arms and little if any skepticism. It is difficult to avoid the conclusion that Holt's desire to prove Davis's guilt had overtaken his usually sound—if stern—judgment. Looking back, even he himself was forced to admit that his confidence in Conover's evidence was greatly "strengthened by my knowledge that it was in accord with and seemed to be, in a large degree, a natural sequence from other facts which had been testified to as having occurred in Canada by witnesses known to the Government and whose reputation has not been and cannot, it is believed, be successfully assailed."[45]

Even as Holt defended his relationship with Conover, he now knew that he had allowed himself to be duped. Still, he insisted to the Judiciary Committee that he could not understand why Conover would engage in such an awful scam, because the man had certainly not been promised a reward for such deception. "I employed him under no contract for any stipulated compensation," Holt declared emphatically. "He had no reason from me to believe that he would receive more for his labor in the event of his success, than in the event of his failure to discover the testimony which he alleged existed."[46] Still, Holt could hardly fail to recognize how much what could now be called the "Conover fiasco" had damaged his case against Davis and the others. He also had to confront the fact that his own proud reputation had been sorely, perhaps irrevocably, tarnished. As his June 18 interview before the Judiciary Committee wound down, Holt personally urged his interrogators to disregard all of the evidence associated with Conover and his witnesses in the case against Jefferson Davis.[47]

Over the next couple of weeks, Holt prepared for Edwin Stanton a detailed report that covered all his dealings with Conover, including their communications since July 1865, as well as letters Holt had received over the months from some of Conover's witnesses. In this report, filed almost exactly a year after the execution of the four convicted conspirators, Holt described the results of the Judiciary Committee's investigations and reiterated his own recommendations. Still, as he had also done before the committee, in closing Holt reasserted his belief in Davis's complicity in the assassination conspiracy, a faith he insisted was supported by an abundance of "other oral and written proofs," in addition to the findings of the military commissioners in the previous summer's trial of the eight conspirators.[48]

As Holt's troubles mounted, Davis, in contrast, was finding signs of hope. At Virginia's Fortress Monroe, his privileges were upgraded again. As of April 26, Andrew Johnson had granted permission for Davis's wife, Varina, to visit him regularly, which she began to do the following week, bringing him a steady supply of good food. Davis was also permitted to move around the prison grounds more freely and to take more exercise. Before long, Varina was actually living at the fort with her husband, and the two were known on occasion to entertain dinner guests in their spacious apartment, with whom they offered toasts to the Confederate dead. Meanwhile, down at Fort Jef-

ferson orders arrived in late July to improve conditions for the convicted Lincoln assassins, so that they might be subject only to "such
punishments as warranted by the condition" of their sentences.[49]

By the late summer of 1866, a beleaguered Joseph Holt seriously
doubted that he could save his case against Jefferson Davis. The damage to the case sustained during the Judiciary Committee's spring
investigations was severe, although it must be noted that the committee ultimately decided to recommend Davis for trial anyway. To
complicate matters further, Representative Andrew Rogers of New
Jersey issued an inflammatory minority report on the Judiciary Committee's findings. Rogers's report, which soon became public,
amounted to a "bitter indictment of Holt's conduct and motives in
relation to the whole conspiracy as well as a challenge to the jurisdiction of the military commission" that had tried the original assassination conspirators. Simultaneously, Holt's fear that the Bureau of
Military Justice would be dismantled now showed signs of being fulfilled. On July 9 the Senate began to debate the possibility of abolishing the Bureau, or at least dramatically reducing its staff, although
the records of approximately 5,000 cases still awaited Holt's final dispensation.[50] For these reasons, Holt had to admit that it was highly
unlikely Davis would ever come before a military commission.
Equally disappointing was the knowledge that if Davis came before a
civil court for treason, Holt would play no official role in the proceedings, and could hope for only limited influence from the side-
lines. Still, a guilty verdict in any venue would provide a measure of
satisfaction.

However, even the possibility of Davis's being tried on a charge of
treason was growing more remote every day, as questions concerning
the location and jurisdiction for such a civil trial remained open, as
sympathy for Davis grew (even in some sectors of the Northern population), and as new concerns were raised about the legitimacy of
Davis's lengthy incarceration without trial, especially in light of the
release on parole of most of his leading associates. Also contributing
to a shift in popular attitudes about Davis was the appearance that
summer of a book entitled *Prison Life of Jefferson Davis*, written by
Johnson supporter and Democrat Charles G. Halpine, but credited to

one of Davis's own doctors; it claimed to expose the extremity of Davis's physical suffering at the hands of his merciless federal captors. By mid-1866, even editor Horace Greeley of the New York Tribune began to use his newpaper's pages to wage a public campaign for Davis's release on bail if he could not be brought to trial soon.[51]

As Holt struggled to come to grips with the fact that his plans regarding Davis would not come to fruition, he grieved as well over the battering his own reputation for honesty, integrity, and fair dealing had taken in recent months. There were, of course, scores of supporters who stood by the judge advocate general and the Bureau of Military Justice without a hint of reservation, even in the wake of the Judiciary Committee's hearings. Among them was Senator Henry S. Lane of Indiana, who attested during the Senate's debate over the continuation of the Bureau to the enviable and "proud historic record" expected someday to "shed a halo of glory around the name of General Holt—a noble man; a patriot; an exception in the midst of his traitorous compeers." Three weeks earlier, a Louisiana correspondent had sent Holt an editorial from the local Republican Party newspaper, the Crescent, which had similarly sung Holt's praises. "I thought it might be pleasant," wrote Holt's friend, "for you to know how much you are loved by the official paper of the state of Louisiana."[52]

Such letters of support brought Holt a measure of solace to be sure. It should come as no surprise, however, that Andrew Johnson's supporters both North and South took advantage of every possible opportunity to damage Holt's reputation further. As early as February Gideon Welles had already begun to express his own doubts about Holt in his diary. "I long since was aware," Welles wrote, "that Holt was severe and unrelenting, and am further compelled to think that . . . he has strange weaknesses. He is credulous and often the dupe of his own imaginings. Believes men guilty on shadowy suspicions, and is ready to condemn them without trial."[53] In response to a growing chorus of criticism, a portion of which appeared in the national press, Holt's supporters displayed their outrage. "I read a number of the rebel deviltries respecting you & felt for them unutterable scorn," wrote his friend Theodore Bell from Louisville. "But for the seething cauldron which Andrew Johnson has set to boiling and fuming, these attacks would have been totally unworthy of notice."[54]

It bears noting that to attack Holt—as Montgomery Blair had done the previous year—was to attack, albeit obliquely, those individuals with whom he was most closely identified, specifically Edwin Stanton. By extension it was also to attack the Radical Republicans' agenda for Reconstruction. Holt himself recognized this. In virtually the same breath with which he struggled to defend his reputation, Holt acknowledged that Johnson's policies for the postwar South had grave implications beyond those relevant to his own (Holt's) future place in the history books. In an August 1, 1866, letter written in the immediate wake of the Conover fiasco, Holt bemoaned the fact that Andrew Johnson "had unleashed 'the barbarism of the rebellion in its renaissance.'" Here he referred explicitly to the second costly race riot to take place in Johnson's supposedly "reconstructed" South, which had occurred in July in New Orleans and which had resulted in the murder of thirty-four blacks and three of their white allies.[55]

In contrast, in his diary Gideon Welles called the New Orleans riot the logical conclusion of the efforts of the Radicals in Congress, and their allies such as Holt, to foment trouble in the South in order to overturn Presidential Reconstruction altogether. "It is part of a deliberate conspiracy and was to be the commencement of a series of bloody affrays through the States lately in rebellion. . . . There is a determination," Welles added, "to involve the country in civil war if necessary, to secure Negro suffrage in the States and Radical ascendancy in the General Government." Welles pointed a particularly damning finger at Secretary of War Stanton, whom he described as "complicated with, if not a prime mover in, the New Orleans difficulties. . . ." Welles at least had the grace to condemn the riot, though his analysis of its origins was grossly misguided. Others' responses bordered on the perverse. To his brother Tom, Samuel Mudd actually expressed pleasure over the news of the riot: "I have been led to believe," he wrote from prison, "the whole South exterminated, or reduced to abject slavery, until news of the recent riot reached us. I am grieved at the occurrence, the loss of valuable lives, but proud to know there is manhood enough left among the people to rebuke the oppression of the interventionists."⁵⁶ From Mudd and Welles to Holt and Stanton, individuals on both ends of the Reconstruction debate quite reasonably believed that a renewed national crisis was at hand.

Nevertheless, being under public attack remained of pressing importance to Holt in early September 1866. As he bitterly noted to a correspondent, a "base endeavor" that had begun with Andrew Rogers's minority report was now under way in the "disloyal press of the country, acting in the interests of Jefferson Davis and the rebellion and in cooperation with Sanford Conover to impress the public mind with the belief" that he, Holt, had not only been duped but in fact had solicited—and perhaps even funded—false testimony in the Davis case. The suggestion was also made that Holt had tried to cover up Conover's chicanery rather than exposing it as soon as it began to be known. Rumors to this effect seem to have appeared first in the *New York Herald* late in the summer, after which they were reprinted by other newspapers around the nation.⁵⁷

Also published was the suggestion that because Conover had testified so problematically at the conspiracy trial in 1865, perhaps Holt had solicited his false testimony then as well, and maybe even the false testimony of other witnesses, too. Seeking to dispel such rumors, Holt urged his assistant Colonel L. C. Turner to provide him with a letter of support for republication, explaining what Turner knew about Conover's trickery and that of his witnesses. Turner readily obliged, adding his own reassurances that, "in my judgment, the base calumnies with which traitors, confessed perjurers and suborners, are pursuing you are as preposterous as atrocious, and will result in increasing instead of lessening the enduring confidence of all true-hearted and honest-minded men in your eminent fidelity and faithfulness as a governmental officer, and your undoubted loyalty as a citizen."⁵⁸

Even Holt's brother Robert, with whom relations continued to be tense since war's end, wrote from Yazoo City, Mississippi, to express his regret at seeing Joseph maligned in public for any reason. Robert urged his brother to fight back, if only to defend the family's honor.

"I write you this with some hesitation," Robert said at the end of August 1866, "because I have understood that I no longer hold my former position in your esteem & affections, and feel that I may subject myself to misapprehension and rebuff." Still, Robert yearned to demonstrate his support, and although he allowed a hint of reproach to cloud his otherwise sympathetic tone—such attacks, Robert noted, were the logical result of Joseph's position in the federal government—what mattered in the end was that he wrote at all.[59] To the deeply troubled judge advocate general, Robert's words must have provided some consolation, as did the many other letters of support and encouragement he received.

Still, it was far from being enough, and on September 11, Holt dispatched a letter of both outrage and anguish to Secretary Stanton. Holt acknowledged the rumors and accusations being circulated about his "official integrity and conduct" as judge advocate general, denied them all as "utterly false and groundless," and then requested that Stanton convene a formal "court of inquiry, composed of officers of high rank and national reputation" to examine the charges and give their opinions.[60]

Around the same time—in much the same way as he had done in the wake of Montgomery Blair's attacks on his prewar record the previous year, and against the advice of a number of supporters, who thought it was both unnecessary and potentially counterproductive— Holt revised for publication and wide distribution the July 3 report he had filed with Stanton concerning the Conover debacle.[61] This, too, produced a stack of letters of support, including one from his longtime associate and colleague Henry Burnett, who summed up the feelings of many when he wrote on September 13 that "the crowning glory of your great life, history will record, was the part you performed in the suppression of this rebellion from the beginning to the close." Of the work Holt and Stanton had struggled to perform since before the war had even begun, Burnett continued loyally:

When the patriotic people of this country cease to remember, that you and he in the beginning grappled almost single handed with the leaders of the rebellion and hurled them from their high

places, and tore loose the fangs they had fastened on the very life
arteries of the Government, when they cease to remember this
and all your great services to the country they will cease to love
liberty or their native land.

Burnett urged his former boss not to pay so much heed to the attacks
on his reputation, and not to dignify them with any further response.
"I have yet to hear," Burnett remarked kindly, "the first man of any
character, loyal or disloyal, speak of this thing except with utter contempt. Not even your enemies, who have any respect for themselves,
have ever uttered a word against your high character for truth, and
your incorruptible official and private integrity."[62]

On the same day that Burnett wrote his letter to Holt, the Union
League of Philadelphia awarded the judge advocate general their sil-
ver medal, "as a mark of their respect and a testimonial of their
appreciation of your gallantry and distinguished services to our
Country in the most perilous days of her history." Not long after, having submitted to Johnson the request for a court of inquiry, Secretary
Stanton informed Holt that the President, too, was "entirely satisfied" with his "honesty and fidelity," and that there was therefore no
need for such a court or any other form of official vindication.
Regardless of his actual policies toward the former Confederacy, it is
clear that Johnson was still dependent for his own credibility on
appearing to support a punitive stance toward Davis and the white
South. In any case, in November Stanton followed up with an official
letter to Holt expressing his own personal regard and his strong faith
that the rumors and charges concerning Holt's professional conduct
over the past eighteen months were "entirely groundless." "So far as
I have any knowledge or information," Stanton wrote with respect,
"your official duties, as Judge-Advocate-General, in the cases referred
to and in all others, have been performed fairly, justly and with distinguished ability, integrity and patriotism, and in strict conformity
with the requirements of your high office and the obligations of an
officer and a gentleman."[63]

Around this time, Sanford Conover was found and arrested by

Holt's special judge advocate, Colonel L. C. Turner, brought to Washington, and indicted by the Judiciary Committee for lying under oath and for encouraging others to do the same. In February 1867 Conover was tried, found guilty, and sentenced to a steep ten years' imprisonment.[64]

The passions of the people are inflamed to war heat against the whole South indiscriminately, while kindness, toleration, and reason are discarded. . . . The great scheme of the Radicals is to inflict vengeance on the whole South . . . regardless of their legal and constitutional rights.

—SECRETARY OF THE NAVY GIDEON WELLES,
November 17, 1866[1]

We are looking with great interest and anxiety for some definite and final action by Congress in reference to the reconstruction of the states South. If they are to be permitted to stand as the President has fixed them up, with all their powers wielded by rebellious hands, as they now are, the result of the war will not prove a Union triumph.

—T. H. DUVAL TO JOSEPH HOLT,
January 23, 1867, from Texas[2]

The president was determined . . . to protect Southern whites from what he considered the horrors of complete racial equality.

—HANS L. TREFOUSSE, *Andrew Johnson* (1989)[3]

Lucky indeed it is for [John Surratt], the boon companion and alleged confidential confederate of J. Wilkes Booth, that his capture occurred after the declaration of peace and the withdrawal of martial law. Indeed, it may be seriously questioned if his successful elusion of pursuit during two years has not resulted in saving his life.

—*New York Times*, of John Surratt Jr., April 8, 1867

8

"A WELL-DRESSED AND
VERY PRESENTABLE YOUNG MAN"
THE TRIAL OF JOHN SURRATT JR.

AROUND THE TIME EDWIN STANTON WAS COMPOSING HIS NOVEMBER 1866 letter to Joseph Holt, reassuring the judge advocate general of his personal and professional respect and support, eligible Americans across the North went to the polls for the midterm elections in which they cast their ballots for those who would serve in the 40th Congress, which was scheduled to convene in December 1867. The elections resulted in a stunning victory for the Republican opposition to Andrew Johnson and its allies. "Was not the result of our elections invigorating?" wrote Holt's good friend Margaret Crosby from New York on November 30.[4] Surely Holt, too, felt encouraged, as were the majority of the members of the 39th Congress. When they reconvened a few days later following a four-month adjournment, the legislators rejoiced that the elections seemed to provide convincing evidence of Johnson's inability to muster sufficient support, at least within the Northern public, for his overly benevolent Reconstruction agenda.

The previous summer, Johnson and his allies had in fact attempted the formation of a new political coalition, dubbed the National Union, which held its first and only convention in Philadelphia in August. The movement was designed to bring together a diverse range of individuals and groups, including both Northern and Southern Democrats and disaffected, pro-Johnson Republicans, who held in common an opposition to the Fourteenth Amendment and to the broader plan for Reconstruction that the Radical Republicans were in the process of designing. The movement collapsed, however, when it became clear that in the newly elected 40th Congress anti-Johnson Republican numbers would so exceed those of Democrats as to guarantee that a presidential veto could be overridden at any time.[5]

Growth of Republican power in Congress also obviated the need for continuing the Joint Committee on Reconstruction after the 39th Congress disbanded, for it meant that debate on the details of Congressional Reconstruction would be limited. At least as encouraging, the midterm elections increased the influence of the Republican Party in every single Northern state as well as in West Virginia, Missouri, and Andrew Johnson's home state of Tennessee, which in July 1866 became the first Confederate state to ratify the Fourteenth Amendment and thus, rather ironically, the first to regain the legislators' approval of its representation in the United States Congress.[6]

Negative public opinion in the North toward Johnson had been reflected as well in the popular response to his pre-election campaign tour, the so-called Swing around the Circle, that Johnson had undertaken with Secretary of the Navy Gideon Welles, the now fully recovered Secretary of State William Seward, and General Ulysses Grant, who for the time being was playing his political cards close to his chest. On that tour, which was unprecedented for an American president, Johnson had spoken "freely, frankly, and plainly"—and to disastrous effect—about his hostility to the Fourteenth Amendment and the Radicals' vision of Reconstruction in general. Even Gideon Welles had quite legitimately worried that the President's brash, confrontational style would alienate many listeners. Welles feared that Johnson's lack of restraint in expressing his opinions would be "misapprehended and misrepresented, that the partisan press and partisan leaders would avail themselves of it and decry him."[7]

Welles was right to be concerned. Holt's friend Margaret Crosby called the President's behavior on the tour a "shocking abasement," far "too serious a wound" to be suffered kindly by Johnson's opponents. It hardly helped that the President, who was "used to the give-

and-take of the stump" from his earlier, less exalted career in Tennessee, responded in kind to hecklers. On one occasion, a member of the audience in Cleveland yelled out that the President should "hang Jeff Davis," to which Johnson reportedly replied: "Why not hang Thad Stevens," referring to one of his most powerful Radical opponents in Congress. On that same occasion, Johnson suggested that a hanging was also in order for Wendell Phillips, an avid abolitionist and now a staunch enthusiast of the Radicals' agenda. In the eyes of many observers, the tour amounted to a bold study in presidential humiliation, even if Johnson himself apparently never voiced a single regret.[8]

It is clear that by the end of 1866 Andrew Johnson and his program for restoring the Union swiftly, painlessly (for most whites anyway), and with virtually no protections for the freedpeople were a long way from being able to claim success. This is not to say that either Johnson or his agenda was defeated. Indeed, there was a good deal of fight left in the stubborn president, who had taken various steps over the past few months to guard his flanks. Among other things, Johnson had finally decided to do what Gideon Welles and others had been recommending for months: purge his top staff of adversaries. "The delicacies and proprieties which should govern the relations that are supposed to exist between a President and his Cabinet associates—his political family, as it were—would indicate to men of proper sensibility the course which they should pursue, if they did not agree with the person whom they were expected to advise in the administration of affairs," Welles had written in his diary on the first anniversary of Lincoln's assassination.[9] However, if they failed to resign on their own, Welles believed, Johnson should fire those cabinet officers who opposed him. Johnson had been reluctant to send his less supportive advisers packing, partly because even the least sympathetic members of the cabinet he had inherited represented a symbolic, legitimizing link between his administration and that of his martyred predecessor.

But as opposition to Johnson's Reconstruction policies grew more vehement and widespread, the President at last began to take Welles's advice. He had used cabinet members' attitudes toward the National

Union movement in the summer of 1866 as a litmus test. In this way Johnson forced Postmaster General William Dennison, Attorney General James Speed, and Secretary of the Interior James Harlan to resign. However, Secretary of War Edwin Stanton, Johnson's sternest and most fervent opponent in the cabinet, refused to quit. And, despite recommendations that he do so, Johnson declined for the time being to throw Stanton out.

He replaced the three departing Cabinet members with men sympathetic to his agenda who in turn employed their patronage power to good effect. Between July 28 and December 6, 1866, for example, the Postmaster General Alexander Randall replaced 1,655 Republican postmasters with Democrats.[10] Other jobs held by Republicans were in jeopardy. In October none other than Louis Weichmann wrote a series of letters to Holt complaining that he was about to lose his government job at the Philadelphia Customs House as a result of the rise of "democratic influence" in that city. Weichmann asked Holt to speak to the secretary of the treasury on his behalf, reminding him to refer only to Weichmann's services to the government at the conspiracy trial, but not to mention anything about party politics.[11]

In Attorney General James Speed's place, Andrew Johnson appointed Henry Stanbery of Ohio, who had already served Johnson's cause well by arguing for Lambdin Milligan before the U.S. Supreme Court. On December 17, 1866, the Court delivered its final statement in this case, which further pleased and encouraged Stanbery, Johnson, and Johnson's supporters, for it "unanimously concluded that martial law was unwarranted where civil courts functioned." As anticipated, the Court not only overturned Milligan's conviction but also cast into serious doubt the legitimacy of military commissions as a whole for trying civilians. The Court's opinion raised additional concerns about the legality and defensibility of any number of the Union army's actions over the past year and a half while serving as the primary agent of law enforcement in the occupied South.[12]

Perhaps not surprisingly, almost as if to prove that he was no friend of the freedpeople, Andrew Johnson dissolved several military commissions that were in place within the borders of the former Confed-

"Pardon and Franchise: Columbia: Shall I Trust these Men. . ."
and its companion, "And not this man?"
both from Harper's Weekly, *August 5, 1865*

eracy. In so doing, he undermined the capacity of a key mechanism that General Grant, as commander of the occupation forces, and the Freedmen's Bureau had employed on the freedpeople's behalf in situations where the civil courts seemed unprepared or disinclined to dispense justice. Taking note of Johnson's obvious willingness to exploit the Supreme Court's decision for a variety of purposes, one of Samuel Mudd's lawyers wrote encouragingly to Mudd's wife that she could now expect some positive developments in her husband's case. The Court's final decision, he wrote, "must secure the liberation of your husband," though he could not predict just when.[13]

As the 39th Congress prepared to convene for its second, "short" session, scheduled to last until its legal expiration on March 4, 1867, the Radical Republicans and those who supported their vision for the postwar South felt ambivalent. Although the November elections had augured extremely well for Republicans generally, those who opposed the President remained convinced of the need to continue devising new strategies to achieve their goals, for clearly the battle for control of Reconstruction was far from over. To this end, and in order to sustain momentum, in January 1867 the legislators passed a bill calling the 40th Congress into session immediately upon the expiration of the 39th (at noon on March 4, 1867), rather than in December. "Radicalism," groaned Gideon Welles to his diary, "desires a perpetual session to override the Executive. We are living in a revolutionary period."[14]

This was not all. Over Johnson's veto Congress passed a bill authorizing black male suffrage in Washington, D.C., for which it had the exclusive right to legislate, and limiting suffrage among formerly pro-Confederate whites residing in the District.[15] Even more dramatic, on January 7, Representative James M. Ashley of Ohio introduced a resolution "to inquire into Johnson's conduct as a preliminary to impeachment" in connection with Reconstruction. Ashley charged Johnson with "high crimes and misdemeanors, usurpation of power, corrupt usage of the appointing, pardoning, and veto power, corruption in disposing of the public property, and interference with elections." By this point, historian Brooks Simpson points out, "debates on how best to shape the postwar South in accordance with Republican principles were giving way to efforts to devise ways to handcuff the chief executive," in order to squelch his stubborn resistance to the Radicals' agenda once and for all. Once the House adopted Ashley's resolution by a party-line vote, it was referred to the Judiciary Committee for consideration. Welles wrote in his diary the next day: "The preliminary step having been taken, backed by strong party vote, the Radicals are committed. . . . It is a necessity for the Radicals to get rid of the President. Unless they do, they cannot carry out their plans of dwarfing the States under the torture of Reconstruction."[16]

Observers on all sides of the debate over Reconstruction were keenly alert to all of these ongoing developments. Not least among those who were paying close attention was Joseph Holt, who was also concerned with the increasing precariousness (proportional to his growing sympathy for the Radical agenda) of Edwin Stanton's hold on his post at the head of the War Department, which seemed like an essential precondition of Holt's own survival at the head of the Bureau of Military Justice. How in this political environment could Holt ever hope to resurrect, let alone complete, his badly tattered campaign to bring Jefferson Davis to justice, especially if Stanton was dismissed as secretary of war?

During the spring of 1866 Holt had banked on his awkward alliance with sympathetic, anti-Johnson Republicans in Congress to provide the additional support and momentum necessary to bring about his desired result in the case against the former Confederate President. Instead, the disastrous hearings before the House Judiciary Committee had deflated Holt's entire case by exposing key witness Sanford Conover's perjury. The hearings had led, moreover, to a significant and dispiriting diversion of Holt's time and energy into the effort to redeem his own reputation. Added to these obstacles now were such adverse developments as the Supreme Court's decision in *ex parte* Milligan, Stanton's growing alienation from Johnson, and the resurgence of many Radical Republicans' original inclination to forgo the targeted punishment of individual rebel leaders in favor of refashioning the South as a whole. Then, to complicate matters further still, on December 3, 1866, John Surratt Jr. was arrested in Egypt.[17]

That Surratt had resurfaced—again—on the other side of the Atlantic Ocean hardly came as a complete surprise to Holt. It will be recalled that Surratt had traveled to Rome, where in January 1866 he enlisted in the papal Zouave guard under the alias John Watson. Coincidentally, a young man named Henri Beaumont de Ste. Marie, who had known Surratt in his youth in Maryland (and who had met him again in Canada), was then also serving in the Vatican guard. Much as Vice Consul Henry Wilding had done back in Liverpool in October 1865, Ste. Marie now tried to alert the federal government that the fugitive had been located. On April 21, 1866, Ste. Marie wrote to inform the U.S. minister to Rome, former Union army general Rufus King, that not only had he spoken to Surratt, but that Surratt had confessed his complicity in the Lincoln assassination conspiracy. Two days later, Rufus King conveyed this news in a letter to Secretary of State Seward, who shared its contents with Holt (then bogged down in the House Judiciary Committee's hearings and the Conover crisis) and Stanton. By the end of May the three men had begun a protracted but not particularly productive discussion of what to do.[18]

The upshot of their communications was that, for the time being, they would do nothing. Meanwhile, well into the summer Rufus King in Rome continued to receive additional communications from Henri de Ste. Marie, whose own motives may have included a measure of patriotic sentiment, but were certainly also tainted by self-interest. Evidence suggests that as late as 1873, Ste. Marie was still trying to collect the balance of the $25,000 reward originally offered for Surratt's capture, but revoked in November 1865.[19] In any case, Rufus King duly passed the word on to the State Department that on more than one occasion, Ste. Marie claimed, Surratt had revealed a connection between the Lincoln assassination and the Confederate leadership in Richmond. At the same time, however, Ste. Marie made it clear that Surratt had consistently denied being in Washington on the night Lincoln was murdered. Regardless of whether he found Surratt's disclaimer credible, Ste. Marie assured King of his own willingness to testify in court against his former friend, whenever the time came.[20]

In the beginning of August King reported that the stage was fully set for bringing Surratt into federal government custody, should the authorities in Washington desire that he do so. The Vatican's own secretary of foreign affairs, Cardinal Giacomo Antonelli, had assured King that he would support Surratt's extradition to the United States, as well as Ste. Marie's release from the papal guard (presumably to serve as a trial witness), as soon as federal government officials made the request. To his surprise, King still failed to receive word on how to proceed.[21]

In the late summer and early fall of 1866, there was little if any incentive or opportunity for Seward, Holt, or Stanton to devote their attention to the fate of John Surratt. Secretary Seward was heading out with Andrew Johnson on his "Swing around the Circle" campaign, and once he joined the tour he fell extremely ill with cholera. For his part, Edwin Stanton was busy trying to bolster the Union army's authority to protect the rights of the freedpeople and their allies in the volatile, occupied South. And Joseph Holt was consumed in a bitter struggle to salvage his own battered reputation, while simultaneously trying to gauge the capacity of the Bureau of Military Justice to bring to justice the enemies of the nation who were already in hand. In relation to this task, the sudden return of John Surratt represented an additional complication. There was no guarantee, after all, that Surratt would implicate Davis under oath, and he might even offer testimony meant to distance Davis and his high-level cohorts from the assassination. Moreover, Surratt's very reappearance in the United States could be counted on to encourage those who were determined to bolster Johnson's plans for the postwar South by painting the President's enemies as ruthless avengers utterly devoid of the spirit of forgiveness. Were they not, after all, responsible for the execution of a woman—a mother!—whose guilt in connection to Lincoln's murder many Americans still doubted? What possible benefit could be derived from reopening the Surratt case?

For all these reasons, for the time being, Holt and Stanton (and perhaps also Seward) hoped to avoid a direct confrontation with Surratt. Their efforts to keep Booth's former associate at a distance began to crumble, however, as soon as Ste. Marie definitively identified him, and the U.S. ambassador to the Vatican engaged in formal negotiations for his capture and extradition. Then, on November 7, apparently without any request from the U.S. government (but with the approval of Pope Pius IX), Cardinal Antonelli had Surratt arrested in Veroli, Italy, and put in prison under heavy guard with plans to transfer him to Rome the following day.[22]

However, during preparations for this transfer, Surratt broke away from his six armed guards, jumped twenty feet from a prison wall onto a ledge cushioned by a pile of "filth from the barracks," and ran for his life. Subsequently, Surratt escaped to Naples, then by steamer to Malta and on to Alexandria, Egypt, where he arrived on November 23. There the authorities finally caught up with him. First quarantined and then confined in prison, Surratt awaited his transfer back to the United States via the steamship *Swatara*. Roughly three weeks later, Henri de Ste. Marie was discharged from the papal guard and given a small reward for providing the information that led to Surratt's arrest.[23]

News of the arrest reached the United States very quickly and it immediately excited popular interest. Among those who were especially eager to see Surratt returned to American soil were those who resented his prior escape from justice, especially in light of his mother's execution, and who hoped to see him hang, too. Others hoped that, given the uncertainty of the future of Reconstruction, a trial of John Surratt would result in his exoneration, thereby undermining the power of those figures within the federal government— particularly Holt and Stanton—who they believed had a history of endorsing vengeance toward the white South rather than forgiveness. And there were others whose interest in Surratt's arrest was almost entirely personal, including Louis Weichmann. On December 5, 1866, Weichmann told Holt in a letter that Surratt's involvement with Booth and the conspiracy against Lincoln had all but destroyed his life, rendering him "an object of mean hatred and suspicion to the copperheads and rebels, and especially to the people of my own church." Anxious to redeem his own reputation, Weichmann yearned for an opportunity to testify against Surratt, though he predictably veiled his desire in the language of patriotic responsibility. "I can not but consider it my duty to do all I can to advance the interests of justice," Weichmann wrote.[24]

Among those who shared with Holt a desire to see Jefferson Davis brought to trial one way or another, Surratt's unexpected capture did offer some measure of hope. Indeed, according to Gideon Welles, news of Surratt's arrest provoked some of the President's staunchest enemies in Congress to revive the dubious theory that Johnson himself had played a supporting role in the Lincoln assassination conspiracy. After all, had not Johnson benefited enormously from his predecessor's untimely death? Welles noted in particular that on December 5, Radical Republican George Boutwell of Massachusetts, a member of the Joint Committee on Reconstruction, went so far as to accuse Johnson of having been involved somehow in Surratt's original escape. For this, Welles remarked approvingly, Boutwell was "rebuked and condemned" by his friends in Congress, who considered the accusation both "intemperate and indecent."[25]

What of Johnson's own response to the news of Surratt's capture and impending return to America? Evidence suggests that the President expressed concern about the possibility that the Radicals might engineer an opportunity to meet with Surratt once he was repatriated. Specifically, Johnson worried that Boutwell and others would attempt to persuade Surratt to testify falsely about his—Johnson's—alleged involvement in the assassination scheme. Indeed, this possibility may already have been on the President's mind when, on December 8, he once again requested that Stanton and Holt provide him with copies of any evidence or testimony they had about the involvement of Jefferson Davis and other Confederate leaders (and, presumably, their sympathizers) in Lincoln's murder. In late January, Johnson was, if anything, even more nervous. "The President," noted Gideon Welles, "remarked . . . that the more reckless Radicals, if they could have access to [Surratt], would be ready to tamper with and suborn him." Thus, Johnson advised that Surratt "should not be allowed to communicate with others, nor should unauthorized persons be permitted to see him."[26]

On February 19, 1867, the *Swatara* docked at the Washington Navy Yard. "The arrival of Surratt," wrote Samuel Mudd cynically to his wife from Fort Jefferson, "will be the advent of a new excitement and the reiteration of every species of lie and slander which were given currency at our trial and subsequently." Still, Mudd hoped that should Surratt actually come to trial, the trial would be "speedy and impartial, and have the effect to clear away many of the mists that surround the tragic affair and lead to my early release from this place of exile and misery, and our once more happy reunion."[27]

Although much pertaining to John Surratt's future remained veiled, at least one crucial detail had been clarified in the weeks since his initial arrest: rather than face a military commission, he would be tried in the criminal court of the District of Columbia. This meant, of course, that regardless of how Joseph Holt would have liked to pursue the case against Surratt, he himself would play no official role

"Landing of John H. Surratt at the Washington Navy-Yard,"
from Harper's Weekly, *March 9, 1867*

bringing this ninth conspirator to justice. Rather, upon Surratt's arrival in Washington, a warrant was issued by Judge George P. Fisher to remand the prisoner to the custody of the civil authorities in the District. On the same afternoon his ship docked, Surratt—still dressed in his Zouave uniform and "looking none the worse for his trip abroad . . . like a man in good heart and hopeful of life"—was taken by hired carriage and under armed guard to the city jail in Washington. The *New York Times* reported the next day that the warden of the jail "has lately fitted up three iron-clad cells . . . which are used for the confinement of murderers and desperate characters." Surratt, the reporter continued, "was placed in one of these cells, from which there is no possible chance of escape, and therefore there need be no doubt about his safe keeping." For the greater part of the next four months, John Surratt awaited trial. Meanwhile, for much of that time, army surgeon George E. Cooper continued to file regular weekly reports with Stanton's War Department on the health of the only man in America possessed of a similar degree of notoriety at the moment: Jefferson Davis, still in federal custody at Fortress Monroe.[28]

It was assumed by many, including President Johnson, that Surratt would be kept in extremely close confinement, forbidden to speak to virtually anyone apart from his lawyers, his jailers, and his sister, Anna, who visited him frequently. Apparently, however, despite the President's orders, a number of other people were also able to gain access to the prisoner. Such was the case for one *New York Times* correspondent, who in early April 1867 published a lengthy article about his meeting with Surratt, whom he characterized as "friendly," "courteous," and "distinguished," a "well-dressed and very presentable young man—and certainly the last one that would be selected from a crowd as a desperate character or a villain."[29]

According to the *Times* article, Surratt's living conditions in the prison were hardly unpleasant. He had plenty of room and freedom to move around within his section of the prison, where he was happily separated from "common prisoners and curious visitors." Only at night was Surratt locked in his cell. Even so, the journalist described Surratt's "cell" as a "commodious apartment, at least ten feet square," although he admitted that the "furniture is scant, consisting merely of a stool, and a mattress laid upon the stone floor." Still, the reporter noted caustically, "such comfortable lodging would have been esteemed a luxury by our soldiers during the war." On top of everything else, Surratt seemed to be provided with an abundance of reading material, and his visitors routinely brought in copious examples of "the choicest of domestic cookery, selected with the sole view of pleasing his palate." Perhaps precisely because he was so comfortable, Surratt proved resistant to any and all efforts to draw him out on the subject of greatest interest—his involvement in the conspiracy to assassinate Lincoln. Instead, he focused on the details of his capture, understandably exhibiting some resentment toward his "treacherous" former friend Henri Beaumont de Ste. Marie.[30]

Apparently, John Surratt hoped to deflect any journalistic inquiries into his possible connection to the murder of Lincoln, as well as any knowledge he might have concerning the complicity with Booth of key Confederate leaders. Nevertheless, a final showdown on these questions was coming. With the return of Surratt to American soil, and especially to the nation's politically embattled capital, a number

John H. Surratt in the uniform
of the papal guard *(Artist's
sketch,* Harper's Weekly, *March 9, 1867;
photograph, Courtesy of
the Library of Congress)*

of mutually reactive, highly combustible elements converged, and plenty of kindling was already in place. It is a separate matter entirely whether any such final showdown would or could be expected, ultimately, to prove illuminating.

Meanwhile, additional political developments served only to further inflame the passions that had been building in Washington for the past two years. Significantly, two weeks after Surratt's return to the District of Columbia, the 39th Congress ended its second and final session with the passage of a bold and far-reaching new Reconstruction Act. This act essentially dismantled the Southern governments that had been created under the auspices of Presidential Reconstruction, and instead carved the former Confederacy (except Tennessee, which had already regained its representation in Congress) into five temporary military districts. These districts were to be under the supervision of military governors and subject to the authority of the occupying Union army. The new Reconstruction Act, which shared a great deal with the plan Edwin Stanton had proposed to Abraham Lincoln three days before Lincoln's death, also redefined the guidelines for the states' reentry to the Union. Of crucial importance, reentry would now fall under Congress's jurisdiction, not the President's. And it would require the adoption of new state constitutions, devised by state conventions whose delegates were elected by "universal" (black and loyal white) male suffrage, and the state's ratification of the Fourteenth Amendment to the federal Constitution.[31] Only when Congress confirmed that the necessary procedures had been followed would a state's elected representatives to the national legislature be readmitted, and that state be deemed officially reconstructed.

The Reconstruction Act indicates beyond a shadow of a doubt that, by early 1867, the executive and the legislature had reached the point of operating virtually independently from each other, neither branch showing concern for the ways in which its actions might obstruct or even nullify the actions of the other. Rather, the two branches of government were equally determined to use the tools at their disposal to shape Reconstruction according to their sharply divergent views.

Still unclear was the way in which the battle would play out. Among other things, victory depended on the outcome of various court cases, particularly those to be brought before the U.S. Supreme Court in the months and years ahead. Also of eminent concern was the matter of the loyalty of the Union army, for the time being the key agent for enforcing law in the postwar South. Did the soldiers in blue and their officers occupying the states of the former Confederacy pledge their allegiance to Andrew Johnson, essentially an unknown element who was, nevertheless, their commander in chief? Or would they follow the orders that came down from the War Department, from Edwin Stanton, whose hard work, dedication, and patriotism, along with those of Lincoln and Grant, had seen them through to victory during the war? The outcome of the battle over Reconstruction also depended on which side more effectively grasped the attention and commitment of the Northern public and their Unionist allies in the South. In the weeks and months ahead, Johnson and the Congress struggled to gain the upper hand on each of these questions.

Not surprisingly, the very day Congress passed it, Andrew Johnson vetoed the Reconstruction Act. Secretary of the Navy Gideon Welles later declared, "It was obvious to my mind that Stanton was an original adviser if not the originator of these laws. He may not have drafted them, but he, and probably Holt in consultation with him, devised the plan of military, despotic government to rule the South."[32] Equally predictably, Congress immediately overrode Johnson's veto; the solid Republican majority was joined by a single Democrat, Reverdy Johnson, Mary Surratt's former lawyer, who expressed frustration over the President's intransigence in the face of what he called the will of the people for a different kind of justice in the South.[33]

Although the huge Republican majority in Congress effectively deprived Johnson of his veto power, the President's opponents remained concerned about his taking a different tack to interfere with their plan for the South. In particular, they worried that Johnson might use his powers as commander in chief to hinder the occupation troops' ability to enforce Congress's laws there. As a result, the President's congressional opponents acted to limit his executive authority over the armed forces. In practical terms, this meant doing whatever they could to guarantee that Stanton would retain his grip on the War Department and on the troops' loyalty, as Stanton's continuation as war secretary seemed essential to the success of Congressional Reconstruction. To secure Stanton in his post, on March 2, the same day they passed their Reconstruction Act, the 39th Congress also passed the Tenure of Office Act, which essentially denied the President the right to dismiss any government official—including any cabinet officer—without Senate approval.

In order to further limit Andrew Johnson's ability to influence the operations of the military forces in the South, the 39th Congress also passed a rider to an army appropriations bill, "providing that all presidential orders to the army must be issued through the general of the army"—namely, Ulysses Grant, who was now also protected by the Tenure of Office Act. Since Johnson's "Swing around the Circle" campaign tour, and in light of his own desire to strengthen the army's powers of law enforcement in the contested South, Grant had begun to show growing sympathy for the Republicans (he would, of course, become their candidate for president in 1868). The legislators aimed to capitalize on Grant's favor if they possibly could. Finally, Congress enacted legislation requiring the President to disband the state militia forces, whose reestablishment and revitalization he had for some time been permitting—and, some would say, encouraging—in the postwar South. Understandably, congressmen who were determined to ensure the safety and welfare of the freedpeople and of Southern Unionists were deeply troubled by Johnson's tacit approval of what amounted to the rearming of former Confederates in the name of state and local security. Such things, they declared, fell within the purview of the Union army's occupying troops, and the legislators aimed to deprive the President of the opportunity to offer unrepentant white Southerners a chance to "help."[34]

In accordance with the special bill passed in January to prevent Congress from going out of session for several months, at midday on March 4, the members of the 39th Congress yielded their seats to the even more Radical 40th Congress. To Johnson's great annoyance, before the end of the month, the 40th Congress had irrefutably displayed its readiness to build on the momentum of the 39th by passing a second Reconstruction Act. This act was designed to move the Reconstruction process along and, perhaps more cynically, to generate immediate support among potential new black voters for the Republican Party. It required that the generals in command of the Southern military districts register eligible voters, both black and white, as a first step toward democratizing the election of delegates to the constitutional conventions already deemed necessary for Southern states to return to the Union by the first Reconstruction Act.[35]

On March 29, T. H. Duval wrote to update Holt on the progress of Reconstruction in Texas, especially in light of the recent actions taken by Congress. In stark contrast with his gloomy letter of the previous December, Duval now seemed optimistic: "I regard the acts of Congress as doing much in the right direction," he commented with enthusiasm. Still, Duval warned, there remained in Texas "thousands of traitors" determined to thwart Congressional Reconstruction, particularly in the portions of the state where "the negro population is greatest, the Union men are weakest, and there is no armed force to protect them." In areas such as this, Duval insisted, unregenerate former rebels would still be elected easily as delegates to the new state convention, where they could be expected to "leave no stone unturned, to retain their control of the state government."[36]

Reading Duval's letter back in Washington, Joseph Holt was hardly unaware that the two-year mark of Jefferson Davis's imprisonment at Fortress Monroe was drawing near. He was also aware that those lobbying for Davis's release had been cheered by rumors that President Johnson was now openly expressing his willingness to pardon the former Confederate leader if requested—perhaps his way of punishing the Radicals for their hijacking of the Reconstruction process and their reauthorization of martial law in the former Confederacy.[37] Holt was nevertheless almost certainly unprepared emotionally for the rapid chain of events destined to bring Davis's case virtually to a close later that spring.

Setting these events in motion was the application made by Charles O'Conor—a New York attorney who had been involved in the Davis

"Trial of Jefferson Davis, May 13, 1867:
Mr. Charles O'Conor Moving
for His Release on Bail,"
from Harper's Weekly, *June 1, 1867*

case since the spring of 1865—for a writ of habeas corpus. In light of
Davis's long incarceration without trial, O'Conor demanded that the
military hand the prisoner over to the civil authorities in Virginia.
After all, President Johnson's peace declaration of April 2, 1866, had
paved the way for the restoration of habeas corpus, which the President reinstated officially by proclamation four months later. Now,
suddenly, it was as if the walls of Fortress Monroe were made of
tissue paper. The writ O'Conor had demanded was granted quickly,
under the authority of Chief Justice of the United States, Salmon
Chase. Almost immediately, on May 8, a much relieved Andrew Johnson issued the order for Davis's release from military custody. Johnson's order was received by Brevet Brigadier General H. S. Burton at
Fortress Monroe on May 10.[38]

The following morning, Jefferson Davis was taken from his cell
and, with his wife, Varina, and a couple of loyal companions, was
placed on board a steamer bound for Richmond. When the steamer

arrived in the former Confederate capital late that afternoon, crowds of well-wishers were present, as well as U.S. army troops ordered to the wharf to prevent trouble. Davis and his small entourage were then taken through streets lined with supporters to the elegant Spotswood Hotel, where he and Varina were allowed to stay under limited guard in rooms they had occupied back in 1861 at the dawn of the Confederacy. The Davises remained at the Spotswood Hotel for two days. Then, at 11:30 A.M. on Monday, May 13, in a crowded courtroom located in the former Confederate White House, and with approximately two hundred armed soldiers standing by outside, Jefferson Davis came before Judge John Underwood of the U.S. circuit court in Richmond. Underwood officially transferred the prisoner to civil custody, then granted Davis's discharge on $100,000 bail (bail was not an option while Davis was in military confinement). To the bail requirement Underwood added only the "condition of recognizance," which meant that Davis must return to the court at the end of November—or whenever the Court reconvened—to face any charges still pending in his case. The gathered crowd exploded with joy, and Davis was escorted back to his hotel room. That very night, Davis and his wife headed north to Canada.[39]

To all intents and purposes, the former president of the Confederate States of America was a free man.[40] It was the fate of the current president of the United States of America that now remained uncertain. Throughout early 1867, Congress had continued to consider Representative James Ashley's January 7 resolution calling for Johnson's impeachment. The Judiciary Committee's investigations into Johnson's conduct began in February and led to the calling of numerous witnesses, including Joseph Holt and Edwin Stanton. Now more than ever the committee was interested in finding out whether there were any credible links between Andrew Johnson and the conspiracy to assassinate Lincoln, links that certainly would have constituted reasonable grounds for impeachment.[41]

Additionally, the committee explored the suggestion that Johnson had somehow suppressed important evidence during the 1865 trial—specifically, that he had perhaps withheld information that might have spared Mary Surratt's life. The committee pursued this particular avenue of inquiry because of pressure from Radical Congressman Benjamin F. Butler, who simultaneously hated Andrew Johnson and condemned the execution of Mary Surratt on the basis that it was her son, not she, who was guilty. Butler hoped that the committee's investigations could be used to prove that the President had single-handedly engineered Mary Surratt's execution, an insupportable theory that was kept alive for a time by the sheer force of Butler's will.

In the end, the Judiciary Committee of the 39th Congress decided that Johnson, though troublesome, was not legally impeachable. Hardly satisfied with this conclusion, Representative Ashley reintroduced his impeachment resolution in the 40th Congress, which once again referred it to the Judiciary Committee. To the frustration of some Radicals, who had hoped to keep Congress in session throughout the summer, the House of Representatives was pleased with the important legislation it had passed during its first four weeks in session and decided to adjourn on March 30. The Senate followed suit on April 20. But, as Gideon Welles noted with disdain in his diary, the members of the Judicary Committee returned to Washington in early May to begin their next round of investigations. After a month, however, Benjamin Butler's determination notwithstanding, committee members still lacked enough hard evidence to indict Johnson on a legitimate impeachment charge. They, too, decided to adjourn, but not before they had divulged to the public a seemingly important bit of information related to the assassination conspiracy: namely, the existence of a diary belonging to John Wilkes Booth, which contained handwritten entries from April 14 and April 21, 1865, and which now appeared to be missing some eighteen pages.[42]

Word that a diary had been found on Booth's dead body had in fact first appeared in the press in the weeks before the original trial of the conspirators began. At that time, newspapers reported that the diary—along with Booth's other possessions—had been turned over to investigators. Two years later, Colonel Everton J. Conger, who had been present at Booth's capture, confirmed this in a letter to Joseph Holt: "I took the Diary from Booth's person and delivered it with the

other things to the Hon. Secretary of War, immediately upon my
return to Washington." After Stanton had a chance to examine the
diary, Holt had also looked it over carefully, then locked it in a safe.
Rightly or wrongly, he and his prosecution team never introduced the
diary as evidence in the 1865 trial, having determined that it did not
serve their purposes. According to one contemporary, Holt expressed
a desire to let the diary "rot with the assassin's memory, as [he] did
not think it proper to publish to the world the defamation of Mr. Lincoln's character which it contained, and the self-glorification of
Booth."[43]

From the vantage point of the present, it appears as if the various
lawyers for the defense, who must have been aware of the diary's existence, would have benefited greatly had they been able to make use
of its contents on their clients' behalf. Among other things, Booth
indicated that he had reached his decision to murder Lincoln only
very shortly before the assassination—perhaps that very morning—
and apparently without the direct and immediate input of any of
the other convicted conspirators. "Until today," Booth wrote shortly
after the assassination "nothing was ever thought of sacrificing to our
country's wrongs," though he acknowledged the kidnap plan and its
failure. "For six months we had worked to capture," Booth continued. "But our cause being almost lost, something decisive and great
must be done." Still, Booth complained that the "others" (whose
names he did not provide) "did not strike for their country with a
heart." Only he himself "struck boldly," and now, "I can never repent
it. . . . Our country owed all her troubles to him, and God simply
made me the instrument of his punishment."[44] Such comments from
Booth's own hand would have done little for the defense of Herold or
Powell, of course, but one is tempted to think that they might have
helped Atzerodt and particularly Mary Surratt escape the noose.
Some prosecution witnesses, it will be recalled, had depicted Mary
Surratt as the mastermind of the plot. Booth's diary made it clear that
Booth had made the decision to kill Lincoln on his own, and at most,
Mary Surratt—and probably even Atzerodt as well—could have been
convicted only for involvement in the conspiracy to kidnap Lincoln.
As such, effective use of the diary might have resulted in their impris-

onment—like Mudd and the others at Fort Jefferson—rather than their executions.

As it turns out, however, according to the law for such trials, if the prosecution failed to introduce evidence, defense attorneys could not introduce it either. If this seems strange, it must be recognized that a document such as Booth's, written after the fact, could hardly be expected to stand up to any sort of serious scrutiny as evidence of his alleged co-conspirators' innocence. After all, Booth might simply have been lying to glorify his own role. At the same time, Booth did not mention his associates by name, and even if he had, the argument could easily be made that he had been trying to protect them once the crime was committed.[45]

In any case, in 1865 the diary was basically forgotten. In contrast, when news of its existence and rediscovery spread in the late spring of 1867, the mutilated diary (which Holt and others persuasively argued was just as they had found it in 1865[46]) achieved sudden and striking importance, not in and of itself but as a weapon in the hands of Johnson's political adversaries. Noted the cynical Gideon Welles in his own diary: "It was a great mystery and was construed to mean whatever any diseased imagination might conceive."[47] Needless to say, a number of Johnson's most hostile critics in Congress hoped to further the cause of impeachment by proving that not only had Johnson known about the diary in 1865, but he had been personally involved in suppressing it in order to ensure that Mary Surratt was convicted along with the others. Some Johnson opponents even suggested that the President had torn out the missing pages himself, which they theorized had contained damning information of one sort or another.

The Booth diary with its mysterious missing pages generated a burst of excitement in the spring of 1867. Ultimately, however, when the Judiciary Committee's members ended their deliberations on Ashley's impeachment resolution in early June, they agreed that whatever pages were now missing had, as Holt and Stanton insisted, been missing at the time of the diary's discovery at Richard Garrett's farm two years before. They also agreed that there was insufficient evidence to demonstrate any sort of malfeasance on the part of the President in relation to the diary, the contents of which the *New York Times* published on May 22.[48]

And so on June 4, the day after the first municipal election in the District of Columbia in which black men were allowed to vote ("The Negroes, under Radical training, have controlled the vote," Gideon Welles complained), the committee confirmed by a 5–4 vote the conclusions of its predecessor in the 39th Congress.[49] Once again, they agreed that the President, though clearly stubborn, oppositional, and extremely difficult for Congress to work with (or even work around), was nevertheless legally unimpeachable. Once again, Johnson's case was put on the back burner. At the same time, a number of questions that had arisen in the context of the committee's investigations, associated with Booth's rediscovered diary, remained unanswered. Many of those same questions would soon be revived in the context of the trial of John Surratt Jr.; his lawyers hoped to use the diary precisely as the defense lawyers back in 1865 might have liked to do, but could not: "as evidence that their client was not implicated in the assassination conspiracy, but was merely cognizant of the plan of abduction."[50]

John Surratt's trial began on June 10, 1867, and lasted for two full months through the same sort of oppressive heat that had prevailed during his mother's trial two years before. Close to three hundred witnesses were called. The day the trial opened and for most of its duration, the courtroom—which held about three hundred people—was packed with eager observers, including "a large number of colored men,"[51] "quite a number of ladies," and several of Surratt's "old schoolmates and personal friends," as well as Surratt's older brother, Isaac, who had absented himself from their mother's trial, and possibly also his sister, Anna. According to the *Times*, the Surratt brothers were a study in contrasts, "John being a quiet, refined, student-looking young man, while Isaac is much stouter, far less intelligent in countenance, with a bold, b'hoyish expression, and far more likely to be picked out as the perpetrator of a desperate deed, though evidently endowed with far less brains."[52]

Although Joseph Holt could have no formal involvement in the prosecution of this case, he observed intently from the Bureau of

Military Justice and made himself available for consultation with the prosecution. The leading lawyers for the District of Columbia were Edwards Pierrepont, a prominent New York attorney, and Edward C. Carrington, the district attorney of Washington, D.C.; they were aided by Assistant District Attorney Nathaniel Wilson and Albert Gallatin (A. G.) Riddle, a former congressman from Ohio. Senator John Bingham provided additional background support to Surratt's prosecutors. On the day the trial began, the *New York Times* claimed that the once cocky Surratt had himself begun to appear increasingly anxious about his fate: "friends of the prisoner," the paper commented, "say that he does not express so much confidence as formerly in his ultimate acquittal."[53]

Especially troubling to Surratt was the broad scope of the four-count indictment that a Washington, D. C., grand jury had handed down against him two weeks before his return to America. Taken together, the four charges contained in the indictment allowed for Surratt's involvement in the murder of Lincoln at every level, from conspiring with his mother, Booth, and the three others who had been executed in July 1865 (as well as others unknown) to kill the President, to killing Lincoln himself with a ten-dollar pistol. Although there was arguably not a shadow of a chance that Surratt could be convicted of actually pulling the trigger, or even of being at Ford's Theater when Booth pulled it, nevertheless the indictment left plenty of room for him to be convicted of having been part of the plot. Surely for the accused this was frightening enough, given that so much evidence of his involvement with Booth and the others had already been presented back in 1865, and given that the death penalty was applicable in his case. Also troubling, perhaps, was the fact that the judge assigned to preside over the case was George Fisher, described by Gideon Welles as a close ally of Stanton and therefore, almost certainly, of Holt as well.[54]

Such things reasonably gave Surratt cause for worry. On the other hand, the prisoner surely took heart from the realization that two full years had passed since the end of the war. If this was not necessarily clear when one considered the struggle over Reconstruction under way between the President and Congress, it was nevertheless the case that among the general public tempers had cooled. Also reassuring was the fact that, thanks to the trial's setting in civil court, Surratt's future depended on the deliberations of a jury made up of twelve civilians rather than a board of nine Union army officers. And then there was the prospect of not having to face as his chief prosecutor the head of the Bureau of Military Justice, whose combination of rage, drive, knowledge of the law, and eloquence might still have swayed any jury, even two years after Appomattox.

Surratt must have experienced some relief when he considered the basic conditions under which his trial would take place. Still, what his former friend Louis Weichmann called the "partisan feeling" of the day could almost certainly be counted on to influence the proceedings. "There probably never was a jury trial in which partisan feeling was so much excited," wrote Weichmann many years later, adding

> President Johnson had returned to the Democratic fold, and though he, perhaps, did not desire to encourage the secession sympathizers in Washington, or elsewhere, to revive the smouldering embers of their hatred for the Government that had destroyed slavery, yet there were hundreds of them at the capital who construed his tergiversation to mean that those whom he had formerly denounced as traitors and determined should take "back seats," might now venture to occupy the amen corner of the political church. Many of these people, as soon as Surratt had been arrested, were active in their endeavors to create sympathy for him.[55]

In a way that his mother would have been unable to do with any confidence during her own trial, Surratt surely hoped that such endeavors would meet with abundant success.

The first few days of the trial were consumed by disputes over the makeup of the jury, to be drawn from (white, male) residents of the District of Columbia. A central feature of the wrangling was the defense team's theory that the prosecution planned to nullify the initially selected jury in favor of one that also included blacks, even though District of Columbia law still prevented blacks from serving on juries. In the end, a new jury was impaneled. This jury included five men of Northern or foreign birth and seven who were Southern born, and if its makeup seemed less than optimal from the prosecution's perspective, it nevertheless reasonably reflected the white male population in the District at the time.[56]

Testimony for the prosecution began on June 17, and it must be noted that although the indictment against Surratt allowed considerable latitude for convicting him, prosecution lawyers somewhat inexplicably took what in the end proved to be a counterproductive approach. They sought to prove that Surratt had not only conspired with Booth and the others to bring about the murder of Lincoln, but that he had in fact been in the District at the time of the assassination, even though much evidence had been presented at his mother's trial to indicate that he had left for Canada more than a week before.[57]

Still, it was possible, of course, that Surratt had returned home by April 14, 1865, if only in order to assist Booth with the assassination. To prove that he had, numerous prosecution witnesses were brought in who claimed to recall having seen Surratt in Washington on April 14. Although a good number of these witnesses gave virtually the same testimony they had given at the trial in 1865, others offered new information, such as Sergeant Joseph Dye who now testified that he had positively seen Surratt outside Ford's Theater just prior to the assassination. David C. Reed, who had known Surratt since he was a child, reported that he, too, had seen Surratt on the day of the murder, dressed in "genteel" clothes and standing near the National Hotel, where Booth had been staying. Former detective John Lee, who was involved in the initial investigation of the murder and knew Surratt by sight on account of his notoriety as a Confederate agent, also claimed to have seen him out walking that day. And Charles H. M. Wood, a barber, testified that he had given Surratt a shave that morning. "Will you tell us who came into the shop with him, if anybody?" asked prosecutor Pierrepont. "Mr. Booth came in, there were four persons who came together," Wood replied. According to his testimony, on that morning Surratt and Booth's companions included O'Laughlen and a "short, thick-set man with a full round head" wearing "dark clothes" and a "black slouched hat," presumably Atzerodt.[58]

Placing Surratt in Washington on April 14 was one of the key goals of the prosecution; placing him at the center of the assassination conspiracy was the other. It was this aspect of John Surratt's trial that revived most dramatically a host of memories and controversies associated with the original trial of the conspirators. As June 1867 drew to a close, a familiar cast of characters paraded through Judge Fisher's courtroom, including John Lloyd, former tenant of the Surratt property in Surrattsville, who had played such an important role in linking Mary Surratt to the conspiracy, but who now "expressed his intention of not giving any evidence about Mrs. Surratt," as she was no longer alive to defend herself, and who, although required to answer questions, offered little illuminating testimony and much that was confusing.[59]

Once again, Louis Weichmann testified calmly and at great length about the involvement in the assassination conspiracy of his former landlady and her son, and apparently he was as persuasive to most observers as he had been two years before. The New York Times correspondent noted on June 27 that Weichmann's "narrative was very clear and connected, and considerably fuller than he gave it on the conspiracy trial, though no new facts were developed. Taken as it stands," however, the reporter conceded, "it is the most convincing and positive proof yet adduced of the very close intimacy of Surratt and his mother with Booth and the other assassins."[60]

Of great value for the prosecution's case, and most problematic for Surratt, was the extensive new testimony given by Lewis McMillan, the surgeon who had met Surratt on board the steamship Peruvian during Surratt's escape from Canada to Europe in September 1865. McMillan recounted in detail the two men's conversations both during the trip and when they reconnected later in Liverpool. According to McMillan, Surratt spoke freely of his work on behalf of the Confederate underground during the war, of carrying dispatches between Richmond and Washington and on up to New York and Montreal, sometimes in the company of a woman, presumably Sarah Slater. On one occasion, McMillan told the court, Surratt described how he, the woman, and several other operatives met five or six ragged, hungry Union soldiers on the way to Richmond. Untouched by their plight, Surratt's female companion suggested they shoot the soldiers, who seemed to have escaped from prisons in the South. Surratt and the other men traveling with them promptly did so, after which they "went right along, paying no more attention to them." Such testimony depicted Surratt in much the same light as Holt had tried in 1865 to depict Booth, his co-conspirators, and the Confederate government in Richmond. In this image, they were all not only murderers of Lincoln, but also perpetrators of a host of hideous crimes against the soldiers of the Union.[61]

Lewis McMillan also spoke of Surratt's many references to his collaboration with Booth and others in the plan to abduct Lincoln, though he claimed that eventually Surratt had admitted realizing that the plan was doomed to failure. "He said, in reference to the abduction," McMillan explained, "that after awhile they found out they could not carry out their plan, and they had to abandon it." Although McMillan confessed that Surratt had not spoken with him at any length about the assassination itself and had not explicitly indicated his involvement in Booth's final plan, his testimony added much to the case the prosecution was trying to build against the defendant as a knowing and active conspirator with Booth (and perhaps also the Confederate leadership in Richmond) in his efforts to do Lincoln serious, and probably mortal, harm.[62]

By cross-examination and frequent objections throughout the prosecution's presentation and examination of its witnesses, Surratt's three attorneys tried to undermine the prosecution's case against their client. The trio of Washington lawyers were Joseph H. Bradley Sr., his son Joseph H. Bradley Jr., and Richard T. Merrick. Two of these men had loose connections to the original trial of the conspirators in 1865: the senior Bradley had been asked to serve as a defense attorney for David Herold, and Richard Merrick had been asked to defend Samuel Mudd. Both had refused, although now, in the summer of 1867, Merrick had become tangentially involved in trying to effect Mudd's release from prison, even as he was serving on Surratt's defense team.[63]

The older Bradley led the team defending Surratt, and he did so in a manner at least one *New York Times* correspondent found thoroughly obnoxious and unnecessarily combative. Describing him as "a bald-headed, full-faced, side-whiskered, double-chinned, rotund man, who, unlike other fleshy men, is petulant and quick-tempered," the writer dubbed Bradley Sr. "the great objector," who, during the presentation of the prosecution's case, "frequently belches out, in sharp, angry tones, a command to a witness not to 'answer that question,' after which, in the same ill-humored vein, he argues the points of his objection." In contrast, the younger Bradley said little and mostly took notes on the evidence, writing so slowly, the *Times* correspondent complained, that he significantly delayed the examination process, thereby giving his father additional time to "badger" witnesses on the stand. Bradley Sr.'s behavior was so rude that it ultimately provoked the ire of Judge Fisher, who reprimanded him on July 2. Later that day, outside the courtroom, the angry judge confronted Bradley about his impertinence and the defense counsel responded with renewed fury. According to observers, the two men almost came to blows before spectators managed to separate them.[64]

No matter what else they were able to achieve during the trial, a primary goal for the defense team was to find a way to fracture the story the prosecution was trying to tell by providing an alibi for John Surratt on April 14, 1865. If they could show that Surratt could not possibly have been in Washington at the time of the assassination, they would have succeeded in stripping away one of the central details on which the prosecution had hung its case. This said, at the time they began to present their witnesses on July 6, the defense had their work cut out for them, because the prosecution had captured the imagination and the confidence of the trial's observers, if not the jury as well. "Among those who have watched the trial thus far," the *New York Times* asserted on June 30, "there is but one opinion about [Surratt], and that is that he is guilty."[65]

To develop Surratt's alibi, the defense employed two interconnected strategies. On the one hand, the attorneys hoped to downplay the significance of Surratt's interactions with the other members of the assassination conspiracy, throwing at least a reasonable doubt in the face of the prosecution's contention that their client had been involved in any specifically anti-Lincoln conspiracy. This was a rather hopeless task, however, given the weight of the accumulated evidence of Surratt's complicity at some level. More effective by far were their efforts to discredit the prosecution's witnesses and their testimony, and to amass evidence that on April 14 Surratt had, in fact, been in Elmira, New York, on assignment for the Confederate government investigating the treatment of rebel prisoners held there.[66] If they could place him in Elmira that day, or at least not in Washington, it would perhaps challenge the allegations contained in the indictment enough to divide the jury.

Throughout the month of July the defense counsel called their witnesses. Among the more important of them was Dr. Augustus Bissell, a New York City physician, who testified he had met and spoken with Surratt on April 14 in Elmira, at a lodging place called the Brainard House.[67] Also important were witnesses like William Failing, J. N. Dunbarry, and Francis Fitch, railroad employees who answered questions pertaining to rail schedules along the relevant lines in mid-April 1865 and whose combined testimony indicated quite conclusively that Surratt could not possibly have been in both Washington, D.C., and Elmira, New York, within the very short span of time necessary to explain how he could have been sighted in both places on April 14.[68] Such detailed testimony worked to confuse the members of the jury. At best, from the perspective of the defense, it provided the necessary reasonable doubt about the prosecution's allegations with respect to their client's whereabouts on that day.

By July 29 the defense had succeeded in calling into serious question the prosecution's claims that Surratt was in Washington on April 14, 1865. At the same time, both defense and prosecution attorneys had managed to effectively discredit the other side's witnesses by using the most vicious tactics. On July 2, for example, defense attorney Richard Merrick challenged McMillan's reliability by accusing him of being paid by the State Department to give his testimony (which McMillan denied) and by suggesting that he was not an upstanding doctor but rather an abortionist. Three weeks later, prosecution attorney Pierrepont similarly suggested that Dr. Bissell was being paid for his testimony, that he was not really much of a doctor either, and that his memory about the layout and location of the Brainard House in Elmira was so flawed as to be utterly untrustworthy. The upshot was that a case which had initially seemed sure to result in a clear victory for the prosecution had collapsed into uncertainty, and there was a growing likelihood that the jury would split.[69]

On August 7, following the closing arguments, Judge Fisher addressed the jury. Fisher's charge to the jury can be interpreted only as expressly favoring the prosecution, filled as it was with words and phrases that would have made even so accomplished an orator, and even so determined a prosecutor of the nation's enemies as Joseph Holt, proud. "Whoso sheddeth man's blood by man shall his blood be shed," Fisher began. He continued: "It is a mistake to suppose that a free people in any country will ever consider it a more heinous crime to kill a king . . . than it is to assassinate a President." Fisher went on to defend with passion the military commission that had tried the original conspirators, as well as the justice of its verdicts. He then described the jurors' duty in the case at hand. The only question they must consider, Fisher informed the twelve men, is "whether the prisoner at the bar participated with John Wilkes Booth and the others named in the indictment, or either or any of them, in this diabolical crime. If, from all the evidence in the case, your minds shall have been convinced beyond a reasonable doubt growing out of that evidence, that the prisoner did cooperate with them . . . in the conspiracy to murder, or," that failing, "in a plot to do some unlawful act which resulted in this foul murder," then they must convict.[70]

The jury met in a heavily guarded upper-story room in the District's somewhat dilapidated City Hall, where the trial had taken place. By midnight on that first night rumors were afoot that the jury was unable to reach a verdict.[71] A large crowd of spectators maintained their vigil in and around the courtroom, and Surratt himself awaited word in his jail cell. [72]

The news finally came three days later, just after 1:00 P.M. At that time, John Surratt was brought from his cell to the courtroom, apparently in good spirits. Judge Fisher then appeared, the court was called to order, and the jury was seated. The chair of the jury made the situation known: despite more than seventy hours in seclusion and discussion, they found themselves "nearly equally divided" (actually 8 to 4 for acquittal) and without any hope of agreeing on a verdict. As one might expect, the split fell essentially along sectional lines, with one Northerner, a native of New York, having joined the Southerners in voting to set Surratt free. As a result of the jury's failure to reach a verdict, Judge Fisher was forced to dismiss them. The defense lawyers initially contested the jury's dismissal in the hope that further deliberation would sway the remaining four toward acquittal. In the end, however, John Surratt was returned to jail. Before parting, Judge Fisher took the opportunity to punish Surratt's lead counsel, Joseph Bradley Sr., one more time for his annoying and unprofessional behavior during the trial. Fisher disbarred him.[73]

The *New York Times* expressed a complete lack of surprise over the trial's outcome. The *Times* reminded its readers that for some time now the certainty that had prevailed early on concerning John Surratt's conviction had been on the decline. The paper was right, moreover, that this was not just a result of the influence of sectional loyalties on the jury's deliberations, and that the trial's outcome was better understood as the logical result of the obvious discrepancies in the evidence, as well as the dubious character of witnesses on both sides. Although most jurors were probably hard-pressed to believe Surratt completely innocent of any association with Booth's conspiracy against Lincoln, this alone did not suffice as proof that he had known of or participated in the murder. The prosecution simply had not succeeded in proving its case beyond a reasonable doubt. In civil court, in order to convict, the prosecutors needed to do better than they had. As such, the trial's conclusion was, as the *Times* put it, "intelligible, if not fair or just."[74]

While the jury in the John Surratt case failed to agree on a verdict, Surratt himself had by no means been exonerated.[75] Indeed there was a possibility he might be brought to trial again, although it was not particularly likely in the current political climate, where other matters seemed so much more pressing. A new trial in a case such as Surratt's would also require that the prosecution discover salient new evidence against the defendant, which hardly seemed possible. Should a second trial be called, there were some who suggested that it might be more fruitful to try Surratt simply for participation in the conspiracy. Perhaps the four-count indictment, which had seemed to leave so much room for conviction, had merely clouded the issues.

It is easy to become so focused on the John Surratt trial itself that one forgets the political turmoil that surrounded and helped to shape it. It is hardly an exaggeration to say, however, as Louis Weichmann did, that the trial was conducted with, and also in the shadow of, the same bitterness that prevailed on both sides of the debate over control of Reconstruction. Particularly noteworthy was the disrespect both sides had displayed toward each other's witnesses, in relation to the credibility of their testimony as well as their character. As one reporter quite accurately pointed out, the very heatedness with which the case was argued, the ill behavior of the lawyers, their vicious attacks on one another and on the witnesses, and even the temper of the judge himself spoke volumes about the "restored calmness of the great majority of the nation" who were yearning to move forward, "as contrasted with the fury still burning in the bosoms of a few extreme men."[76] In turn, the failure of the jury to agree on a verdict reflected the angry divisions still awaiting resolution in the nation's capital, regarding punishment for the Confederacy's past deeds and the program for the South's future. Watching from Fort Jefferson, Samuel Mudd hoped that at last the day of his release was drawing near.[77]

Two days before Judge Fisher turned John Surratt's case over to the jury for deliberation, on August 5, 1867, a thoroughly exhausted and disheartened Joseph Holt, who had been feeling unwell and had been suffering from insomnia for months, began a thirty-day leave of absence. That same day, Andrew Johnson wrote to Secretary of War Stanton demanding his resignation. Stanton refused, and a week later Johnson suspended the secretary, transferring Stanton's powers, *ad interim*, to General Grant. In Gideon Welles's opinion, getting rid of Stanton was hardly sufficient. Rather, Johnson should dispose of Holt and Stanton at the same time. "It would be more effective and proper to remove the two together," Welles declared. It was time, he added, to "strike an effective blow against Radical usurpations."[78]

Seldom have revolutionists been offered remission on more generous terms—the establishment of equal civil rights for everyone regardless of race and a guarantee that for a reasonable time the national government would continue under the control of the party that had won the war.

—BENJAMIN P. THOMAS AND HAROLD M. HYMAN,
Stanton (1962)[1]

I suppose that the removal of your friend, Secretary Stanton, will lead to your resignation of the high office you have held, with so much honor to yourself, & advantage to the country. I, therefore, beg to assure you, that you have the *full approbation,* the *esteem & love* of *all the honest, & true-hearted Union* men in *these Southern States*, and the sterling integrity, devoted & self-sacrificing patriotism—& disinterested love of justice & truth, which have in all cases been pre-eminent in your [career] will secure the gratitude of posterity, and redeem the honor of your name, from the miserable calumnies with which vanquished, & malignant Rebels have tried to surround it.

—WILLIAM H. DOHERTY TO JOSEPH HOLT,
from North Carolina, August 10, 1867[2]

There is among the Radicals neither statesmanship, sagacity, nor sense. Hate, revenge, thirst for power govern them. To oppress and persecute the white population of the Southern States is their delight; to place negro regiments over them by the aid of the military is their intention.

—GIDEON WELLES, diary entry of January 20, 1868[3]

9

"THE WICKED MAN
NOW ACTING AS PRESIDENT"
THE TRIAL OF ANDREW JOHNSON AND
THE COLLAPSE OF HOLT'S AGENDA

JOSEPH HOLT'S MUCH NEEDED LEAVE OF ABSENCE IN UPSTATE NEW YORK was deeply colored by the news that President Johnson had suspended his boss, Edwin Stanton, as secretary of war.[4] Because Congress had passed the Tenure of Office Act in March specifically to protect Stanton by requiring congressional approval for his removal, for the time being, Johnson was only suspending, not firing, Stanton, or so the President and his supporters argued. Still, the news was bad, and many of his correspondents, and probably even Holt himself, were sure he would be the next to go. Holt's friend Thomas Shankland wrote from Brooklyn: "The rumors are that you are to be displaced which is perfectly in accordance with the President's programme and persistent endeavours to overthrow the union sentiment to subserve the cause of Treason. . . . Now Montgomery Blair will rejoice, and all Rebeldom with him." Shankland reassured Holt that "the rejoicings of the wicked are but for a moment."[5]

Johnson's reasons for trying to push Stanton out of the cabinet were clear: the secretary of war vigorously opposed the lenient plan for Southern restoration that Johnson was attempting to enact. Stanton, after all, had drawn up the original blueprint for temporary military rule in the South, he supported the Reconstruction Acts passed by Congress, and he openly endorsed the proposed Fourteenth

Amendment to the Constitution. He was also known to support the idea of black male suffrage, at least in the states of the former Confederacy. In short, Stanton was a force for opposition within what Secretary of the Navy Gideon Welles had called Johnson's "political family," the cabinet, and he was hardly an insignificant force, for to all intents and purposes he had the military behind him.[6] Moreover, not only did the army support Stanton, but it appears that a majority of the army's top brass were also now inclined to support the vision for the postwar South articulated by the Republicans in Congress. Getting rid of Stanton, therefore, was essential if Johnson wanted to have any chance to save his own plan for national restoration.

Still, given the climate of mutual antagonism and hostility in which Johnson was operating, he could hardly declare his true motivation explicitly, so he found other ways to justify his decision to force Stanton out. At the same time, Johnson apparently did not anticipate—or care—how thoroughly his own schemes would generate further disdain in many quarters for his presidency. As Johnson biographer Hans Trefousse has explained, "Once Johnson made up his mind, he could be stubborn, and now that he had decided finally to defy his opponents and get rid of Stanton and his radical subordinates, he moved with firm deliberation" rather than caution.[7]

In his determination to dispose of Stanton (and, if possible, Holt), Johnson latched on to two separate but interrelated controversies that arose conveniently against the backdrop of John Surratt's trial. The first was a new and complicated scandal involving the convicted perjurer Sanford Conover, the judge advocate general, and, by association, the secretary of war. The second was a dispute over who was really responsible for the execution of Mary Surratt. This question had become increasingly nettlesome over time, a vivid reflection of the tensions associated with the debate over vengeance or forgiveness on the part of the federal government, and the North generally, toward the former Confederacy. In this dispute as it shaped up in early August 1867, Johnson disingenuously attempted to claim the moral high ground. To do so, he took the stance that Holt, the Bureau of Military Justice, and the Department of War were at fault, and that he had been falsely led to endorse their version of justice in her case.

The Conover scandal exploded in late July. Conover, who had recently begun serving his sentence for perjury, sent a woman who claimed to be his wife to the White House with some startling news. In a private meeting, "Mrs. Conover" conveyed to Andrew Johnson a tale of "promises and assurances of pardon" that had been offered to her husband if he assisted the prosecution's case against John Surratt, and indirectly against Jefferson Davis. (The parties who had urged Conover to do this were subsequently revealed to be two of the President's staunchest opponents in Congress, Benjamin Butler and James Ashley.) These "parties," Conover's "wife" reported, had even brought with them to Conover's prison cell what turned out to be a genuine recommendation for clemency in his case, which was signed by none other than Joseph Holt and accompanied by a supporting note from Congressman Ashley. A second note of support was also attached, signed by A. G. Riddle, one of the prosecution lawyers in the Surratt case and an associate of Stanton.[8]

According to Gideon Welles's account of the events in his diary, Conover's "wife" brought all the relevant documents to the White House. After perusing them on his own, Johnson then shared them with his cabinet (except Stanton, of course). Over the next few days Johnson and his advisers pondered how to interpret the documents and Conover's claims, and what to do next. The general consensus within the cabinet was that Congressmen Ashley and Butler, presumably supported from the start by the ill-intended Holt and Riddle, must have approached Conover in order to cast a negative light on Johnson for failing to prosecute him. But Conover had apparently decided to earn his pardon another way, by directly exposing to the President the treachery of the congressmen and their allies in the War Department and elsewhere. Welles reports that after much discussion Johnson indicated that he was prepared simply to pardon Conover for having come forward in this way. But his cabinet persuaded the President to postpone any such decision, instead encouraging him to pursue rapid and widespread publication of the scandal's details in order to undermine the Radicals' credibility, to embarrass Holt thoroughly, and to drum up support for Secretary of War Stanton's permanent removal.[9]

It is not clear whether, when Holt participated in the attempt to elicit Conover's testimony against Surratt and Davis, he did so cynically or with the explicit goal of suborning perjury in order to harrass Andrew Johnson. One needs to recall that Holt genuinely, if nevertheless naïvely and even desperately, believed that the volatile and unpredictable Conover truly was a treasure trove of valuable evidence against both Davis and Surratt. At the same time, however, one must also acknowledge Holt's long-standing and misguided support for his prevaricating former witness. There is no doubt that Holt signed the problematic pardon recommendation, on July 23, of his own free will.[10]

Some two months before this scandal broke, rumblings of trouble were being heard. On May 17, a man who identified himself as Francis McFall made a sworn statement before a New York notary public in which he claimed that Conover had informed him in August 1866 that he (Conover) and Holt had "become involved in a quarrel" over Conover's fundamental responsibility for Holt's damaged reputation following the Judiciary Committee's hearings that spring and summer. (McFall's statement referred back to the previous year's controversy, which had so embarrassed Holt and led him to produce his original public "vindication.") According to McFall, Conover said that Holt, angry and wounded when he first discovered Conover's duplicity, had begun "persecuting him with the vindictiveness of a fiend"—although there is no evidence to indicate that this was the case, and certainly Holt's subsequent willingness to sign a recommendation for Conover's pardon suggests the opposite. Nevertheless, by way of "retribution," Conover—now with the assistance of Benjamin Wood, the former editor of the *New York Evening News*, and former Confederate general Roger A. Pryor—had decided to do whatever he could to undermine the judge advocate general's reputation even further and at the same time promote the cause of Jefferson Davis's release from prison. Forgotten, apparently, was the resentment Conover had expressed toward Davis for having ordered him incarcerated during the war at Castle Thunder, a Richmond prison, and having supposedly "insulted" his wife. Now, explained McFall, Conover's plan was to have various individuals sign affidavits accusing Holt of asking each of them to produce a written deposition implicating Davis in Booth's conspiracy. For this deceit Conover, Wood, and Pryor would pay the men generously. McFall had initially done as Conover requested, but he had subsequently decided to come forward and expose the subterfuge, noting that in fact he had never even met Joseph Holt, let alone been pressured by him to give false testimony against Jefferson Davis.[11]

At the same time, several other individuals made similar statements under oath in which they confessed their involvement in the two-pronged scam of Sanford Conover, Roger Pryor, Benjamin Wood, and other "friends of Jefferson Davis" supposedly to "punish Judge Holt for his animosity" toward Conover and to "bring upon him and the Bureau of Military Justice such a measure of public condemnation as to warrant the President . . . in setting . . . Davis at liberty." All these statements indicated that Conover, Pryor, and Wood had promised their recruits large sums of money for their affidavits, which helps to explain why McFall and the others initially agreed to cooperate. Moreover, according to one deponent, James E. Matterson, at first it seemed reasonable to participate in trying to bring Holt down, because it seemed clear "from the statements and representations of Conover, Pryor, and others and from articles which appeared in the newspapers that an atrocious and murderous conspiracy had been formed with Judge Holt at its head to convict and shed the blood of Mr Davis on the gallows by means of bogus witnesses and false testimony." Matterson had therefore "believed that he was performing a humane, Christian act in assisting in this way," since it seemed to be the only possible means by which "to defeat the diabolical machinations of the supposed conspirators." Subsequently, however, Matterson and the others had thought better of what they were doing and now pledged to own up.[12] Why exactly they changed their minds is unclear, though it seems naïve to chalk it up to simple moral compunction.

The statements of confession regarding Conover's earlier plot against Holt were taken and notarized in mid-May 1867, but it is impossible to know when they actually came into Holt's hands.[13] What is certain is that they remained out of reach of the nation's press. However, once Andrew Johnson decided to publicize the news of "Mrs. Conover's" visit to the White House, predictably these statements about Conover and the conflict in his relationship with Holt came to light. In Johnson's mind, the most important thing was that he had found an opportunity to expose the perfidiousness of his opponents in Congress and—even more important at the moment—their allegiance with Holt and with the troublesome and oppositional Edwin Stanton. To Johnson, this latest Conover scandal would serve its purpose if it offered a defensible excuse for suspending his sole remaining opponent in the cabinet, while further damaging Holt's reputation.

Unfortunately for Johnson, however, although scandal did erupt, it did not play out as he had planned. Johnson's supporters rallied to the cause, but Holt's supporters did likewise. The national press raged with news of the scandal that August, but it offered Johnson anything but a clear victory for his strategy.[14]

Conveniently, a second opportunity arose that the President believed he could also exploit for the purpose of justifying his suspension of Stanton while at the same time attacking Holt. During the trial of John Surratt Jr., the public was reminded more than once that among the nine military commissioners who had sentenced Mary Surratt to hang were five who had recommended mercy. It may be recalled that their petition, for her sentence to be converted to life in prison because of her age and her sex, had been signed on June 30, 1865; it was taken by Joseph Holt to the White House on July 5 along with the rest of the relevant papers for Johnson's approval and signature.

On July 7, 1865, the day of the execution, the New York Times noted the existence of the clemency petition, which means that the petition's existence must have been known to the newspaper's correspondent the previous day. Thus, it can safely be assumed that Johnson, too, was fully aware of its existence by July 6, giving him plenty of time to stay the executioner's hand had he wanted to. He chose not to. Instead, Johnson adamantly refused to entertain any of the several pleas for mercy for Mary Surratt that came his way in that two-day period.

THE WICKED MAN NOW ACTING AS PRESIDENT 271

Nevertheless, when word of the clemency petition resurfaced toward the end of the John Surratt trial, it created a popular sensation, much as John Wilkes Booth's diary had done. On Thursday, August 1, in his closing argument on Surratt's behalf, Richard Merrick made a point of invoking the memory of the defendant's mother, as he and the defense team had done repeatedly throughout the trial. "Mrs. M. E. Surratt was not guilty," Merrick declared with passion, "the proof against her was not sufficient to have hung a dog." In order to stimulate additional sympathy for his client, Merrick reminded the jury, in highly emotional language, that the poor woman might have been saved had the clemency petition been approved. Then, as if to prove that John Surratt's own situation was not just an offshoot of the 1865 trial of the assassins, but was also a consequence of the bitter political disputes raging in Washington over Reconstruction, Merrick stunned his listeners by accusing not Andrew Johnson but Joseph Holt of ensuring that the petition would in fact go by the wayside. Merrick claimed that Holt had intentionally withheld the petition from Johnson on the assumption that had Johnson read it, he would certainly have approved it. Thus, according to Merrick, Mary Surratt's blood was on the vengeful judge advocate general's hands rather than the President's. On Judgment Day, Merrick intoned dramatically, "when Mrs. Surratt is called to testify against Joseph Holt, what will he in vindication say?"[15]

The matter did not rest there. During his own extended closing argument over the next few days, prosecutor Edwards Pierrepont furiously returned to the subject. Pierrepont's main purpose in addressing the question of the clemency petition was to defend the honor of the military commission, as well as the honor of Joseph Holt, the Bureau of Military Justice, his own friend Stanton, and the War Department, against those who supported the President. Pierrepont also hoped to shame John Surratt Jr.'s defense counsel for their repeated invocation of Mary Surratt's ghost and for their frequent suggestions that she had been wrongly convicted and executed and that her son now faced a similarly unjust fate. Unlike John Surratt's lawyers, declared Pierrepont, "I have not come here for the purpose of proving that Mrs. Surratt was guilty, or that she was innocent."

Rather, he went on, "I do not understand why that subject was lugged into this case in the mode that it has been." Pierrepont hoped to dissuade the jury from permitting allegations of Mary Surratt's innocence to undermine the strong evidence he and the prosecution team had presented against her son and to point out that the case against her was closed. At the same time, Pierrepont strove to make it clear to the jury—and the American public—that Mary Surratt's conviction and execution had been sanctioned not just by Edwin Stanton and Joseph Holt, but by Andrew Johnson himself. It was Johnson who had signed her death warrant, in spite of any pleas for mercy on her behalf.[16]

When word of the clemency petition hit the press, it fueled the powerful emotions already rife among those who had come to believe Mary Surratt's hanging to have been an injustice, even if they were not entirely sure of her innocence. Equally, it encouraged those who sought any means available to prove that Holt, Stanton, and the Radicals in Congress were far more eager to punish than to forgive the errant South and its sympathizers. Hoping to capitalize on this sentiment, after the closing arguments Andrew Johnson demanded with apparent outrage that Stanton produce for review the relevant original documents from the 1865 trial, including the clemency petition. W. Winthrop handled the matter at the Bureau of Military Justice (Holt had just gone to New York on leave) and took the papers to the Executive Mansion himself.[17]

For several days Johnson held on to the documents. He then boldly told the press that he had never in fact seen the clemency petition until Winthrop delivered the documents to his office on the afternoon of August 5, 1867. To Johnson's advantage, it turns out that he had never actually signed the original clemency petition, even to indicate that he had read it, although he had affixed his signature to several other relevant papers Holt had brought in with it. In 1867, however, the absence of the President's signature made Johnson's claim somewhat more credible, at least among those who were predisposed to support him anyway. At the same time, Johnson's vehement protestations of innocence to the press made those who were inclined to believe Holt and Stanton more adamant than ever. "Among those who know you, as you are," wrote loyal assistant Winthrop to Holt on August 12, "I have not heard the slightest expression of doubt as to the question of veracity between you & the President. They *know* that you *must* be right—that it is *impossible* that it can be otherwise." Years later, August Kautz, who had been a commissioner at the 1865 trial, wrote that Johnson's claim that he had not seen the clemency petition that year simply "did not seem to be very sincere, in view of the fact that within a day or two after the adjournment of the Commission," on June 30, 1865, "the recommendation . . . was published in the daily papers." And it is worth recalling that, even if one accepts the virtually unimaginable scenario of Johnson's being kept in the dark about the clemency petition until after Mary Surratt was dead, historian Thomas Reed Turner is surely on the mark when he notes that nothing the President said or did in the time between the end of the trial and the hanging indicates that he would have spared her under any circumstances.[18]

Still, in some minds the announcement raised new doubts about Holt, who was undeniably the original bearer of the papers to Johnson. More important in immediate practical terms, it provided Johnson with additional ammunition to explain why he was removing Edwin Stanton from the War Department. It even bolstered the President's courage to attack other key figures who opposed his Reconstruction plan. Among the individuals Johnson next targeted were Philip Sheridan and Daniel Sickles. In commanding military districts in the South, these two generals had proven themselves more loyal to Stanton and the Radical Republican agenda than to the President himself. Against General Grant's advice and will, Johnson removed Sheridan shortly after he suspended Stanton on August 12, and before the month was over he replaced Sickles as well.[19]

In his *Personal Memoirs*, Ulysses Grant wrote of all these developments in a manner that reflected how much his own attitude toward the former Confederacy, and his ideas about Reconstruction, had come to diverge from Johnson's. During the years of his presidency, said Grant, Johnson came to "regard the [white] South not only as an oppressed people, but as the people best entitled to consideration of any of our citizens." This was "more than the people who had secured to us the perpetuation of the Union were prepared for, and they became more radical in their views," which increasingly centered around the importance of enfranchising the freedmen for their own protection, as well as for the sake of the Republican Party's survival. Black male suffrage, Grant explained, which had been neither an original war aim nor an aim of most Northerners in the first year or so after the war ended, "became an absolute necessity . . . because of the foolhardiness of the President and the blindness of the Southern people to their own interest."[20]

Put another way, Grant believed that the President's intransigence, rather than immediately guaranteeing white supremacy and the "continued subordination of the blacks to their former masters" in a rapidly restored South, transformed the Republican Party and its supporters like Holt and Stanton—perhaps even to some extent unwittingly—into the "country's vanguard for racial justice" (in the end, of course, their goals, too, remained unfulfilled). As historian Hans Trefousse writes, had the efforts of the Radical Republicans and their supporters "to reconstruct Southern society met with success, they might have brought about a lasting adjustment of relations between the races. All Americans, white and black, would have been the winners."[21] Instead, by suspending Stanton in the summer of 1867, the President dealt the Radicals and their allies what he hoped would be a stunning and perhaps even fatal blow. In this he was disappointed, because his recklessness pushed Grant even closer to the Radicals' position. This was important because of Grant's control of the Union occupying troops and, after Stanton's suspension, temporarily also of the War Department. Johnson's actions also stimulated new sentiment in favor of his impeachment.

Meanwhile, Edwin Stanton assumed that his suspension could not be countermanded until Congress came back into session in December. He made plans to go on an extended "vacation"; before leaving Washington, he ordered Winthrop to send a telegram to Joseph Holt in Pawling, New York, summoning him back to the Bureau of Military Justice. Stanton was annoyed with Ulysses Grant because of the general's having accepted the interim leadership of the War Department (though evidence clearly indicates that Grant did so to keep

Johnson in check and protect the military forces in the South). As a result, Stanton wanted Holt to keep an eye on Grant, making sure the general did not lose his political footing and slip into the Johnson fold. He also wanted to ensure that Holt himself was not removed from office while he was out of town.[22]

Stanton's concerns were hardly without foundation. Frank Ballard wrote to Holt on August 13 that New York City newspapers were already predicting that Johnson would remove Holt at the first opportunity. "The Gods evidently wish to destroy the President," Ballard commented acidly, "if they have maddened him to this extent." At the same time, Ballard continued, Stanton's stock was actually rising. "The President has . . . immortalized him by this mark of his fear and hate," and he predicted that Stanton might even become president at some point in the future. Home in Washington, Holt received many other letters of support, and many words of warning. His friend W. C. Dodge urged him to make sure he had copies of all the important documents in the possession of the Bureau of Military Justice, and that the copies be kept in a safe spot. "It is obvious," Dodge wrote, "that the wicked man now acting as President, and his associates, desire to get you out of the way, as well as Stanton; and in their madness, they will stop at nothing."[23]

Despite the staunch encouragement of his supporters, the weary and battle-worn Joseph Holt was preparing to lay down his sword. Everywhere he turned he saw signs that much of what he had fought for over the past several years now verged on defeat. He might rejoice that the Union had been preserved, but Lincoln was dead, and although his actual murderer, Booth, was also dead, only eight of Booth's co-conspirators had been convicted and punished. The only other figure "properly" penalized for all of the other crimes that had been committed against the Union and its army during the Civil War was Henry Wirz, the commander of Andersonville Prison. Meanwhile Jefferson Davis and all of his high-level cronies had essentially gone free, and John Surratt Jr. seemed likely to do so as well.

Moreover, although the Union army had won the war and freed the slaves, an unrepentant South now seemed eager and ready, with the help of Andrew Johnson, to thwart any meaningful outcome of that victory and any efforts on behalf of the future security of the freed-people. "Nothing but violence and brutality remain," wrote General John Pope on August 10. Pope, a Republican from Holt's native Kentucky, was in Atlanta commanding a military district under the March Reconstruction Act. "Justice is unknown here," he declared, "and personal rights are as little regarded as oaths. . . . I do not believe that the Southern whites to-day are fit for self government. . . . I doubt too whether they ever will be." Pope added with what was meant to be kindness, "The trouble with the blacks is that they do not possess a character sufficiently savage and ferocious to hold their own against the Southern whites without powerful aid for a long time to come."[24] Andrew Johnson seemed bound and determined to deny them that aid.

It is true that in August 1867 Holt, like Stanton, still enjoyed the respect and reverence of many who knew how much each man had sacrificed for the nation's sake. Yet increasingly Holt had to ask himself what tangible evidence there was to suggest that those sacrifices—which included his reputation—had truly been worthwhile. Nor was he reassured by Andrew Johnson's next proclamation of amnesty, drafted by his stalwart supporter Gideon Welles. Issued on September 7, this proclamation extended full pardon to all former Confederates, with the exception of individuals linked to the assassination of Lincoln or any plot connected with it. Practically speaking, this meant denying the possibility of amnesty only to John Surratt Jr. in Washington, D.C., Jefferson Davis in Canada, and the convicted conspirators still in prison at Fort Jefferson in the Dry Tortugas (their number soon reduced to three, with the death from yellow fever of Michael O'Laughlen that month). Noted Welles in his diary shortly after the proclamation appeared in the national press, "The Radicals are full of sensation and malignity" over Johnson's latest act of forgiveness. "They see in it incipient monstrosities, and the leaders declare that the President shall now certainly be impeached."[25]

Indeed, from the perspective of the Radicals and their allies, the only hope for a turnaround in political affairs seemed to rest with the return of the 40th Congress in December, and the sure revival of calls for Johnson's impeachment. In the meantime, Holt concentrated once more on shoring up his reputation, this time by soliciting letters and statements of support from those who could confirm his proper handling of the clemency petition back in July 1865.[26] Surely the judge advocate general also observed with interest the slow, steady razing of most of the buildings at the Old Arsenal Penitentiary at Greenleaf's Point, where the 1865 conspiracy trial had taken place. In the process of this "improvement" of the Old Arsenal grounds, the remains of John Wilkes Booth, Mary Surratt, David Herold, George Atzerodt, Lewis Powell, and Henry Wirz were exhumed and reinterred in a common trench along a wall in a large room at the northeast corner of what was known as Warehouse No. 1. New headboards were installed, and the room was locked.[27]

The state and local elections of November 1867 were relatively quiet, but they were not without consequence. In the South, Republicans managed considerable gains, thanks in large part to Congress's Reconstruction Acts, whose provisions—including those pertaining to voter registration and election policies—the Union army's occupation troops struggled to enforce. Across the North, however, there were signs that the Radicals' attempts to enforce a stern vision of Reconstruction along with civil and political rights for the freedpeople were producing something of a backlash. North of the Mason-Dixon line the elections actually resulted in pro-Johnson Democrats and moderate Republicans regaining a sizable portion of the ground lost to the Radicals the previous year.[28]

Sensing what appeared at the local level to be a shift across the North back in Johnson's direction, the 40th Congress returned to Washington aware that their time to act on several fronts was growing short, and they immediately got down to work. Indeed, the House Judiciary Committee had convened even before Congress officially reopened, recommencing efforts to link Andrew Johnson to the conspiracy to assassinate Lincoln or to the suppression of evidence against the Confederate leadership. The committee also reexamined the question of Jefferson Davis's complicity in the assassination, which, if demonstrated, could be used to bring the former Confederate president to justice, and also to attack Johnson for having allowed Davis to walk out of prison in the first place. (In November, Davis had returned from Canada to appear in court in Virginia, where government lawyers requested and received a continuance in the case until March 1868.) The Judiciary Committee examined new witnesses and considered the report of William H. Gleason, who had been engaged by what was being called the Committee on the Assassination, organized by the relentless Benjamin Butler, to travel to Fort Jefferson to interview the three surviving conspirators convicted in 1865: Samuel Mudd, Samuel Arnold, and Edman Spangler.[29] On December 19, Gleason came before the Judiciary Committee to answer questions and to turn over the prisoners' statements, which essentially offered nothing new. In the end, it seemed, nothing the prisoners told Gleason, and nothing that was revealed during the Judiciary Committee's examination of other witnesses in the fall of 1867, could be used to further the cause of Holt, Stanton, or the Radicals against either Davis or Johnson.[30]

The Judiciary Committee went ahead and recommended Johnson's impeachment anyway.[31] Once again, however, finding no indictable evidence, the House of Representatives as a whole felt compelled to reject the committee's recommendation. Despite this, the momentum in favor of impeachment continued to build, provoked in part by Johnson's year-end replacement of two more generals commanding military districts in the South. By way of counterattack, in mid-January 1868, on the basis of the Tenure of Office Act, the Senate Military Committee overruled Secretary Stanton's suspension. Much to Johnson's surprise and displeasure, Ulysses Grant immediately turned over the keys to the war secretary's office, an act that resulted in a permanent breach between the general and the president. "There is no doubt that Grant has been in secret intrigue in this business," commented Gideon Welles, "acting in concert with and under the direction of the chief conspirators."[32] Welles hoped that, having been duly reinstated, Stanton would now resign. But he did not expect it.

Evidence suggests that Stanton did initially intend to resign once he was returned to office, and had confided that plan to his wife and sister. However, his concern over the possible implications of leaving the War Department, the army, and the enforcement of Congress's Reconstruction laws in the hands of Johnson and his allies held him at his post. Holt, for his part, stood steadfastly by. "I am glad in my heart, that you remain in your important official position in this government," wrote friend D. P. Henderson to Holt from Chicago on January 15. "There is some hope to our hearts, amid all the treachery, when we know *you* are there."[33]

By now, however, although Stanton seemed determined to resist being forced out, Johnson resolved to be done with Lincoln's war secretary once and for all. He was even unwilling to wait and see if the local- and state-level gains enjoyed by Democrats and moderate Republicans across the North in the fall elections would, come the following November, turn out to have been a harbinger of a full-scale popular rejection of the Radicals, their allies, and their plan for the South. Instead, on February 21, 1868, when Congress was still in session, Johnson boldly suspended Stanton again. This time he turned to Adjutant General Lorenzo Thomas to fill Stanton's post until a new war secretary could be nominated. But the aging and mild-mannered Thomas found himself unable to gain access to the Secretary's War Department files. On the advice of a number of supporters, likely including Holt, Stanton had locked himself in his office and now refused to surrender his keys. According to his biographers, Benjamin Thomas and Harold Hyman, in the current climate "there can be no doubt that Stanton saw himself as the savior of the nation's best, most patriotic interests. This man of unheroic mold was now, in his own mind, a knight engaged in struggle with a despised dragon of reaction."[34]

Meanwhile, General Grant in effect placed the army in direct opposition to the President by publicly throwing his support behind Stanton and positioning armed guards around the War Department building. This immediately gave rise to anxious rumors that violence, and perhaps a new civil war, was about to erupt in the capital. Up on Capitol Hill Congress exploded over the latest example of Johnson's disregard for Stanton, the Tenure of Office Act, and the Radicals' plan for Reconstruction, while those who had been hoping for legal means by which to oust the President rejoiced over the opportunity that his suspension of Stanton provided. On February 22, Gideon Welles noted that, upon learning of Stanton's second suspension, the

Senate "at once stopped all business and went into executive session, where a fierce and protracted debate took place, extending far into the night" and ultimately producing a resolution to the effect that "the President had no constitutional or legal power to remove the Secretary of War and appoint another."[35]

Three days later, the House of Representatives impeached Andrew Johnson by a party-line vote of 126–47, marking the first time in American history that a sitting president had been challenged in this manner. The legislators immediately organized a board of prosecutors to try Johnson; this board, it should be noted, included some of the most radical men in Congress, such as Thaddeus Stevens, George Boutwell, and Benjamin Butler. Meanwhile, the war secretary remained holed up in his office (despite the urgings of his wife that he come home), and Lorenzo Thomas halfheartedly attempted to assume control of Stanton's department. "The alleged cause of impeachment," commented Welles bitterly, "is the removal of a con-tumacious, treacherous, and unprincipled officer, who intrudes him-self into the War Department under the authority of a law . . . [designed] to fetter the President and deprive the Executive of his rights."[36]

Overseen by Chief Justice Salmon Chase, Andrew Johnson's trial began in the Senate on February 25, 1868. It lasted about eleven weeks, during which time, at the government attorneys' request, Jef-ferson Davis's treason case before Justice Chase's court in Virginia was again postponed, this time until May, and the Davises returned to Canada. "The loyal men of this state," wrote Holt's longtime friend T. H. Duval from Texas on March 8, "are watching with deep interest the progress of the impeachment measure." Hopeful that Johnson might finally be removed from office, Duval nevertheless feared that the crisis might foment another war. Still, he wrote, "this will be preferable to the condition of affairs that would result from his acquittal." An acquittal, Duval noted, in language Holt himself might have used, would mean that "the war for the Union will have been fought for nothing, the freedmen will again be slaves in fact, loy-alty at the South will be crushed out, and treason and traitors will be everywhere triumphant." Duval put his faith in Congress, however, to have the "nerve and patriotism" to convict the President and send him packing.[37]

The Radical Republicans were not to have their day. The trial ended in late May with Johnson's acquittal on all counts. Thirty-five senators voted to convict the President, one vote short of the two-thirds majority required by the Constitution. Many people had anticipated that Johnson would be convicted.[38] In the end, however, the fears of many in Congress that impeachment would only inflame national passions beyond the possibility of control contributed to Johnson's victory. So, too, did a widespread dislike for and distrust of arch-Radical Republican Benjamin Wade, who as president pro tempore of the Senate would, by law, have succeeded Johnson—who had no vice president—in the Executive Mansion. Also important was the fact that the charges against him were poorly framed. Most of the eleven articles of impeachment had to do with Stanton's removal from office and Johnson's attempt to replace him with Lorenzo Thomas. The ninth charge, which addressed the question of the President's challenges to the authority and the respectability of Congress, was surely the most revealing, for without question the real reason the legislators put Johnson on trial was because they resented his attempts to obstruct their Reconstruction plan. Still, none of the charges cited an indisputably impeachable offense—for example, a high crime or misdemeanor. Even if Johnson had violated the Tenure of Office Act, the Supreme Court was in the process of considering its constitutionality (it would be overturned). Moreover, because of the way the act was written, it was arguably possible to interpret it to apply only to cabinet officers Johnson himself had appointed, which would not include Stanton, a Lincoln holdover.[39]

Even Welles, who had anticipated conviction, had never believed the charges constituted valid grounds for Johnson's ouster. In February 1868 he had commented that "those who may vote to convict upon these articles would as readily vote to impeach the President had he been accused of stepping on a dog's tail." When the Radicals' effort to unseat Johnson failed, Stanton seems to have lost the will to fight any longer. On May 26, he resigned, unwilling and simply too exhausted to continue the struggle. Meanwhile, guns of celebration were fired and victory parades and fireworks displays were arranged by Johnson's exultant supporters across the white South. On June 1, 1868, General John Schofield took Stanton's place, his nomination having been expeditiously confirmed by Congress, and the grateful Lorenzo Thomas returned to his duties in the adjutant general's office.[40] Observing all this from his post at the Bureau of Military Justice, a saddened Joseph Holt kept his own counsel.

Johnson's supporters in the South still hoped to reap the benefits of his lenient Reconstruction policies. Indeed, there was evidence that despite Congress's best efforts to the contrary, Johnson's success in holding on to the Executive Office would continue to produce favorable results for the general cause of forgiveness toward the former Confederacy and its chief agents.

Meanwhile, on May 12, just four days before the senators cast their votes on the first article of impeachment, John Surratt asked to be released on bail. His request was refused. But on June 22, less than a month after Johnson was acquitted, Surratt's second request met with approval and he was released from custody on $40,000 bail, although he technically remained under indictment. Even before the release of Surratt, Jefferson Davis's trial was postponed again, this time until late November, and Davis began to express his certainty that he would be able to avoid a trial altogether.[41]

Other evidence, however, such as the proceedings of the Republican Party's nominating convention in Chicago, suggested that Johnson's opportunities for shaping Reconstruction were on the wane. On May 21, after Johnson had escaped conviction on one charge and with the foreboding that he would almost certainly avoid conviction altogether, the Republicans selected Ulysses S. Grant as their candidate for the presidency. Pro-Johnson forces were deeply distressed by the nomination of Grant, who understandably commanded enormous confidence and support across the Republican Party. Grant endorsed a platform demanding black male suffrage in the states of the former Confederacy, but leaving the same question up to the discretion of the states in the North, as many moderate Republicans had hoped he would. In his diary, the ever faithful Gideon Welles derided the nomination of Grant, whom he had come to dislike almost as intensely as he disliked Stanton. In harsh words that belied their four years of struggling together during the war to save the Union, the secretary of the navy now described Grant as a "man of low instincts, not of a nice sense of honor nor of proper self-respect . . . wanting in truthfulness and sincerity, and . . . grossly, shamefully ignorant of the Constitution and the structure of the government."[42]

Undoubtedly what irked Welles most of all was the fact that Grant's nomination virtually ensured his election and perhaps even a Republican sweep at the polls in November. He was, after all, the general most responsible for winning the war, and the loyal Northern states' votes would dominate the election. Practically speaking, it made sense to anticipate Grant's ascension to the Executive Mansion and to assume that as president he would act to dismantle Johnson's plan for redeeming the former Confederacy. Still, Johnson and his supporters refused to give in, although they now came to an important conclusion: there was simply no point anymore in retaining Andrew Johnson as their standard bearer. Probably no Democrat could win against Grant, but Johnson surely never would. And so, in July, when they gathered for their own convention, the Democrats turned to a man who was even more openly racist than the President himself, Horatio Seymour. A New Yorker, Seymour was famous for having addressed the violently antiblack New York City draft rioters of 1863 as "my friends."[43]

If the nomination of Seymour alone fails to make explicit the Democratic Party's attitudes toward Congressional Reconstruction and the so-called Negro problem, the man the convention chose as Seymour's running mate provides clarity: they selected Frank Blair, the brother of Montgomery Blair, who had attacked Holt and Stanton in his widely reprinted August 1865 speech. Significantly, the vice presidential nominee had recently written an open letter asserting that a Democratic president "could restore 'white people' to power in the South by declaring the new governments" that had been formed since March 1867 under the Congressional plan for Reconstruction "null and void," and by "using the army to disperse them."[44] The Democrats also promptly adopted a platform whose sole purpose was explicitly to oppose Radical Congressional Reconstruction.

Despite the shameless efforts of the Democratic Party in 1868 to capitalize on persistent racism along with popular feelings of discomfort about some of the bolder measures contained in the Radicals' plan for Reconstruction, the possibility that Seymour and Blair might actually be elected must have seemed extremely remote in the face of Grant's nomination. Supporters of the Republican Party and of Radical Reconstruction nevertheless heaved a great sigh of relief when, on July 28, the Fourteenth Amendment was finally ratified, legally guaranteeing civil rights to the freedpeople, and paving the way for suffrage for the freedmen (this would be accomplished by means of the Fifteenth Amendment, ratified in March 1870). "I am greatly rejoiced at the ratification," wrote T. H. Duval to Joseph Holt a few days later. "It fixes and settles, forever I hope, most important principles, and is the basis upon which all the reconstruction measures rest."[45]

Andrew Johnson remained defiant, having issued on July 4 yet another amnesty proclamation, this time drafted by none other than Secretary of State Seward, who tried his best to negotiate a middle-of-the-road position between Johnson and Johnson's opponents. The new amnesty proclamation covered all former Confederates with the exception of any still under indictment, implicitly Jefferson Davis and John Surratt. According to Welles, Johnson had initially hoped to strike the restrictive clause altogether, in order to bring an end to what Welles termed "this unhappy controversy" and offer an "unqualified amnesty to all, without any exception." However, some cabinet members had persuaded the President not to provoke an already angry Congress again.[46]

Still, down at Fort Jefferson the three remaining convicted conspirators felt encouraged anew by this latest proclamation, coming as it did on the heels of Johnson's acquittal and the discharge of John Surratt from custody. "Surratt having been virtually released finally," Samuel Mudd wrote his wife on July 5, "I can't perceive the slightest justification for holding me and the others." Determined to make the most of Johnson's remaining days in office (on the assumption that if elected, Grant would most likely sustain their convictions and abandon them to Fort Jefferson indefinitely), Mudd, Arnold, and Spangler hired a lawyer to fight for their freedom. Not surprisingly, the legal basis for their case was the Supreme Court's 1866 decision in *ex parte* Milligan, and on August 28 their attorney argued before Judge Thomas Jefferson Boynton of the District Court of the United States for the Southern District of Florida that the military commission by which the men had been convicted had acted without proper jurisdiction. For good measure, the lawyer also posited that the President's amnesty proclamations, especially the most recent one, in effect pardoned the men, so they should be set free. Eager for liberation at any cost, Mudd wrote hopefully to his wife that their lawyer required "one hundred dollars in hand, and one hundred dollars each upon release."[47]

The time had not yet come. To the prisoners' utter disbelief and frustration, in September, Judge Boynton refused to release them. Around the same time, Washington District Attorney Edward Carrington, who had led the prosecution team in 1867, learned that a new indictment he issued against John Surratt in June (this time for conspiracy) could not be prosecuted because of the statute of limitations. Thus, whereas Mudd, Arnold, and Spangler had been disappointed once again, John Surratt and his supporters could breathe easily as the case against him continued to dissolve and he remained free on bail. Wrote Mudd to his wife with great bitterness: "It is clearly of no interest of the Government to prosecute the man. . . . They tried him for murder and proved, without doubt, the innocence of his unfortunate mother. . . . It is a wonder the papers don't take up the subject of the legality of our imprisonment, especially since the developments made in the trial of Surratt."[48] For his part, Joseph Holt resisted public comment; his official role in connection with John Surratt, after all, had come to a close the moment Surratt's case was transferred to civil court in early 1867. For the time being, Holt devoted his attention instead to sustaining his own position as judge advocate general in the wake of Stanton's departure from the War Department, and he looked forward to Grant's election.

As Mudd, Spangler, and Arnold bided their time at Fort Jefferson, the rest of the nation prepared for the upcoming November elections. All but three of the states of the former Confederacy (Virginia, Mississippi, and Texas) had reentered the Union by complying with the demands of Congressional Reconstruction, which were being enforced as well as could be expected by those federal army troops who were still assigned to occupation duty in the South.[49] It was unclear when the return of the three unreconstructed states to the national fold would occur. Holt's friend T. H. Duval wrote pessimistically from Austin on July 23: "You ask me if there is any chance of completing the work of reconstruction in Texas, before the Presidential election. I think none whatever. . . . The rebel element in Texas is so encouraged and emboldened by the attitude of the Democratic party in the North, and so confident of their success, that its whole strength would be united against the acceptance of any thing coming from the *radicals.*" Moreover, wrote Duval, "if Seymour can be elected over Grant, the loyal men of the State, black & white, will be at once the victims of the most intolerable tyranny and persecution." Therefore, Duval concluded that "what we now need, and shall need, until after the Presidential election, is military law in Texas, and a large increase to the Federal force."[50]

While Duval crossed his fingers and hoped for the arrival of reinforcements from the Union army, the enemies of Radical Reconstruction did their best to increase the Democratic Party's chances. In August, the once greatly feared Confederate cavalry raider Nathan Bedford Forrest, now the leader of the newly formed Ku Klux Klan, warned Republicans and their supporters across the South that any attempts to use state militia forces to oppose the Klan would be harshly and violently opposed. Especially in Louisiana, Georgia, and Arkansas, the KKK resorted to alarming tactics, including killing over a thousand people—most of them blacks—in order to frighten black voters and Republicans generally into abandoning their political demands.[51]

In the end, the Democratic ticket failed, though Seymour and Blair carried eight states, including New York. "Will you receive congratulations for the country in general," wrote Joseph Holt's friend Margaret Crosby, "from a miserable inhabitant of New York State, and still worse, from a citizen of New York City?" The Republicans (if not necessarily the Radicals among them) had retained their two-thirds majority in the House, which, combined with their four-fifths majority in the Senate, and their control of the Executive Mansion, ensured that Congressional Reconstruction could continue, at least for the time being. "Don't we feel as if we should have smooth sailing now—" wrote Margaret Crosby enthusiastically, "such a President and such a Congress!" And she added, "I know your unselfish heart is full of thanks."[52]

Thankful for the election of Ulysses Grant to the presidency, Holt was nevertheless dismayed, though hardly surprised, by developments in the case against Jefferson Davis. Late in November 1868, lawyers debated in the Virginia court about the feasibility of pursuing a conviction of any sort against the former president of the Confederacy. On this occasion Davis's defense attorneys argued that Davis was being subjected to "double jeopardy" now that the Fourteenth Amendment to the Constitution in effect already punished their client by forbidding him to hold office on account of his having sworn an oath to uphold the U.S. Constitution and then having engaged in rebellion against it. The next month, Chief Justice Chase and Judge Underwood failed to reach an agreement on the proper course to pursue, and the government's attorneys decided to suspend their efforts against Davis indefinitely.[53]

For the four months remaining before Grant's inauguration, a despondent Joseph Holt chose to keep a very low profile. His most important and powerful ally and supporter, Stanton, had departed from the War Department, and his hopes of bringing Jefferson Davis and John Surratt Jr. to justice seemed utterly barren. "Your kind letter came last night," Margaret Crosby wrote Holt on February 28, just a few days before Grant was to take office. "I sat for an hour thinking it over and shed tears to think of your heart weariness."[54]

Meanwhile, Andrew Johnson continued to find both practical and symbolic ways to express his desire for a generous and forgiving redemption of the former Confederacy. As had been true since the end of May 1865, when he issued his first proclamations concerning the future of the postwar South, at least some of Johnson's expressions of mercy toward the former Confederacy specifically targeted individuals associated in one way or another with the Lincoln assassination conspiracy. Notably, on December 25, 1868, Johnson issued yet another proclamation of amnesty, this time including "all former insurgents," even those still under indictment, though by now the point was essentially moot.[55]

In early February 1869, with only a month left to go in his presidency, Johnson granted the requests of Anna Surratt and others that those buried in the common trench in the Old Arsenal Penitentiary's Warehouse No. 1 be returned to their families. The disinterment of the remains of Henry Wirz, John Wilkes Booth, David Herold, George Atzerodt, Lewis Powell, and Mary Surratt momentarily captured the attention of some of the nation's leading journalists, including George Alfred Townsend, who described the event in detail for the *Boston Traveler*: "They had been buried in ammunition boxes of common pine wood, six feet long, two feet wide and two feet deep," wrote Townsend. "When the lid was lifted from Booth's coffin, his face was perfect," though Townsend claimed that Booth's head "dropped off from the body" when it was placed "in a handsome rosewood coffin supplied by his mother." As for Mary Surratt, "her face and form were perfect," too, "and she looked like on[e] in a happy, dreamless sleep." Powell's body, on the other hand, "was greatly wasted," and the German immigrant Atzerodt, who had been the subject of the most critical press reports all along, "was the worst of all; for when the army blanket that covered his remains was lifted up, it revealed a shapeless mass of blackened bones and ashes, with a bald and separated skull in one corner." The remains of Mary Surratt and Henry Wirz were then transferred to plots at Washington's Mount Olivet Cemetery; Booth's were buried in his family plot at Greenmount Cemetery in Baltimore; Herold's went into the family plot at Washington's Congressional Cemetery; Atzerodt's were placed "in the public vault" at Glenwood Cemetery in Washington; and the remains of Lewis Powell were transferred to the Holmead Cemetery, also located in the District of Columbia.[56]

Having returned Wirz and the dead assassination conspirators to their families, Johnson now concentrated on the living ones. "Every body seems to think that Johnson will release you, beyond a doubt, before his term of office expires," Mudd's wife had written encouragingly on January 30, "and for myself I can't see how he can possibly get out of it, after all the petitions and appeals which have been made in your behalf." Even the soldiers at Fort Jefferson had composed a statement supporting Mudd's release, in recognition of his "great services" to the garrison in his capacity as a doctor during the yellow fever epidemic of fall 1867. "He inspired the hopeless with courage," the statement read, "and by his constant presence in the midst of danger and infection, regardless of his own life, tranquillized the fearful and desponding." Many there were, the soldiers' statement continued, who "doubtless owe their lives to the care and treatment they received at his hands." Written the previous October, it is unclear when this statement reached Andrew Johnson's desk. What is clear is that now, in the few weeks remaining before he was to turn over the Executive Mansion to Grant, Johnson felt free to respond favorably to it. He therefore issued a full and unconditional pardon to the three remaining conspirators. For good measure, on February 9 Johnson also pardoned the infamous perjurer Sanford Conover and sent him on his way, while Joseph Holt observed in bitter silence. And on February 26, Attorney General William Evarts informed Jefferson Davis's defense attorneys that the former president of the Confederacy, who had just left on a pleasure trip to London with his wife, "no longer faced the threat of federal prosecution."[57]

"The abject Man of Iniquity," Thomas Shankland wrote to Joseph Holt on February 11, 1869, "has but a few days yet to occupy and disgrace the exalted position which a conspiracy and an assassin helped him to occupy." This longtime friend encouraged Holt to stand by for a possible cabinet appointment in the Grant administration. After all, he wrote with genuine kindness and admiration, "Your name is a tower of strength throughout the land, and among all good men and true, it is spoken with the greatest respect and reverence." On the day before Grant's inauguration, D. P. Henderson of Chicago also wrote to Holt with considerable optimism: "Tomorrow is the coming day of promise to the people of this nation. . . . God grant us men of peace, wisdom, piety and principle at the head of our nation!" The following morning, Ulysses S. Grant took the oath of office at the United States Capitol, as his predecessor had done almost four years before, under much more somber conditions in the room at the Kirkwood Hotel where George Atzerodt had planned to murder him. Andrew Johnson did not attend.[5]

Let us have done with Reconstruction. The country is tired and sick of it.

—*New York Tribune*, April 18, 1870

The fact . . . that a President of the United States, in order to avoid the responsibility of his own act, sought by falsehood & treachery, to destroy the reputation of a subordinate officer holding a confidential interview with him, is a fact of such astounding wickedness, that in my judgment, it concerns the national honor & should not be allowed to perish from the memories of men.

—JOSEPH HOLT, February 27, 1883[1]

Among those great men who in those trying days gave themselves, with entire devotion, to the service of their country, one who brought to that service the ripest learning, the most fervid eloquence, the most varied attainments, who labored with modesty and shunned applause, who in the day of triumph sat reserved and silent and grateful . . . was Joseph Holt, of Kentucky.

—JAMES G. BLAINE, September 1881[2]

EPILOGUE

———

WHEN ULYSSES S. GRANT BECAME PRESIDENT OF THE UNITED STATES ON March 4, 1869, he initiated a new phase of Reconstruction in which Republican control of both the White House and the national legislature seemed to augur well for realizing a more just vision for the postwar South, including guaranteeing civil rights for the former slaves and suffrage for the freedmen. Indeed, even as Jefferson Davis's lawyers were receiving word at the end of February that their client was no longer subject to federal prosecution, and before Andrew Johnson had vacated the Oval Office and the Executive Mansion, Congress began to consider yet another amendment to the federal Constitution, the Fifteenth, which was designed to cement the freedmen's right to vote. Republican legislators across the spectrum rightly anticipated the new Grant administration's support for the amendment. It was ratified in just over a year, on March 30, 1870.

Tragically, over the months and years to follow, new obstacles arose that ultimately helped to undermine much of the Radicals' agenda for the postwar South. Among many other problems, the Republican Party itself was unable to establish an enduring presence in the South. As historian James McPherson has explained, the party "had no indigenous roots in the region," and "most whites perceived it as an alien instrument of hateful change" whose leaders were either profit-minded invaders from the North, or anti-Confederate Southern Unionists who continued to betray their section.[3] Former Confederates railed against these "carpetbaggers" and "scalawags" as hostile enemies smitten with the "Negro cause," against whom all good white Southerners should rise up. And many did, not only in formal political challenges to the Republican Party, but also by means of violent hate organizations such as the Ku Klux Klan.

Meanwhile, in Washington, Grant proved himself a much better general than executive officer of the federal government. He struggled to contend with mounting resistance to Congressional Reconstruction in the South, including the rise of the KKK, while also trying to hold the Northern wing of the Republican Party together in the face of a series of political patronage scandals. At least as troublesome was the looming backlash against what many Northern voters were coming to consider the relentless extremism of Radicals such as Benjamin Butler and Charles Sumner. Hints of this backlash had first been evident at the local level in the elections of 1867. By 1872, a new party called the Liberal Republicans had formed. Its members included disaffected Republican moderates and also Democrats, and they increasingly called for sectional reconciliation rather than radicalism and "bayonet rule" in the South.[4]

The most deplorable development was that so many Northern whites were losing interest in the whole question of the freedpeople's future security and prosperity. Emancipation was one thing, and that, after all, had been achieved. Social and political equality was something else altogether. Persistent racism in the resentful South made it clear that these goals were going to take a much longer time to achieve; and persistent racism in the victorious North undermined white folks' patience with the whole project. And so, even by the early 1870s Radical Reconstruction was well on the wane. But in March 1869, when Ulysses Grant replaced Andrew Johnson, it appeared to many who had stood with the Radicals through four grueling years of battle with Johnson and his supporters, as D. P. Henderson wrote to Joseph Holt, that the "day of promise to the people of this nation" had finally arrived.[5]

Two weeks after Grant took office, Samuel Mudd returned home to Maryland. According to his daughter Nettie, who years later published a memoir of her father's life, Mudd's health had been severely compromised by the time he was reunited with his family. Although he lived for almost fourteen more years, he never recovered his original vitality. At the same time, having protested his innocence repeatedly during the years of his imprisonment, Mudd now seems to have fallen silent on the matter. Instead of struggling to redeem his deeply—perhaps permanently—tarnished name, Mudd devoted his energy to rebuilding his medical practice and to restoring his farm operations, which had essentially collapsed during the war. As a result of emancipation, wrote Nettie with resentment, "There were no laborers to cultivate the farm." In addition, "the fences had fallen down or been destroyed by the Federal soldiery," leaving the fields "unprotected against intrusive cattle." Also, many of the farm's buildings had fallen into disrepair, and "money [was] almost unobtainable." Still, over time conditions improved: Mudd's farm and his medical practice both revived to a considerable extent, and between 1870 and 1878 he and his wife Sarah produced five additional children, beyond the four Mudd had left behind in 1865. Then, at the age of forty-nine, while tending to some ill neighbors, Samuel Mudd contracted pneumonia. He died on January 10, 1883.[6]

Of the three convicted Lincoln assassins who survived the 1867 yellow fever outbreak at Fort Jefferson, Mudd was actually the second to go. He followed Edman Spangler, who had traveled to Baltimore after his discharge. Spangler spent the next four years working there for his former employer and longtime advocate, John T. Ford.[7] For reasons that are not entirely clear, in 1873 Spangler left Baltimore to reappear unexpectedly at the Mudd farm. His former cell mate, to whom he had become very attached during their four years' imprisonment together, generously granted him five acres of land for his own use.

For the next eighteen months Spangler farmed the land, assisted the Mudds' gardener with chores, and did some carpentry work for various individuals in the vicinity. Mudd's daughter Nettie recalled, "He was a quiet, genial man, greatly respected by the members of our family and the people of the neighborhood. His greatest pleasure seemed to be found in extending kindness to others, and particularly to children, of whom he was very fond." On February 7, 1875, Spangler died of an unknown illness, leaving behind little more than a written statement that contained some details of his life and reiterated his innocence of the crime for which he had been imprisoned. Samuel Mudd found the document tucked into Spangler's tool chest.[8]

Convicted conspirator Samuel Arnold lived on into the early twentieth century. After returning to Maryland with his father in 1869, Arnold largely kept to himself, refusing interviews with the press and, as he later put it, "abiding my own time to give to the public any and all facts which I possessed" concerning the Lincoln assassination conspiracy. In 1904, now seventy years old, Arnold composed a lengthy statement defending his own character, once again admitting his involvement in the original abduction scheme, but denying any connection to (or knowledge of) Booth's plan to murder Lincoln. At the end of his life Arnold clearly remained bitter over what he described as his "unjust trial, torture and condemnation." He died of tuberculosis in 1906.[9]

Samuel Arnold's death closed the book on the eight individuals who had been found guilty of conspiracy with John Wilkes Booth in 1865. John Surratt, however, lived on for another decade. Released from prison on bail in June 1868, Surratt rejoiced when all charges against him were finally dropped fifteen months later. For the next several years, Surratt insisted that his nervous system had been permanently damaged in the wake of his 1867 trial. He further claimed that the expenses he had incurred during the trial—which apparently included hiring private detectives to follow the government's detectives around, in order to ensure that the latter did not falsify or destroy evidence favorable to his case—had cast him into financially desperate straits.[10] Perhaps this is why Surratt attempted to capitalize on his notoriety by giving paid lectures on the abduction and assassination conspiracies with which his name was indelibly associated.

The first such lecture took place at the courthouse in Rockville, Maryland, on December 6, 1870. Adult attendees paid fifty cents (children were half price) to hear Surratt describe the dramatic events of the spring of 1865. They also heard him declare his innocence in connection with the actual murder of the President, and then recount his adventures while on the lam in Canada and Europe. One thing they did not hear was a strong and pointed defense by Surratt of his mother's innocence. At best, he defended Mary Surratt indirectly by attacking Louis Weichmann, whom he declared "a base-born perjurer" and "a murderer of the meanest hue! . . . Give me a man who can strike his victim dead," Surratt demanded, "but save me from a man who, through perjury, will cause the death of an innocent person. . . . Hell possesses no worse fiend than a character of that kind."[11]

John Surratt repeated the lecture to audiences at Cooper Union in New York City and at Concordia Hall in Baltimore, but his lecture career came to a halt less than a month after it began. On December 30, Surratt had planned to give the same basic speech at the Odd Fellows Hall in Washington, D.C., just a few blocks from both the former Surratt boardinghouse and Ford's Theater. This time, however, Surratt clearly overestimated the enthusiasm with which a speech by one so intimately linked to the assassination of Abraham Lincoln would be received in the town—indeed, the very neighborhood—where the murder took place. At the last minute, responding to a widely circulated petition urging that Surratt's lecture be canceled, the Odd Fellows and then the mayor of Washington himself withdrew their support. The talk was indeed canceled, and Surratt subsequently retired from the public eye.

For most of the next thirty years, John Surratt quietly focused on his private and professional life. He taught school briefly in Rockville and then Emmitsburg, Maryland, and in 1872 married Mary Victorine Hunter. Surratt and his wife had seven children. Eventually the family moved to Baltimore, where Surratt's brother, Isaac, and his sister, Anna, also lived, she with her husband, William P. Tonry, and their four children.[12] John Surratt took employment there at the Old Bay Line steam packet company, becoming a freight auditor and then the company's treasurer.

In 1898 Surratt resurfaced briefly, having agreed to an extended interview with journalist Hanson Hiss, which was then published in the *Washington Post*. In essence, the interview repeated the contents of his 1870 lecture: Surratt spoke of his involvement with the Confederate underground, and of Booth, but he continued to distance himself from the assassination itself. As before, Surratt also made the most of his adventures while avoiding capture both in Canada and in Europe, as well as the drama ultimately associated with his arrest, repatriation, and trial. As in the past, he substituted an attack on Louis Weichmann for a defense of his mother. He pronounced Weichmann's testimony "from beginning to end . . . outrageously false." Weichmann, insisted Surratt, was a "moral coward" who had "made up his story out of whole cloth" in order to save his own neck. Not unlike Samuel Arnold, thirty years after his release from prison John Surratt remained an extremely bitter man. He retired from the Old Bay Line company in 1914, and died on April 21, 1916, at the age of seventy-two.[13]

Long since deceased by then was another man whose name had been linked consistently to the assassination of Abraham Lincoln: Jefferson Davis. Once Davis was no longer subject to prosecution for either treason or conspiracy to assassinate Lincoln, he and his wife, Varina, embarked on an extended period of wandering in Canada, Europe, and the American South, while Davis engaged in a variety of basically unsuccessful business ventures. In 1876, the man whom Joseph Holt had more than once referred to as the "arch rebel" finally settled in Mississippi. There he set to work on his memoirs, an egocentric and unrepentant two-volume work, in which Davis represented himself as the central figure in the Lost Cause tragedy. *The Rise and Fall of the Confederate Government* was published in 1881. In subsequent years, Davis entertained countless guests and attended as many events commemorating the war and the Confederacy as his health permitted. Even in his daily life he routinely dressed in Confederate gray. Jefferson Davis died of natural causes in December 1889, at the age of eighty-one.[14]

Former Secretary of War Edwin Stanton predeceased Davis by twenty years. He died on December 24, 1869, only a few days after his fifty-fifth birthday and his confirmation as a justice of the United States Supreme Court. Stanton had spent much of the period since his

May 1868 resignation from the War Department struggling to regain
the health he had sacrificed on the nation's behalf during and after the
war, while reviving his legal practice. He was unsuccessful. An asth-
matic all his life, in the end Stanton's respiratory system failed before
his professional life was fully restored. Although he died of heart failure, rumors began to circulate among Stanton's enemies that he had
committed suicide out of guilt over the role he had played in the 1865
trial, and particularly his association with the execution of Mary Surratt. Such rumors were sheer nonsense. Although Stanton was
exhausted at the end of his life, he was neither broken nor consumed
by remorse. Those who met with him shortly before he died spoke of
his good cheer and his excitement about his future prospects.[15]

As for Andrew Johnson, after refusing to attend Grant's inauguration, the former president returned to his home state of Tennessee,
where he participated in local politics. Soon, however, Johnson
yearned to return to the national stage and he decided to make a bid
as a Democrat for a seat in Congress. In doing so, the former president could hardly avoid confronting the ghosts of his political past,
most important that of Mary Surratt, for whom popular sympathy
had continued to grow over the years. This was especially true in
Johnson's native South, where for many unrepentant former Confederates she symbolized the cruel lengths to which the federal government and its agents (notably Holt and Stanton) had proved willing to
go when the war ended. In the context of his efforts in the early 1870s
to persuade Tennesseans to send him back to Washington, Johnson
found it necessary to try to lay to rest any and all claims that he was
to blame for the unjust federal government murder of this "innocent"
woman, whose political sympathies had so clearly rested with the
now vanquished South.

Among his potential Democratic constituents Johnson could
hardly afford to reaffirm the faith in Mary Surratt's guilt that he had
shown in July 1865, nor could he reiterate the justice of the sentence
that had been carried out, on his order, against her. Instead, Johnson
chose to recirculate for mass consumption his August 1867 claim that
Joseph Holt had failed to make him aware of the military commissioners' recommendation to clemency in her case. Once again, John-

son insisted that he had become aware of the clemency petition only when its existence was revealed during John Surratt's trial, and therefore he could not be held responsible for her death.[16] As before, Johnson's implication was that the vindictive Holt had suppressed or withheld the recommendation to mercy purely in order to guarantee that Johnson, who now depicted himself as benevolent and forgiving, agreed to Mrs. Surratt's execution.

If Johnson had hoped that reopening this debate would boost his chances for immediate electoral success, he was mistaken. Instead, he was defeated in two separate races (one for Senate, one for a seat in the House) before finally being elected to the U.S. Senate by the Tennessee state legislature in January 1875. But Johnson hardly had an opportunity to enjoy his comeback. Back in Tennessee following a brief trip to the nation's capital in March, he had a massive stroke. Andrew Johnson died on July 31, 1875.[17]

Johnson's revival of the debate over Mary Surratt's clemency petition did him little if any good politically. It did succeed, however, in further embittering the last years of Joseph Holt's tenure as judge advocate general. Indeed, it powerfully altered the tone of the last two decades of Holt's life. As Holt saw it, rather than fading into well-deserved oblivion after his departure from the Executive Mansion, the cowardly, self-serving, obstructionist Andrew Johnson had thrown down the gauntlet again. In so doing, this thoroughly unworthy successor to the great Abraham Lincoln had left Holt with no choice. With Stanton dead and the Radicals' influence over the future of the South in decline, Holt turned his energy, and what remained of his own stores of self-respect and patriotism, to vindicating his reputation once more. In defending himself, he also defended the Bureau of Military Justice and its efforts over the years to exact fair punishment on all who had threatened the life and future of the nation, preeminently those Holt had identified as Lincoln's assassins. When Andrew Johnson publicly insisted in 1873, as he had in the summer of 1867, that Joseph Holt's hands and not his own bore the stains of the innocent blood of Mary Surratt, Holt launched a furious counterattack. He mustered evidence from all relevant sources to prove Andrew Johnson a liar.[18]

By late that summer, Holt's latest "vindication" began to take shape in the form of a long letter to Secretary of War W. W. Belknap, in which Holt adamantly refuted Johnson's charges. "For me to have attempted the suppression or concealment of the [petition] from the President," wrote Holt, "would have argued a stupidity on my part verging upon idiotcy." Soon thereafter Holt published his response to Johnson in the *Washington Chronicle*, and subsequently as a pamphlet. His *Vindication of Judge Advocate General Holt* contained a detailed statement of self-defense as well as numerous letters from supporters, colleagues, and significantly involved parties bolstering his claim to have done his full duty back in July 1865. One of the more important items Holt included was a February 1873 letter from John Bingham, his former assistant judge advocate, in which Bingham declared that he himself had been informed by both Stanton and Secretary of State Seward that Johnson had not only seen the clemency petition prior to the execution, but had also discussed it in a cabinet meeting, where those present had agreed unanimously to reject it. By publishing Bingham's letter in his *Vindication*, along with many other items of supporting evidence, Holt hoped to make clear once and for all that when Andrew Johnson signed the execution order for Mary Surratt, he did so with all the relevant material at hand.[19]

Throughout the fall of 1873 and into 1874, Holt sent copies of his *Vindication* to any and all who requested them. As in the past, he received in turn a flood of letters and other signs of encouragement and endorsement. "The vindication is full and complete," telegraphed James A. Ekin, one of the commissioners at the original conspiracy trial. "It confirms what was known to your friends, it pulverizes your enemies." David Hunter, who had presided over the 1865 trial, wrote, "I have not the least doubt President Johnson saw this petition. . . . No one who witnessed the amiable manner in which you conducted yourself during this long and tedious trial, will for a moment believe that you could have concealed this recommendation to mercy."[20] Holt was hardly so sure.

Meanwhile, having reopened Pandora's box, the politically ambitious Andrew Johnson published a formal reply to Holt's *Vindication* in November 1873 in which he boldly restated his own innocence in connection with Mary Surratt's execution. Predictably, Holt responded with a lengthy public "Rejoinder," which he then also distributed far and wide.[21] At the same time, although he was bone weary (he took a thirty-day leave of absence beginning on September 29, 1873, and two subsequent leaves in 1874 and 1875[22]), Holt relentlessly labored to drum up additional evidence in his own behalf. On this score, Holt solicited in particular the aid of his fellow Kentuckian and once good friend, Lincoln's Attorney General James Speed, who had resigned in protest from the Johnson administration in 1866 following Johnson's veto of the Freedmen's Bureau bill.

Unfortunately for Holt, Speed stubbornly and frustratingly opted to remain above the fray. Holt's hope had been that Speed, as one of Johnson's cabinet members, could and would provide direct evidence of Johnson's having discussed the clemency petition with his closest advisers—which would of course require that he had seen it—shortly before the execution. (On this point, John Bingham's February 1873 letter was only hearsay.) Instead, although Speed freely admitted to having seen the clemency petition himself prior to the execution, for reasons that remain a mystery, he clung to the principle that a president's communications with his cabinet were inviolably confidential, and for the time being he consistently failed to give Holt the satisfaction he so desperately desired.

Many years later, however, in a speech to the Loyal Legion in Cincinnati in 1887, the seventy-five-year-old Speed finally made a statement that seemed to clear Holt's name once and for all. In referring to Holt's conduct of the original conspiracy trial and its outcome, Speed described Holt as having "performed his duty kindly and considerately," and in a manner that was "just and fair" in every way. "This I know," Speed added, "Judge Holt needs no vindication from me nor anyone else." Although Speed's words at this late date offered some solace, it was typical of Holt that he refused to be satisfied with anything short of a complete and final exoneration. By this time, Holt had been retired from the post of judge advocate general for over ten years. Deeply saddened by his inability to recapture the unqualified public trust and honor that had been his hallmark through so much of his professional career, Holt had resigned on December 1, 1875, just four months after the death of Andrew Johnson.[23]

More than a decade into his retirement, Holt doggedly refused to let the issue go. At his request, in 1888 the *North American Review* published his empassioned correspondence (dating back to 1883) with James Speed, who had died shortly after his speech in Cincinnati. This correspondence revealed again both Holt's eagerness for vindication and Speed's almost perverse determination to maintain silence on the matter of cabinet discussions, despite the fact that Johnson was long dead by the time Speed and Holt were exchanging letters. Holt wrote to the editor of the *Review*, "It will be gratifying if through your kind instrumentality the legal or moral principle discussed can be brought to the notice of the American people . . . whether a Cabinet officer is justified in withholding & so suppressing, testimony of the innocence of an officer of the government charged with an infamous offense merely because the accuser of such officer was the President of the United States."[24]

Holt's supporters continued to rally to his defense during his later years. In 1889, Henry L. Burnett gave a speech before the Military Order of the Loyal Legion in New York, in which he defended his onetime boss in no uncertain terms, displayed an abundance of evidence in Holt's favor, and decried Johnson's deceit as the most "cruel and treacherous betrayal" that was "ever committed by a man in high official position." In 1890, Holt's longtime friend Horatio King extended the discussion in an article in *Century Magazine*. As others had also done, King pointed out that even if one could prove that Johnson never saw the clemency petition, the fact remained that the President had on several occasions openly expressed his disdain for Mary Surratt, and his firm belief that she was guilty and should be punished. King wrote that "there was no man living" in the summer of 1865, "who more firmly believed in her guilty participation in the assassination of Abraham Lincoln than President Johnson, who . . . said at the time to Rev. J. George Butler of St. Paul's Church, Washington, that he could not be moved; for, in his own significant language, '*Mrs. Surratt kept the nest that hatched the egg.*'"[25]

To the end, Holt conducted his campaign to clear his name from his Washington home. According to one source, Holt's final years were characterized by continued estrangement from much of his family back in Kentucky, which sometimes included refusing to answer their letters or returning those letters unread. Historian William Hanchett reports that Holt's fellow citizens often saw him sitting on his porch, "a massive man with shaggy eyebrows and a full head of gray-white hair," wearing an expression so solemn that one observer described him as "the personification of gloom." The evidence nonetheless suggests that Holt maintained an active presence in Washington, attending public events, keeping up social contacts with his friends, and producing a substantial amount of correspondence. When he died at home, at 2:50 A.M. on August 1, 1894, Holt was eighty-seven years old.[26]

According to the New York Times obituary "Judge Holt was in very good health until a few days ago. He was descending a stairway in his house, and, when near the bottom, made a misstep. His nervous system was considerably jarred by the unexpected shock, and from that time he began to sink rapidly." That same afternoon, an announcement of his death was issued by the adjutant general's office on behalf of the secretary of war, and two days later, cavalry troopers escorted Holt's funeral cortege to the railroad station for his final return to Kentucky. Meanwhile, in his honor the War Department lowered its flag to half staff with orders to hold it there until the late judge advocate general's remains "shall have passed beyond the boundaries of the city." An editorial in the New York Times on August 2 noted, "The death of Joseph Holt severs one more of the ties that link the present generation to those who fought the war for the Union. . . . In the trying time when public sentiment was unformed and unaroused, and when the love of country which became swiftly irresistible was still latent, the eloquent and stirring voice of this sincere and devoted Unionist rang through the land." Although the writer did not refer explicitly to Holt's postwar career or his pursuit of Lincoln's assassins, he did add that throughout Holt's professional life, "he remained as modest and unselfish as in the hour of trial he had been courageous and faithful."[27]

If such words failed to tell the whole story of Holt's career at the

Bureau of Military Justice, they certainly held true for a significant piece of it. A deeply—even rigidly—principled man, Holt committed his uncompromising support to the Union virtually at the moment his native South began to secede from it. When John Wilkes Booth murdered Abraham Lincoln four years later, he guaranteed that in Judge Advocate General Holt, his co-conspirators would face a wrathful and determined avenger. Holt understood the crimes of April 14, 1865, to be the grotesque culmination of countless other crimes committed by the Confederacy during the war. For this reason, Holt and his many loyal associates worked together with enormous passion and dedication, if not always the highest degree of discernment and good judgment, to exact retribution. At the same time, they struggled to transform the South in ways they believed to be just, and also necessary if such crimes were to be prevented in the future. In avenging the murder of Lincoln, and the crimes of the Confederacy as a whole, Holt and his colleagues across the federal government sacrificed much—in some cases perhaps even a measure of their own respectability—for their cause. Such successes as they were able to enjoy were, for the most part, achieved in opposition to the very man Lincoln's murder placed in the Executive Mansion: Andrew Johnson, the only Southern senator to have remained loyal to the Union throughout the war, who as president became the former Confederacy's most powerful and generous friend.

NOTES
___

These shortened forms are used throughout the notes for frequently cited sources:

Butler Papers   Report 104 of the House of Representatives (Judiciary Committee's investigations relating to Jefferson Davis and Clement Clay in the spring of 1866), 39th Congress, 1st session, 1866. (I thank James Hall for sharing with me his microfilmed copy of this report, which he found in the Butler Papers, Library of Congress, Washington, D.C.)

Holt-HL   Joseph Holt Papers, Huntington Library, San Marino, California.

Holt-LC   Joseph Holt Papers, Library of Congress, Washington, D.C.

Kautz Papers   August V. Kautz Papers, Library of Congress, Washington, D.C.

M-599   RG 153, the Records of the Judge Advocate General, Investigation and Trial Papers Relating to the Assassination of President Lincoln, Microfilm no. 599 (16 rolls), National Archives, Washington, D.C.

Official Records   The War of the Rebellion: The Official Records of the Union and Confederate Armies (Washington, D.C.: Government Printing Office, 1881–1902).

Stanton Papers   Edwin M. Stanton Papers, Library of Congress, Washington, D.C.

1. "THAT FEARFUL NIGHT"
THE ASSASSINATION AND THE MAKING OF AN AVENGER

1. M. W. Jacobus to Joseph Holt, May 9, 1865, in container 47, Holt-LC.
2. *New York Commercial Advertiser*, April 22, 1865.
3. Ibid.
4. Ibid.
5. Needless to say, numerous accounts of the murder of the President exist, both contemporary and modern. For two thorough versions of quite recent vintage, see Roy Z. Chamlee, *Lincoln's Assassins: A Complete Account of Their Capture, Trial, and Punishment* (Jefferson, N.C.: McFarland & Company, 1990), pp. 5–7, and Edward Steers, *Blood on the Moon: The Assassination of Abraham Lincoln* (Lexington: University Press of Kentucky, 2001), pp. 113–18.
6. Leon Q. Prior, "Lewis Payne, Pawn of John Wilkes Booth," *Florida Historical Quarterly* 43 (1964), pp. 13–14; Louis J. Weichmann, *A True History of the Assassination of Abraham Lincoln and of the Conspiracy of 1865* (New York: Alfred A. Knopf, 1975), p. 142; Benn Pitman, *The Assassination of President Lincoln and the Trial of the Conspirators* (1865; reprint, New York: Funk & Wagnalls, 1954), pp. 154–56; Glyndon Van Deusen, *William Henry Seward* (New York: Oxford University Press, 1967), pp. 412–14. Initially Secretary Seward was expected, like Lincoln, to die of his wounds. In her diary on April 15, New Yorker Maria Lydig Daly echoed popular belief about Seward's condition: "The Secretary is old already, weakened from having broken his arm; he will scarcely survive. God save us all. What may not a day bring forth!" (Harold Earl Hammond, ed., *Diary of a Union Lady, 1861–1865* [New York: Funk & Wagnalls, 1962], p. 354). Secretary Seward did indeed survive, as did his wounded sons, but the emotional trauma of the attack greatly debilitated Seward's wife, who died only about two months later, before Seward himself was able to resume the full duties of his office. His daughter, Fanny, was also shattered by the events of April 14; she died in October 1866 (Van Deusen, *William Henry Seward*, p. 416; Margaret Leech, *Reveille in Washington, 1860–1865* [New York: Harper & Brothers, 1941], p. 395). See also Patricia Carley Johnson, ed., "I Have Supped Full on Horrors," *American Heritage* 10 (October 1959), pp. 60–65 and 96–101, for Fanny Seward's account of April 14.
7. Michael Maione and James O. Hall, "Why Seward? The Attack on the Night of April 14, 1865," *Lincoln Herald* 100 (Spring 1998), pp. 29–34.
8. Benjamin P. Thomas and Harold M. Hyman, *Stanton: The Life and Times of Lincoln's Secretary of War* (New York: Alfred A. Knopf, 1962), pp. 20, 64–66, 381–83, 394. There has been considerable debate over the years on the topic of Stanton's relationship with Lincoln, with perhaps the most

extreme example of a negative interpretation coming from Otto Eisen-schiml, whose provocative if severely distorted book, *Why Was Lincoln Murdered?* (New York: Grosset & Dunlap, 1937), absurdly fingered Stanton as the mastermind of the assassination conspiracy. As Thomas and Hyman point out, it is clear that in his first encounter with Lincoln in 1855, when the two were assigned to work together on a legal case, the more experienced Stanton treated Lincoln in a manner that was "rude, snobbish, and supercilious," and he apparently referred to his junior colleague as "that giraffe." Over the course of the war, however, Stanton and Lincoln became not only allies on behalf of the nation, but also good friends, and by 1865 it is clear that Stanton's affection and respect for Lincoln ran deep.

9. Jay Winik, *April 1865: The Month That Saved America* (New York: HarperCollins, 2001), p. 261.

10. Howard K. Beale, ed., *Diary of Gideon Welles: Secretary of the Navy Under Lincoln and Johnson* (New York: W.W. Norton, 1960), 2:289–90.

11. See Stanton's April 20, 1865, order transferring responsibility for the investigations, and the prosecution of the accused, to Holt, in the Stanton Papers.

12. *New York Times*, August 2, 1894; Mary Bernard Allen, "Joseph Holt: Judge Advocate General (1862–1875): A Study in the Treatment of Political Prisoners by the United States Government During the Civil War" (Ph.D. diss., University of Chicago, 1927), pp. 48–49; undated autobiographical statement of Joseph Holt, in container 117, Holt-LC; Roger J. Bartman, "The Contribution of Joseph Holt to the Political Life of the United States" (Ph.D. diss., Fordham University, 1958), pp. 5–13.

13. *New York Times*, August 2, 1894; Allen, "Joseph Holt," pp. 48–49; undated autobiographical statement of Joseph Holt, in container 117, Holt-LC; Bartman, "Contribution of Joseph Holt," pp. 52–65.

14. Allen, "Joseph Holt," pp. 48–50; Bartman, "Contribution of Joseph Holt," pp. 72–75.

15. Virginia Clay-Clopton, *A Belle of the Fifties* (New York: Doubleday, Page, 1904), pp. 54–55; Allen, "Joseph Holt," pp. 50–52; *New York Times*, September 3, 1861, and August 2, 1894; undated autobiographical statement of Joseph Holt, in container 117, Holt-LC; William Hanchett, *The Lincoln Murder Conspiracies* (Urbana: University of Illinois Press, 1983), p. 62. Holt's good friend of almost thirty years, Theodore S. Bell of Louisville, agreed: "It would be as easy to make the sun swerve from its orbit," wrote Bell to Holt on the occasion of his shift into the War Department, "as to get you to fail in duty or to swerve from the line of integrity" (T. S. Bell to Joseph Holt, January 8, 1861, in container 26, Holt-LC).

16. John G. Nicolay and John Hay, *Abraham Lincoln: A History* (New York: Century, 1904), 3:76, 89.

17. Bartman, "Contribution of Joseph Holt," pp. 158–64; Thomas and Hyman, Stanton, pp. 89–97.

18. Philip Auchampaugh, *James Buchanan and His Cabinet on the Eve of Secession* (Boston: J.S. Canner, 1965), p. 35.
19. *New York Times*, January 1, 1861; William H. Freehling, *The South vs. the South: How Anti-Confederate Southerners Shaped the Course of the Civil War* (New York: Oxford University Press, 2001), p. 52; Bartman, "Contribution of Joseph Holt," p. 65.
20. *New York Times*, January 1, 1861; Louis T. Wigfall to M. L. Bonham, January 2, 1861, in *Official Records*, ser. 1, vol. 1, p. 252; Allen, "Joseph Holt," p. 64; Bartman, "Contribution of Joseph Holt," pp. 14, 65, 62; Clay-Clopton, *Belle of the Fifties*, p. 54. See also W. M. Gwin to C. Benham, February 8, 1861, *Official Records*, ser. 2, vol. 2, p. 1015.
21. To an old law partner from his days in Vicksburg, Mississippi, Holt wrote with resignation on January 14, 1861: "I concur with you that the South was determined to separate from the North. . . . They will succeed. The union is passing away, like a bank of fog before the wind." Still, Holt firmly believed that the South's own destruction would follow. The South's fate, he prophesied, "will be that of Sampson. She will pull down the temple, but she will perish amid its ruins" (Allen, "Joseph Holt," p. 62; spelling as in the original).
22. Robert Holt to Joseph Holt, January 10, 1861, in container 26, Holt-LC; spelling as in the original.
23. Unknown correspondent to Joseph Holt, January 5, 1861, in container 26, Holt-LC.
24. Nicolay and Hay, *Abraham Lincoln*, 3:90; Thomas and Hyman, *Stanton*, p. 105.
25. Quoted in Nicolay and Hay, *Abraham Lincoln*, 3:109.
26. Thomas and Hyman, *Stanton*, pp. 105–6.
27. Nicolay and Hay, *Abraham Lincoln*, 3:130, 159–61, 170–72; Dr. H. Wigand to Joseph Holt, January 24, 1861, in container 26, Holt-LC.
28. Joseph Holt to James Buchanan, February 18, 1861, *Official Records*, ser. 1, vol. 51, pt. 1, pp. 436–38.
29. Ibid.; Nicolay and Hay, *Abraham Lincoln*, 3:149–52; Michael Burlingame, ed., *An Oral History of Abraham Lincoln: John G. Nicolay's Interviews and Essays* (Carbondale: Southern Illinois University Press, 1966), p. 76.
30. Robert Holt to Joseph Holt, February 11, 1861, in container 27, Holt-LC.
31. *New York Times*, September 3, 1861.
32. Undated autobiographical statement of Joseph Holt, in container 117, Holt-LC; Nicolay and Hay, *Abraham Lincoln*, 3:376. See also William Seward to Joseph Holt, March 6, 1861, in container 28, Holt-LC.
33. Gayla Koerting, "For Law and Order: Joseph Holt, the Civil War, and the Judge Advocate General's Department," *Register of the Kentucky Historical Society* 97 (Winter 1999), p. 7; Abraham Lincoln to Joseph Holt, March 12, 1861, in container 28, Holt-LC. See also Mary K. Stephens to Maggie

Holt [actually deceased at the time], February 28, 1861, and Dr. H. Wigand to Joseph Holt, January 24, 1861, in container 27, Holt-LC.

34. Quoted in Freehling, *The South vs. the South*, p. 82. As James M. McPherson notes, other sources claim to quote Lincoln expressing the belief that "while he hoped to have God on his side, he must have Kentucky" (James M. McPherson, *Ordeal by Fire: The Civil War and Reconstruction* [New York: McGraw-Hill, 1992], p. 157).

35. McPherson, *Ordeal by Fire*, p. 157.

36. Bartman, "Contribution of Joseph Holt," pp. 139–51, 207, 212, 214; *New York Times*, July 13, 1861. See also *New York Times*, July 18 and July 20, 1861, which contain reports of Holt's speeches in Kentucky.On October 12, 1861, *Frank Leslie's Illustrated Newspaper* published a photograph of "Camp Jo Holt," a military post for Kentucky volunteers in the Union army, named in his honor, and established just across the Ohio River in Jeffersonville, Indiana.

37. *New York Times*, August 6, 1861. See also notices and descriptions of Holt's speeches elsewhere during this period, in *New York Times* of August 21, September 3, and September 4, 1861; *Boston Post*, August 27, 1861; and *Boston Courier*, August 28, 1861.

38. Freehling, *The South vs. the South*, p. 54. Theodore S. Bell to Joseph Holt, September 19, 1861, in container 30, Holt-LC. According to Freehling, Kentucky sent twice as many soldiers into the Union army as into the Confederate forces.

39. Joshua F. Speed to Joseph Holt, December 8, 1861, in container 31, Holt-LC.

40. *New York Times*, August 2, 1894; Edwin M. Stanton to Joseph Holt, January 25, 1862, in Holt-HL.

41. *New York Times*, August 2, 1894, November 13, 1862. See also Joseph Holt to Edwin M. Stanton, June 29, 1864, in RG 94, Records of the Adjutant General's Office, 1780s–1917, Letters Received by the Commission Branch of the Adjutant General's Office, 1863–1870, Roll 96, H834 CB 1864, National Archives, Washington, D.C. Holt scholar Mary Allen writes: "Moderates throughout the country who relied on Holt's judgment were inspired with confidence in Stanton's ability because of his friend's manifest confidence in him" (Allen, "Joseph Holt," p. 84).

General Orders No. 270, of October 11, 1864, defines the "duties and functions of the Bureau of Military Justice." See *Official Records*, ser. 3, vol. 4, p. 774.

During his tenure as judge advocate general, Holt refused a number of nominations for cabinet positions, including the attorney generalship, which Lincoln offered him in late 1864. On that occasion, Holt, "with that modesty and conscientiousness which formed the most striking trait of his character, believed that the length of time which had elapsed since he had

retired from active service at the bar had rendered him unfit for the preparation and presentation of cases in an adequate manner before the Supreme
Court, and therefore declined the appointment" (Nicolay and Hay, Abraham Lincoln, 9:72–73, 346–47; see also Joseph Holt to Abraham Lincoln,
November 1864, in Holt-HL).

42. E. B. Long, The Civil War Day by Day (New York: Da Capo Press, 1971),
pp. 270–71. Lincoln originally suspended the writ of habeas corpus on
April 27, 1861, specifically in response to the crisis in Maryland, where the
secessionist legislature threatened to take action that would isolate Washington from the North. In May 1861, the Supreme Court of the United
States, led by Chief Justice Roger Taney, ruled this suspension unconstitutional, but Lincoln refused to recognize or bend to the ruling. The September 24, 1862, proclamation suspending the writ again amounted to a
restatement and expansion of Lincoln's previous position and was
grounded in the notion that "the Constitution provided for suspension [of
the writ] in cases of rebellion or invasion where public safety required it"
(ibid., p. 79). As will be discussed below, President Andrew Johnson
restored the writ of habeas corpus on April 2, 1866.

43. New York Times, August 6, 1861.

44. Hanchett, Lincoln Murder Conspiracies, p. 63. Adds Hanchett: "Holt interpreted this [latter] very broadly. . . . He was thus the principal agent by
which Lincoln extended military control over political prisoners." See also
Thomas Bland Keys, "Were the Lincoln Conspirators Dealt Justice?," Lincoln Herald 80 (1978), pp. 38–46, and Allen, "Joseph Holt," pp. 86–95.
Regarding military commissions, Keys writes: "The army first had
employed military commissions to try civilians in the Mexican War. Thousands of citizens were tried by military commissions during the Civil War
and Reconstruction. . . . Their authority, lacking statute law, was based on
the vague laws of war—the military commander's powers under martial
law. Their membership of five to thirteen officers included a trial judge
advocate, who was both prosecutor and member. To impose the death sentence, a two-thirds vote was required. Verdicts were not subject to review
by civil courts, although the system was in the process of being challenged
in the federal judiciary." And he adds: "Military commissions were conducted generally according to the same rules as courts-martial. Those rules
considered defendants to be incompetent witnesses, and they were not permitted to testify in their own defense." (Keys, "Were the Lincoln Conspirators Dealt Justice?," p. 38.)

45. Official Records, ser. 1, vol. 12, pt. 2, pp. 507–12.

46. McPherson, Ordeal by Fire, p. 272.

47. Frank L. Klement, The Limits of Dissent: Clement L. Vallandigham and the
Civil War (New York: Fordham University Press, 1998), p. 259.

48. Ibid. See also Frank L. Klement, Dark Lanterns: Secret Political Societies,

Conspiracies, and Treason Trials in the Civil War (Baton Rouge: Louisiana State University Press, 1984). Klement devoted much of his scholarly career to challenging the credibility of the view that Holt (whom he takes on directly) and others held regarding the potential and real impact on the war and the nation's life of Copperheadism and of secret societies such as the Knights of the Golden Circle. Others, including James M. McPherson and William Hanchett, have taken Klement to task, as Holt surely would have done, arguing that such political trends and organizations were, in fact, extremely significant. See Klement, *The Limits of Dissent*, p. xxii.

Milligan dodged the noose when Andrew Johnson converted his sentence to life imprisonment in May 1865. Less than a year later, the United States Supreme Court ruled in *ex parte* Milligan that Milligan's trial by a military commission had been illegal, in light of the fact that "the civil courts had been operating and unobstructed" at the time. This final dispensation of the Milligan case is discussed at greater length in chapter 7.

49. Joseph Holt to Edwin M. Stanton, March 2, 1865, *Official Records*, ser. 2, vol. 4, p. 1216; Joseph Holt to Edwin M. Stanton, November 13, 1865, *Official Records*, ser. 3, vol. 5, p. 490; E. D. Townsend to Joseph Holt, July 12, 1864, *Official Records*, ser. 1, vol. 52, pt. 1, pp. 567–68; Joseph Holt to Edwin Stanton, July 31, 1864, *Official Records*, ser. 1, vol. 39, pt. 2, pp. 213–14. According to Holt, in an 1875 interview with John Nicolay, the judge advocate general's office processed approximately 30,000 cases a year during the war (Burlingame, ed., *Oral History of Abraham Lincoln*, p. 68).

50. Joseph Holt to Edwin M. Stanton, October 8, 1864, *Official Records*, ser. 2, vol. 7, pp. 930–53. See also two less extensive letters from Holt to Stanton regarding his investigations in the West: Joseph Holt to Edwin Stanton, July 31, 1865, *Official Records*, ser. 1, vol. 39, pt. 2, pp. 212–15; and Joseph Holt to Edwin Stanton, August 5, 1864, *Official Records*, ser. 3, vol. 4, pp. 577–79.

2. "A Vindictive Clique of Villains"
The Pursuit and Capture of the Suspects

1. W. G. Snethen to Joseph Holt, April 4, 1865, in container 47, Holt-LC.
2. Howard K. Beale, ed., *Diary of Gideon Welles*, 2:293–94; newspaper article quoted in Joseph George Jr., "Nature's First Law: Louis Weichmann and Mrs. Surratt," *Civil War History* 28 (1982), p. 108.
3. H. L. Burnett to Edwin Stanton, May 2, 1865, *Official Records*, ser. 2, vol. 8, p. 523.
4. *New York Times*, May 2, 1865; William Hanchett, *The Lincoln Murder Conspiracies* (Urbana: University of Illinois Press, 1983), p. 65.
5. *New York Times*, August 6, 1861.

6. Otto Eisenschiml, *Why Was Lincoln Murdered?* (New York: Grosset & Dunlap, 1937), p. 102; Michael Kauffman, "David Edgar Herold: The Forgotten Conspirator," in *In Pursuit of . . . : Continuing Research in the Field of the Lincoln Assassination* (Clinton, Md.: The Surratt Society, 1990), pp. 23–26; *Philadelphia Inquirer*, May 19, 1865; *Richmond Times*, April 24, 1865; *New York Times*, May 1, 1865; Laurie Verge, "That Trifling Boy," *The Surratt Courier* 27 (January 2002), p. 5. See also the statement of Thomas Chissen outlining the makeup of the Herold family, M-599, roll 14; "Voluntary Statement" of Herold to John A. Bingham, April 27, 1865, in M-599, roll 4; and statement of Jane Herold, April 20, 1865, M-599, roll 4.

7. Kauffman, "David Edgar Herold," pp. 24–25; *New York Times*, May 1, 1865; *Baltimore American*, July 9, 1865; *Richmond Times*, April 24, 1865; Eisenschiml, *Why Was Lincoln Murdered?*, p. 132; Report of Officer C. H. Rosch, April 26, 1865, M-599, roll 4; Voluntary Statement of Herold, April 27, 1865.

8. See *Official Records*, ser. 1, vol. 46, pt. 1, pp. 1317–22, for a number of documents pertaining to the escape and capture of Booth and Herold. There are also numerous secondary accounts of Booth's and Herold's escape and final capture. See in particular Edward Steers, *Blood on the Moon: The Assassination of Abraham Lincoln* (Lexington: University Press of Kentucky, 2001), pp. 183–206.

9. Kauffman, "David Edgar Herold," pp. 24–25; Elizabeth Steger Trindal, *Mary Surratt: An American Tragedy* (Gretna, La.: Pelican, 1996), p. 137; David M. DeWitt, *The Judicial Murder of Mary E. Surratt* (1895; reprint, St. Clair Shores, Mich.: Scholarly Press, 1970), p. 13; Michael Kauffman, "Fort Lesley McNair and the Lincoln Conspirators," *Lincoln Herald* 80 (1978), p. 176; Roy Z. Chamlee, *Lincoln's Assassins: A Complete Account of Their Capture, Trial, and Punishment* (Jefferson, N.C.: McFarland & Company, 1990), p. 218.

10. *New York Times*, April 17, April 18, and April 22, 1865; *Washington Evening Star*, April 15 and April 17, 1865; *Lewiston* (Maine) *Daily Evening Journal*, April 18, 1865; Benn Pitman, *The Assassination of President Lincoln and the Trial of the Conspirators* (1865; reprint, New York: Funk & Wagnalls, 1954), pp. 121–23; Statement of Officer Sampson, M-599, roll 2; Report of John A. Foster, M-599, roll 5; Kauffman, "Fort Lesley McNair," p. 176; Leon Q. Prior, "Lewis Payne, Pawn of John Wilkes Booth," *Florida Historical Quarterly* 43 (1964), p. 16. See also Interview with Honora Fitzpatrick, April 28, 1865, M-599, roll 5, and Statement of C. H. Rosch, M-599, roll 6, regarding Powell's arrest.

11. Betty O. Gregory, "Lewis Powell: Mystery Man of the Conspiracy," in *In Pursuit of . . .* , pp. 15–16; Betty Ownsbey, *Alias "Paine": Lewis Thornton Powell, the Mystery Man of the Lincoln Conspiracy* (Jefferson, N.C.: McFarland & Company, 1993), pp. 3–6; Prior, "Lewis Payne," pp. 1–2.

12. Gregory, "Lewis Powell," pp. 16–17; William E. Doster, *Lincoln and Episodes of the Civil War* (New York: G. P. Putnam's Sons, 1915), pp. 272–73; Ownsbey, *Alias "Paine,"* pp. 5–9.
13. Gregory, "Lewis Powell," p. 17; Prior, "Lewis Payne," pp. 3–4; Jerry H. Maxwell, "The Bizarre Case of Lewis Paine," *Lincoln Herald* 81 (1979), pp. 226; Ownsbey, *Alias "Paine,"* pp. 15–34.
14. James O. Hall, "The Story of Mrs. Mary Surratt," unpublished paper in the Surratt Society Archives, Clinton, Maryland, pp. 1–5; Trindal, *Mary Surratt*, pp. 13–17; Francis X. Busch, *Enemies of the State* (Indianapolis: Bobbs-Merrill, 1954), p. 16.
15. Hall, "Story of Mary Surratt," pp. 5–6; Trindal, *Mary Surratt*, pp. 19–20.
16. Hall, "Story of Mary Surratt," pp. 6–9; Busch, *Enemies of the State*, pp. 16–18; Trindal, *Mary Surratt*, pp. 35–65. See also Joseph George Jr., "'A True Childe of Sorrow': Two Letters of Mary E. Surratt," *Maryland Historical Magazine* 80 (Winter 1985), pp. 402–5.
17. Ownsbey, *Alias "Paine,"* p. 60; Hall, "Story of Mary Surratt," pp. 9–10; Busch, *Enemies of the State*, pp. 17–18; Trindal, *Mary Surratt*, pp. 62–80; Chamlee, *Lincoln's Assassins*, p. 19.
18. James O. Hall and Edward Steers, "George Andrew Atzerodt," in *In Pursuit of. . . ,* p. 29; Pitman, *Assassination of President Lincoln*, p. 149; *Philadelphia Inquirer*, July 10, 1865; Royal States Attorney, in Tuhl, Germany to William W. Murphy (U.S. Consul General), May 26, 1865, M-599, roll 7; William W. Murphy to William Hunter, May 17, 1865, in container 92, Holt-LC.
19. Hall and Steers, "George Andrew Atzerodt," pp. 29–30; Busch, *Enemies of the State*, p. 19; Pitman, *Assassination of President Lincoln*, pp. 130–39; *Philadelphia Inquirer*, July 10, 1865; Osborn H. Oldroyd, *The Assassination of Abraham Lincoln* (1901; reprint, Bowie, Md.: Heritage Books, 1990), pp. 164–65. See also Deposition of John A. Foster, M-599, roll 3; Deposition of M. E. Martin, M-599, roll 5; Deposition of Nora Fitzpatrick, M-599, roll 5; Examination of Mary Surratt, M-599, roll 6; Examination of Anna Surratt, M-599, roll 6; and Testimony of Louis Weichmann, M-599, roll 8. See also miscellaneous documents, M-599, roll 7, regarding the Atzerodts' coach-making and painting business.
20. Hall and Steers, "George Andrew Atzerodt," p. 30; Eisenschiml, *Why Was Lincoln Murdered?*, pp. 166–67; Pitman, *Assassination of President Lincoln*, pp. 144, 146; Deposition of R. R. Jones, M-599, roll 2; Deposition of Washington Briscoe, M-599, roll 2; Deposition of John Greenwalt, M-599, roll 2.
21. Lincoln assassination specialist Edward Steers writes, "Most important to the case of the Lincoln conspirators, a person may be a member of an unlawful conspiracy without knowing all of the details of the conspiracy or even all of the other members. If a person understands the unlawful nature

of a plan and willingly joins the plan, even if only on one occasion, it is sufficient to convict the individual for conspiracy even though that person
played only a minor role" (*Blood on the Moon*, p. 210).

22. Hall and Steers, "George Andrew Atzerodt," pp. 30–31; Trindal, *Mary Surratt*, pp. 123–24; Eisenschiml, *Why Was Lincoln Murdered?*, p. 195; Pitman, *Assassination of President Lincoln*, pp. 148, 149, 152; *New York
Times*, April 18, April 21, and April 26, 1865; *Official Records*, ser. 1, vol.
46, pt. 3, p. 783. See also C. G. B. Drummond to A. A. Porter, April 20,
1865, M-599, roll 2; Deposition of Zachariah Gemmill, M-599, roll 3;
Deposition of Francis Kerns, M-599, roll 3; Report of John A. Foster, M-
599, roll 3; Deposition of William R. Gaither, M-599, roll 3; Deposition of
Lucinda A. Metz, M-599, roll 3; Deposition of John L. Caldwell, M-599,
roll 3; Deposition of Robert Murray, M-599, roll 6; Deposition of Frank
Munroe, M-599, roll 1; Statement of John Lee, April 16, M-599, roll 2; and
"Inventory of Articles Found in Room No. 126 . . . ," M-599, roll 2.

23. Chamlee, *Lincoln's Assassins*, p. 15.

24. Michael Kauffman, ed., *Samuel Bland Arnold: Memoirs of a Lincoln Con-
spirator* (Bowie, Md.: Heritage Books, 1995), p. 43; Percy E. Martin, "The
Hookstown Connection," in *In Pursuit of. . .* , p. 117; Chamlee, *Lincoln's
Assassins*, pp. 14–16; Louis J. Weichmann, *A True History of the Assassination of Abraham Lincoln and of the Conspiracy of 1865* (New York:
Alfred A. Knopf, 1975), pp. 101, 400–401; Oldroyd, *Assassination of
Abraham Lincoln*, pp. 55, 57, 59; Pitman, *Assassination of President Lincoln*, pp. 235, 236, 240; "Sketches of Sam'l B. Arnold, Michael O'Laugh-
lin . . . ," M-599, roll 3.

25. Scholars of the conspiracy have usually spelled O'Laughlen's name
"O'Laughlin" because the 1865 indictment of the conspirators mistakenly
spelled it that way. In fact, the O'Laughlen family Bible and the stone over
Michael's grave spell the name with an "e" (see *In Pursuit of. . .* , p. iii).

26. Weichmann, *True History*, pp. 44, 78, 380, 400, 471; Pitman, *Assassination of President Lincoln*, pp. 222, 232; Chamlee, *Lincoln's Assassins*, pp.
67–68; Samuel Bland Arnold, *Defense and Prison Experiences of a Lincoln
Conspirator* (Hattiesburg, Miss.: Book Farm, 1943), pp. 18–19; Statement
of Charles J. Clarke, M-599, roll 2.

27. Weichmann, *True History*, pp. 45, 73, 381, 382; Arnold, *Defense and
Prison Experiences*, pp. 19, 20; Statement of L. P. D. Newman, M-599, roll
2; Statement of Mrs. Mary Van Tyne, M-599, roll 6; Chamlee, *Lincoln's
Assassins*, p. 68; Hanchett, *Lincoln Murder Conspiracies*, p. 44.

28. Weichmann, *True History*, pp. 382, 383; Hanchett, *Lincoln Murder Conspiracies*, p. 49; Arnold, *Defense and Prison Experiences*, pp. 22, 42, 45,
46; Statement of John Howard, M-599, roll 6; Edward Steers, *His Name Is
Still Mudd: The Case Against Dr. Samuel Alexander Mudd* (Gettysburg,
Pa.: Thomas Publications, 1997), pp. 15–16.

29. Arnold, *Defense and Prison Experiences*, p. 46; Hanchett, *Lincoln Murder Conspiracies*, pp. 49–50; Steers, *His Name Is Still Mudd*, p. 16. See also John Surratt's account of the kidnap scheme, and how it turned out, quoted in Weichmann, *True History*, p. 432.
30. Weichmann, *True History*, pp. 44, 181, 380, 400–401; Oldroyd, *Assassination of Abraham Lincoln*, pp. 55, 61; Chamlee, *Lincoln's Assassins*, pp. 13–15; Martin, "Hookstown Connection," p. 117; "Sketches of Sam'l B. Arnold, Michael O'Laughlin . . . ," M-599, roll 3; Arnold, *Defense and Prison Experiences*, pp. 15, 18, 26, 27, 36, 52 (spelling as in the original); John C. Brennan, "The Confederate Plan to Abduct President Lincoln," in *In Pursuit of. . .* , p. 145; Percy E. Martin, "The Six-Hour War of Samuel B. Arnold," *Lincoln Herald* 88 (1986), pp. 134–36; Pitman, *Assassination of President Lincoln*, p. 236; *Washington Evening Star*, April 15, 1865.
31. Pitman, *Assassination of President Lincoln*, pp. 221–23; Statement of Thomas H. Carmichael, M-599, roll 4. In his 1904 recollection of the events of 1865, Arnold wrote that as soon as he learned of Lincoln's death he knew that "my former connection and intimacy with Booth would lead to my arrest and to be even suspected was, I felt, almost equivalent to death. Had I been differently situated or been where I felt the law would have protected me, I would have surrendered myself (in my entire innocence) into the hands of the Government, but as it was, I determined to let affairs pursue their own course and quietly . . . await my arrest" (Arnold, *Defense and Prison Experiences*, p. 51).
32. Arnold, *Defense and Prison Experiences*, pp. 52–57.
33. Although referred to in the formal charges and the trial records as "Edward," Spangler's birth certificate actually lists the name "Edmund," and he spelled his own name "Edman" (see *In Pursuit of. . .* , p. iii).
34. Oldroyd, *Assassination of Abraham Lincoln*, p. 47; Chamlee, *Lincoln's Assassins*, p. 540; Pitman, *Assassination of President Lincoln*, pp. 97, 102–3. See also the Internet site members.aol.com/RVSNorton/Lincoln25.html, which includes a photograph of Spangler's gravestone, erected by the Surratt and Mudd Societies, on which is carved the same birth date, and the death date of February 7, 1875.
35. Pitman, *Assassination of President Lincoln*, pp. 74, 78, 104, 106; Chamlee, *Lincoln's Assassins*, pp. 476, 540.
36. Pitman, *Assassination of President Lincoln*, pp. 70–83; Hanchett, *Lincoln Murder Conspiracies*, p. 37 .
37. Statement of Edman Spangler, April 15, 1865, M-599, roll 6; Pitman, *Assassination of President Lincoln*, p. 74; Statement of John C. Bohrur [Joseph Burroughs], M-599, roll 4.
38. Pitman, *Assassination of President Lincoln*, pp. 108–9.
39. Statement of Edman Spangler, April 15, 1865; *New York Times*, April 19, 1865. Many individuals connected with Ford's Theater, including John T.

Ford and others in his family, were arrested in connection with the assassination, but Spangler was the only one charged.

40. Pitman, *Assassination of President Lincoln*, p. 98; Report of John A. Foster to Henry L. Burnett, April 29, 1865, M-599, roll 2; Oldroyd, *Assassination of Abraham Lincoln*, p. 84.

41. Steers, *His Name Is Still Mudd*, p. 28.

42. Statement of Thomas Davis, April 29, 1865, M-599, roll 4; Statement of Samuel A. Mudd, undated, M-599, roll 5.

43. Statement of Samuel A. Mudd, April 21, 1865, M-599, roll 2. See also H. H. Wells to Christopher C. Augur, April 22, 1865, M-599, roll 1; Statement of Thomas Davis, April 29, 1865; Statement of Samuel A. Mudd, undated, M-599, roll 5; Statement of Frank Washington, M-599, roll 6; Steers, *His Name Is Still Mudd*, pp. 28–30; Oldroyd, *Assassination of Abraham Lincoln*, pp. 142–44.

44. Wells to Augur, April 22, 1865; Steers, *His Name Is Still Mudd*, pp. 30–38; Chamlee, *Lincoln's Assassins*, pp. 134, 149. See also a copy of Stanton's instructions to Winfield S. Hancock regarding the transfer of the prisoners and the conditions under which Stanton wanted them held at the Old Arsenal (Edwin M. Stanton to Winfield S. Hancock, April 29, 1865, Stanton Papers).

45. *Philadelphia Inquirer*, May 4, 1865 (the article is datelined May 2).

46. Edwin Stanton to Joseph Holt, May 2, 1865, ser. 1, reel 14, in the microfilmed Andrew Johnson Papers, Library of Congress, Washington, D.C.

47. *New York Times*, April 20, 1865.

48. William A. Tidwell, *Come Retribution: The Confederate Secret Service and the Assassination of Lincoln* (New York: Barnes & Noble, 1988), pp. 20, 189, 192; Ben Perley Poore, ed., *The Conspiracy Trial for the Murder of the President* (Boston: J.E. Tilton, 1865), 1:7.

3. "A DISPOSITION TO PRESERVE LAW AND ORDER"
JOSEPH HOLT AND THE FIRST TRIAL OF THE ASSASSINS

1. T. B. Peterson, *The Trial of the Assassins and Conspirators* (Philadelphia: Peterson & Brothers, 1865), p. 16. This version of the trial record reprinted the testimony as it was recorded for publication by the special correspondents to the *Philadelphia Inquirer* who were assigned to the courtroom.

2. William Hanchett, *The Lincoln Murder Conspiracies* (Urbana: University of Illinois Press, 1983), pp. 21–22; Benn Pitman, *The Assassination of Abraham Lincoln and the Trial of the Conspirators* (1865; reprint, New York: Funk & Wagnalls, 1954), pp. 17–18; Ben Perley Poore, ed., *The Conspiracy Trial for the Murder of the President* (Boston: J.E. Tilton, 1865), 1:5; Roy Z. Chamlee, *Lincoln's Assassins: A Complete Account of Their*

Capture, Trial, and Punishment (Jefferson, N.C.: McFarland & Company, 1990), pp. 215–16, 247; David M. DeWitt, *The Judicial Murder of Mary E. Surratt* (1895; reprint, St. Clair Shores, Mich.: Scholarly Press, 1970), pp. 24–26.

3. Poore, *Conspiracy Trial*, 1:10; Louis J. Weichmann, *True History of the Assassination of Abraham Lincoln and of the Conspiracy of 1865* (New York: Alfred A. Knopf, 1975), p. 235; Chamlee, *Lincoln's Assassins*, pp. 225–26; August V. Kautz Diary, May 30, 1865, Kautz Papers; August V. Kautz, "Memoir," vol. 2, Kautz Papers; A. E. King to G. W. Gile, April 28, 1865, *Official Records*, ser. 1, vol. 46, pt. 3, p. 1002.

4. Chamlee, *Lincoln's Assassins*, pp. 218–19; Kautz Diary, Kautz Papers; Kautz, "Memoir," vol. 2, Kautz Papers.

5. Osborn H. Oldroyd, *The Assassination of Abraham Lincoln* (1901; reprint, Bowie, Md.: Heritage Books, 1990), pp. 12, 119.

6. The *New York Times* of May 16, 1865, noted that the reading of the previous day's proceedings took three hours of the court's time. On May 27, the paper reported that about half the day was occupied "by the reading of the voluminous journal of yesterday's proceedings."

7. The fact that the defendants were allowed to appear in court, at least initially, without the benefit of defense counsel was one of several features of a military commission that distinguished it from a civil trial in 1865. In the case of the assassination conspirators, it contributed to the theory—to which I do not subscribe—that the eight defendants would have received fairer treatment, and would have perhaps been exonerated, had they been tried in civil court.

8. Kautz Diary, May 10, 1865, Kautz Papers; Kautz, "Memoir," vol. 2, Kautz Papers; Pitman, *Assassination of President Lincoln*, pp. 18–21 (according to Pitman, the accused actually first received notice of the charges against them on May 8, from General Hartranft); Poore, *Conspiracy Trial*, 1:14–19; *Official Records*, ser. 2, vol. 8, pp. 696–98; *New York Times*, May 10 and May 11, 1865; Chamlee, *Lincoln's Assassins*, p. 235.

9. Oldroyd, *Assassination of Abraham Lincoln*, p. 115. For an early public discussion of the relevant points in the debate over the jurisdiction of the court, see *New York Times* of May 16, 1865, in which the *Times*, which supported the military commission, opposed the view presented by the rival, *New York World*. The *Times* correspondent wrote: "The assassination of Mr. Lincoln was the murder of a military officer, in actual command, during actual war, in a fortified camp, and for the purpose of aiding the enemy; what more was needed to give the military tribunals complete cognizance of the case?" See also the *Lewiston* [Maine] *Daily Evening Journal*, May 12, 1865; Edward Steers, *Blood on the Moon: The Assassination of Abraham Lincoln* (Lexington: University Press of Kentucky, 2001), p. 212; and Gabor S. Boritt and Norman O. Forness, eds., *The Historian's Lincoln:*

Pseudohistory, Psychohistory, and History (Urbana: University of Illinois Press, 1988), p. 372.

10. Pitman, *Assassination of President Lincoln*, pp. 251–63; Hanchett, *Lincoln Murder Conspiracies*, p. 66; Lorie Ann Porter, "Not So Strange Bedfellows: Thomas Ewing II and the Defense of Samuel Mudd," *Lincoln Herald* 90 (1988), pp. 91–101.

11. In his memoir, Kautz defended the commission's jurisdiction from the perspective of efficiency as much as anything else. See Kautz, "Memoir," vol. 2, Kautz Papers.

12. Charles A. Dana to Edwin Stanton, May 22, 1865, Stanton Papers (see also the accompanying regulations for the prisoners); Mrs. C. C. Clay to Joseph Holt, May 23, 1865, in container 48, Holt-LC. For vivid accounts of the capture of Davis, see William C. Davis, *Jefferson Davis: The Man and His Hour* (New York: HarperCollins, 1991), pp. 635–44; and William J. Cooper, *Jefferson Davis, American* (New York: Alfred A. Knopf, 2000), p. 534.

13. *New York Times*, May 16, 1865; Poore, *Conspiracy Trial*, 1:52; Chamlee, *Lincoln's Assassins*, p. 247.

14. Pitman, *Assassination of Abraham Lincoln*, pp. 21–22; Poore, *Conspiracy Trial*, 1:51–62; Kautz Diary, May 13, 1865, Kautz Papers; Chamlee, *Lincoln's Assassins*, p. 247; Kautz, "Memoir," vol. 2, Kautz Papers. For an extended account of the discussion about Johnson's right to serve, see also *New York Times*, May 14, 1865.

15. Kautz, "Memoir," vol. 2, Kautz Papers; Francis X. Busch, *Enemies of the State* (Indianapolis: Bobbs-Merrill, 1954), pp. 35, 38; Pitman, *Assassination of President Lincoln*, pp. 22, 251–63.

16. See Mary Bernard Allen, "Joseph Holt: Judge Advocate General (1862–1875): A Study in the Treatment of Political Prisoners by the United States Government During the Civil War" (Ph.D. diss., University of Chicago, 1927), p. 138.

17. *Pittsburgh Commercial*, April 17, 1865. The next day the paper quoted a speech given by Pennsylvania's former governor, who said: "This greatest crime of this or any other age belongs to the hell-born spirit of slavery. It is the legitimate and unavoidable result of its workings, teachings, and designs" (*Pittsburgh Commercial*, April 18, 1865). See also Hanchett, in Boritt and Forness, *The Historian's Lincoln*, p. 325.

18. Chamlee, *Lincoln's Assassins*, pp. 296–97.

19. Peterson, *Trial of the Assassins*, p. 16; Kautz, "Memoir," vol. 2, Kautz Papers; Kautz Diary, May 16 and May 31, 1865, Kautz Papers; *New York Times*, May 23, 1865.

20. Poore, *Conspiracy Trial*, 1:62–69.

21. Peterson, *Trial of the Assassins*, p. 7; Pitman, *Assassination of President Lincoln*, pp. 24, 35; Poore, *Conspiracy Trial*, 1:22–23, 34–35, 42, and 3:83-115.

22. Prosecution witness Henry Von Steinacker also provoked a good deal of controversy, for similar reasons—see, for example, Pitman, *Assassination of President Lincoln*, pp. 38, 64–69. I choose to focus here on Conover, however, because of his importance after the 1865 trial and, through the next few years, in connection with Holt's efforts to punish everyone whom he considered significantly connected with the Lincoln assassination. On the Von Steinacker controversy, see Joseph George Jr., "'Old Abe Must Go Up the Spout': Henry Von Steinacker and the Lincoln Conspiracy Trial," *Lincoln Herald* 94 (1992), pp. 148–56.

23. Poore, *Conspiracy Trial*, 3:115–43.

24. Pitman, *Assassination of President Lincoln*, pp. 28–34; Chamlee, *Lincoln's Assassins*, p. 388; Hanchett, *Lincoln Murder Conspiracies*, pp. 72-73; Poore, *Conspiracy Trial*, 3:115–43.

25. John A. Dix to Edwin Stanton, June 24, 1865, Stanton Papers.

26. As I will discuss in detail below, although Conover's reasons for lying on the stand in 1865 were never entirely clear, they were revealed in part over the weeks and months ahead as he sought to exploit Holt's gullibility for his own selfish purposes.

27. Hanchett, *Lincoln Murder Conspiracies*, p. 73; Pitman, *Assassination of President Lincoln*, pp. 42–43. See Chamlee, *Lincoln's Assassins*, pp. 387–89, for a concise summary of the Conover controversy during the conspiracy trial. For a thorough study of the connection between the Confederate leadership and the assassination of Lincoln, see William A. Tidwell, *Come Retribution: The Confederate Secret Service and the Assassination of Lincoln* (New York: Barnes & Noble, 1988). On the Lon letter, of whose fabrication for the sake of the prosecution's case Holt seems to have had at least some indication early on, see Joseph George Jr., "Subornation of Perjury at the Lincoln Conspiracy Trial? Joseph Holt, Robert Purdy, and the Lon Letter," *Civil War History* 38 (1992), pp. 232–41; W. H. Emory to Brigadier General Morgan, June 4, 1865, in container 92, Holt-LC; and Statement of Lon McAleer, June 7, 1865, in container 92, Holt-LC.

28. Weichmann's testimony covers pp. 69–110, 135–37, and 369–90 in vol. 1 and pp. 42–44 in vol. 2 of Poore, *Conspiracy Trial*. See also Pitman, *Assassination of President Lincoln*, pp. 113–20.

29. Weichmann, *True History*, pp. xiv, 12, 405–7; Joseph George Jr., "'The Days Are Yet Dark': L. J. Weichmann's Life After the Lincoln Conspiracy Trial," *Records of the American Catholic Historical Society of Philadelphia* 95 (1984), p. 67; Oldroyd, *Assassination of Abraham Lincoln*, p. 159; Louis J. Weichmann to H. L. Burnett, M-599, roll 3; Poore, *Conspiracy Trial*, 1:69. "Wiechmann" is the original spelling of the family name, but the name was commonly misspelled in the United States, and Louis eventually adopted the spelling "Weichmann" for his own use (*In Pursuit of . . .* , p. iii).

30. *Anderson* [Indiana] *Herald*, June 6, 1902; Louis J. Weichmann to Joseph

Holt, November 12, 1865, in container 50, Holt-LC; Weichmann, *True History*, pp. xiv–xv, 15–17; Oldroyd, *Assassination of Abraham Lincoln*, p. 155; Statement of Louis J. Weichmann, April 30, 1865, M-599, roll 7.

31. Weichmann, *True History*, pp. 13, 443; Poore, *Conspiracy Trial*, 3:69; *Washington Post*, April 3, 1898.

32. Weichmann, *True History*, pp. 18–20.

33. Ibid., pp. xiv–xv, 13–14, 22–27; Louis J. Weichmann to Henry de Ste. Marie, April 1863, M-599, roll 3.

34. Weichmann, *True History*, pp. 28–29; James O. Hall, "The Story of Mrs. Mary Surratt," unpublished paper in the Surratt Files, Surratt Society Archives, Clinton, Maryland, p. 10; Poore, *Conspiracy Trial*, 1:70.

35. Weichmann, *True History*, p. 30.

36. Ibid., pp. 21, 29–30. Edward Steers writes that the Surratt house in Surrattsville, "according to a Confederate Signal Bureau document located in the National Archives . . . was a specific stop along the underground route into the District of Columbia" (Steers, *His Name Is Still Mudd: The Case Against Dr. Samuel Alexander Mudd* [Gettysburg, Pa.: Thomas Publications, 1997], p. 20; see also Tidwell, *Come Retribution*, p. 6).

37. Weichmann, *True History*, pp. 33–34.

38. Ibid.; Hall, "Story of Mrs. Mary Surratt," p. 12; Poore, *Conspiracy Trial*, 1:70–71, 94–98, 100–101, 103–4, 389–90; Statement of Louis J. Weichmann, undated, M-599, roll 6.

39. "Clara" to Louis J. Weichmann, February 1865, M-599, roll 6; Weichmann, *True History*, pp. 29, 30, 32, 34, 35, 103. Weichmann added coldly, "During the whole period of my acquaintance with Booth, I had no intimacy with him whatever. I never wrote him a letter or exchanged correspondence of any kind with him. . . . I was friendly with him only because he was the friend of my friend. . . that was the limit of my friendship for him" (ibid., p. 104).

40. Atzerodt's treatment by the press throughout the conspiracy trial in 1865, and by historians subsequently, matched his treatment by Weichmann. The *New York Times* of April 26, 1865, declared that "the general contour of his features stamp him as a man of low character, who would stoop to any action, no matter how vile, for money." The *Philadelphia Inquirer* of July 7, 1865, called him a "vulgar looking creature . . . just the man to commit a murder, and then fail on coming to the point." The *Richmond Times* of April 24, 1865, called him "a villainous-looking man," and the *Washington Evening Star* of April 21, 1865, described him as having "a thoroughly bad face and repulsive manners." Assassination scholar Osborn Oldroyd claimed that Atzerodt had "a stupid expression" (*Assassination of Abraham Lincoln*, p. 133), and Francis X. Busch called him an "awkward, rough-looking stranger" (*Enemies of the State*, p. 19). Most sources tellingly and prejudicially link Atzerodt's presumably unpleasant and

rugged appearance with his German birth—including, ironically, fellow German Otto Eisenschiml, who described Atzerodt as "a shrinking little man of German ancestry and no breeding" (*Why Was Lincoln Murdered?* [New York: Grosset & Dunlap, 1937], p. 250).

41. Weichmann, *True History*, pp. 75–76, 85–86; Hall, "Story of Mrs. Mary Surratt," p. 13; Poore, *Conspiracy Trial*, 1:72–73, 75–76, 79–80, 88–89, 108–9, 374–76, 381–83.

42. Weichmann, *True History*, pp. 27, 34, 78. Weichmann was enrolled in Company G of the regiment, which was drawn from among the male clerks of various War Department offices, and may not have been entirely voluntary. On the evening he and Surratt met Booth and Mudd on 7th Street, Weichmann later claimed, he had been wearing his "military suit," which consisted of blue pants, a light blue cloak with cape, and a U.S. army cap. If this was indeed the case, it may have been a reason that the three other men left him out of some of their conversations that night (ibid., pp. 138–39).

43. Ibid. pp. 96–99; Hall, "Story of Mrs. Mary Surratt," p. 14; Louis J. Weichmann to Henry L. Burnett, May 5, 1865, M-599, roll 6; Poore, *Conspiracy Trial*, 1:76–78, 107–8.

44. Weichmann, *True History*, pp. 99–103; Poore, *Conspiracy Trial*, 1:370–72, 374, 376.

45. D. H. L. Gleason, "The Conspiracy Against Lincoln," *The Magazine of History* 13 (February 1911), p. 59; Weichmann, *True History*, pp. 103–9; Poore, *Conspiracy Trial*, 1:77, 89–91, 384–85, 388–89, and 2:43–44.

46. Weichmann, *True History*, pp. 121–22, 433, 435; Hall, "Story of Mrs. Mary Surratt," pp. 16–17; Poore, *Conspiracy Trial*, 1:80–82, 91–92, 369.

47. Weichmann, *True History*, pp. 127, 134, 165–70; Hall, "Story of Mrs. Mary Surratt," pp. 18–20; Weichmann to Burnett, May 5, 1865; Poore, *Conspiracy Trial*, 1:82, 84–87, 104, 105, 372–73.

48. Weichmann, *True History*, pp. 172–75; Hall, "Story of Mrs. Mary Surratt," p. 20; Statement of Mary Surratt, M-599, roll 6; Poore, *Conspiracy Trial*, 1:87, 92–93.

49. Weichmann, *True History*, pp. 178–79.

50. Ibid.; Hall, "Story of Mrs. Mary Surratt," p. 21; Poore, *Conspiracy Trial*, 1:376–78.

51. More than three decades after the assassination and the trial of the conspirators, in the wake of a published interview with John Surratt Jr. in which Surratt defended himself and accused Weichmann of complicity with the conspirators, Weichmann and Richards engaged in a protracted correspondence. In their letters they recalled the events of the spring and summer of 1865, and their roles therein. Richards's letters, dating from April 1898 to November 1901 (eight months before Weichmann's death, in June 1902), were published in Weichmann's memoir. Throughout, it must be acknowl-

edged, Richards expressed complete faith in Weichmann's honesty and praised him abundantly for his stand on behalf of the federal government. See Weichmann, *True History*, pp. 408–28.

52. Ibid., pp. 179–221; Poore, *Conspiracy Trial*, 1:104–5; Joseph George Jr., "Nature's First Law: Louis Weichmann and Mrs. Surratt," *Civil War History* 28 (1982). Not all of those involved in the investigations approved of Richards's decision to let Weichmann accompany the detectives to Canada (see O. H. Olcott to H. L. Burnett, April 25, 1865, M-599, roll 2). Weichmann also went with detectives to the home of David Herold in Washington on the morning of April 15, helping them to procure a photograph of the suspect (Testimony of Louis J. Weichmann, M-599, roll 8). It is worth noting that according to assassination scholar Roy Chamlee, "Mrs. Herold was in a similar position" to Mary Surratt, "yet she was never jailed or even suspected. The conspirators occasionally met at Mrs. Herold's boardinghouse, even as they did at Mrs. Surratt's." Chamlee points out, however, that there were significant differences in the two women's cases. For one, "Mrs. Herold never fraternized with them. They never came to her house when her son was not at home, and there was no evidence that she was connected with questionable activities. Furthermore," Chamlee adds for good measure, Mrs. Herold "cooperated with the investigators," as he clearly believes Mary Surratt did not (*Lincoln's Assassins*, p. 145).

53. Weichmann, *True History*, pp. 225–28, 230; George, "Nature's First Law," p. 108. See also Henry L. Burnett to J. Ingraham, May 4, 1865, M-599, roll 1; Weichmann to Burnett, May 5, 1865.

54. *New York Times*, May 22, 1865. The very next day the *Times* did publish testimony from the trial that seemed to indicate Davis's involvement in the conspiracy. The point here is that the cases against most of the prisoners at the bar were, in many people's minds at least, easily sewn up, whereas proof of a larger conspiracy continued to be elusive. As the *Times* Washington correspondent put it on May 23: "The link in the chain of evidence that directly connects Booth and the prisoners in an agreement with Davis to murder Mr. Lincoln and Mr. Seward, has not been produced on this trial, but may yet be offered before the government closes its testimony. In contrast, the *Pittsburgh Commercial* actually pronounced the case against Davis and the rebel leadership closed as early as May 20. "The evidence now in," exclaimed the *Commercial*, "connects the rebel leaders . . . not with the assassination only, but with a long standing and elaborately matured plot to murder, burn and destroy on an extensive scale, and in many places. We consider the complicity of Jeff. Davis and the rebel leaders . . . has been fully made out, and an impartial jury would so declare, even without another word of testimony."

4. "A STUPENDOUS RETRIBUTION"
CONVICTION AND PUNISHMENT OF EIGHT CO-CONSPIRATORS

1. David M. DeWitt, *The Judicial Murder of Mary E. Surratt* (1895; reprint, St. Clair Shores, Mich.: Scholarly Press, 1970), p. 15.
2. Lew Wallace, *Lew Wallace: An Autobiography* (New York: Harper & Brothers, 1906), 2:849.
3. Joseph George Jr., "Trial of Mrs. Surratt: John P. Brophy's Rare Pamphlet," *Lincoln Herald* 98 (1996), pp. 17, 18, 20. See also Joseph George Jr., "Nature's First Law: Louis Weichmann and Mrs. Surratt," *Civil War History* 28 (1982), pp. 116–17. As George, a late-twentieth-century scholar of the assassination, notes, after the trial Weichmann and Brophy engaged in a bitter, public battle of words in the Philadelphia and Washington newspapers over the issue of Weichmann's truthfulness.
4. Report of John A. Foster, M-599, roll 3; Louis J. Weichmann to Henry L. Burnett, May 28, 1865, M-599, roll 3; Louis J. Weichmann, *A True History of the Assassination of Abraham Lincoln and of the Conspiracy of 1865* (New York: Alfred A. Knopf, 1975), pp. 267, 284, 285.

   Historian Joseph George writes, "There is good evidence that Weichmann was terrorized by his imprisonment," and by the intense and frequent interrogation he experienced, which among other things would have shown him how much of a suspect he himself had become in the course of the accumulation of evidence, and would have driven him to be even more likely to try and save his own neck by giving evidence against others (George, "Nature's First Law," p. 111).
5. Ben Perley Poore, ed., *The Conspiracy Trial for the Murder of the President* (Boston: J.E. Tilton, 1865), 1:471–80, and 2:3–9, 31–32.
6. *Philadelphia Inquirer*, May 4, and May 9, 1865; spelling as in the original.
7. This was the horse, blind in one eye, that Booth had purchased some time back from an acquaintance of Samuel Mudd near Bryantown.
8. Poore, *Conspiracy Trial*, 1:110–14, 62–69, 165–66, 176–79, 326–41. See also the April 23, 1865, report of John A. Foster on the evidence he had thus far collected in the case, M-599, roll 5; Fletcher's own pretrial statement, M-599, roll 5; Deposition of R. R. Jones, M-599, roll 2; Benn Pitman, *The Assassination of President Lincoln and the Trial of the Conspirators* (1865; reprint, New York: Funk & Wagnalls, 1954), pp. 159–60; and the statement of William H. Bell, M-599, roll 4.
9. *Philadelphia Inquirer*, May 10, 1865; Poore, *Conspiracy Trial*, 1:117–18. Lloyd's testimony covers pp. 115–34 and 137–39 in vol. 1 of Poore, *Conspiracy Trial*, and pp. 85–87 in Pitman, *Assassination of President Lincoln*.
10. Poore, *Conspiracy Trial*, 1:116–20; Statement of John M. Lloyd, April 22, 1865, M-599, roll 2. See also the statement of John Lloyd, April 28, 1865, M-599, roll 5.

11. Poore, *Conspiracy Trial*, 1:139–43, 149–62, 163–65, 166–69, 181–87, 198–203, 209–16. Reporting on Arnold's arrest on April 21, 1865, the *Washington Evening Star* noted that the suspect "denies any knowledge of the plot to assassinate the President, but confesses that he was concerned with Booth and other parties, about seven in all, in a plot to kidnap the President and deliver him to the Richmond authorities. . . . He says he withdrew from the gang, when Booth threatened to shoot him." See also *Lewiston* [Maine] *Daily Evening Journal*, April 21, 1865.

12. Poore, *Conspiracy Trial*, 1:258–72, 281–93, 435–48, and 2:46–55, 150–68, 170–74.

13. Poore, *Conspiracy Trial*, 2:174; Pitman, *Assassination of President Lincoln*, pp. 24–65, passim.

14. William E. Doster, *Lincoln and Episodes of the Civil War* (New York: G.P. Putnam's Sons, 1915), p. 257.

15. "Voluntary Statement of David Herold," April 27, 1865, M-599, roll 4; *New York Times*, April 18 (reprint of an article from the day before), May 1, and May 22, 1865; *Richmond Times*, April 24, 1865; Anonymous to Edwin M. Stanton, April 21, 1865, M-599, roll 2; *Washington Evening Star*, April 17, 1865.

16. Some, of course, did not interpret Booth's actions in Garrett's barn very heroically at all. The *Pittsburgh Commercial* called it "a dog's death" on May 1, 1865, noting that Booth's "stage tricks were taken out of him before he sought shelter—lamed, bruised, stripped of his paint and feathers—in a shed along with one of his wretched accomplices."

17. Pitman, *Assassination of President Lincoln*, pp. 97, 274–75.
It was asserted in the press during the trial that President Lincoln had had prescriptions filled at Thompson's drugstore near the Executive Mansion, and the theory was floated that "the plan of the conspirators was to get Harrold a place in this drug store . . . for the purpose of placing a poison" in one of Lincoln's prescriptions (*Lewiston* [Maine] *Daily Evening Journal*, May 20, 1865 [spelling as in the original]; see also Weichmann, *True History*, p. 43). Years later Weichmann wrote derisively of Herold: "How such an insignificant and puny character could have mustered courage enough to nerve himself for his terrible deeds is to those who knew him best and who saw him in the court for nearly sixty days utterly incomprehensible" (Weichmann, *True History*, pp. 247–48).

18. August V. Kautz, "Memoir," vol. 2, Kautz Papers; Affidavit of Frank Munroe, M-599, roll 2; Deposition of Robert Murray, M-599, roll 6; Undated report of John A. Foster, M-599, roll 3; Confession of George Atzerodt, April 25, 1865, M-599, roll 3; Inventory of Articles Found in Room No. 126, Kirkwood House, M-599, roll 2; *Richmond Times*, April 24, 1865; *New York Times*, April 26, 1865.

19. *Philadelphia Inquirer*, May 16, 1865; Pitman, *Assassination of President Lincoln*, pp. 150–53; Poore, *Conspiracy Trial*, 2:506–7.

20. Pitman, *Assassination of President Lincoln*, pp. 150–53, 304; Poore, *Conspiracy Trial*, 2:506, 507, and 3:416. Historian Bell Wiley noted that German-born soldiers in the Union army had "a reputation for cowardice," though he insists that it was unfounded (Bell I. Wiley, *The Life of Billy Yank, the Common Soldier of the Union* [Indianapolis: Bobbs-Merrill, 1952], p. 308).

21. Doster, *Lincoln and Episodes*, pp. 264–66; Pitman, *Assassination of President Lincoln*, p. 156.

22. Pitman, *Assassination of President Lincoln*, pp. 166–67; Poore, *Conspiracy Trial*, 3:143–46.

    A concise summary of Powell's [a.k.a. Paine's] military career is found in Jerry H. Maxwell, "The Bizarre Case of Lewis Paine": "During the bloody battles of the Peninsular Campaign, Lewis Powell served in Jubal Early's Brigade. He also fought with Robert E. Lee's army at Second Manassas in August 1862. He was one of Stonewall Jackson's soldiers who participated in the famous capture of Harper's Ferry during the Maryland Campaign of September, 1862. The following spring Lewis fought in the Battle of Chancellorsville. In July of 1863 Lewis served in Brigadier General Edward A. Perry's Brigade at Getttysburg" (Maxwell, "The Bizarre Case of Lewis Paine," *Lincoln Herald* 81 [1979], p. 226). See also Leon Q. Prior, "Lewis Payne, Pawn of John Wilkes Booth," *Florida Historical Quarterly* 43 (1964), pp. 4–5, and Betty Ownsbey, *Alias "Paine": Lewis Thornton Powell, the Mystery Man of the Lincoln Conspiracy* (Jefferson, N.C.: McFarland & Company, 1993), pp. 10–34.

    According to William Tidwell, "Powell came into a Union encampment at Fairfax Court House, Fairfax County, Virginia, on 13 January 1865. Under the alias Lewis Paine, he applied to the provost marshal there, a Lieutenant Maguire, to protect him as a civilian refugee from Fauquier County. It must have been a gem of a story. Maguire accepted it and sent 'Paine' along to headquarters in nearby Alexandria. At Alexandria he took his oath of allegiance and was discharged from custody" (Tidwell, *Come Retribution: The Confederate Secret Service and the Assassination of Lincoln* [New York: Barnes & Noble, 1988] p. 339).

23. Pitman, *Assassination of President Lincoln*, pp. 167–68, 311–13; Kautz, *Diary*, June 21, 1865, Kautz Papers. In his memoir, Doster later recalled that his impassioned final argument on behalf of Powell failed to move at least one of the commissioners, who at lunch following the conclusion of the argument remarked simply, "Well, Payne [Powell] seems to want to be hung, so I guess we might as well hang him" (*Lincoln and Episodes*, p. 263). The testimony of two guards at the Old Arsenal Penitentiary—John

B. Hubbard and John E. Roberts—indicated that while in prison Powell had indeed expressed a desire to die; as Hubbard put it, Powell said that "he was tired of life, and would rather be hung than come back here in the court-room" (Pitman, *Assassination of President Lincoln*, p. 166). There were also reports that Powell had tried to commit suicide in his cell—see John A. Gray, "The Fate of the Lincoln Conspirators: The Account of the Hanging, Given by Lieutenant-Colonel Christian Rath, the Executioner," *McClure's Magazine* 37 (October 1911), p. 633.

On July 10, shortly after the execution of Powell and the others, the *Lewiston* [Maine] *Daily Evening Journal* published sentiments that echo those Doster strove to generate during his summary argument. "Lewis Thornton Powell," the paper exclaimed, "was the only one of these men worth saving. He had character. He was frank and generous, simple and honest, and, under other influences and surroundings than those his boyhood knew, would have grown into worthy and commanding manhood. While giving thanks that his crime has met its just punishment, give also pity that slavery wasted his young life, clothed his heart with garments of hate, and put into his hand the assassin's knife."

24. Pitman, *Assassination of President Lincoln*, pp. 124–38; T. B. Peterson, *The Trial of the Assassins and Conspirators* (Philadelphia: Peterson & Brothers, 1865), p. 156; Poore, *Conspiracy Trial*, 2:192–96, 342–69.

Joseph George observes that Holt's assistant Henry Burnett "was disturbed enough to have an interview with Weichmann that very day (May 28) to discuss Howell's testimony. Apparently on that occasion Burnett was so severe in questioning Weichmann that the latter found it prudent to send him a letter offering 'a few necessary additional statements concerning Howell.'" He assured the assistant judge advocate that he could redeem his character "ten thousand times" and "argued that Burnett should pay no heed to Howell" or anything he said (George, "Nature's First Law," pp. 114–15). Burnett must have been satisfied, for on the very next day Weichmann was released from custody, where he had been held for questioning and his own safety (ibid., p. 116).

Other witnesses also testified that Lloyd was extremely drunk on April 14. See Poore, *Conspiracy Trial*, 2:482–85; Peterson, *Trial of the Assassins*, pp. 124, 154.

25. Peterson, *Trial of the Assassins*, p. 156; Poore, *Conspiracy Trial*, 2:184–85, 188, 485–96, and 3:467. See also Mary Surratt's depositions to investigators, M-599, roll 6.

26. *Philadelphia Inquirer*, May 10, 1865.

27. Poore, *Conspiracy Trial*, 2:174, 179, 219–22.

28. Pitman, *Assassination of President Lincoln*, pp. 132, 137.

29. *New York Times*, May 31, 1865. See also Henry Kyd Douglas, *I Rode with Stonewall* (Chapel Hill: University of North Carolina Press, 1940), p. 346.

30. Peterson, *The Trial of the Assassins*, p. 156; Poore, *Conspiracy Trial*, 2:181, 183, 496–501.
31. *Philadelphia Inquirer*, May 4, 1865. For more on this topic see, among other things, my *All the Daring of the Soldier: Women of the Civil War Armies* (New York: W.W. Norton, 1999), and my "Mary Surratt and the Plot to Assassinate Abraham Lincoln," in Joan Cashin, ed., *The War Was You and Me* (Princeton: Princeton University Press, 2002).

On July 8 the *Inquirer* reiterated its condemnation of pro-Confederate women and identified the now deceased Mary Surratt as one of their order. "During the Rebellion," the *Inquirer* reminded its readers, "the South has been cursed by the malignant fierceness of she devils. They have been from the first the wild inciters of rebellion. . . . There has been no crime too barbarous to shock the sentiments of the Southern women. From spitting at Union officers in weak spitefulness, to wearing the bones of slaughtered Unionists as personal ornaments, and from plotting treason up to the encouragements of horrid murders, they have not shrunk. They have been transformed by their passions into fiends, and in the long catalogue of the woes of the South the hands of female plotters and assassins have been busy." Mary Surratt, the article continued, "was a type of these Jezebels."
32. *Philadelphia Inquirer*, May 11, 1865; *Lewiston* [Maine] *Daily Evening Journal*, May 16, 1865; *Harper's Weekly*, June 3, 1865.
33. Pitman, *Assassination of President Lincoln*, p. 298.
34. Ibid. pp. 228–33, 240–43, 344.
35. In his closing argument for Arnold and O'Laughlen, Cox pointed out that had O'Laughlen in fact murdered Grant on April 13, it would have undermined the rest of Booth's plan, "for it would have put every one else on his guard" (Pitman, *Assassination of President Lincoln*, p. 346).
36. Poore, *Conspiracy Trial*, 1:149–65, and 2:196–215; Pitman, *Assassination of President Lincoln*, pp. 344, 347, 350.
37. Pitman, *Assassination of President Lincoln*, pp. 99–113; Statement of Edman Spangler, April 15, 1865, M-599, roll 6. See also the testimony of John F. Sleighman, Joseph Burroughs, Mary Ann Turner, Mary Jane Anderson, John Miles, J. L. Dubonay, and Jacob Ritterspaugh, in Pitman, *Assassination of President Lincoln*, pp. 73–75, 81, 97, 105–6. See also the statements of "John C. Bohrur" (Joseph Burroughs) and John Miles, M-599, rolls 4 and 5, respectively, and John L. Foster to H. L. Burnett, April 23, 1865, in M-599, roll 5.
38. Poore, *Conspiracy Trial*, 2:531; Pitman, *Assassination of President Lincoln*, pp. 74, 100; Osborn H. Oldroyd, *The Assassination of Abraham Lincoln* (1901; reprint, Bowie, Md.: Heritage Books, 1990), pp. 12, 55.
39. Pitman, *Assassination of President Lincoln*, pp. 73–77, 102, 105, 111–12, 277, 282, 288; *New York Times*, May 22, 1865. Years later Commissioner Kautz recalled of Spangler that he did not seem "to have been a conspirator

knowingly. . . . His greatest crime was his ignorance, and that he did not see the ends to which he was being used" (Kautz, "Memoir," vol. 2, Kautz Papers).

40. *New York Times*, May 14, 1865.

41. Pitman, *Assassination of Abraham Lincoln*, pp. 178–217; Poore, *Conspiracy Trial*, 2:258–68, 386–403, 422, and 3:288, 294; Statements of Samuel A. Mudd, M-599, roll 2 and roll 5.

42. Poore, *Conspiracy Trial*, 1:436, and 2:263, 294–300, 306; Kautz, "Memoir," vol. 2, Kautz Papers.

43. Pitman, *Assassination of President Lincoln*, pp. 318–32.

44. Ibid., pp. 351–402; William Hanchett, *The Lincoln Murder Conspiracies* (Urbana: University of Illinois Press, 1983), p. 68.

45. *Richmond Times*, May 19, 1865; Doster, *Lincoln and Episodes*, pp. 257–59. John Clampitt recalled, "The Commission was organized to convict" (John W. Clampitt, "The Trial of Mrs. Surratt," *North American Review* 131 [September 1880], p. 230).

    On the dubious theory that a different kind of trial (especially a civil trial) at a different place might have produced a different result in the spring and early summer of 1865, see especially the very persuasive work of Thomas Reed Turner, *Beware the People Weeping: Public Opinion and the Assassination of Abraham Lincoln* (Baton Rouge: Louisiana State University Press, 1982).

46. Kautz, "Diary," July 2, 1865, Kautz Papers; Howard K. Beale, *Diary of Gideon Welles: Secretary of the Navy Under Lincoln and Johnson* (New York: W.W. Norton, 1960), 2:324. As will be seen, given the firestorm that would ensue later in connection with the commissioners' findings, Johnson's approval, and the subsequent carrying out of the sentences, one could argue that Johnson's illness was either premature or prophetic.

47. Frances X. Busch, *Enemies of the State* (Indianapolis: Bobbs-Merrill, 1954), p. 72; *New York Times*, July 7, 1865; *Philadelphia Inquirer*, July 7, 1865. See also the documents relating to the military commission's final deliberations, in container 92, Holt-LC.

48. *Philadelphia Inquirer*, July 7, 1865; *New York Times*, July 7, 1865.

49. *Philadelphia Inquirer*, July 7 and July 8, 1865.

50. Ibid. Powell's father did write to William Doster in September, thanking him for his work on behalf of his son's defense and explaining that he had learned of his son's fate only shortly before the execution and had not sufficient time to travel north to see him (Doster, *Lincoln and Episodes*, p. 272).

51. See the statement of John P. Brophy, enclosed in a letter from Charles Mason to Andrew Johnson, July 7, 1865, in the microfilmed Andrew Johnson Papers, ser. 1, reel 16, Library of Congress, Washington, D.C.

52. *Philadelphia Inquirer*, July 7 and July 8, 1865.

53. Clampitt, "The Trial of Mrs. Surratt," p. 235.

54. *Philadelphia Inquirer*, July 7 and July 8, 1865; George, "Nature's First

Law," pp. 118–19; Sarah F. Mudd to Joseph Holt, September 4, 1865, in container 49, Holt-LC.

55. *Philadelphia Inquirer*, July 8, 1865.

56. Doster, *Lincoln and Episodes*, p. 276.

57. *Philadelphia Inquirer*, July 8, 1865; *New York Times*, July 8, 1865; *Harper's Weekly*, July 22, 1865; Gray, "The Fate of the Lincoln Conspirators," p. 636. According to the *Inquirer* article, "at as early an hour as eight A. M." on the seventh, "people commenced to wend their way down to the prison, and the boats to Alexandria, which ran close by the jail, were crowded all day by those who took the trip in hopes of catching a glimpse of the gallows, or of the execution."

Booth's body had been buried within the walls of the Old Arsenal on the night of April 27, in order to prevent it from becoming "a relic for souvenir hunters" (Michael Kauffman, "Fort Lesley McNair and the Lincoln Conspirators," *Lincoln Herald* 80 (1978), p. 178).

58. *Philadelphia Inquirer*, July 8, 1865.

5. "IN VIOLATION OF THE LAWS AND CUSTOMS OF WAR"
GOING AFTER HENRY WIRZ OF ANDERSONVILLE

1. T. S. Bell to Joseph Holt, July 7, 1865, in container 48, Holt-LC.

2. Samuel Bland Arnold, *Defense and Prison Experiences of a Lincoln Conspirator* (Hattiesburg, Miss.: Book Farm, 1943) p. 17.

3. Thomas Ewing Jr. to Sarah Mudd, July 31, 1865, quoted in Nettie Mudd, ed., *The Life of Dr. Samuel A. Mudd* (New York: Neale, 1906), pp. 112, 115. See also *New York Times*, August 4, 1865; Louis J. Weichmann, *A True History of the Assassination of Abraham Lincoln and of the Conspiracy of 1865* (New York: Alfred A. Knopf, 1975), p. 284; Gary Planck, "Lincoln's Assassination: More 'Forgotten' Litigation—Ex parte Mudd (1868)," *Lincoln Herald* 76 (1974), p. 87; Memo of John F. Hartranft, July 16, 1865, Stanton Papers; Arnold, *Defense and Prison Experiences*, pp. 17, 62, 63, 66; and Roy Z. Chamlee, *Lincoln's Assassins: A Complete Account of Their Capture, Trial, and Punishment* (Jefferson, N.C.: McFarland & Company, 1990), pp. 482–83.

4. *Harper's Weekly*, August 26, 1865; Arnold, *Defense and Prison Experiences*, pp. 67–68; Planck, "Lincoln's Assassination," p. 87.

5. *New York Times*, August 4, 1865.

6. Ibid. Chamlee says that this is not the first time Mudd confessed, that he had done so as well to a visiting reporter at the Old Arsenal on July 17. Steers also makes a strong case for Mudd's confession. Clearly, however, I find the notion of Mudd actually confessing to be incongruous, not only with his previous denials of involvement, but also with the federal govern-

ment's failure to retry and convict him, if in fact he had volunteered new information pertaining to his guilt. (Chamlee, *Lincoln's Assassins*, p. 482. See also Edward Steers, *Blood on the Moon: The Assassination of Abraham Lincoln* [Lexington: University Press of Kentucky, 2001], pp. 235ff.)

7. Weichmann, *True History*, p. 258; Mudd, *Life of Dr. Samuel A. Mudd*, pp. 42–48.

8. Chamlee, *Lincoln's Assassins*, p. 482.

9. Arnold, *Defense and Prison Experiences*, pp. 68–69, 77.

10. Peggy Robbins, "'I Am Ashamed of My Conduct': Dr. Samuel Mudd's Attempt to Escape from Fort Jefferson," *Civil War Times Illustrated* 16 (1978), p. 14; Mudd, *Life of Dr. Samuel A. Mudd*, p. 139; Anne Catherine Pierce, "A Letter from Spangler," in *In Pursuit of. . . : Continuing Research in the Field of the Lincoln Assassination* (Clinton, Md.: The Surratt Society, 1990), pp. 277–78 (spellings as in the original). In early November, some of the black soldiers were replaced again by whites (Mudd, *Life of Dr. Samuel A. Mudd*, pp. 139, 143).

11. Chamlee, *Lincoln's Assassins*, p. 488; Planck, "Lincoln's Assassination," p. 87; Arnold, *Defense and Prison Experiences*, pp. 79–80; Mudd, *Life of Dr. Samuel A. Mudd*, pp. 119–27, 131–34, 161.

12. Chamlee, *Lincoln's Assassins*, p. 488; Planck, "Lincoln's Assassination," p. 87; Arnold, *Defense and Prison Experiences*, pp. 79–80; Robbins, "'I Am Ashamed'"; Mudd, *Life of Dr. Samuel A. Mudd*, pp. 119–27, 131–34, 161.

13. V. O. Taylor to Joseph Holt, July 7, 1865, in container 48, Holt-LC; Margaret Crosby to Joseph Holt, July 10, 1865, in container 49, Holt Papers.

14. See, for example, H. S. Olcott to Joseph Holt, September 15, 1865, in container 49, Holt Papers. See also Lafayette C. Baker's rather self-serving discussion of the controversy over the rewards, in his *History of the United States Secret Service* (Philadelphia: L. C. Baker, 1867), pp. 564–65. Chamlee reports that disputes over the reward moneys lasted well into 1866 (Chamlee, *Lincoln's Assassins*, pp. 491–92).

15. Weichmann, *True History*, p. 284; *New York Times*, July 7, 1865. For the commissioners' reports and the clemency petition, dated June 29 and June 30, see container 92, Holt-LC.

16. I discuss this debate at considerable length in chapter 9.

17. See the habeas corpus petition, and Andrew Johnson's response, July 7, 1865, in container 92, Holt-LC.

18. Kautz, "Memoir," vol. 2, Kautz Papers; *New York Times*, July 13, 1865. Andrew Johnson also received a number of letters praising him for his firm stance throughout the conspiracy trial and for following through on the execution. See, for example, Thomas Laurie to Andrew Johnson, July 8, 1865, in the microfilmed Andrew Johnson Papers, ser. 1, reel 16, Library of Congress, Washington, D.C. Laurie wrote in a postscript: "I rejoice especially that misguided evil doers of the other sex have been taught that

womanhood is no excuse for crime, but rather an aggravation of its wickedness."

19. See the Statement of John P. Brophy, enclosed in a letter from Charles Mason to Andrew Johnson, July 7, 1865, ser. 1, reel 16, Andrew Johnson Papers, Library of Congress; *Philadelphia Inquirer*, July 17, 1865.

20. *Philadelphia Inquirer*, July 8 and July 17, 1865; *New York Times*, July 13, 1865.

21. Joseph George Jr., "Nature's First Law: Louis Weichmann and Mrs. Surratt," *Civil War History* 28 (1982), p. 119. In the latter portion of his life, Weichmann wrote a massive account of the assassination and the conspiracy trial, which was published only in 1975, for reasons that are debatable. The book is avowedly a work of self-defense and self-justification: "I write this history," noted Weichmann, "in personal vindication of myself" (*True History*, p. 4). Throughout the book, of course, Weichmann insists on the absolute truthfulness of his testimony at the conspiracy trial in the summer of 1865 and elsewhere.

22. *Philadelphia Inquirer*, July 21, 1865.

23. *New York Times*, July 14, 1865; *Philadelphia Inquirer*, July 21, 1865; Alfred Isacsson, "The Case of Jacob Walter," *Lincoln Herald* 89 (1987), p. 21. See also the several documents relating to this debate in the James Allen Hardie Papers, Library of Congress, Washington, D.C. , including a letter of July 21 from Reverend E. Q. Waldron of Pikesville, Maryland, who explicitly linked the controversy concerning Father Walter with pro-Southern resentment toward the government. Waldron commiserated with Hardie with regard to such absurd attacks as Father Walter's and expressed confidence that, "the conduct of the government towards these conspirators and their senseless sympathizers is so prudent and admirable we can afford for the future to let them [the government's various opponents] go on so long as the result of their foolish course remains so harmless."

24. Sarah F. Mudd to Joseph Holt, September 4, 1865, in container 49, Holt-LC.

25. *New York Times*, May 7, 1865. The same issue of the paper also included a public denial of complicity from W. W. Cleary.

26. J. M. McAlpine to Joseph Holt, May 18, 1865, in container 47, Holt-LC; V. O. Taylor to Joseph Holt, July 7, 1865, in container 48, Holt-LC. Added McAlpine enthusiastically, "I would like to see you President, & if all hands felt towards you as I do, you would be the next President without any trouble." See also Mary Stephens to Joseph Holt, August 10, 1865, in container 49, Holt-LC (spelling as in the original).

27. William Hanchett, *The Lincoln Murder Conspiracies* (Urbana: University of Illinois Press, 1983), p. 75; Howard K. Beale, ed., *Diary of Gideon Welles: Secretary of the Navy Under Lincoln and Johnson* (New York: W.W. Norton, 1960) 2:307, 335–39.

28. Clement Clay to Edwin Stanton, August 19, 1865, Stanton Papers.

29. Joseph Holt to Edwin Stanton, November 13, 1865, *Official Records*, ser. 3, vol. 5, pp. 490–94.

30. Unknown to Edwin Stanton, May 14, 1865, Stanton Papers.

31. Beale, *Diary of Gideon Welles*, 2:364; William J. Cooper, *Jefferson Davis, American* (New York: Alfred A. Knopf, 2000), pp. 542, 553; William C. Davis, *Jefferson Davis: The Man and His Hour* (New York: HarperCollins, 1991), pp. 641, 645.

32. Francis Lieber to Joseph Holt, September 15, 1865, in container 49, Holt-LC; spellings as in the original.

33. *Lewiston* [Maine] *Daily Evening Journal*, May 29, 1865; Roger J. Bartman, "The Contribution of Joseph Holt to the Political Life of the United States," (Ph.D. diss., Fordham University, 1958), pp. 262–63.

34. See Sanford Conover to Joseph Holt, November 1, 1865, in container 92, Holt-LC. See also Sanford Conover to Joseph Holt, July 26, August 2, August 24, September 1, September 4 (two letters), October 10, and November 11, 1865; all in container 92, Holt-LC. See also the correspondence of Joseph Holt and Sanford Conover from this period, contained in Holt-HL.

35. James M. McPherson, *Ordeal by Fire: The Civil War and Reconstruction* (New York: McGraw Hill, 1992), p. 450.

36. Patricia L. Faust, ed., *Historical Times Illustrated Encyclopedia of the Civil War* (New York: HarperCollins, 1991), p. 837; John Hitz to Andrew Johnson, November 9, 1865, *Official Records*, ser. 2, vol. 8, pp. 792–93; Susan Banfield, *The Andersonville Prison Civil War Crimes Trial: A Headline Court Case* (Berkeley Heights, N.J.: Enslow, 2000), pp. 20–21; Henry Wirz to J. H. Wilson, May 7, 1865, *Official Records*, ser. 2, vol. 8, pp. 537–38; John Hitz to Andrew Johnson, *Official Records*, ser. 2, vol. 8, pp. 793–94.

37. McPherson, *Ordeal by Fire*, pp. 450–56.

38. Ben Perley Poore, ed., *The Conspiracy Trial for the Murder of the President* (Boston: J.E. Tilton, 1865), 2:130–36.

39. Ibid., 2:241–43 and 3:500, 502. See also the testimony of James Young, ibid., 2:243–46.

40. Ibid., 2:133–34, 242, and 3:502; spellings as in the original.

41. Henry Wirz to J. H. Wilson, May 7, 1865, *Official Records*, ser. 2, vol. 8, pp. 537–38.

42. J. H. Wilson to the Adjutant General, May 16, 1865, *Official Records*, ser. 1, vol. 49, pt. 2, p. 800; George H. Thomas to the Adjutant General, May 26, 1865, *Official Records*, ser. 2, vol. 8, p. 538.

43. General Court Martial Orders No. 607, *Official Records*, ser. 2, vol. 8, pp. 784–89; H. T. Drinkhouser to Joseph Holt, August 28, 1865, in container 49, Holt-LC (spelling as in the original).

44. In contrast with the findings of the commission in his case, there is some documentary evidence to suggest that Wirz did, at least on a couple of occasions, try to ameliorate the horrible conditions at Andersonville (see H. Wirz to R. D. Chapman, June 6, 1864, *Official Records*, ser. 2, vol. 7, p. 207). Other documents, however, only enhance Wirz's image as a "brutal monster" who nevertheless slightly favored Union prisoners of German birth (see statement of Prescott Tracy, August 19, 1864, *Official Records*, ser. 2, vol. 7, p. 622). Still other documents show Wirz as commandant defending himself against reports from within the Confederacy itself suggesting the extreme nature of the Andersonville horrors (see H. Wirz to J. H. Winder, September 24, 1864, *Official Records*, ser. 2, vol. 7, pp. 758–60).

45. Joseph Holt to Andrew Johnson, October 31, 1865, *Official Records*, ser. 2, vol. 8, pp. 775–81, 789–92; Joseph Holt to Edwin Stanton, November 3, 1865, *Official Records*, ser. 2, vol. 8, pp. 782–83.

    According to Susan Banfield in her study of the trial, the original charges against Wirz named Jefferson Davis and Robert E. Lee as co-conspirators with Wirz but Stanton told Holt to omit their names. Banfield claims that the War Department "had gotten cold feet about naming the popular Jefferson Davis as a co-conspirator" (Banfield, *Andersonville Prison Civil War Crimes Trial*, p. 39). My own research leads me to the conclusion that while Stanton may have been developing some vague doubts about the possibility of successfully prosecuting Davis, Holt was still fully persuaded and absolutely determined to try.

46. *Official Records*, ser. 2, vol. 8, pp. 773–74; 791–95. These documents reveal that Schade also tried to persuade Johnson that the proceedings of the military commission had been biased and unfair to his client and had included false testimony. He insisted that Wirz had been "almost a prisoner himself at Andersonville" and that he had tried without success to improve the conditions there.

47. *Official Records*, ser. 2, vol. 8, pp. 791–95.

6. "FORBEARANCE AND FORGIVENESS"
ANDREW JOHNSON'S VISION FOR SOUTHERN RESTORATION

1. Daniel E. Sutherland, ed., *A Very Violent Rebel: The Civil War Diary of Ellen Renshaw House* (Knoxville: University of Tennessee Press, 1996), p. 190.

2. Mary K. Stephens to Joseph Holt, August 10, 1865, in container 49, Holt-LC; spelling as in the original.

3. Hans L. Trefousse, *Andrew Johnson* (New York: W.W. Norton, 1989), p. 232.

4. Joseph Holt to Edwin Stanton, November 13, 1865, *Official Records*, ser. 3, vol. 5, pp. 490–94.
5. Ibid.
6. Ibid.
7. William J. Cooper, *Jefferson Davis, American* (New York: Alfred A. Knopf, 2000), p. 542.
8. See Sanford Conover to Joseph Holt, July 26 and November 1, 1865, in container 92, Holt-LC. See also Sanford Conover to Joseph Holt, August 2, August 24, September 1, September 4 (two letters), October 10, and November 11, 1865; all in container 92, Holt-LC. And see the depositions of William Campbell (November 4, 1865), Joseph Snevel (November 4, 1865), John McGill (August 17, 1865), and Farnum B. Wright (November 23, 1865), among others, all in container 92, Holt-LC; and the depositions of Sarah Douglass and Mary Knapp in container 93, Holt-LC.
9. Sarah Mudd to Joseph Holt, September 4, 1865, in container 49, and November 27, 1865, in container 50, Holt-LC. See also Anna Surratt to Edwin Stanton, July 8, 1865, Stanton Papers.
10. Louis J. Weichmann to Joseph Holt, October 10, November 12, and December 18, 1865, in container 50, Holt-LC. See also Louis J. Weichmann to Joseph Holt, November 25, 1865; and Louis J. Weichmann to James A. Ekin (one of the military commissioners at the conspiracy trial), November 21, 1865, both also in container 50, Holt-LC.
11. Robert S. Holt to Joseph Holt, August 25, 1865, in container 49, Holt-LC; Thomas Holt to Joseph Holt, October 17, 1865, in container 50, Holt-LC.
12. *New York Times*, September 16, 1865.
13. Howard K. Beale, ed., *Diary of Gideon Welles: Secretary of the Navy Under Lincoln and Johnson* (New York: W.W. Norton, 1960), 2:364, 370–71.
14. *New York Times*, September 16, 1865.
15. Ibid.
16. Beale, *Diary of Gideon Welles*, 2:374; Frank Ballard to Joseph Holt, September 15, 1865, and W. G. Snethen to Joseph Holt, September 15, 1865, both in container 49, Holt-LC. See also Frank Ballard to Joseph Holt, September 5, 1865, in container 49, Holt-LC. As it turns out, this was not even the first postwar attack on Holt by a member of the Blair family. A July 1865 letter to Holt suggests that Montgomery Blair's brother, Frank, had launched an earlier salvo in July, in a speech in Lexington, Kentucky (see C. B. New to Joseph Holt, July 19, 1865, in container 49, Holt-LC).
17. Beale, *Diary of Gideon Welles*, 2:370; D. H. Hoopes to Joseph Holt, September 18, 1865, in container 50, Holt-LC; C. B. New to Joseph Holt, July 19, 1865.
18. D. H. Hoopes to Joseph Holt, September 18, 1865; Beale, *Diary of Gideon Welles*, 2:370.

19. H. L. Burnett to Joseph Holt, September 5, 1865, in container 49, Holt-LC.

20. Hans L. Trefousse, *Impeachment of a President: Andrew Johnson, the Blacks, and Reconstruction* (New York: Fordham University Press, 1999), p. 3.

21. Hans Trefousse writes, "Speedy restoration of the Southern states to their former rights in Congress would eventually result in the supremacy of the [largely Southern and pro-Southern] Democratic party, a contingency the victorious Republicans could hardly view with equanimity. Moreover, the lapse of the three-fifths compromise, which had based representation on all free persons and three-fifths of all slaves, would result in an increase of Southern representation now that all slaves were free. Northerners could hardly be expected to be ready so lavishly to reward their recent foes" (Trefousse, *Andrew Johnson*, p. 214). See also Benjamin B. Kendrick, *The Journal of the Joint Committee of Fifteen on Reconstruction* (1914; reprint, New York: Negro Universities Press, 1969), pp. 198–99; Trefousse, *Impeachment of a President*, pp. 3–4.

22. Trefousse, *Andrew Johnson*, p. 208.

23. Eric Foner, *Reconstruction: America's Unfinished Revolution, 1863–1877* (New York: Harper & Row, 1988), p. 177; James M. McPherson, *Ordeal by Fire: The Civil War and Reconstruction* (New York: McGraw-Hill, 1992), pp. 393, 407, 631; Beale, *Diary of Gideon Welles*, 2:289–91; Benjamin P. Thomas and Harold M. Hyman, *Stanton: The Life and Times of Lincoln's Secretary of War* (New York: Alfred A. Knopf, 1962), p. 400; Trefousse, *Andrew Johnson*, p. 194.

24. Trefousse, *Andrew Johnson*, p. 192.

25. Foner, *Reconstruction*, p. 178.

26. According to Trefousse, early on Wade even expressed some concern that Johnson might be "too extreme," based on comments Johnson made in conversation about wanting to execute leading Confederates (*Andrew Johnson*, p. 198).

27. Ibid.

28. Ibid., p. 197; Thomas and Hyman, *Stanton*, p. 439; Foner, *Reconstruction*, p. 180.

29. McPherson, *Ordeal by Fire*, p. 496. Thomas and Hyman write that Johnson's "own stern struggle to rise in life had instilled in him a hatred of monopoly and privilege. He shared Stanton's biting scorn for the planter aristocrats and came to the presidency breathing fire and slaughter against them for bringing on the war" (*Stanton*, p. 440).

30. Foner, *Reconstruction*, p. 181.

31. McPherson, *Ordeal by Fire*, p. 496; Thomas and Hyman, *Stanton*, pp. 446–47; Trefousse, *Andrew Johnson*, p. 175; Foner, *Reconstruction*, pp. 182, 190, 199; Trefousse, *Impeachment of a President*, p. 13; Nettie Mudd, ed., *The Life of Dr. Samuel A. Mudd* (New York: Neale, 1906), p. 155.

32. Thomas and Hyman, *Stanton*, pp. 440–41.

33. Trefousse, *Andrew Johnson*, p. 22. According to Johnson, the "black race of Africa were inferior to the white man in point of intellect—better calculated in physical structure to undergo drudgery and hardship—standing, as they do, many degrees lower in the scale of gradation that expressed the relative relation between God and all that he had created than the white man" (ibid., pp. 57–58).

34. Ulysses S. Grant, *Personal Memoirs of U. S. Grant* (1885; reprint, New York: Penguin Putnam, 1999), p. 616.

35. Glyndon Van Deusen, *William Henry Seward* (New York: Oxford University Press, 1967), p. 419; Foner, *Reconstruction*, p. 217; Trefousse, *Andrew Johnson*, p. 216.

36. Trefousse, *Andrew Johnson*, p. 215.

37. Beale, *Diary of Gideon Welles*, 2:347–48.

38. Foner, *Reconstruction*, p. 159.

39. In a January 4, 1866, letter to Andrew Johnson (*Official Records*, ser. 2, vol. 8, p. 844), Stanton noted that three members of Jefferson Davis's cabinet had been paroled: G. A. Trenholm (secretary of the treasury), James A. Seddon (secretary of war), and John H. Reagan (postmaster general). Stanton also noted the parole granted to Assistant Secretary of War John A. Campbell.

40. McPherson, *Ordeal by Fire*, pp. 502, 504; Trefousse, *Andrew Johnson*, pp. 218, 227, 231, 232; Foner, *Reconstruction*, p. 191. Trefousse notes that some of these former Confederates had not even been pardoned at the time they were elected; Johnson pardoned them after the fact, however, "in order to enable them to take office" (*Andrew Johnson*, p. 231). According to Secretary of the Navy Gideon Welles, Johnson swore as late as August 11 that he would not pardon any of the former members of the Confederate cabinet, or Davis, or Stephens (Beale, *Diary of Gideon Welles*, 2:358). Foner notes: "By 1866, over 7,000 Southerners excluded from amnesty under the $20,000 clause had received individual pardons" from Johnson (*Reconstruction*, p. 191).

41. Trefousse, *Andrew Johnson*, p. 222; Foner, *Reconstruction*, p. 216.

42. Foner, *Reconstruction*, p. 223; Beale, *Diary of Gideon Welles*, 2:375.

43. Tal. P. Shaffner to Joseph Holt, June 27, 1865, in container 48, Holt-LC; C. B. New to Joseph Holt, July 19, 1865; A. Burwell to Joseph Holt, August 18, 1865, in container 49, Holt-LC; Mary K. Stephens to Joseph Holt, August 10, 1865, in container 49, Holt-LC. See also J. W. Kincheloe to Joseph Holt, September 20, 1865, in container 50, Holt-LC.

44. Other government documents suggest that the State Department was aware of Surratt's whereabouts even earlier, while he was preparing to leave Canada for Europe. See Thomas Michael Martin, "The United States Government Versus John Harrison Surratt: A Study in Attitudes" (Master's thesis: Old Dominion University, 1996), pp. 43–45.

45. Louis J. Weichmann, *A True History of the Assassination of Abraham Lincoln and of the Conspiracy of 1865* (New York: Alfred A. Knopf, 1975), p. 438.
46. Ibid. pp. 326–27. According to Weichmann, Joseph Holt received no information about this proposition (ibid., p. 327). Even if he had, it seems unlikely he would have agreed to such an arrangement.
47. Gary R. Planck, "Lincoln Assassination: The 'Forgotten' Litigation—Shuey v. United States (1875)," *Lincoln Herald* 75 (1973), p. 87; Alexandra Lee Levin, "Who Hid John H. Surratt, the Lincoln Conspiracy Case Figure?," *Maryland Historical Magazine* 60 (1965), pp. 175–84; Weichmann, *True History*, pp. 330ff, 437–40, 445; Martin, "United States Government Versus John Harrison Surratt," pp. 37–39.

    In 1870, now a free man, John Surratt denied assertions that he had deserted his mother "in the direst hour of her need." Rather, he said, when he left Montreal he believed she was safe, that "there was no cause for uneasiness on my part," and that his friends' letters repeatedly assured him that "all would be well." He affirmed that he had sent a messenger to a friend in Washington, who returned with word that Surratt should not worry, that to become involved in his mother's case at this point would only make things worse. "What else could I do but accept these unwavering assurances?" Surratt asked. Then, only after the execution was over did he learn his mother's fate, at which point, he recalled, "It would be folly for me to attempt to describe my feelings" (Weichmann, *True History*, pp. 438–40).
48. Planck, "Lincoln Assassination . . . Shuey," p. 87; Martin, "United States Government Versus John Harrison Surratt," pp. 40–42. See also General Orders No. 164, dated November 24, 1865, *Official Records*, ser. 1, vol. 49, pt. 2, p. 1116.
49. See the testimony of Edwin Stanton to the Judiciary Committee, January 1867, Stanton Papers.
50. Martin, "United States Government Versus John Harrison Surratt," pp. 45–47.
51. *New York Times*, September 16, 1865.

7. "TRAITORS, CONFESSED PERJURERS AND SUBORNERS" THE UNRAVELING OF REVENGE

1. Joseph Holt to Edwin Stanton, November 23, 1865, *Official Records*, ser. 2, vol. 8, p. 865.
2. Howard K. Beale, ed., *Diary of Gideon Welles: Secretary of the Navy Under Lincoln and Johnson* (New York: W.W. Norton, 1960), 2:437–38.
3. Eric Foner, *Reconstruction: America's Unfinished Revolution, 1863–1877* (New York: Harper & Row, 1988), p. 215.

338 NOTES (PP. 192–199)

4. Glyndon Van Deusen, *William Henry Seward* (New York: Oxford University Press, 1967), pp. 562–63.
5. Foner, *Reconstruction*, p. 224.
6. T. H. Duval to Joseph Holt, December 4, 1865, in container 50, Holt-LC. See also T. H. Duval to Joseph Holt, January 14, 1866, in container 51, Holt-LC.
7. Foner, *Reconstruction*, pp. 224–25.
8. Ibid., p. 229; James M. McPherson, *Ordeal by Fire: The Civil War and Reconstruction* (New York: McGraw-Hill, 1992), pp. 510–11. The remaining members of the Joint Committee were Republicans Thaddeus Stevens (Pa.), Roscoe Conkling (N.Y.), George S. Boutwell (Mass.), James W. Grimes (Iowa), Ira Harris (N.Y.), Jacob Howard (Mich.), George H. Williams (Ore.), Elihu B. Washburne (Ill.), Justin S. Morrill (Vt.), and Henry T. Blow (Mo.); and Democrats Andrew J. Rogers (N.J.) and Henry Grider (Ky.). Benjamin B. Kendrick writes that in the end, "it was the members of this committee who, from December, 1865, to March, 1867, determined the principles of reconstruction that finally were carried into effect in the South" (Kendrick, *The Journal of the Joint Committee of Fifteen on Reconstruction* [1914; reprint, New York: Negro Universities Press, 1969], p. 18).
9. As Eric Foner has written, "Johnson would never quite understand that, [even] to mainstream Republicans . . . , the freedmen had earned a claim upon the conscience of the nation. . . . Their fate had become identified with the outcome of the Civil War. Many Northerners who did not share the Radicals' commitment to black political rights insisted the freedmen's personal liberty and ability to compete as free laborers must be guaranteed or emancipation would be little more than a mockery" (*Reconstruction*, p. 225). Writing early in the twentieth century, historian Benjamin Kendrick noted that Johnson, in contrast, wanted the Southern states to agree only to "a guarantee of the perpetuity of the Union, and the destruction of the institution of slavery. These were the only objects for which the war had ever at any time been professedly waged, and Johnson believed that a war could have no political results different from the objects for which it had been waged" (*Journal of the Joint Committee*, p. 152).
10. Beale, *Diary of Gideon Welles*, 2:387, 395–97.
11. Ibid. 2:395–97.
12. Ibid. 2:387, 395–97. Sumner's lack of interest in punishing Davis was not uncommon among the Radicals in Congress. As Eric Foner explains, "While some constituents . . . demanded the execution of Southern leaders as punishment for treason, only a handful of Radical leaders echoed these calls. Rather than vengeance, the driving force of Radical ideology was the utopian vision of a nation whose citizens enjoyed equality of civil and political rights, secured by a powerful and beneficent national state" (*Reconstruction*, p. 230).

13. Joseph Holt to Edwin Stanton, November 23, 1865, *Official Records*, ser. 2, vol. 8, pp. 862–66.
14. Ibid.
15. William C. Davis, *Jefferson Davis: The Man and His Hour* (New York: HarperCollins, 1991), p. 654.
16. Nettie Mudd, ed., *The Life of Dr. Samuel A. Mudd* (New York: Neale, 1906), pp. 148–50.
17. Davis, *Jefferson Davis*, p. 647. Eric Foner writes, "Why the President so quickly abandoned the idea of depriving the prewar elite of its political and economic hegemony has always been something of a mystery. . . . Did flattery by planters and their wives play upon the Presidential ego and lead Johnson to abandon a planned assault upon the Confederacy's elite? More likely, he came to view cooperation with the planters as indispensable to two interrelated goals—white supremacy in the South and his own reelection as President" (*Reconstruction*, p. 191).
18. Joseph Holt to Edwin Stanton, December 6, 1866, *Official Records*, ser. 2, vol. 8, pp. 855–61. During this period, reports on the health of Clay and Davis were arriving in Washington on a regular basis—see Nelson A. Miles to E. D. Townsend, January 2, 1866, ibid., p. 842; see also Miles to Townsend, January 11, January 12, January 13, January 15, and January 18, 1866, ibid., pp. 846–47, 867. How much Holt cared about the health of Clay and Davis is unclear. Surely his primary concern was simply that they remain healthy enough to stand trial whenever the time came.
19. Andrew Johnson to the Senate of the United States, January 5, 1866, ibid., p. 843; James Speed to Andrew Johnson, January 4, 1866, ibid., pp. 844–45.
20. Edwin Stanton to Andrew Johnson, January 4, 1866, ibid., pp. 843–44.
21. William J. Cooper, *Jefferson Davis, American* (New York: Alfred A. Knopf, 2000), pp. 556–57.
22. Mudd, *Life of Dr. Samuel A. Mudd*, p. 158.
23. Beale, *Diary of Gideon Welles*, 2:422.
24. Foner, *Reconstruction*, pp. 243–51; Benjamin P. Thomas and Harold M. Hyman, *Stanton: The Life and Times of Lincoln's Secretary of War* (New York: Alfred A. Knopf, 1962), p. 477; McPherson, *Ordeal by Fire*, pp. 505, 510–12; Beale, *Diary of Gideon Welles*, 2:474, 480–81, 581; Hans L. Trefousse, *Impeachment of a President: Andrew Johnson, the Blacks, and Reconstruction* (New York: Fordham University Press, 1999), p. 31. Foner notes: "Johnson's rejection of the Civil Rights Bill has always been viewed as a major blunder, the most disastrous miscalculation of his political career. If the President aimed to isolate the Radicals and build up a new political coalition around himself, he could not have failed more miserably. Moderates now concluded that Johnson's policies 'would wreck the Republican party'" (*Reconstruction*, p. 251).

25. Mudd, *Life of Dr. Samuel A. Mudd,* pp. 165–66.

26. Joseph Holt to Edwin Stanton, March 20, 1866, *Official Records,* ser. 2, vol. 8, pp. 890–92.

27. Thomas and Hyman, *Stanton,* p. 478; C. R. Woods to Joseph Holt, April 4, 1866, and Edwin Stanton's response, *Official Records,* ser. 3, vol. 5, p. 933.

28. Beale, *Diary of Gideon Welles,* 2:423.

29. Frank L. Klement, *Dark Lanterns: Secret Political Societies, Conspiracies, and Treason Trials in the Civil War* (Baton Rouge: Louisiana State University Press, 1984), pp. 227–28; Brooks Simpson, *The Reconstruction Presidents* (Lawrence: University Press of Kansas, 1998), p. 98. See chapter 1 for more on the Milligan case.

30. Mudd, *Life of Dr. Samuel A. Mudd,* p. 174.

31. E. D. Townsend to Nelson A. Miles April 17, 1866, *Official Records,* ser. 2, vol. 8, p. 899.

32. *Official Records,* ser. 2, vol. 8, p. 842, footnote; Beale, *Diary of Gideon Welles,* 2:404, 436, 472, 478.

33. James F. Wilson to Edwin Stanton, April 17, 1866, *Official Records,* ser. 2, vol. 8, pp. 898–99; McPherson, *Ordeal by Fire,* p. 527.

34. Mudd, *Life of Dr. Samuel A. Mudd,* pp. 180–81, 187.

35. Butler Papers. I am extremely grateful to Lincoln assassination conspiracy expert James O. Hall for sharing with me his microfilmed copy of the Judiciary Committee's investigations relating to Jefferson Davis and Clement Clay in the spring of 1866, officially Report 104 of the House of Representatives, 39th Congress, 1st session, 1866.

36. See Holt's April 13 and April 14, 1866, testimony to the House Judiciary Committee, Butler Papers.

37. McPherson, *Ordeal by Fire,* pp. 631–32; Kendrick, *Journal of the Joint Committee,* p. 183; Beale, *Diary of Gideon Welles,* 2:494, 498. Benjamin Kendrick describes Bingham, in his basic attitude toward Reconstruction, as being more similar to the moderate Fessenden than to the Radical Thaddeus Stevens. Like Fessenden, Bingham wished to avoid a breach with the President, but he was unwilling to sacrifice his principles simply for the sake of harmony. Moreover, "he particularly desired to have the civil rights of the individual put into the keeping of the National Government, and it is not too much to say that had it not been for his untiring efforts the provision for nationalizing civil rights would not have found a place in the fourteenth amendment" (*Journal of the Joint Committee,* pp. 183–84).

38. Hans L. Trefousse, *Andrew Johnson* (New York: W.W. Norton, 1989), pp. 251–52.

39. Butler Papers.

40. Foner, *Reconstruction,* pp. 261–62. The riot began on May 1, and some forty-six blacks and two whites were killed.

41. Butler Papers.

42. Ibid.

43. L. C. Turner's deposition, June 2, 1866, in container 52, Holt-LC; Louis J. Weichmann's May 26, 1866, testimony to the House Judiciary Committee, Butler Papers.

44. Holt's June 18, 1866, testimony to the House Judiciary Committee, Butler Papers.

45. Ibid.

46. Ibid.

47. Ibid.

48. Joseph Holt to Edwin Stanton, July 3, 1866, *Official Records*, ser. 2, vol. 8, pp. 931–45.

49. Davis, *Jefferson Davis*, pp. 649–50; Mudd, *Life of Dr. Samuel A. Mudd*, p. 190.

50. Mary Bernard Allen, "Joseph Holt: Judge Advocate General (1862–1875): A Study in the Treatment of Political Prisoners by the United States Government During the Civil War" (Ph.D. diss., University of Chicago, 1927), p. 153. See also a copy of the debate concerning the future of the Bureau of Military Justice, dated July 9, 1866, in container 52, Holt-LC.

51. Davis, *Jefferson Davis*, pp. 653–54; John J. Craven, *Prison Life of Jefferson Davis* (New York: Carleton, 1866).

52. Senate debate over the continuation of the Bureau of Military Justice, July 9, 1866, in container 52, Holt-LC; H. C. [full name illegible] to Joseph Holt, June 19, 1866, in container 52, Holt-LC.

53. Welles saw Stanton in much the same light. "Stanton," he wrote, "has sometimes brought forward singular papers relating to conspiracies, and dark and murderous designs in which he had evident faith, and Holt has assured him in his suspicions" (Beale, *Diary of Gideon Welles*, 2:423–24).

54. T. S. Bell to Joseph Holt, September 13, 1866, in container 53, Holt-LC. Not surprisingly, Samuel Mudd also enjoyed the opportunity to criticize Holt anew. "I believe sincerely there are parties at the head of the different departments of the Government," he wrote his wife on August 22, "who delight in human affliction and suffering, especially when they can by any pretext prosper their own, or their party's cause. I cannot view the conduct of Judge Holt otherwise" (Mudd, *Life of Dr. Samuel A. Mudd*, pp. 202–03).

55. Foner, *Reconstruction*, p. 263. Writes Johnson biographer Hans Trefousse, "Johnson's assertion that he had peacefully restored the South and that law and order reigned in the former Confederacy was shown" by the New Orleans race riot "to be a gross exaggeration" (*Andrew Johnson*, p. 258).

56. Beale, *Diary of Gideon Welles*, 2:569–70; Mudd, *Life of Dr. Samuel A. Mudd*, pp. 206–7.

57. See L. C. Turner to Joseph Holt, November 8, 1866, *Official Records*, ser. 2, vol. 8, pp. 973–74.

58. L. C. Turner to Joseph Holt, September 10, 1866, ibid., pp. 962–65. Samuel Mudd seems to have had a particular dislike for Turner, whom he associated with what he liked to call the "Bureau of *Military Injustice*." When Turner died in the spring of 1867, Mudd was delighted. In contrast with the newspaper reports indicating that Turner had died of apoplexy, Mudd asserted to his wife that Holt's former associate must have poisoned himself as a result of his "guilty conscience" in connection with the 1865 trial of the conspirators (Mudd, *Life of Dr. Samuel A. Mudd*, pp. 231–32).

59. Robert S. Holt to Joseph Holt, August 21, 1866, in container 52, Holt-LC.

60. Joseph Holt to Edwin Stanton, September 11, 1866, *Official Records*, ser. 2, vol. 8, pp. 964–65.

61. See W. W. Winthrop to Joseph Holt, August 6, 1866, in container 53, Holt-LC.

62. Henry L. Burnett to Joseph Holt, September 13, 1866, in container 53, Holt-LC.

63. Document from the Union League of Philadelphia, September 13, 1866, in container 53, Holt-LC; Reply of Edwin Stanton, undated, *Official Records*, ser. 2, vol. 8, p. 965; Edwin Stanton to Joseph Holt, November 14, 1866, in container 53, Holt-LC. Welles agreed that a court of inquiry was unnecessary in Holt's case, but his tone in his diary was considerably less sympathetic and supportive than Stanton's. On the one hand, Welles feared that such an inquiry would open a dreadful can of worms; on the other, he thought Holt was acting unduly distressed. "I regretted his sensitiveness," wrote Welles on September 28 (Beale, *Diary of Gideon Welles*, 2:601, 604).

64. Roy Z. Chamlee, *Lincoln's Assassins: A Complete Account of Their Capture, Trial, and Punishment* (Jefferson, N.C.: McFarland & Company, 1990), pp. 512–13; William Hanchett, *The Lincoln Murder Conspiracies* (Urbana: University of Illinois Press, 1983), p. 81. Under examination, Conover "confessed" that he had "coached" others to lie about Davis's complicity in the Lincoln assassination in order to get revenge against Davis "by whose order he had been imprisoned for six months" during the war "in Castle Thunder," a notorious Confederate prison in Richmond, and who had also, purportedly, "insulted" Conover's wife. Given Conover's history of shameless duplicity, it is impossible to know how much to credit his own claims about his motivations for acting as he did. See also L. C. Turner to Joseph Holt, November 8, 1866, *Official Records*, ser. 2, vol. 8, p. 973.

8. "A WELL-DRESSED AND VERY PRESENTABLE YOUNG MAN"
THE TRIAL OF JOHN SURRATT JR.

1. Howard K. Beale, ed., *Diary of Gideon Welles: Secretary of the Navy Under Lincoln and Johnson* (New York: W.W. Norton, 1960), 2:616–19.

2. T. H. Duval to Joseph Holt, January 23, 1867, in container 55, Holt-LC.

3. Hans L. Trefousse, *Andrew Johnson* (New York: W.W. Norton, 1989), pp. 267, 272.

4. Margeret E. Crosby to Joseph Holt, November 30, 1866, in container 54, Holt-LC.

5. Eric Foner, *Reconstruction: America's Unfinished Revolution, 1863–1877* (New York: Harper & Row, 1988), p. 267.

6. Beale, *Diary of Gideon Welles*, 2:558.

7. Ibid., 2:588–89.

8. Margaret E. Crosby to Joseph Holt, November 30, 1866, in container 54, Holt-LC; Foner, *Reconstruction*, p. 265; Brooks Simpson, *The Reconstruction Presidents* (Lawrence: University Press of Kansas), pp. 108–9.

9. Beale, *Diary of Gideon Welles*, 2:482.

10. Trefousse, *Andrew Johnson*, p. 276. According to Eric Foner, "Friends of moderate Congressmen" who had benefited previously from Republican Party patronage "fared no better than those who owed their posts to Radicals" (*Reconstruction*, p. 266). Johnson replaced Harlan with Orville H. Browning of Illinois. According to Roy Z. Chamlee, Browning had been a behind-the-scenes adviser to defense counselor Ewing during the 1865 trial of the conspirators. (Chamlee, *Lincoln's Assassins: A Complete Account of Their Capture, Trial, and Punishment* [Jefferson, N.C.: McFarland & Company, 1990], p. 428).

11. See Louis J. Weichmann to Joseph Holt, October 10, October 19, and October 23, 1866, in container 54, Holt-LC.

12. Simpson, *Reconstruction Presidents*, p. 105; Benjamin P. Thomas and Harold M. Hyman, *Stanton: The Life and Times of Lincoln's Secretary of War* (New York: Alfred A. Knopf, 1962), pp. 516–17.

13. Simpson, *Reconstruction Presidents*, p. 111; Nettie Mudd, ed., *The Life of Dr. Samuel A. Mudd* (New York: Neale, 1906), p. 217.

14. James M. McPherson, *Ordeal by Fire: The Civil War and Reconstruction* (New York: McGraw-Hill, 1992), p. 520; Beale, *Diary of Gideon Welles*, 3:17–18.

15. Trefousse, *Andrew Johnson*, p. 273. Horrified, Gideon Welles noted to his diary that such a bill was punitive to certain whites, elevating "ignorant, vicious, stupid negroes who have flocked hither" to superior status (Beale, *Diary of Gideon Welles*, 3:3–8).

16. Thomas and Hyman, *Stanton*, p. 520; Hans L. Trefousse, *Impeachment of a President: Andrew Johnson, the Blacks, and Reconstruction* (New York: Fordham University Press, 1999), p. 55; Simpson, *Reconstruction Presidents*, p. 112; Beale, *Diary of Gideon Welles*, 3:8, 12.

17. Beale, *Diary of Gideon Welles*, 2:630.

18. Thomas Michael Martin, "The United States Government Versus John Har-

rison Surratt: A Study in Attitudes" (master's thesis: Old Dominion University, 1996), pp. 49–53.

19. Planck, "Lincoln Assassination: The 'Forgotten' Litigation—Shuey v. United States (1875)," *Lincoln Herald* 75 (1973), pp. 87–88. See also the *New York Times*, December 13, 1867, which reported on an "application of H. B. Sainte Marie for compensation for information furnished by him which led to the capture of John H. Surratt. Judge-Advocate General Holt," the paper noted, "thinks he ought to be paid."

20. Martin, "United States Government Versus John Harrison Surratt," pp. 53–58.

21. Ibid. pp. 58–59.

22. Ibid. pp. 65, 67.

23. Ibid. pp. 67, 78; *New York Times*, January 8, 1867. See also Osborn H. Oldroyd, *The Assassination of Abraham Lincoln* (1901; reprint, Bowie, Md.: Heritage Books, 1990), pp. 230–34; and Surratt's own account of his European adventures, quoted in Louis J. Weichmann, *A True History of the Assassination of Abraham Lincoln and of the Conspiracy of 1865* (New York: Alfred A. Knopf, 1975), pp. 445–50.

24. Louis J. Weichmann to Joseph Holt, December 12, 1866, in container 54, Holt-LC. Ever eager to inflate his own importance, Weichmann took credit for introducing Surratt to Ste. Marie in the first place, in April 1863, when all three were in Little Texas, Maryland (*True History*, p. 329).

25. Beale, *Diary of Gideon Welles*, 2:634.

26. Joseph Holt to Edwin Stanton, December 15, 1866, *Official Records*, ser. 2, vol. 8, pp. 976–78; Beale, *Diary of Gideon Welles*, 3:31.

27. Mudd, *Life of Dr. Samuel A. Mudd*, pp. 220, 227.

28. *New York Times*, February 20, 1867; *Lewiston* [Maine] *Daily Evening Journal*, February 21, 1867. See also letters from George E. Cooper to the commanding officer of the Military District of Fort Monroe, dating from December 26, 1866, to May 1, 1867, *Official Records*, ser. 2, vol. 8, pp. 980–83.

29. *New York Times*, April 8, 1867.

30. Ibid.

31. Eric Foner writes, "Black suffrage, of course, was the most radical element of Congressional Reconstruction, but this too derived from a variety of motives and calculations. For Radicals, it represented a culmination of a lifetime of reform. For others, it seemed less the fulfillment of an idealistic creed than an alternative to prolonged federal intervention in the South, a means of enabling blacks to defend themselves against abuse, while relieving the nation of that responsibility" (*Reconstruction*, p. 278).

32. Beale, *Diary of Gideon Welles*, 3:110. That Holt firmly supported the Fourteenth Amendment—if not necessarily entirely for the sake of blacks them-

selves—is evidenced by a letter from W. G. Suellen in April 1867. "I believe with you that the dawn is breaking," wrote Suellen, "and that we shall owe our salvation to the Negro vote in the elections, as we did to his bullet in the field" (Suellen to Holt, April 29, 1867, in container 56, Holt-LC). Once a slaveholder himself, Holt had since the start of the war become increasingly hostile toward the institution of slavery ("a crime worthy of death"), and increasingly supportive of blacks' rights. By the fall of 1862, he came out publicly in favor of emancipation, and at least by July 1864 Holt was enthusiastic about the recruiting of black troops for the Union army. See Joseph Holt to Hiram Barney, October 25, 1862, quoted in *New York Times*, November 13, 1862; and Joseph Holt to Edwin Stanton, July 31, 1864, *Official Records*, ser. 1, vol. 39, pt. 2, pp. 213–14.

33. Foner, *Reconstruction*, p. 276.
34. McPherson, *Ordeal by Fire*, pp. 518–20. See also Trefousse, *Andrew Johnson*, pp. 276–77; and Thomas and Hyman, *Stanton*, pp. 514–15, 524–25.
35. McPherson, *Ordeal by Fire*, p. 520.
36. T. H. Duval to Joseph Holt, March 29, 1867, in container 55, Holt-LC.
37. William C. Davis, *Jefferson Davis: The Man and His Hour* (New York: HarperCollins, 1991), p. 655.
38. Ibid. p. 651; Thomas Bland Keys, "Were the Lincoln Conspirators Dealt Justice?" *Lincoln Herald* 80 (1978), p. 39; George C. Gorham, *The Life and Public Services of Edwin M. Stanton* (Boston: Houghton Mifflin, 1899), 2:209.
39. See various collected documents pertaining to the transfer to civil custody and the release on bail of Jefferson Davis in *Official Records*, ser. 2, vol. 8, pp. 983–86. See also William J. Cooper, *Jefferson Davis, American* (New York: Alfred A. Knopf, 2000), pp. 565–68; and Davis, *Jefferson Davis*, pp. 654–56.
40. Notes William Hanchett, "The release of Davis naturally raised questions about the justification of the 1865 prosecution, conviction, and punishment of the eight individuals with whom he was supposed to have conspired" (Gabor S. Boritt and Norman O. Forness, eds., *The Historian's Lincoln: Pseudohistory, Psychohistory, and History* [Urbana: University of Illinois Press, 1988], p. 324).
41. Trefousse, *Andrew Johnson*, p. 283. According to the U.S. Constitution, the President, like all federal officers, can be impeached only for treason, bribery, or (unspecified) "high crimes and misdemeanors," and the decision to go to trial requires a simple majority vote in the House; the trial, in the Senate, requires a two-thirds majority vote to remove from office.
42. Foner, *Reconstruction*, p. 308; Beale, *Diary of Gideon Welles*, 3:75, 84, 90; Trefousse, *Impeachment of a President*, p. 74; Trefousse, *Andrew Johnson*, pp. 284–85. See also James O. Hall, "Booth's Diary: Missing Pages," unpublished paper in the Surratt Society Archives, Clinton, Maryland.

In the spring of 1867 Benjamin Butler spearheaded the formation of yet another congressional committee, the Committee on the Assassination, dedicated exclusively to uncovering links between the President and the assassination conspirators. Its findings were "inconclusive at best, and no report was forthcoming. According to William Hanchett, Butler "later conceded that there was no case against Johnson" (Boritt and Forness, *The Historian's Lincoln*, p. 324).

Also according to Hanchett, it was Lafayette C. Baker who first raised the issue of the existence of Booth's diary to the Judiciary Committee in January 1867 (Hanchett, *The Lincoln Murder Conspiracies* [Urbana: University of Illinois Press, 1983], pp. 83–86).

43. E. J. Conger to Joseph Holt, April 13, 1867, in container 56, Holt-LC; *New York Times*, May 22 and May 24, 1867.

44. The entire contents of Booth's diary appeared in the *New York Times*, May 22, 1867.

45. I am very grateful to assassination expert Michael Kauffman who recently explained to me, in conversation, the legal obstacles the defense faced in trying to make any use of Booth's diary in 1865. See also Hanchett, *Lincoln Murder Conspiracies*, pp. 83–85, and Chamlee, *Lincoln's Assassins*, p. 288.

46. *New York Times*, May 22, 1867. At least one fraudulent version of the missing pages has surfaced, only to be debunked conclusively by assassination expert James O. Hall. This version and Hall's comments ("Booth's Diary: Missing Pages") are contained in the Surratt Files, Surratt Society Archives.

47. Beale, *Diary of Gideon Welles*, 3:95.

48. *New York Times*, May 22, 1867.

49. Thomas and Hyman, *Stanton*, p. 539; Beale, *Diary of Gideon Welles*, 3:102.

50. Beale, *Diary of Gideon Welles*, 3:102; *New York Times*, May 30, 1867.

51. *New York Times*, May 28, June 11, June 22, and June 30, 1867. According to Louis Weichmann, at least some of these men were present at Secretary Stanton's request, as symbols of the federal government's (or at least the Republican Party's) cause in the case, to serve as a "restraint on the element" in the courtroom whose sympathies lay with the white South, and also "to take care that the Government witnesses should not be insulted or subjected to bodily harm" (*True History*, p. 376).

52. *New York Times*, June 11, June 22, and June 30, 1867. Weichmann wrote with disgust, "On one occasion about twenty students from St. Charles College . . . came into court. All of them were permitted, by the marshal of the court, to approach the prisoner and to shake hands with him, and this in the presence of the jury" (*True History*, p. 377).

53. *New York Times*, May 24, May 28, and June 10, 1867. See also Surratt's own account of the trial, quoted in Weichmann, *True History*, pp. 450–51.

54. *Trial of John H. Surratt in the Criminal Court for the District of Columbia* (Washington, D.C.: Government Printing Office, 1867), 2:1380—83; Beale, *Diary of Gideon Welles*, 3:160. See also Martin, "United States Government Versus John Harrison Surratt," p. 86, where he calls Fisher "Stanton's surrogate."

55. Weichmann, *True History*, pp. 375-376.

56. *Lewiston* [Maine] *Daily Evening Journal*, June 14, 1867; *Trial of John H. Surratt*, 1:3–117. See also Martin, "United States Government Versus John Harrison Surratt," pp. 86–94, 134. The members of the jury are identified as W. B. Todd (foreman), Robert Ball, J. Russell Barr, Thomas Berry, George A. Bohrer, C. G. Schneider, James Y. Davis, Columbus Alexander, William McLean, Benjamin F. Morsell, B. E. Gittings, and W. W. Birth (*Trial of John H. Surratt*, 2:1379).

57. See *Trial of John H. Surratt*, 2:1380–83. See also Martin, "United States Government Versus John Harrison Surratt," pp. 92–94.

58. Trial of John H. Surratt, 1:136–62, 195–203, 494–98.

59. Ibid. 1:276–87; *New York Times*, June 25, 1867.

60. *Trial of John H. Surratt*, 1:369-436, 437–60, *New York Times*, June 28, 1867.

61. *Trial of John H. Surratt*, 1:461–84, 493–94.

62. Ibid.

63. Chamlee, *Lincoln's Assassins*, pp. 219, 517. Merrick, a "member of a distinguished legal family and a prominent Washington lawyer," had "served privately as advisory counsel for Dr. Mudd" in 1865, and now, in the wake of Mudd's imprisonment, he "actively sought Mudd's release." In 1868, Merrick would serve as Andrew Johnson's counsel at his impeachment trial. (Ibid., p. 486.)

64. *New York Times*, June 30 and July 3, 1867.

65. *New York Times*, June 30, 1867.

66. *New York Times*, August 20, 1867.

67. *Trial of John H. Surratt*, 2:863–92.

68. Ibid. 2:769–78.

69. *New York Times*, July 25 and July 29, 1867; *Trial of John H. Surratt*, 1:478–79.

70. *Trial of John H. Surratt*, 2:1368–78.

71. It is unclear how this rumor got started. The *New York Times* reporter later noted on August 10, 1867, that the guard around the jury room was such that it was "impossible to approach the door of their room near enough to overhear their deliberations or conversations."

72. *New York Times*, August 8, 1867.

73. *New York Times*, August 11, 1867.

74. *New York Times*, August 13, 1867.

75. *New York Times*, August 11, 1867. The *Lewiston* [Maine] *Daily Evening*

Journal reported that some observers expected the jury to divide along religious lines. "A disagreement of the jury is looked for," the paper reported on August 2, "as one or two of them are too firm Catholics, it is alleged, to convict one of their own faith in a Protestant court."

76. *New York Times*, August 12, 1867.
77. Mudd, *Life of Dr. Samuel A. Mudd*, p. 255.
78. Document signed by E. D. Townsend, August 3, 1867, granting Holt a leave of absence, in container 56, Holt-LC; Thomas and Hyman, *Stanton*, pp. 549–51; Beale, *Diary of Gideon Welles*, 3:163 (see also pp. 167–68 and 171, in which Welles again condemns Stanton and Holt for being in league with each other and with the Radicals in Congress). And see the letters from Dr. John F. Gray to Joseph Holt (particularly April 5, April 15, and May 19, 1867), concerning Holt's health, in container 56, Holt-LC.

9. "THE WICKED MAN NOW ACTING AS PRESIDENT"
THE TRIAL OF ANDREW JOHNSON AND THE COLLAPSE OF HOLT'S AGENDA

1. Benjamin P. Thomas and Harold M. Hyman, *Stanton: The Life and Times of Lincoln's Secretary of War* (New York: Alfred A. Knopf, 1962), p. 506.
2. William H. Doherty to Joseph Holt, August 10, 1867, in container 57, Holt-LC.
3. Howard K. Beale, ed., *Diary of Gideon Welles: Secretary of the Navy Under Lincoln and Johnson* (New York: W.W. Norton, 1960), 3:264.
4. Although he was away on leave, Holt kept tabs on developments in Washington as best he could. Just hours before Stanton was suspended, Holt's assistant W. Winthrop wrote informing him that no one expected any action to be taken against Stanton for the time being, and promising that he would telegraph the judge advocate general should he learn of "any imperative reason why you should return" (W. Winthrop to Joseph Holt, August 12, 1867, in container 57, Holt-LC).
5. Thomas Shankland to Joseph Holt, August 13, 1867, in container 57, Holt-LC.
6. According to Welles, "the best men" in the Union army "generally disliked" Stanton personally (Beale, *Diary of Gideon Welles*, 3:173). Whether this statement reflects the truth or Welles's own antipathy toward Stanton is not clear. Surely Stanton was known for being cranky and hard to deal with. But one suspects that the war secretary's personality did not affect most soldiers' respect for his politics and his leadership.
7. Hans L. Trefousse, *Andrew Johnson* (New York: W. W. Norton, 1989), p. 292.
8. A. G. Riddle to Andrew Johnson, July 23, 1867, in container 57, Holt-LC

(copy). See also a note, in Holt's handwriting, dated July 23, 1867 (in container 57, Holt-LC), in which Holt does indeed call for the pardon of "Charles A. Dunham" in return for his having given valuable service to the prosecution during Surratt's trial.

9. Trefousse, *Andrew Johnson*, pp. 291, 293. 298, 300; Beale, *Diary of Gideon Welles*, 3:143, 145, 149–52; Roy Z. Chamlee, *Lincoln's Assassins: A Complete Account of Their Capture, Trial, and Punishment* (Jefferson, N.C.: McFarland & Company, 1990), pp. 513–16; Hans L. Trefousse, *Impeachment of a President: Andrew Johnson, the Blacks, and Reconstruction* (New York: Fordham University Press, 1999), p. 80.

10. See a draft of this recommendation in Holt's handwriting, in container 57, Holt-LC.

11. Deposition of Francis McFall, May 17, 1867, in container 56, Holt-LC.

12. Depositions of John Martin, James E. Matterson, and Nathan Auser, in container 56, Holt-LC.

13. In the massive collection of Joseph Holt's papers held in the Library of Congress in Washington, D.C., the statements are filed with other materials from that same time period. This does not mean, however, that Holt actually had the statements in hand at that time, and certainly some other documents in his enormous collection seem to be misfiled in one way or another. What is certain is that Holt was a man who kept his ear close to the ground on matters that most deeply concerned him; it therefore seems likely that he must have been aware that this latest scandal was brewing some time before it boiled over.

14. The Holt Papers contain copies of numerous undated articles from this period (many misfiled with documents from August 1866), detailing the Conover scandals and, predictably, offering strong defenses of Holt and Stanton and equally strong invective against Johnson. See, for instance, "The Johnson-Conover Conspiracy" (*Cincinnati Gazette*), "The Conover Swindle" (*Baltimore American*), and "Fat and Foul Disclosures" (*Cincinnati Gazette*) in container 53, Holt-LC. See also Beale, *Diary of Gideon Welles*, 3:172, 175. In his diary, Welles went so far as to accuse Holt of originating the "fraudulent affidavits" produced by McFall, Matterson and the others for his own purposes.

15. *Trial of John H. Surratt in the Criminal Court for the District of Columbia* (Washington, D.C.: Government Printing Office, 1867)2:1209, 1245. See also *New York Times*, August 1, 1867, which described Merrick's speech as "very violent . . . denouncing the Government officials connected with the trial of the assassins . . . as murderers, proclaiming Mrs. Surratt as an innocent woman." The *Times* had actually mentioned the clemency petition earlier in the trial, on July 2, 1867, but only in August did the issue erupt into controversy.

16. *Trial of John H. Surratt*, 2:1249.
17. See *New York Times*, August 5, August 9, August 10, and August 12, 1867; W. Winthrop to Joseph Holt, August 12, 1867.
18. W. Winthrop to Joseph Holt, August 12, 1867; August V. Kautz, "Memoir," vol. 2, Kautz Papers. See also the undated articles "Holt vs Johnson" (*Missouri Democrat*), "The President Again Cornered" (*Cincinnati Gazette*), and "A Presidential Plotter" (*Cincinnati Gazette*), in container 53, Holt-LC. Thomas Reed Turner, "Public Opinion on the Assassination of Abraham Lincoln" *Lincoln Herald* 78:2 (1976), p. 69.
19. Trefousse, *Andrew Johnson*, p. 295. Sheridan's post was given to Winfield Scott Hancock; Sickles's was given to Edward R. S. Canby.
20. Ulysses S. Grant, *Personal Memoirs of U. S. Grant* (1885; reprint, New York: Penguin Putnam, 1999), pp. 616–17.
21. Trefousse, *Impeachment of a President*, pp. 17, 32.
22. W. Winthrop to Joseph Holt, August 13, 1867, in container 57, Holt-LC.
23. Frank Ballard to Joseph Holt, August 13, 1867, and W. C. Dodge to Joseph Holt, August 19, 1867, in container 57, Holt-LC.
24. John Pope to Joseph Holt, August 10, 1867, in container 57, Holt-LC.
25. Beale, *Diary of Gideon Welles*, 3:183, 194, 198–99; Gary Planck, "Lincoln's Assassination: More 'Forgotten' Litigation—Ex parte Mudd (1868)," *Lincoln Herald* 76 (1974), p. 87; Samuel Bland Arnold, *Defense and Prison Experiences of a Lincoln Conspirator* (Hattiesburg, Miss.: Book Farm, 1943), p. 112; Louis J. Weichmann, *A True History of the Assassination of Abraham Lincoln and of the Conspiracy of 1865* (New York: Alfred A. Knopf, 1975), p. 390; Nettie Mudd, ed., *The Life of Dr. Samuel A. Mudd* (New York: Neale, 1906), p. 267. During the epidemic, Samuel Mudd tended not only to his cell mates but also, following the death of the surgeon in charge, to virtually the entire garrison, soldiers as well as prisoners. (Overall numbers at the fort had shrunk dramatically by this time to well under a hundred.) To his credit, Mudd seems to have experienced genuine grief over O'Laughlen's death—see his letters of September 22 and 23 to his wife, and Mudd's description of the epidemic itself, in Mudd, *Life of Dr. Samuel A. Mudd*, pp. 266–67, 286–95. After his death, O'Laughlen's body was returned to his mother in Baltimore.
26. See, for example, James A. Ekin to Joseph Holt, August 26, 1867, in container 57, Holt-LC. In this letter Ekin, who was one of the military commissioners at the 1865 trial, recalled a conversation with Andrew Johnson shortly after the end of the trial in which Johnson had manifested particular interest in the clemency petition and had informed Ekin that "he could not accede to, or grant the petition, for the reason, that there was no class in the South more virulent in the expression and practice of treasonable sentiments than the rebel women . . . and he . . . considered that the interests

of the country demanded that an example should be made which would act as a summary check upon and corrective of female disloyalty."

27. *Baltimore Gazette*, October 26, 1867, quoted in the *Surratt Courier* 27 (November 2002), p. 7; *New York Times*, October 4, 1867; Michael Kauffman, "Fort Lesley McNair and the Lincoln Conspirators," p. 185.

28. Eric Foner, *Reconstruction: America's Unfinished Revolution, 1863–1877* (New York: Harper & Row, 1988), pp. 314–15.

29. Trefousse, *Andrew Johnson*, p. 300; William J. Cooper, *Jefferson Davis, American* (New York: Alfred A. Knopf, 2000) p. 571.

30. Mudd, *Life of Dr. Samuel A. Mudd*, pp. 296–97. See also the testimony of Henry H. Hine, November 1867; the statements of Samuel Arnold, Samuel Mudd, and Edman Spangler, December 3, 1867; and the statement of William H. Gleason, December 19, 1867, all in the Butler Papers. Gleason had left Washington for Florida early in the fall, but the yellow fever epidemic that killed Michael O'Laughlen delayed his visit to Fort Jefferson until the end of November.

31. "Boutwell," grumbled Gideon Welles to his diary, "who made the report to the House, is a fanatic, impulsive, violent, and ardent, narrow-minded partisan, without much judgment" (Beale, *Diary of Gideon Welles*, 3:238).

32. Trefousse, *Andrew Johnson*, pp. 302, 304; James M. McPherson, *Ordeal by Fire: The Civil War and Reconstruction* (New York: McGraw-Hill, 1992), p. 527; Beale, *Diary of Gideon Welles*, 3:259, 261.

33. Thomas and Hyman, *Stanton*, pp. 561, 572; D. P. Henderson to Joseph Holt, January 15, 1868, in container 58, Holt-LC.

34. Thomas and Hyman, *Stanton*, pp. 574, 578.

35. Ibid., pp. 587, 593; Beale, *Diary of Gideon Welles*, 3:285. According to Thomas and Hyman, Stanton "secretly ordered that if Thomas tried to take the war office by force, it was to be surrendered at once, so that bloodshed might be avoided" (*Stanton*, p. 593).

36. Beale, *Diary of Gideon Welles*, 3:292; McPherson, *Ordeal by Fire*, p. 527; Thomas and Hyman, *Stanton*, p. 598.

37. Cooper, *Jefferson Davis*, p. 575; T. H. Duval to Joseph Holt, March 8, 1868, in container 58, Holt-LC. According to Cooper, the government's lawyers feared that Davis would be acquitted, "humiliating the government" (*Jefferson Davis*, p. 576).
  The full story of Johnson's impeachment has been told well and in great detail elsewhere—see, for example, Trefousse, *Impeachment of a President*.

38. Beale, *Diary of Gideon Welles*, 3:324. Welles wrote, "The Senate seems debauched, debased, demoralized, without independence, sense of right, or moral courage. It is, to all intents and purposes, a revolutionary body. . . . It is like slaughtering, shooting down, the faithful sentinel because of his fidelity in standing to his post" (ibid.).

39. Trefousse, *Andrew Johnson*, pp. 329–31; Brooks Simpson, *The Reconstruction Presidents* (Lawrence: University Press of Kansas, 1998), pp. 125, 335; McPherson, *Ordeal by Fire*, pp. 527–29.

40. Beale, *Diary of Gideon Welles*, 3:299; Trefousse, *Andrew Johnson*, pp. 332–33; Thomas and Hyman, *Stanton*, pp. 608, 611.

41. T. M. Harris, *Assassination of Lincoln: A History of the Great Conspiracy* (1892; reprint, Bowie, Md.: Heritage Books, 1989), p. 252; Alfred Isacsson, *The Travels, Arrest, and Trial of John H. Surratt* (Middletown, N.Y.: Vestigium Press, 2003), p. 32; Cooper, *Jefferson Davis*, p. 577. See also *New York Times*, January 21 and February 20, 1868, for brief comments concerning the ongoing attempt to prosecute Surratt.

42. Thomas and Hyman, *Stanton*, p. 607; Foner, *Reconstruction*, pp. 315–16; Beale, *Diary of Gideon Welles*, 3:363.

43. Quoted in Foner, *Reconstruction*, p. 340.

44. Ibid.

45. McPherson, *Ordeal by Fire*, pp. 631–32; T. H. Duval to Joseph Holt, August 5, 1868, in container 59, Holt-LC.

46. Trefousse, *Andrew Johnson*, p. 337; Beale, *Diary of Gideon Welles*, 3:394–95.

47. Mudd, *Life of Dr. Samuel A. Mudd*, p. 312. See *New York Times*, September 23, 1868, for a brief comment on the possible implications of the July 4 amnesty proclamation for the case against John Surratt Jr.

48. Thomas Bland Keys, "Were the Lincoln Conspirators Dealt Justice?," *Lincoln Herald* 80 (1978), p. 41; Planck, "Lincoln's Assassination," p. 89; Harris, *Assassination of Lincoln*, p. 252; Isacsson, *Travels, Arrest, and Trial of John H. Surratt*, p. 32; Mudd, *Life of Dr. Samuel A. Mudd*, p. 314.

49. Simpson, *Reconstruction Presidents*, p. 129. These three states were finally readmitted to the Union in 1869. Georgia, which originally had been "reconstructed" in June 1868, was then briefly remanded by Congress to military rule, and finally reentered the Union in March 1870 (McPherson, *Ordeal by Fire*, p. 541).

50. T. H. Duval to Joseph Holt, July 23, 1868, in container 59, Holt-LC.

51. McPherson, *Ordeal by Fire*, p. 538. See also Beale, *Diary of Gideon Welles*, 3:460–62, on the situation in Arkansas during the fall of 1868.

52. Margaret E. Crosby to Joseph Holt, November 4, 1868, in container 60, Holt-LC.

53. Cooper, *Jefferson Davis*, pp. 581–82.

54. Margaret E. Crosby to Joseph Holt, February 28, 1869, in container 60, Holt-LC.

55. Trefousse, *Andrew Johnson*, p. 347.

56. See Anna Surratt to Andrew Johnson, February 5, 1869, ser. 1, reel 36, in the microfilmed Andrew Johnson Papers, Library of Congress, Washington, D.C.; *Boston Traveler*, February 9, 1869 (see also the *Washington Star* of

the same date); Kauffman, "Fort Lesley McNair," p. 185. According to
Kauffman, "When Holmead was disbanded in 1887, the records were scat-
tered, and the whereabouts of Powell's body are now unknown" (ibid.).
57. Mudd, *Life of Dr. Samuel A. Mudd*, pp. 282–83, 317–18; Keys, "Were the
Lincoln Conspirators Dealt Justice?," p. 44; William Hanchett, *The Lincoln
Murder Conspiracies* (Urbana: University of Illinois Press, 1983), p. 89;
Beale, *Diary of Gideon Welles*, 3:145; Cooper, *Jefferson Davis*, p. 582.
Johnson issued his pardons of Mudd, Arnold, and Spangler in February,
and the men returned home in March.
58. Thomas Shankland to Joseph Holt, February 11, 1869, and D. P. Hender-
son to Joseph Holt, March 3, 1869, in container 60, Holt-LC; Trefousse,
Andrew Johnson, p. 351; Beale, *Diary of Gideon Welles*, 3:540–42.

EPILOGUE

1. Joseph Holt to Allen Thorndike Rice, February 27, 1883, in container 82,
Holt-LC.
2. Quoted in Louis J. Weichmann, *A True History of the Assassination of
Abraham Lincoln and of the Conspiracy of 1865* (New York: Alfred A.
Knopf, 1975), p. 236.
3. James M. McPherson, *Ordeal by Fire: The Civil War and Reconstruction*
(New York: McGraw-Hill, 1992), pp. 548–59.
4. Ibid., p. 563.
5. D. P. Henderson to Joseph Holt, March 3, 1869, in container 60, Holt-LC.
6. Nettie Mudd, ed., *The Life of Dr. Samuel A. Mudd* (New York: Neale,
1906), pp. 320–21, 326; Edward Steers, *His Name Is Still Mudd: The Case
Against Dr. Samuel Alexander Mudd* (Gettysburg, Pa.: Thomas Publications, 1997), pp. 88, 154.
7. In June 1865, Ford even published a pamphlet containing the trial testimony pertaining to Spangler, in order to generate support for his employee
and to try to redeem the reputation of the theater itself. See James L. Swan-
son and Daniel R. Weinberg, *Lincoln's Assassins: Their Trial and Execution*
(Santa Fe: Arena Editions, 2001), p. 92.
8. Mudd, *Life of Dr. Samuel A. Mudd*, pp. 294–95, 321–26; Weichmann, *True
History*, p. 491; Roy Z. Chamlee, *Lincoln's Assassins: A Complete Account
of Their Capture, Trial, and Punishment* (Jefferson, N.C.: McFarland &
Company, 1990), p. 540.
9. William Hanchett, *The Lincoln Murder Conspiracies* (Urbana: University
of Illinois Press, 1983), p. 89; Samuel Bland Arnold, *Defense and Prison
Experiences of a Lincoln Conspirator* (Hattiesburg, Miss.: Book Farm,
1943), pp. 7, 125, 133.
10. Weichmann, *True History*, p. 451.

11. Ibid., p. 435.
12. Anna Surratt and William Tonry, a doctor, were married in June 1869 by Reverend Jacob A. Walter, the priest who had attended Mary Surratt at the end of her life. When his bride's identity became known to his employer four days after the wedding, Tonry was fired from his position at the surgeon general's office (then located, ironically, at Ford's Theater). Soon after, the Tonrys moved to Baltimore, where he established his own laboratory. Anna died in October 1904 at the age of sixty-one. (Elizabeth Steger Trindal, *Mary Surratt: An American Tragedy* [Gretna, La.: Pelican, 1996], p. 231; Joseph George Jr., "Trial of Mrs. Surratt: John P. Brophy's Rare Pamphlet," *Lincoln Herald* 98 [1996], p. 17).
13. Weichmann, *True History*, pp. 450–51; Chamlee, *Lincoln's Assassins*, pp. 531, 535; Joseph George Jr., "A True Childe of Sorrow: Two Letters of Mary E. Surratt," *Maryland Historical Magazine* 80 (Winter 1985), p. 405; *Surratt Courier* 25 (March 2000), p. 6; Alexandra Lee Levin, "Who Hid John H. Surratt, the Lincoln Conspiracy Case Figure?," *Maryland Historical Magazine* 60 (1965), p. 184. Surratt's Rockville lecture is reprinted in its entirety in Weichmann, *True History*, pp. 428–40, followed by the Hiss article on pp. 441–51.
14. William C. Davis, *Jefferson Davis: The Man and His Hour* (New York: HarperCollins, 1991), pp. 660–88, 705.
15. Benjamin P. Thomas and Harold M. Hyman, *Stanton: The Life and Times of Lincoln's Secretary of War* (New York: Alfred A. Knopf, 1962), pp. 625–39.
16. Hans L. Trefousse, *Andrew Johnson* (New York: W. W. Norton, 1989), pp. 365–66.
17. Hans L. Trefousse, *Impeachment of a President: Andrew Johnson, the Blacks, and Reconstruction* (New York: Fordham University Press, 1999), pp. 189–90; Trefousse, *Andrew Johnson*, p. 377.
18. See, among others, Joseph Holt to John A. Bingham, February 11, 1873, Frederick Seward to Joseph Holt, May 24, 1873, and R. D. Mussey to Joseph Holt, August 19, 1873, all in container 66, Holt-LC. See also Joseph Holt to James Speed, March 30, 1873, and Joseph Holt to R. D. Mussey, July 9, 1873, in container 100, Holt-LC.
19. Joseph Holt to W. W. Belknap, August [date illegible], 1873, in the Surratt Society Archives, Clinton, Maryland (spelling as in the original); Joseph Holt, *Vindication of Judge Advocate General Holt* (Washington, D.C.: Chronicle, 1873); Trefousse, *Andrew Johnson*, p. 365.
20. James A. Ekin to Joseph Holt (telegram), August 29, 1873, David Hunter to Joseph Holt, November 24, 1873, T. S. Bell to Joseph Holt, August 27, 1873, Horatio King to Joseph Holt, August 28, 1873, John A. Bingham to Joseph Holt, October 13, 1873, all in container 66, Holt-LC.
21. "Rejoinder of J. Holt, Judge Advocate General, to Ex-President Johnson's Reply to His Vindication of 26th August Last," in container 116, Holt-LC.

22. See Joseph Holt to W. W. Belknap, November 20, 1875, and General Orders No. 98, both in RG 94, Records of the Adjutant General's Office, 1780s–1917, Letters Received by the Commission Branch of the Adjutant General's Office, 1863–1870, Roll 96, H834 CB 1864, National Archives, Washington, D.C.
23. See A. M. Brown to Joseph Holt, June 12, 1889, in container 85, Holt-LC; Joseph Holt to W. W. Belknap, November 20, 1875, in RG 94, Records of the Adjutant General's Office.
24. "New Facts About Mrs. Surratt," *North American Review* 147 (July 1888), pp. 83–94. See also Joseph Holt to Allen Thorndike Rice, February 27, 1883, in container 82, Holt-LC.
25. www.tiac.net/users/ime/famtree/burnett/holt/holt.htm; Horatio King, "Judge Holt and the Lincoln Conspirators," *Century Magazine* 39 (April 1890), p. 958.
26. Hanchett, *Lincoln Murder Conspiracies*, p. 99. Among those with whom Holt was in regular contact toward the end of his life was Louis J. Weichmann, who was writing his own memoirs and sought Holt's opinion of the manuscript, among other favors.

    Holt's attending surgeon notified the adjutant general in a memo later that day: "Sir, I have the honor to report that Brigadier General Joseph Holt U. S. Army (retired) died at his residence in this city at 2:50 A.M. Immediate cause of death—exhaustion resulting from fracture of femur caused by a fall" (Attending Surgeon [name illegible] to Adjutant General, August 1, 1894, in RG 94, Records of the Adjutant General's Office).
27. *New York Times*, August 2, 1894; Adjutant General George D. Ruggles to Commanding Officer, Fort Myer, Virginia, August 3, 1894, and Adjutant General's Office's Announcement of Holt's Death, August 1, 1894, both in RG 94, Records of the Adjutant General's Office. See also the *Louisville Courier Journal*, August 4, 1894.

INDEX

Page numbers in *italics* refer to illustrations.

357

Ewing, Thomas, Jr., 73, 125,
127–28, 138, 214

Failing, William, 259
Fair Oaks (Seven Pines), Battle of,
153
Fessenden, William Pitt, 196
Fifteenth Amendment, 284, 291
First Delaware Cavalry, U.S., 45
First Maryland Infantry Volun-
teers, CSA, 49
Fisher, George P., 240, 253, 256,
258, 260–61, 262
Fitch, Francis, 259
Fitzpatrick, Honora, 94, 119,
120
Fletcher, John, 107
Florida, 40–41, 179, 199
Florida, U.S.S., 138, 139
Floyd, John B., 14, 16–17, 20
Foner, Eric, 179, 185
Ford, Henry Clay ("Harry"), 56
Ford, John T., 55, 56, 209, 293
Ford's Theater, 4, 7, 36, 55–56,
59, 81, 94, 96, 253, 255,
295
Forrest, Nathan Bedford, 286
Fort Jefferson, 138, 180, 200,
209, 276, 278, 288–89
conditions in, 140–41, 220–21
Fortress Monroe, 75, 86, 101,
135, 137, 149, 150–51, 201,
204, 220, 240, 247
Fort Sumter, 3, 14–16, 17, 19–20,
23, 64, 169, 170, 171
Foster, John A., 105
Foster, Lafayette S., 8
Foster, Robert S., 68, 143
Fourth Louisiana Infantry Regi-
ment, C.S.A., 153

Fourteenth Amendment, 215–17,
230, 243, 284, 287
Fourteenth Veteran Reserves, U.S.,
133–34
Fourth Michigan Cavalry, U.S., 75
Fowle, James H., 218
Freedmen's Bureau, 184, 200,
208–9, 233, 300
freedpeople, 187, 236–37, 292
reclaimed lands issue and, 184
in Reconstruction debate,
173–74, 179–80, 181, 197,
231, 232, 276, 277, 284
voting rights for, 174, 182, 183,
185–86, 207, 223, 234, 252,
274, 284, 291

Garrett, Richard, 38, 251
Gemmill, Zachariah W., 48
Georgia, 16, 179, 286
Gifford, James, 55
Gleason, D. H., 95–96
Gleason, William H., 278
Grant, Ulysses S., xiii, 3, 7, 25,
56, 57, 70, 84, 110, 123,
139, 182, 214, 230, 233,
245, 262–63, 279, 289, 291,
292, 297
in 1868 election, 282–84, 285,
286
Johnson's break with, 278
Reconstruction position of,
273–74
in War Department, U.S., 274–75
Welles's dislike of, 282–83
Greeley, Horace, 222
Greenhow, Rose, 121–22

habeas corpus, writ of:
Davis's incarceration and, 246–47

Lieber, Francis, 151, 216
Limits of Dissent, The (Klement), x
Lincoln, Abraham, 31, 57, 64, 77, 111, 151, 165, 166, 173, 184, 206, 243, 253, 255, 275, 276, 294, 298, 303
   Amnesty and Reconstruction Proclamation of, 174, 177, 178
   assassination of, xii, 4–5, 7–9, 98
   attempted kidnapping of, 49–53, 90
   Fort Sumter crisis and, 23
   funeral of, 33, 35, *35*
   habeas corpus suspended by, 26–27, 34
   Holt appointed to Bureau of Military Justice by, 26–27
   Holt's conversation with, 23
   inauguration of, 21, 22
   Johnson's relationship with, 9–10
   Reconstruction vision of, 4, 56, 174–75, 176, 180–81
Lincoln, Mary Todd, 4–5
Lloyd, John, 44, 97, 100, 107–8, 131, 255
   testimony of, 107–9, 118–19
"Lon letter," 85–86
Louisiana, 179, 222, 286
Louisville Advertiser, 12
Louisville Journal, 24
Lovett, Alexander, 62, 111
Loyal Legion, 300, 301

McAlpine, J. M., 147
McAleer, Leonidas (Lon), 86
McClellan, George B., 28, 77
McDevitt, James, 99

McFall, Francis, 268–69
McGill, John, 168
McMillan, Lewis J. A., 188–89, 256–57, 259
McPhail, James L., 54
McPherson, James M., 23, 154, 291–92
Mallory, Stephen R., 199
March Reconstruction Act, 276
Marvin, William, 199
Maryland, 16, 23, 77
Matterson, James E., 269
Merrick, Richard T., 257, 259–60, 271
Metropolitan Police, 9, 33, 34, 58, 98
Miles, John, 110
Miles, Nelson, 75–76
Milligan, Lambdin P., 28–29, 34, 211–14, 232, 235, 284–85
Minnesota, 185
Mississippi, 16, 179, 285
Missouri, 16, 23, 30, 230
Montauk, U.S.S., 39, 40, 48, 58, 113
Montreal, 188
Mosby, John Singleton, 41
Mudd, George, 62, 126
Mudd, Henry L., 60
Mudd, Nettie, 293–94
Mudd, Samuel A., 9, 36, *61,* 73, 99, 109, 110, 134–35, 146, 168, 180, 200, 206–7, 209–10, 213, 214, 223–24, 233, 239, 251, 257–58, 262, 278, 284–85, 294
   arrest of, 62–63
   background of, 59–62
   Booth's leg treated by, 60–62, 125

Blair controversy and, 169–70,
172, 173
Booth's diary and, 250, 251–52
Conover scandal and, 267
death of, 296–97
"grand" conspiracy theory of,
10–11
Holt's alliance with, 202–3
Holt's reports to, 165–67, 190,
220, 225
Johnson's suspension of, 232,
262, 265, 270, 273, 274–75,
278–80, 281
resignation of, 281–82
Stanton (Thomas and Hyman),
264
Star of the West, U.S.S., 19–20,
170
State Department, U.S., 189, 190,
236, 259
Stephens, Alexander H., 185, 214
Stephens, Mary, 164
Stevens, Thaddeus, 183, 196, 231,
280
Stewart, K. J., 151
Stone, Fredrick, 73, 114, 115, 214
Stonestreet, Charles H., 120
Streett, Samuel, 110
Sumner, Charles, 127, 198–99,
292
Supreme Court, U.S., 28, 74, 244,
281, 296
Milligan decision of, 211–14,
232, 235, 284–85
Surratt, Elisabeth Susanna (Anna),
43, 44, 88–89, 92, 94, 120,
131, 132, 135, 143, 240,
252, 288, 295
Surratt, Isaac, 43, 252, 295
Surratt, John H., Jr., xi, xiii, 36,

39, 42, 43–44, 70, 84, 86,
100, 104, 105, 107, 109,
110, 111, 125, 126, 127,
135, 146, 147, 168, 176,
211, 213, 218, 228, 239,
267, 275, 276, 284, 287
arrest of, 235, 237–38
awaiting trial, 240–41
as fugitive, 187–90, 256
post-trial life of, 294–96
released from custody, 282, 287
trial of, *see* Surratt, John, Jr.,
trial of
Weichmann's friendship with,
87–90, 98–99
in Weichmann's testimony,
87–97, 101
Surratt, John Jr., trial of, 252–62,
266
civil jurisdiction of, 238–40, 254
defense counsel in, 257–58
defense strategy in, 258–60
Holt and, 252–53
indictment in, 253, 255
jury in, 254–55
Mary Surratt's clemency petition
in, 270–72, 298
political turmoil surrounding,
262
prosecution counsel in, 253
testimony for prosecution in,
255–57
verdict in, 260–61
Surratt, John H., Sr., 42–43, 46,
48, 51, 89
Surratt, Mary E., 36, 45, 48, 58,
59, 62–63, 69, 73, 77, 79,
137, 140, 159, 167, 196,
213, 244, 248–49, 250, 251,
256, 268, 295